"Anoushiravan Ehteshami combines the rich contextual knowledge of an area specialist with a masterful grasp of the rapidly changing dynamics of international politics. The result is an indispensable study of the impact of globalization on the geopolitics of the Middle East. This book will be welcomed as a major addition by specialists on the region, but Ehteshami's lucid style also makes it an accessible–indeed, inviting–introduction for non-specialists. Hopefully, it will garner the attention of policy-makers as well."
  Ian Shapiro, Sterling Professor of Political Science at Yale University and author of 'Containment: Rebuilding a Strategy against Global Terror'

"This useful survey of the dilemmas that confront the vast and complex region between Morocco and Central Asia in this era of rapid and worldwide change–and of the corresponding opportunities and challenges that the region itself represents for the world as a whole–should be useful for both beginning students and long-time observers of the Middle East."
  Lisa Anderson, Dean of the School of International and Public Affairs, Columbia University

"Anoushiravan Ehteshami brings together the disciplinary focus of the social scientist and the expertise of the Middle Eastern specialist to provide a uniquely area-specific study of globalization. Thoroughly informed and always lucid, this book examines globalization's impact on perhaps the most critical region of the world, and convincingly argues that geopolitics can explain both the uncertain unfolding of and resistance to wider changes in the local context. It powerfully demonstrates that the interdependence and transnationalism of the Middle East are dependent on strategic events such as the war on terror and the invasion of Iraq – a perspective of immense analytical and policy significance."
  James Piscatori, Oxford Centre for Islamic Studies, University of Oxford

Globalization and Geopolitics in the Middle East

This book explores the impact of globalization in the greater Middle East – including North Africa – in the context of the powerful geopolitical forces at work in shaping the region today. Discussion of globalization has often neglected to consider its impact on the Middle East. However, despite the relative lack of foreign direct investment, and the dysfunctional state of trade and regional co-operation, this book shows that globalization has had an impact on the Middle East, although its character and implications have been profoundly different from other regions such as East Asia. It demonstrates that, unlike in other regions, geopolitics has been a critical factor in driving globalization in the Middle East. It argues that whereas elsewhere globalization has opened up the economy, society, culture and attitudes to the environment, in the Middle East it has had the opposite effect, with poor state formation, little inter-regional trade, foreign and inter-regional investment, and reassertion of traditional identities. The author also explores the many dimensions and challenges of the region's being able to integrate fully into the globalized system. Overall, this book provides a much needed assessment of the impact of globalization on the polities, economies and social environment of the greater Middle East, in the context of the region's position as the central site of global geopolitical competition into the twenty-first century.

Anoushiravan Ehteshami is Professor of International Relations and Head of the School of Government and International Affairs at Durham University, UK. He is also a Fellow of the World Economic Forum. He was Vice-President of the British Society for Middle Eastern Studies (BRISMES) from 2000–03. He is the author of numerous books and articles on politics, international relations, strategic studies and political economy of the Middle East.

Durham Modern Middle East and Islamic World Series
Series Editor: Anoushiravan Ehteshami, University of Durham

Economic Development in Saudi Arabia
Rodney Wilson, with Abdullah Al-Salamah, Monica Malik and Ahmed Al-Rajhi

Islam Encountering Globalisation
Edited by Ali Mohammadi

China's Relations with Arabia and the Gulf, 1949–99
Mohamed Bin Huwaidin

Good Governance in the Middle East Oil Monarchies
Edited by Tom Pierre Najem and Martin Hetherington

The Middle East's Relations with Asia and Russia
Edited by Hannah Carter and Anoushiravan Ehteshami

Israeli Politics and the Middle East Peace Process, 1988–2002
Hassan A. Barari

The Communist Movement in the Arab World
Tareq Y. Ismael

Oman – The Islamic Democratic Tradition
Hussein Ghubash

The Secret Israeli–Palestinian Negotiations in Oslo
Their Success and Why the Process Ultimately Failed
Sven Behrendt

Globalization and Geopolitics in the Middle East
Old Games, New Rules
Anoushiravan Ehteshami

Globalization and Geopolitics in the Middle East

Old Games, New Rules

Anoushiravan Ehteshami

LONDON AND NEW YORK

First published 2007
Paperback edition first published 2009
by Routledge
2 Park Square, Milton Park, Abingdon, Oxon OX14 4RN

Simultaneously published in the USA and Canada
by Routledge
270 Madison Ave, New York, NY 10016

Routledge is an imprint of the Taylor & Francis Group, an informa business

© 2007, 2009 Anoushiravan Ehteshami

Typeset in Times by Taylor & Francis Books
Printed and bound in Great Britain by
Biddles Digital, King's Lynn

All rights reserved. No part of this book may be reprinted or
reproduced or utilised in any form or by any electronic, mechanical, or
other means, now known or hereafter invented, including
photocopying and recording, or in any information storage or retrieval
system, without permission in writing from the publishers.

British Library Cataloguing in Publication Data
A catalogue record for this book is available from the British Library

Library of Congress Cataloging in Publication Data
A catalog record for this book has been requested

ISBN10 0-415-42632-4 (hbk)
ISBN10 0-415-47712-3 (pbk)
ISBN10 0-203-96253-2 (ebk)

ISBN13 978-0-415-42632-9 (hbk)
ISBN13 978-0-415-47712-3 (pbk)
ISBN13 978-0-203-96253-4 (ebk)

Contents

List of Tables		viii
Preface		ix
	Introduction: Globalization and Geopolitics in the Middle East	1
1	Globalization: System or Process?	20
2	Globalization and Strategic Interdependence	33
3	The MENA Regional System in Crisis	47
4	Geopolitical Tectonics: The Greater Middle East on the Margins of Eurasia	60
5	Government and Governance in the Era of Globalization	109
6	Economic Internationalization and the Changing Balance of Economic Power in the Middle East	130
7	Culture Clash: Globalization and the Geopolitics of Identity in the Middle East	149
8	Globalization and International Politics of the Greater Middle East	165
9	Globalization and the Middle East in Perspective	185
	Notes	197
	Select Bibliography	229
	Index	242

List of Tables

4.1	Main global economic players, mid-1990s	65
4.2	Foreign direct investment flows to developing countries by region, 1995	68
4.3	Inter-Arab trade relations in the mid-1990s (US$ million)	73
4.4	Euro–Mediterranean trade, 1992 (US$ billion)	74
4.5	Military profile of main non-EU Mediterranean armed forces, 2003	82
4.6	The conventional domains of power (late 1990s)	93
5.1	Selected Arab defence and security spending as percentage of current expenditure, 1997–2002	114
5.2	Number of elections in the MENA region, 1989–99	116
6.1	Average annual GDP growth in selected MENA countries, 1965–80	133
6.2	MENA oil income, 1946–64 (US$ million)	134
6.3	Oil dependence in trade and GDP (late 1990s) (%)	139
6.4	Selected Persian Gulf States – value of total and petroleum exports, 1973–90 (US$ billion)	139
6.5	Value of total and petroleum exports in OPEC North Africa, 1973–90 (US$ billion)	140
6.6	External debt of main Arab debtors, 1970 and 1988 (percentage of GDP)	140
6.7	Oil imports of the oil-importing developing countries, 1972–75	141
6.8	MENA trade openness: selected countries (percentage of GDP)	142
6.9	MENA economies in transition, 1960–81 (percentage of GDP)	142

Preface

This book was initially conceived as an introductory text on the globalization debate in the Middle East (which, for my purposes, also includes North Africa), but the work soon acquired the dimensions of a major research monograph on the impact and consequences of globalization on this highly dynamic and relatively unstable region. In its original form, it was to fill an obvious gap in the literature on globalization and the Middle East and North Africa (MENA) region. It was clear to me that much of the commentary, research and even speculation about globalization and its regional (geopolitical) aspects in the 1990s either inadvertently, or quite deliberately, chose to bypass the Middle East. Second, when MENA-related observations were made, these tended to be at the economic level, seemingly bereft of the historical, political, socio-economic and geopolitical context of the region. By its exclusion from debate and analysis, it seemed, the region's 'exceptionalism' was being proved. There existed, therefore, a real need for a comprehensive analytical text on the phenomenon of globalization and its multifaceted dimensions in what is today being referred to as the greater Middle East (GME).

The mission was twofold. First, to attempt to bridge the ever-widening gap between 'area studies' and the social science disciplines of international relations and political economy, and also to contextualize the multi-faceted debate about globalization as a global force in and around the Middle East, which is a strategically significant but vulnerable subsystem of the international system. The second task was to try and illustrate the unique characteristics of the region in the light of the unitary global force we now call globalization. Operationally, in the debates about globalization, regionalization has been presented as more-or-less its Siamese twin. The rapid integration and expansion of the European Union, the strengthening of the North American Free Trade Area, NAFTA's South American equivalent, and even the emergence of a Pacific Rim Forum have been explained in terms of the consolidation of regions in response to the globalization of the world economy and its transformation into a single system. But two regions of the international system – sub-Saharan Africa and the GME – have not fitted the analytical mould very easily. For me, while the African case is interesting and reflective of many of the arguments made in this book, for geostrategic reasons an exploration of the MENA case is even more enriching. The GME is, in geostrategic terms, at the heart of the international system, and part and parcel of one of its most dynamic and fast-changing components. As will be shown, the GME's place in Eurasia gives this region a huge weight in determining the fate and direction of change in this vast continental landmass.

The other major assumption made about globalization is its linear penetration across the globe. Its universality seems to be taken for granted, and debates focus on the nature of responses to it. In the GME, however, one is all too aware of the very real geopolitical, geocultural and even geo-economic tensions that correspond to the reach of globalization. While globalization, in terms of information and communication technologies and rapidity of movement, is readily observable, the causes of resistance to the general globalization of the region remain understudied. In the GME, for example, foreign direct investment remains very small, and regional co-operation and trade in a dysfunctional state. This is the case despite the fact that some of the region's economies – notably the region's hydrocarbon exporters – have been vertically integrated into the world economy for decades. So it is possible to argue that globalization has not taken root. Furthermore, the point has to be made that geopolitical conditions do have a direct impact on responses to globalization. It is ironic that while, conceptually, globalization throws up geopolitics as a variable, so much of the debate about the former conveniently overlooks the impact the latter could have on the operationalization of globalization. In the GME, it will be argued here, geopolitics is a major determining factor.

Indeed, geopolitics struck with a vengeance – as I started writing this book, the size of the task ahead of me was inflated by the intensity of events in the region. Yet the delay has been useful, for it gave me time to build on the (albeit still few) exceptional studies on the subject that have now appeared. But time elasticity also enabled me to develop a longer-term view of the debates, and helped me in broadening my remit to also take account of the consequences of the more recent significant strategic developments affecting the region.

The book analyses the impact of globalization in the geopolitical context of the region – on the polities, economies and social environment of the Muslim-dominated MENA arena. But it does this in the context of the shifting strategic map of the region, and therefore looks at globalization's impact through the lens of geopolitics. The impact of the MENA-related events beyond the region on the Middle East itself cannot be underestimated either; following the devastating 9/11/2001 terrorist attacks on American soil it is impossible to talk about the post-Cold War geopolitics of the region in isolation from the international system. That single event, and its dramatic regional and global consequences, has returned the region into the centre of world politics, where I believe it is likely to remain for much of the twenty-first century. Indeed, just as it was in the twentieth century – with oil putting the Middle East at the heart of international politics – today oil and the threats to its safe exploration and passage, and the threat of international terrorism sustained by authoritarian regimes and undemocratic societies, form the other main planks of concern, which also include proliferation, social unsustainability, rapid population growth, and the march of political Islam. The key difference from the past, though, is that the world has become a far more integrated place, and power too diffuse for any single actor to try and 'manage', or even contain, the Middle East's many complexities. Interdependence, along with transnationalization of the network of states and social communities, has turned the relationship between the GME and the rest of the system into a major security complex. In the meantime, globalization has continued to erode the certainties of life for the average MENA citizen without necessarily providing the benefits of integration. For this area, in addition to uncertainties of globalization itself, the geopolitical fall-out from 9/11 will have to be added to any serious study. The effects and vagaries of globalization must be evaluated with an eye on the geopolitical consequences of 9/11 and the deeply destabilizing war on terror.

This book owes much to the debates I have had the privilege of conducting with prominent thinkers, senior corporate and government policy leaders and advisors on the fringes of the World Economic Forum summits and meetings. They have collectively provided the international fabric for my thoughts, and many of them have played an active part in shaping my ideas. Colleagues in Durham and those elsewhere in the UK research community (Exeter, Lancaster, Leeds, London, Oxford, Sheffield, St Andrews), in addition to those from the USA, Finland, Germany and France, have been unselfishly supportive and helpful throughout. The warmth and generosity of a large number of wonderful friends and colleagues in the region itself – from Egypt, Iran, Jordan, Lebanon, and Tunisia, to Turkey, the UAE and Saudi Arabia – actually made writing the book a pleasant experience. Colleagues from, or based in, these countries have played a critical role in crystallizing my thoughts on the relationship between geopolitics and globalization. The end of this book is perhaps the first stage of this ongoing dialogue.

In addition, I owe a big debt of gratitude to a whole host of students in my Master's classes, who over the years have helped me to fine-tune many of the themes with which I have grappled in this book. Their collective effectiveness as a sounding board cannot be exaggerated. To all the students who have walked through the doors of my classes in the past decade or more, I express my deepest thanks. To my research students, whose research often had a 'globalist' dimension, I also say thank you! They, over 20 of them so far, have contributed greatly in keeping me intellectually fresh and mentally alert. This book owes much to their challenging work and intellectual enquiries. While none of the above share any of the shortcomings the reader may find in the book's analysis – that is entirely my responsibility – they have been partners in revealing insights that the reader may find interesting.

Last, but not least, I am indebted to my wife, Emma, for supporting me in every stage of this undertaking. I dedicate this book to her, as much as to my two little boys, Ardeshir and Kasra, who have brought so much joy to us. They will never know how secretly grateful I have been for the sleepless nights that they kindly passed my way in their attempts to keep my writing programme on schedule. My sister, Nadereh, and my niece, Noosha, also need a special mention for being there for me at the crucial final stages of this book. To them, and all my colleagues who have helped my intellectual development over the years, I convey my deepest gratitude!

Anoush Ehteshami
Durham,
Summer 2006

Introduction
Globalization and Geopolitics in the Middle East

The world economy is composed of its constituent producer, consumer, trader, financial, national, regional, local, sectoral, enterprise and individual parts; but like the proverbial whole, it is more than the sum of its parts. Any of its parts may be affected by others and by what is going on in the whole. To understand what is going on ... it is essential not to lose sight of the forest for looking at the trees. For the forest has a life of its own – growth, evolution, decay – beyond that of its constituent trees. Moreover, the development of the forest – through the interaction of the individual trees with each other and the forest as well as with their physical environment – determines more in the life of each tree than its life cycle affects the whole forest.

Andre Gunder Frank, 'East–West–South Relations in the World Economy', in Kofi Buenor Hadjor (ed.) *New Perspectives in North–South Dialogue: Essays in Honour of Olof Palme* (London: I.B. Tauris, 1988).

The Debate

To speak about globalization in the greater Middle East (GME) immediately opens up the debate about the context and the very nature of social and political organization in the Muslim world. Globalization is not the only prime mover here, and the much-neglected geopolitical context needs to be understood if emerging trends and major changes taking place in the region are to be properly understood.[1] This study aims to place globalization in a geopolitical frame of analysis, arguing that the realities of the latter help shape the globalizing forces now bombarding this region. By geopolitics, it understands that 'nations or states are engaged in a perpetual struggle for life, the key to which is control over "spaces" into which the earth is divided. Development of these "spaces" is subject to "laws" which can be derived from the study of geography and history and successfully applied to foreign policy'.[2] Once such critical space with well developed and complex laws is the region known as the Middle East and North Africa (MENA), and the wider geographical area to its east, which today forms the 'greater' Middle East. On the Middle East space and its laws, Carl Brown produced a pioneering study, which has informed the debate about the international politics of the Middle East to this day.[3] In it he showed that the apparently confused state of international politics of the Middle East could be reduced to a discernible pattern – hence the 'old rules, dangerous game' of his subtitle. For me, though, the current situation could be better captured by the term 'old games, new rules'. Some of the old games, or even old rules, are of course still to be found in the international politics of the region, but for a fuller picture political economy, as part of the new rules, cannot be ignored.

This study therefore gives credit to the importance of political economy in shaping the modern Middle East. In doing this, it seeks to undertake a concurrent assessment of the key junctions of the encounters between globalization and this strategically significant region, notably in the broad realms of economics, politics and culture. The international politics of this area will provide the context for the impact that globalization could be having on regional politics, and on the relationship of the GME with the rest of the world. In this book I rapidly move from the general to the particular – after presenting an analysis of the geopolitical and geostrategic realities shaping the region, I follow the broad debates about globalization to locate this analysis in a regional framework, taking stock of the broader geopolitical environment in which the Middle East states operate, their neighbouring regions, and the huge role the USA plays in shaping the region's many pressing agendas. I begin by laying the foundations, and asking what the concept of globalization actually means – at least to me. Then I explore how its paraphernalia and various dimensions affect the GME region.

There is real fear of globalization in this part of the world, and it is seen as a threatening force in many quarters.[4] The problem lies in the fact that, while MENA regimes of all ideological persuasions have accepted the principle of economic liberalization and the need for adoption of World Trade Organization standards, few have been prepared to absorb the consequences of economic globalization for their countries' socio-economic fabric. With weak economic systems and crumbling infrastructure, it is not surprising that several MENA regimes object to the unbridled economic force of globalization. Globalization, after all, would invite foreign investment, competition and transparency in economic relations. But, at the same time, it could also challenge the existing clientelist, corporatist and often authoritarian structures of the ruling systems, the region's rentier socio-economic relationships, its subsidy-driven distribution systems, and the 'coupon-clipping' capitalist enterprises of most Middle East economies, in which profit from speculation more often than not takes precedence over profit from production.

The concerns of all less-developed countries about economic globalization are, of course, headed by fears of loss of control, which in political economy terms can translate into domination by the large transnational corporations, and loss of economic sovereignty and control over economic planning and cycles. Many of these fears are well founded, given the interdependencies that already exist between separate economic units (states and corporations) and the level of penetration of foreign capital in the most vibrant economic regions of the world. Economic globalization thus indicates 'not only flows of finance, capital investment, technology and labour, but also an expanding web of transnational regulatory institutions ... [whose] autonomy from national governmental control has increased ... Individual nation-states, in this sense, are confronted not only by transnational economic power, but also, and in large measure, by transnational regulatory institutions'.[5] The combination of economic penetration and imposition of international regulatory regimes on the ground pose unyielding challenges to the authority, if not the autonomy, of the MENA state, particularly where the political elite finds itself in charge of the national economy as well.

The debate about the erosion of the territorial state, in which the degree of state control over the economic process has been hotly contested for some time, is symptomatic of the perceived nature of the threat posed by globalization. In no other developing region, I would argue, is sovereignty (economic, political and cultural) more fervently defended than in the Middle East, which again raises deep suspicions in this part of the world about the corrosive impact of globalization on Muslim societies. At such junctions, the forces of globalization encounter their geopolitical counterparts. Holton has noted that challenges to the national integrity of a people as the cornerstone of a state immediately puts the spotlight on questions of cultural identity.[6] In the Muslim Middle East, which has a unique and historically distinct cultural make-up, compared with many other regions, globalization's penetration means that the challenge is felt more profoundly at state level than elsewhere.

'Islamic nationalism', even in its most militant form, could therefore be seen as a direct response to this side-effect of economic globalization. Richard Falk's observation that where the state becomes subordinated to 'the logic of global capital, many people [react] by re-emphasising their traditional identities, including that of religion' is of direct relevance to the Middle East, where culture and religion, or political economy and religion, are never too far apart.[7] In this setting, a de-territorialization of politics and culture can, under certain circumstances, be seen as enhancing the Arabist/Islamist tendencies of most of its peoples in ways that the 1960s generation of Arab nationalists failed to advance. Subordination of the Muslim state to global capitalist forces can, on the other hand, also trigger a sense of rootlessness and isolation that could only be comforted through resistance and an indulgence in tradition.

The universalism of globalization, ironically, at the MENA regional level breeds parochialism and entrenchment of the forces of 'tradition'. In a dialectical process, at the same time it also breeds universalism of Islam itself. The 'Islamic' response, in turn, reinforces the perception of Middle East 'exceptionalism' – its uniqueness. Although religious-based political responses have been recorded elsewhere in the developing world,[8] it is in the Middle East that the combination of the political economy of rentierism and religion produce a volatile and unpredictable mix.

Unique the region may be, but its exceptional status is tested in its inability to manage the challenges posed by globalization. As Hinnebusch notes, Middle East responses to globalization should be seen as 'a function of a changing interaction between the systemic (inter-state) and state (domestic) levels'.[9] At this level, the region faces seemingly insurmountable challenges. In other words, it is in the exploration of the interaction between the inter-state and domestic levels that we understand better the nature of state responses to globalization. The state itself, though, can only be understood within its own geopolitical and historical setting. As Halliday has observed, it is not always the future of the Middle East, 'but its past, that ... poses the greatest challenge'.[10]

Furthermore, while global capital would probably appreciate the more open and competitive labour relations that the resultant fracturing of social systems brings, the Muslim peoples, with their tightly knit social relations, would find the prospect of a co-opted state so threatening as to take refuge in the very spaces that come to confront globalization. This is the paradox of our time with regard to the cultural impact of globalization on Muslim states of the GME: any rapid opening up to the West, in cultural, political and economic terms, can ignite an Islamist backlash and, under certain circumstances, force a reversal.

But the remarkable fact is that the MENA region is generating strong politico-cultural responses to globalization when it is actually the least exposed of regional systems in terms of foreign direct investment and international trade. At the same time, its hydrocarbon exports are consumed worldwide, and it imports everything from ideas, to food, science, technology and know-how, to tools, cars, shoes and clothing. Even many of the handicrafts it sells as its own, in its local bazaars, are made elsewhere. The region is not by any means a backwater. It is not a global financial or industrial hub, certainly, and where financial and services hotspots do exist they are located in Dubai, Manama, Doha, and a handful of other relatively small Gulf Arab cities – but nor is it closed off from the rest of the world.

Could its relative economic autocracy be feeding its rejectionist sentiments, or is the state deliberately taking up the cause of culture as its shield – its *pardah*, veil – against globalization? Is culture a barrier to further economic integration, or a handy tool in the struggle for defence of national rights and core identities? Are the costs seen to outweigh the benefits of an open-door policy, even in the absence of other alternatives? If this were to be the case, could we then argue that the defence of the nation-state is actually little more than an instrumental element of the mercantilist instinct of MENA elites? Finally, how does this apparent resistance fare in the face of growing regionalization of the world economy, and the push by some

MENA states for the deepening of regional relations (in terms of inter-MENA trade, investment and labour mobility) as a response to the internationalization of economic processes that globalization brings? These questions must be addressed, once we have located the region historically and strategically.

Globalization in History

In its simplest form, globalization suggests interdependence and interregional connection. Such interdependencies have a particular resonance in the MENA region. In geopolitical terms, this region has been an open regional system for generations, interactive with regard to its pre-modern social organizations, and highly extrovert as far as its pre-Islamic and Islamic empires are concerned. Its expansive reach and cosmopolitan nature in earlier times have been underlined by the presence of the profitable trade highway across Asia – the famous Silk Road – and the prosperity of such substantial urban centres as Baghdad, Damascus, Cairo, Saba, Samarqand, Cordoba, and Granada. Even before the emergence of the Silk Road and the cities that it nurtured, Alexandria in Egypt had established itself as the most cosmopolitan and open city in the world, where Egyptians traded exotic products from Arabia and Asia with their northern Mediterranean counterparts. Alexandria was also an important seat of learning, home to the world's largest library at the time.

The early contacts between the Pharaoh's kingdom in Egypt and Europeans, in the millennia before the rise of Christianity, presaged more direct and lasting cultural exchanges between the 'East' (the Near East) and the 'West' (Europe) as far back as 500 BC, when the Greeks and the Persians battled for control of the Near East. Since the defeat on the battlefield of the Achaemenids by Alexander the Great, and the Greeks' deliberate integration of various Eastern practices into their polity, the Middle East has been a tapestry of cultures. Consequently as much a product of geography and geopolitics as of war and trade, one of the enduring features of the MENA region since pre-modern times has been its rich cultural diversity, which has grown from the cultural fusion of various Eastern and European empires, and the penetration of the region by outside forces. Cultural fusion, in which Graeco–Persian competition led to the integration of Hellenic ways with western Asian cultures, has been the norm in this part of the world.[11] Later, Persian–Roman rivalries, and Roman domination of the region for several hundred years, also led to intensive exchanges between the peoples occupying the common borders of Europe and Asia. This, in turn, encouraged further exchanges between the European and Asiatic worlds, although not always friendly ones, judging by the bloody encounters between the Byzantine and Persian states, and of course the role the Crusades played in shaping perceptions across the Mediterranean.

That this region has been cosmopolitan from the rise of the first world empires should be heavily underlined, therefore; as indeed should its role in shaping the first globalized system. John Hobson asserts that globalization in fact started as far back as the sixth century, and that it did so in the East. He takes 500 CE as the starting point of what he terms 'oriental globalisation'. After 500, he notes, 'the Persians, Arabs, Africans, Javanese, Jews, Indians, and the Chinese created and maintained a global economy down to about 1800, in which the major civilisations of the world were at all times interlinked'.[12]

Far from being insular, the Near East has been on the crossroads of different cultures from time immemorial, constantly absorbing cultural invaders from any quarter – even reaching out to other cultures and regions. Goldschmidt explains that the Sasanids, for example, 'sent out scholars to many other countries to collect books, which were translated into the Pahlavi (Middle Persian) language, and to collect scientific and technical lore. Many foreign scholars were attracted to Persia, a tolerant kingdom in which Nestorian Christians, Jews, and Buddhists could worship and proselytize freely. Driven from a bigoted Byzantine Empire, in the fifth century, Nestorian savants found refuge at the legendry Persian academy of Jundishapur, a center for the preservation of Hellenistic culture ... Scholars and students came from all parts of Europe and Asia to teach and study there, unhindered by racial prejudice, religious dogma, or political restrictions'.[13] That Hellenic civilization was consciously being protected by a non-European power should provide some concrete evidence for the thesis that the Middle East has been not just big on cultural interaction, but also tolerant and welcoming of other ways of life. On the western flanks of the region, links were also being sought with Europe, culminating in the rise of Muslim kingdoms in Andalusia from the ninth century. What is clear from even a cursory examination of the MENA civilizations is that none ever emerged or grew in geographical or cultural isolation; the Egyptians, Phoenicians, Assyrians, Persians, and Muslim Arab empires hailing from these lands expanded their realms of influence through assimilation and interaction with their neighbours. Muslim empires, in particular, enjoyed a sophisticated economic system that was built on the efforts of merchants and the principles of commerce. As Maxine Rodinson has noted, 'the density of commercial relations within the Muslim world constituted a sort of world market ... of unprecedented dimensions. The development of exchange had made possible regional specialisation in industry as well as in agriculture, bringing about relations of economic interdependence that sometimes extended over great distances. A world market of the same type was formed in the Roman empire, but the Muslim "common market" was very much bigger ... Not only did the Muslim world know a capitalistic sector, but this sector was apparently the most extensive and highly developed in history before the establishment of the world market created by the western European bourgeoisie, and this did not outstrip it in importance until the sixteenth century'.[14]

Islamic empires, in other words, had already made great strides towards integration of vast territories through trade before Europe had even awakened to the very real new economic opportunities presented beyond its borders: 'the birth of oriental globalisation', maintains Hobson, 'owes much to the Islamic [world]. The Muslims (and Negroes) of Africa as well as Muslims of the Middle East were the real global capitalist pioneers, serving to weave together a global economy of significant scale and importance'.[15] This early global economy, the heart of which was in the Near East, extended far, into China and Polynesia in the east, and the Eurasian landmass and western European sea-lanes in the west.

With the rise of Islam and the establishment of the tradition of the annual Pilgrimage, Mecca and Medina emerged as the new cosmopolitan cultural centres of the Middle East, providing new bridges between the region and the rest of the world. Soon Muslims from all over Asia would be rubbing shoulders with each other, exchanging ideas and learning from each other's traditions – the types of exchange that still take place during the annual Hajj festival. Other Islamic cities far removed from the nerve-centre of the faith, such as Karouwan in Tunisia, served a similar purpose. These trans-national links were so rich and intensive that Abd-El-Kader Cheref has even suggested that 'the first Islamic state established by Prophet Muhammad was ... the commencement of globalization of the human society'.[16]

As is evident, then, the Middle East has been exposed to outside forces for a longer time than there have been modern states; on the surface globalization, following the colonial and imperial storms of recent centuries, should have posed no real new threat to the region, or at least should not be seen as threatening by these societies. Yet globalization has been seen across the MENA region as posing both a challenge and a new kind of existential threat to the 'Muslim way of life'. It is therefore being resisted in the same vein that colonialism and imperialism once were, perhaps even more vigorously, given the responses to it since the late 1980s. Against the backdrop of an inclusive and enlightened environment surrounding the rise of Islamic empires since the seventh century, why globalization should been seen with such open hostility is one of the paradoxes of our time. For all the region's open borders through the ages and its extensive cultural interactions, globalization is being resisted by several governments and movements as the bearer of a challenge greater than colonialism, and a threat greater than ungodly Marxism. Understanding what it is about globalization that causes so much anxiety, how globalization is formulated in the Middle East, and what people in the region mean by this term will be crucial in any attempt to make sense of the nature of the policy and intellectual debates in the region. This is a prerequisite, it seems, for any assessment of the impact of globalization on the Middle East.

Dar el-Islam Fights Back?

Fanon was one of the main authorities drawing attention to the corrosive power of colonial/imperial cultures in the less-developed countries, but also wrote in a semi-romantic fashion of an 'Arab awakening' in the 1950s and 1960s. Arab writers, he said, 'reminded their people of the great pages of their history [in] reply to the lies told by the occupying power'. This awakening, he argued, was the antithesis of the colonial cultural imposition: 'The struggle for national liberty has been accompanied by a cultural phenomenon known by the name of the awakening of Islam ... The Arab leaders have tried to return to the famous Dar El Islam which shone so brightly from the twelfth to the fourteenth century'.[17] For Fanon, Dar el-Islam represented a 'firebreak' against colonialist/imperialist culture. As one traces the intellectual evolution of such debates, it is interesting that Fanon's version of the political importance of Dar el-Islam in colonial times has, since the 1970s, been transplanted onto a new political–religious force, commonly known as the revivalist Islamic movements – or political Islam. But Fanon's Dar el-Islam and political Islam do not share the same social space or, strictly speaking, the same function. Fukuyama aptly noted that the strength of political Islam or, as he says, Islamic revival, 'can only be understood if one understands how deeply the dignity of Islamic society had been wounded in its double failure to maintain the coherence of its traditional society and to successfully assimilate the techniques and values of the West'.[18] While the appeal of Dar el-Islam to Fanon was clearly in its power, in the hands of Arab nationalist elites, to present an authentic and indigenous force against imperialism, the Islamic revivalists of today represent a very different strand, more of a counter-cultural fight back from within the Muslim *umma* – a defensive response to the power of the authoritarian ruling state on the one hand, and to globalization on the other. As Mandaville notes, 'hegemony in its Western guise is not the only obstacle contemporary Islam needs to negotiate; there is also hegemony within'.[19] This is very much a local–global challenge, and will need to be revisited in several ways. The cultural realm of the debate is still with us, but takes a slightly different shape when presented within the globalization paradigm.

Returning to the broader debate of earlier times about imperialism and cultural domination, the culture-specific arguments developed in the 1950s and 1960s by such authorities as Fanon and Sartre ran counter to the views expressed by the father of radical political economy, Karl Marx. Marx had done more than any thinker to expose the links between the economics and the cultural underpinnings of capitalism – which today form the fundamental elements of the globalization debate. For Marx, the 'Asiatic' world was both despotic and, in historical terms, primitive. His was an unguarded Eurocentric view of the world. In 1853, for instance, he cautioned readers of the *New York Daily Tribune* that 'we must not forget that these idyllic village communities, inoffensive though they may appear, had always been the solid foundation of Oriental despotism, that they restrained the human mind within the smallest possible compass, making it the unresisting tool of superstition, enslaving it beneath traditional rules, depriving it of all grandeur and historical energies'.[20] As Carrere d'Encausse and Schram have observed, to say that the Asian countries 'are still at a phase corresponding to the dawn of civilization, and that they would never have emerged from their stagnation without Western intervention, is to condemn in advance any attempt by the peoples of these countries to modernize while retaining their own personalities'.[21] If Marx could speak to us today, he might argue that globalization was the catalyst for civilization change that the less-developed world needed. But he might also add that the developing world was incapable of managing the advances brought by globalization. He could indeed see the reinforcement of despotism as a reaction to global capitalism.

Others, notably Bill Warren, put forward an alternative view: that capitalism was indeed the liberating force Marx had identified it to be. In his classic, *Imperialism: Pioneer of Capitalism*, Warren deliberately adopted an 'early Marxian' methodology in his analysis of capitalist development outside Europe, to argue that imperialism was indeed the most effective way of introducing the dialectical energies of capitalism into the developing world. In this he could be classed as an early advocate of globalization and a strong critic of exceptionalism as a virtue. Capital export, far from being a feature of capitalist stagnation, as Lenin had suggested, was in fact an important measure of its success and dynamism, and a 'significant feature of industrial capitalism since its inception'.[22] Capital export (leading to growth of industry and manufacturing) was the same energy seen in the less-developed countries in the post-1945, post-colonial world. Imperialism (read globalization) was a 'powerful engine of progressive social change [which had brought] substantial industrialisation and capitalist transformation' to the developing world, said Warren.[23]

A century after Marx's judgement came the biggest challenge to Marx's Eurocentric perspective, when the Chinese Communist Party finally triumphed over its domestic foes and imperial powers, and founded Asia's first and largest Peoples' Republic. Mao's China saw the emergence of the biggest theoretical challenge of all to classical Marxism, that of 'Asiocentric communism'. The birth of the Peoples' Republic of China created fundamental geopolitical and intellectual challenges for the Soviet Marxist–Leninists who had come to believe in the supremacy of the working class, the proletariat, over all other 'oppressed' classes, and had come to see this class as the most likely revolutionary class. Thus by the mid-twentieth century we had come full circle, and parted very significantly from the perspectives first enunciated by Marx in the 1850s and 1860s about the absence of socio-economic vibrancy in the less-developed world and Asiatic society's lack of potential for political development. Today the same debates are being rehearsed in the context of globalization debates and the Middle East and its purported 'exceptionalism'.

Thus the debate regarding globalization and the Middle East is subject to similar culturally driven, as well as political economy, arguments. The region is seen by some as backward in political and economic terms because it has suffered social deprivation, thanks to despotic elites and religious fanaticism. An important work on the 'prospects of democracy', for example, has posed the question 'whether some characteristics of Muslim culture make democratization more difficult in Islamic countries than in the countries of other cultural areas'. An explanation of a wealth of empirical data presented offers the following conclusion: 'because Muslim culture unites the countries of the [MENA and Central Asia] regional group and separates them from most countries of the other regional groups, one could argue that some features of Muslim culture strengthen the concentration of political power. It may be that power-holders can increase their control of intellectual power resources by identifying themselves with Islam just like the former Christian rulers in Europe were allied with the Church'.[24] Mirroring earlier debates, Muslim culture is again being portrayed as nurturing and nourishing despotism. The assertion is that the cultural realm has stifled progress on the political front, while the problems resulting from the unique political economy of the region have contributed to holding back progressive social forces. Repression of women can be seen as a classic example of how religion might have helped keep the region 'backward' and seemingly detached from the global forces around it.

The tendency towards concentrating political power in the hands of a few men is what Hisham Sharabi labelled a unique form of neo-patriarchy in the Arab world. This is a patriarchal form which is 'neither European nor Asiatic, as Marx has characterized these', but one that has 'its own peculiar history and structure, which can be identified as distinctively Arab (Islamic), not merely Asian or non-European'.[25] This Arab (Islamic) neo-patriarchy is now facing the forces of globalization, and far from being a progressive force in the way Fanon had depicted, is today perceived as an outmoded and reactionary one that is not only unable to respond positively to challenges of the domestic arena, but is also incapable of mediating the pressures of an ever-changing and dynamic regional and international environment.

The Strategic Context: 9/11, Globalization and the Greater Middle East

For the purposes of broader discussion it is assumed here that MENA is a regional system, but the term 'system' is used loosely and does not imply the existence of a cohesive regional order. 'System' is used to refer to the existence of a set of interactive and dynamic relationships between the group of Arab countries in this region; between these and a set of non-Arab actors (Iran, Israel, Turkey, and also Afghanistan, Pakistan, and parts of Central Asia); and between the entire group of states and non-state actors from Morocco in the west to the northern shores of the Arabian and Caspian seas in the east and north-east. This is today's broader or GME, forming a unique strategic unit. At critical junctures, one can identify concert in action among the subsets of the GME states, and even some policy congruence over what are perceived to be region-wide security issues. But this tends to be the exception rather than the rule, for the geopolitics of this area encourages competition and rivalry as one of its inherent drivers.

As already noted, there is a need to explore the multifaceted impact that globalization is – and is perceived to be – having on the region. Globalization is a phenomenon that exists, and is the essence of what Bill and Chavez have called 'incoherence' and 'chaotic turbulence'.[26] We therefore also need to understand why 'probably no area in the world resists ... globalization to an extent equating that of the Islamic Middle East [and why] the majority of regimes, opposition movements, and intellectuals in the region are consciously anti-globalization'.[27]

Moreover, we must note the strategic consequences of the region's antiglobalists' position of seeing the USA as its main enemy. Somewhat simplified, the prevailing line of thinking goes as follows: since the end of the Cold War the USA has dominated the international system and, because it no longer has a global counterweight, it has been able to lead globalization unhindered. The USA is therefore pursuing global domination through military force and economic penetration. As the Muslim world, particularly its heartland in the Middle East, provides the strongest base of resistance to US designs, it has been targeted by Washington, whose aggressive intentions have become more pronounced since 9/11. In this region, it is heard, the USA is only interested in securing Israel's regional hegemony and in monopolizing the Muslim world's core asset, its hydrocarbon deposits. So everything it does will – inevitably, according to this line of thought – be driven by a deep desire to weaken the Muslim states and to break down their resistance. In practical terms, the struggle over Iraq's future subsequent to the fall of Baghdad to Anglo–American military forces in spring 2003 has largely been seen in this light by the USA's enemies.

Examples of this line of Islamist-leaning, but also nationalist, thinking can be gleaned from a wide range of speeches and statements issued by representatives of such forces. But in order to demonstrate the depth of this line of reasoning, we can illustrate the classic position through the words of a British Muslim, who stated in early 2003 that 'it is generally believed the real American objective behind an invasion [of Iraq] is to change the political map of the Middle East, appropriate its oil wealth and appoint Israel as a regional superpower exercising total hegemony over the entire Middle East and beyond'.[28] This has been an often-repeated Muslim view. Lord Heseltine (a former British deputy prime minister and a member of the establishment) has reflected on this sentiment and concluded that 'in the Middle East there is the beginning of a holy war because there is a focus of discontent which, if we don't get a grip, will fester and grow'.[29] The two views, although expressed from the opposite poles of the debate, convey the same message: Western action is seen as a direct challenge to the integrity of the Muslim world.

But, ironically, the debate about globalization in the immediate aftermath of 9/11 focused more on the limits of globalization.[30] Indeed, 9/11 was viewed in some business circles as a real dampener on globalization. The argument was made that the terror attacks could result in a reduction in the pace of integration, travel, and communication, which would ultimately weaken the globalization process. Undoubtedly 9/11 has made it harder for goods, people, and services to travel across borders, particularly in and out of the Western countries. But is this sufficient evidence to argue the demise of globalizing forces?[31] Proponents of globalization, who see it as the articulation of a series of economic-related systems dependent on the continuing mobility of capital, certainly do not think so. The 9/11 terrorist attacks have not disrupted the flow of capital across any border.

As 9/11 came to emphasize the cultural distance between the world's regions, globalization had already substantially narrowed the intellectual and commercial gap between them. For capital there was no option but to attack other markets; this had been the fundamental logic of capitalism from its inception. In the course of the twentieth century Western capital, in all its forms, exported itself to all corners of the globe, respecting neither communism nor planned economic systems. The terrorist attacks, witnessed live or in near-real time by many millions around the globe, may have changed the backdrop for the debate about globalization, but have not affected its onward march.

If we accept the premise that globalization carries within it the two-dimensional force of simultaneous but opposite movements of global integration and local separation, then it is possible to maintain that challenges from the global level will generate their own counter-forces from below. Thus for every global actor, like the USA, there will necessarily be a local rebel, an often-violent Spartacus. In the geopolitical framework of the GME, post-9/11, the global actor has to cope not only with the national insecurities that follow global integration (in the shape of al-Qaeda's reach to America's heartland and that of its global allies), but also the challenges posed by radical Islam in this strategically vital region – whether in Pakistan, Uzbekistan, Saudi Arabia, Iraq, Jordan, or in Algeria, Morocco, or Tunisia.

So, on the American side, 9/11 has not only raised new suspicions about the faith of Islam and Muslims in general; has not only forced the instinctively introvert Bush administration to revitalize the USA's international role; has not only led it to military intervention in the affairs of more than one weak and vulnerable Muslim state (Afghanistan, Iraq); has not only encouraged it to perceive the Muslim world (and the Middle East in particular) as backward and therefore in urgent need of active modernization and development (democratization); but has also, in the light of information coming to the fore about the nationality of the hijackers and their associational links with the al-Qaeda network, caused it to re-evaluate its relations with some of its closest allies in the Arab world. As we will see, America's reassessment of its Arab partnerships has had a direct impact on the security narrative of the region, and has left a mark on the domestic politics of many of its regional partners. The White House's declaration that the region was in need of renewal and reform – in need of intervention – has formed the basic platform of the USA's relationships and priorities in the GME region.[32]

In this mission, the administration received intellectual support from several important quarters, forces that within weeks of the fall of the Berlin Wall in 1989 had already raised the spectre of radical Islam as a deadly foe of the West, and the prospects of a clash of cultures and civilizations.[33] 'A new spectre is haunting America', Douglas Streusand warned in 1989, 'one that some Americans consider more sinister than Marxism–Leninism ... That spectre is Islam'.[34] Daniel Pipes had warned the West in 1990 that the 'Muslims are coming!'[35] These analysts, notes Gerges, invoked familiar Cold War concepts 'to sharpen public concern and fear about a new Islamic threat'.[36] Moreover, well before 9/11, these figures had drawn a dangerous image of rampant Islam in an unstable MENA region, in which terrorism and proliferation combined to create a direct challenge to the safety of the West.

In September 2001, their seemingly prophetic warnings about the 'green peril' had come to pass; their chance to shape the agenda on Islam had come. The discourse on globalization and the political relations between the USA and the Muslim world were now hostages to the battle against international–transnational Islamic terrorism. Huntington stated that the 'contemporary global politics is the age of Muslim wars. Muslims fight each other and fight non-Muslims far more than do peoples of other civilizations. Muslim wars have replaced the cold war as the principal form of international conflict'.[37]

As already noted, 9/11 ignited a much wider debate in the West, particularly in the USA, about the 'problems' of the Muslim world, the place of Islam as a seventh-century phenomenon in a modern society, the role of Islam in the socialization process and politicization of Muslim populations, the educational role Islam played in curricula around the Muslim world, and the relationship between Islam and culture and politics in Muslim societies.[38] In some Western circles it became imperative to reinforce the secular (and Western) underpinnings of the state. Thus, in 2004 in France, all outward, public signs of religious symbolism were banned, and to the dismay of many hundreds of pious French Muslims the wearing of the Islamic veil, along with the display of other religions' symbols, was outlawed. Paris's policy generated an angry response from all corners of the Muslim world, and even led al-Qaeda to declare that the ban 'is new evidence of the extent of the Crusaders' hatred for Muslims, even if they brag about democracy, freedom and human rights. France, the country of liberty defends only the liberty of nudity, debauchery and decay, while fighting chastity and modesty'.[39]

On the Middle East side, the terrorist acts were received with genuine shock and horror. But beyond sympathies with the human tragedy that had unfolded, many in the region saw in the Bush administration's responses a reinforcement of their perceptions of the USA as the hegemonic and anti-Islam power of our time – the New Rome – whose mission was to destroy Muslim culture and way of life, to dominate Muslim lands and societies, and to usurp its natural and other resources. The perception is, said Malaysia's prime minister Mahathir Mohamad, 'that Muslim countries seem to be the target everywhere – Libya, Sudan, Somalia, Chechnya, Iran, Iraq ... It is a question of injustice. It seems that it is all right for Palestinians to die, or Afghans to die. Thousands of Bosnians died, 200,000 died, and the world watched on TV and did nothing ... But if you kill anybody else that is wrong'.[40] Mahathir Mohamad, it should be noted, was no anti-Western fanatic: he was one of the few Muslim leaders who had not only embraced globalization, but had been a close partner of the West in the Far East.

The war on terror, moreover, was said to be 'a campaign to wrench Muslim societies from their religious roots'.[41] In this climate of fear and suspicion, the already strong perception that globalization was a Western tool for subjugation of the developing world was reinforced. Unfortunately, the security responses to 9/11 in the USA and the West in general further reinforced the impression of globalization as an American agent for the destruction of Islam and Muslims. A typical position was that of a group of 209 prominent Muslims from across the Arab world, who in a statement issued in November 2002, argued that the USA was intent on 'wiping out the Islamic identity, spread American culture in the region, control its oil wealth and cover up for its failure in Afghanistan'. In a telling combination of geopolitical and cultural analysis, the signatories stated that the USA 'wants to plunge the region into turmoil, prevent development and protect Israel and ensure its superiority'.[42]

In short, in the aftermath of the September 2001 attacks, the vigorous debate on the intricacies of globalization and Middle Eastern encounters with the process were slowly relegated to a subdivision of the discussions of Islam as a faith, its place in the global village, and the essence of Muslim–Western relations.

To the radical Islamists, on the other hand, 9/11 had not only 'taught the Americans a lesson' for what was to be its arrogant behaviour and unjust policies towards the Middle East; it had at the same time provided the excuse for the Americans to unleash their power against Islam. The battle, at last, had been joined. As a leading Egyptian Islamist put it, 'What the US is trying to do is change Islam from within. The campaigns against Afghanistan, Iraq, Palestine, Kashmir and Sudan [show this, but will also] definitely awaken the sleeping giant'.⁴³ The persistent claim that the USA was seeking to 'change Islam from within' was symptomatic of two related developments. First, an acknowledgement by the Islamists that the USA's reach in the region was indeed extensive – that although it was a global power, it had also become a local actor. And second, that the greater Middle East was already highly penetrated and greatly vulnerable to the pressures that global forces could bring to its societies. Globalization was, in America's hands, the vehicle for this two-pronged attack.

Terrorism and Geopolitics: The 9/11 Effect

While the 'war on terror' campaign of the USA was no doubt an understandable security response to an unprecedented crisis, its formulation, which directly targeted parts of the Muslim world, coupled with the sentiment expressed by President George W. Bush that 'if you are not with us then you are against us', left little doubt in many minds in the Muslim world that the real target was indeed their realm.⁴⁴ The president's statement merely added fuel to fires already raging. An example is the comments made by a highly respected Egyptian intellectual on US motives: 'I don't think the US has a new map for the region yet, a new Sykes–Picot formulation', he wrote, 'But what it does want is to shake up established customs and ways of doing things. It is already putting pressure on Arab and Islamic countries to alter curricula, liberate the economy, allow more freedom of expression, change the status of women, and restrain the role of at least some religious institutions ... the US is engaged in policies aimed at undermining movements antagonistic to the US or to reform imposed from abroad. There are attempts to create a deeper sense of humiliation, either through [deliberately] insulting comments by US officials or through disrupting the efforts of Arab and Islamic countries to help the Palestinians ... The aim is to deprive these regimes of any chance to regroup or rehabilitate the Arab regional system. The US is using all its strength to get Arab and Islamic countries to capitulate, one after another ... Washington will continue until the Islamic and Arab community loses cohesion, Islam's penchant for *jihad* ebbs, and the pan-Arab movement runs out of steam. At which time the 'greater Middle East', promised by President Bush ... will finally materialise'.⁴⁵

The Arab and Muslim fears of the USA's motives were further raised when, within weeks of the atrocities, other voices in the USA, particularly evangelical preachers from the vast American religious establishment, began to criticize Islam in their television broadcasts and other communications. The theme of the commentaries was straightforward: 'Islam is at war with us', as stated by Paul Weyrich, an influential Washington figure. Three individuals, in particular, were singled out by Islamic groups and Muslim leaders for expressing the most offensive anti-Islam views: Jerry Falwell, Pat Roberston, and Franklin Graham (the son of well known televangelist Billy

Graham). In an interview broadcast in early October 2002 on CBS television's *60 Minutes* news programme, Falwell joined the fringe of Islam-bashers by calling Prophet Mohammed 'a terrorist'. Barely a year earlier, Franklin Graham had been criticized for stating in November 2001 that Islam was 'a very evil and wicked religion'. For his part, Pat Robertson had said in February 2002 that Islam was a religion of violence seeking to 'dominate and then, if need be, destroy'. His words were echoed in the political establishment by a member of the Pentagon's Defense Policy Board, Kenneth Adelman, who stated that 'the more you examine the religion [Islam], the more militant it seems. After all, its founder, Mohammed, was a warrior, not a peace advocate like Jesus'.[46] Such views, articulated by prominent American parsons and commentators, underlined the gulf that 9/11 had opened up between the world of Islam and the USA, for a similar line of attack on the USA was daily being reinforced by the traditional and radical Islamist forces across the vast territories of Asia, Africa, and Europe, where most Muslims lived.

At the conceptual level, also, we can find reasons why the USA should be emerging as the single most important target of anti-Western/anti-globalization radical forces in the Muslim world. Part of the answer may lie in the analysis of Levy, who had shown back in the 1960s that since the rise of the less-developed world, the late-developer (late-modernizing) countries have tended to follow the example set by their 'modern' (that is to say Western) counterparts. Today, the society to emulate and imitate in terms of innovation, technological and industrial achievements is of course the USA which, according to Levy, represents 'the most extreme example of modernization' in the world.[47] For its dynamism and global reach, the USA would surely make an easy target for those forces that resist the march of globalization. If one adds to this Sklair's observation that the USA is the only country in the world 'whose agents, organizations and classes are hegemonic in all three spheres' of politics, culture and economics,[48] then one can again develop a real focus for the depth of animosity between radical Islamist forces and the USA. In no uncertain terms, these groups see the USA as the ultimate hegemon – a powerful and unrivalled bully who is also the guardian of the contemporary international system, with all the inequities, cultural deprivation and plundering that this global system breeds.

But amidst the confusion, 9/11 also brought a badly needed sense of purpose to the Muslims, whose own civilization was already tearing itself apart over ideology, purpose, governance, distribution of political and economic power, and control of the Muslim agenda in a post-bipolar world. Before 9/11, an intensive 'clash of civilizations' was already going on in Afghanistan between various Muslim states supporting or fighting the Taleban. A flavour of the ferocity of the inter-Islamic clashes can be gleaned from a semi-official Iranian publication on international Islamic developments. This article is significant for its assessment of the rise of the Taleban in Afghanistan and the tenor of its analysis with regard to Iran's Muslim neighbours:

> Thus, with American arms and with petrodollars from certain oil-rich [Gulf Arab] states, the Inter-Services Intelligence (ISI) of the Pakistani armed forces created the schools that had mushroomed with Saudi money in Afghan refugee camps for the spread of schismatic Wahhabi beliefs ... [The Taleban] first made their appearance on the Afghan scene in 1995 with Pakistani military advisors in their train. However, their record ... shows that the Taleban are neither Islamic nor all of them are Afghans.[49]

On one hand, it was claimed that the Taleban was created in order to discredit Islam; on the other, it was argued that the Taleban was manufactured in Pakistan and Afghanistan by some Muslim states as a tool in their own battles against other Islamic traditions. The 9/11 attacks did not affect these differences much, but they did have a very direct impact on the geopolitics of Islam after the USA unleashed its military might against the al-Qaeda bases in Afghanistan and their Taleban backers. As the war unfolded, the Taleban as a viable political force was extinguished, support from two key Gulf Arab states (Saudi Arabia and the United Arab Emirates) ceased, the military government in Pakistan drew nearer to the USA, and the presence of anti-American radical Islam in South and Southeast Asia, the Arabian Peninsula, and the former Asian republics of the Soviet Union intensified. The 9/11 attacks also intensified the battle within Islam as Salafi forces and al-Qaeda affiliates increased their attacks on Shias after the fall of the Sunni-dominated regime in Baghdad in April 2003.

Cultural Geography and American Power

A direct, and perhaps inevitable, consequence of these developments has been the confrontation (sometimes political and sometimes violent) that has appeared at the intersections of contact between the USA and the Muslim countries. It is at these crossroads that radical Islam, initially in the shape of al-Qaeda, has been able to sharpen its angle of attack. In Pakistan in October 2002, for instance, it was the alliance of six anti-American Islamic groups that emerged to form the single most important opposition force in Pakistan's parliamentary elections. The Muttahida Majlis-e-Amal (MMA) is no friend of the West or the ruling establishment in Islamabad. It not only views the Taleban with favour, but is vehemently opposed to any interaction with the USA. Its leader, Qazi Hussain Ahmed, has said that he 'will not accept US bases and western culture'.[50] The MMA's general secretary (Mian Aslam) stated shortly after the poll that 'The Taliban are our brothers. They are good people. The idea [that] they are bad is a misconception of the West'.[51] Their electoral success, it has been evident for some time, has not only hampered the hunt for al-Qaeda members in Pakistan and Afghanistan, but also threatened the stability of Pakistan's government and its foreign partnerships.

The second instance of the web of confrontation between the two took place just 2 days later, when a massive car bomb destroyed a popular entertainment district in the holiday resort of Bali (Indonesia), killing hundreds of Western tourists and dozens of others. The fact that the attack might have been linked to a darker al-Qaeda plot emerged in the context of bin Laden's earlier comments about Australia's role in harming the land of Islam in Indonesia. He had said, back in November 2001, that the Australians were part and parcel of the same Christian 'crusaders' who had entered Muslim lands.[52] Under the guise of United Nations peace-keeping operations in East Timor, the Australians had set foot on sacred Muslim soil and were part of 'a long series of conspiracies, a war of annihilation [against Islam]'. The Australians were part of the conspiracy to dismember Muslim Indonesia, he claimed, and were an active member of the same United Nations organization that had, in 1947, 'surrendered the land of Muslims to the Jews'. They were therefore guilty by action as well as association, and therefore their citizens were viewed as a legitimate target.

Both events introduced a new political factor in Washington's relations with these important Muslim countries, particularly as, combined, they came to exercise significant influence on the geopolitics of Islam in very unpredictable ways. The front against militant Islam had broadened in dangerous ways, and the governments of these countries were forced to make unpalatable choices between their domestic agendas and management of power relations at home, and their security obligations towards the international community. These governments, and many others like them across the Muslim world, have tried to postpone the unpalatable choice between security and democracy for as long as possible, but with its choice of targets across many lands al-Qaeda has persistently tested the stability of the balance being sought by moderate Muslim governments between legitimacy at home and the provision of security.[53] Such precarious conditions considerably complicate the politics of globalization in the Muslim world, which up to this point had been subsumed within the basket of cultural concerns. Domestic politics, and with it national security, after the autumn of 2001 had been caught up in the geopolitical firestorm generated by 9/11.

So, by the time the USA attacked Afghanistan in October 2001, the geopolitical impact of 9/11 had helped increase the sense of siege in the two contending poles of Islam and the West, and had sharpened the debate in the Middle East about globalization. The impression that globalization was an intrusive and imposed force in turn reinforced the notion that a clash of cultures was indeed taking place, in ways that Samuel Huntington had been severely criticized for suggesting in 1993. But if Islam is believed to be both religion and state, it would stand to reason that the clash would also be between

Islam and the globalization spearheaded by the West, for globalization targets both the state and its cultural and socio-economic underpinnings.

In the aftermath of 9/11, the MENA region presented the West with both a huge security challenge and a golden opportunity to smash the residues of resistance to true modernization – to 'marketization'. Here was a historic chance to shape the region in the mould of the advanced countries fit for the twenty-first century. To even whisper the words 'regime change' in the mid-twentieth century and during the birth of the post-colonial era would have been interpreted as a direct assault on another country's sovereignty; to openly pursue it in the twenty-first century, as the USA did with regard to Iraq and others, demonstrates on the one hand the erosion of the sanctimonious state as the inviolable unit of international politics, and on the other the impact globalization has had on the constellation of international forces. In the post-9/11 international order, regimes and regions that posed a challenge to the security of the West and its regional interests have themselves been challenged without impunity. Force has been mobilized to effect change (Afghanistan and Iraq), and pressure has been applied elsewhere in order to expedite it (Saudi Arabia, Iran, Libya, Syria, Sudan), all with grave and unforeseen geopolitical consequences.

It is being accepted that, in the highly interdependent and globalized international system of the twenty-first century, local and regional insecurities need to be dealt with at source, for they can easily escalate into clear and present dangers for the entire system. It was noted earlier that the local–international dichotomy is a natural by-product of the globalization process itself, for the operating assumption here is that globalization is 'a two-dimensional process engendering simultaneous but opposite movements – towards global integration and an enhanced focus on the local. For every new self there is a new other, for every global truth there is a local dissent, for every global lord there is a local rebel'.[54] Given this dichotomy, it is not at all surprising that 9/11 has caused a sudden shift in the world's new East–West boundaries, and has brought the globalism of America to the heart of the 'particularist' Middle East. As explored throughout this book, in the greater Middle East 'glocalization' is at its sharpest edge.

1 Globalization
System or Process?

At any given time, globalization has limits set by the state of technology, social organization, and conceptualization, and by the costs it imposes and the resistance it provokes. How far and fast globalization extends, how deeply it penetrates, are functions of the balance between impulse and resistance – but both are always there. By that definition, during its first millennium Islam was the world's most powerful engine, and vehicle of globalization, and it was also globalization's most sharply contested battleground.

Thomas W. Simons Jr, *Islam in a Globalizing World* (Stanford, CA: Stanford University Press, 2003).

Globalization and the Capitalist Project

Globalization has proved to be one of the hardest modern concepts to define unambiguously, let alone to encapsulate fully in a set of operating principles. Even finding a universally acceptable set of variables for its content has proved difficult, with different disciplines assigning their own values to it. To some, it is no more than a new way of evaluating the international march of capital, and as such is not novel at all. Others, though, view the phenomenon as a new, 'post-modern' development, associated only indirectly with the 500-year march of capitalism. Still others see globalization as a symbol of, and testimony to, the cultural victory of the West over the rest – the supremacy of 'Western values and value systems'. In this regard, it has also come to depict the political domination of the West in the international arena, seen by foe and friend alike to be headed and managed by the USA. It was in the late twentieth century that the unexpectedly rapid and sustained American economic expansion,[1] coupled with the demise of the Soviet bloc, came to symbolize, particularly in the Muslim world, the triumph of American cultural, political and economic power in the world.

Some observers even saw the victory of the West over the Soviet bloc as the 'end of history' and the prelude to the dawn of 'universal history'. The collapse of the Berlin Wall in 1989 captured the mood of the moment very well – the end of the historic struggle between competing powers in the international arena in favour of the Western-style liberal democratic model. But for many in the Muslim world, radical, conservative or traditionalist, the view that 'liberal democracy remains the only coherent political aspiration that spans different regions and cultures around the globe' seemed to represent more a of threat – a call to arms – than promise of a brighter future.[2] With good reason, one might say, as many observers in less-developed countries equated the universal history thesis with that of the 'universal values' one, in which the West would be aiming to impose its own interests and agendas on the Muslims.[3] Fear of socio-cultural domination again reared its head, a fear that the Islamists have used expertly in their efforts to mobilize support for rebutting the West. Sceptical sentiments rising in the Muslim world found similar echoes in other non-Western societies. For many, whether Western or purely American, cultural hegemony was not a welcome by-product of the end of the Cold War. Even in Europe, and nowhere more so than in France, the prospect of American socio-cultural hegemony generated serious anxiety, inviting widespread opposition to the USA's corporate presence in the European Union's heartland.

At one level, it had become apparent across the world that the battle was being lost – the march of capitalism was unstoppable. But, on another level, when people saw their economic and political uniqueness being lost, and their cultural identity apparently undermined, they seem to have turned to the spiritual space as their sole remaining vehicle for self-preservation.[4] They have increasingly also utilized the spiritual as the vehicle capable of mounting a cultural–political fight back against US-led globalization. Nowhere were such struggles more manifest and dramatic than in the Middle East heartland of the Muslim world, where political/radical and traditionalist Islam joined hands in an effort to try and blunt the instruments of globalization, which they saw not just in cultural terms, but also in political, security and socio-economic terms. For them, globalization should receive the same treatment that imperialism had a century earlier.

Globalization, it could also be claimed, may in addition have acted as the chief midwife of the al-Qaeda terrorist network. First, globalization provided the rationale for a bloody fight against the USA and its allies; second, globalization provided the means for a fight back. In the course of the late 1990s, when Afghanistan was no more than a medieval Islamic emirate under the Taleban student-rulers of the country, the extra-territorial al-Qaeda and its global network took root there and learnt to adapt the first rule of globalization – think global, but act local – for its own terror campaign. Al-Qaeda proceeded from this beginning to use the tools of globalization – open borders, low barriers to movements of capital and people, the information superhighway, remote targeting – against Islam's perceived enemies. Terrorism experts have even talked in terms of the movement being a corporate entity. The prominent security expert Peter Bergen, for example, opined after the 28 November 2002 terror attack on an Israeli-owned hotel in Mombasa, Kenya that 'Al-Qaida has relaunched itself, a rebranding that presages a second phase in its war against the west'.[5] In a similar vein, another terrorism expert noted in 2004 that bin Laden himself is 'best viewed as terrorist CEO, essentially having applied business administration and modern management techniques learned at university and in the family construction business to the running of a transnational terrorist organization ... Just as large, multinational business conglomerates moved during the 1990s to more linear, flatter and networked structures, bin Laden did the same with al-Qaeda'.[6] The language is unmistakably of the type used by economic forecasters, hinting at the enmeshed nature of al-Qaeda with globalization.

Like everything else in the GME region, therefore, globalization has acquired baggage.

What's in a Name?

Globalization has conjured up in the minds of many the same confused images that imperialism had done in the late nineteenth/early twentieth centuries. Early in the twentieth century, imperialism stood for everything evil about capitalism and its operations in the lands beyond western Europe. Lenin, in chastising many of his contemporaries for their lack of understanding of imperialism, had firmly set the conceptual agenda for the early debates about the phenomenon in his *Imperialism, The Highest Stage of Capitalism*. His conceptual focus was unashamedly political–economic; in the preface to the French and German editions of his pamphlet, for instance, he pointedly attacked several of his German counterparts for their comprising conceptualization of imperialism, writing: 'Capitalism has grown into a world system of colonial oppression and of the financial strangulation of the overwhelming majority of the population of the world by a handful of "advanced" countries. And this "booty" is shared between two or three powerful world plunderers armed to the teeth'.[7] This image of the early twentieth century is visited daily across the Muslim world of the twenty-first, in terms of American power, Western domination, and a sense of powerlessness in the face of neo-colonial aggression facilitated through globalization.

Lenin, the architect of modern anti-imperialism, is at his best towards the end of his famous pamphlet, where he exposes the reader to a vintage analysis of modern capitalist forces at work. As his conclusions still reverberate in intellectual circles, it is worth quoting him in full.

> When a big enterprise assumes gigantic proportions, and, on the basis of an exact computation of mass data, organises according to plan the

supply of primary raw materials to the extent of two-thirds, or three-fourths, of all that is necessary for tens of millions of people; when the raw materials are transported in a systematic and organised manner to the most suitable places of production, sometimes situated hundreds or thousands of miles away from each other; when a single centre directs all the consecutive stages of processing the material right up to the manufacture of numerous varieties of finished articles; when these products are distributed according to a single plan among tens and hundreds of millions of consumers ... then it becomes evident that we have socialisation of production.[8]

Re-reading this passage carefully, one could be forgiven for thinking that Lenin's concept of 'socialization of production' was indeed an allusion to what we today call globalization. However, if Lenin had been preoccupied with the mechanisms of modern capitalism, the next generation of commentators were more directly concerned with the issue of cultural invasion and the social and political manipulative power of imperialism (and its sister, colonialism). So, we find some of the prominent radical sociologists of the 1950s and 1960s focusing on culture as the great battleground between colonialism/imperialism and the less-developed world. In this vein, in his preface to Franz Fanon's famous *The Wretched of the Earth*, Jean-Paul Sartre explains that the imperial mother country of Europe is engineering colonized societies and their cultures to its own advantage, 'satisfied ... to keep some feudal rulers in her pay [here]; there, dividing and ruling she has created a native bourgeoisie, sham from beginning to end; elsewhere she has played a double game: the colony is planted with settlers and exploited at the same time. Thus Europe has multiplied divisions and opposing groups, has fashioned classes and sometimes even racial prejudices, and has endeavoured by every means to bring about and intensify the stratification of colonized societies'.[9]

This view of Europe of the past century is articulated today in many parts of the less-developed world in terms of the USA of today: a hungry empire seeking to dominate the world militarily and culturally for economic gain. But to understand the complexities of this relationship better, we ought to be clear in our minds what globalization is, what it is not, and how to evaluate its impact.

Globalization: Conceptual Framework or Endgame?

We must begin by identifying the rubrics of definitions for this much-contested concept. Here I will try and draw out the (inter)disciplinary roots and conceptual basis of the many definitions on offer, as well as the context for the definitions being provided. What I intend to do here is draw out the many facets of definitions for globalization, and the areas of human activity purportedly affected by it. In so doing, I will, implicitly at first, identify the most salient features of the phenomenon when contextualized in the Middle East. Later, I will explore the realities of the region set against the analytical framework of globalization. The following is thus a series of reflections, signposts if you will, on my reading of the literature and the way that I believe the phenomenon could be interacting with the GME region.

Ian Clark has observed that globalization is a concept still bearing 'the birthmarks of its multi-disciplinary paternity', making it almost impossible to discern a simple meaning for it.[10] This is indeed true, given globalization's mixed intellectual parentage. Globalization can, at times, appear to be all things to all men and women.[11] From the Internet to a hamburger, the term can easily encompass it all, according to Susan Strange.[12] It is even a shorthand for some people's 'entire philosophy of life'.[13] One commentator has distilled its meaning into one comprehensive sentence: 'globalization refers to all those processes by which peoples of the world are incorporated into a single global society'.[14] Use of the term 'global society' is particularly interesting, for in this new world, state actors are diminished to a secondary role and 'region states', which may or may not fall within the borders of a given sovereign country, contends Kenichi Ohmae, take centre stage. States, as our world's political aggregates and chief unit of analysis for over a century, are increasingly less relevant, it is claimed. The glue holding nation-states together 'has begun to dissolve'.[15] The vulnerability of states illustrates the trans-border power of globalization, which is arguably replacing the traditional cross-border relations between states and corporations. At its most abstract level, therefore, globalization implies evolution from the merely 'international' to the 'universal', a global system in which one will find 'high levels of differentiation, multicentricity and chaos ... [where] culture ... will be extremely abstract expressing tolerance for diversity and individual choice ... Importantly, territoriality will disappear as an organising principle for social and cultural life, it will be a society without borders and spatial boundaries'.[16]

To a sceptical few, though, globalization is no more than a myth.[17] 'Although we live in an era of impressive technological, and to some extent social and political, change' argues Lentner, 'evidence for fundamental transformation remains scant'.[18] Even where its presence is acknowledged, its extent is said to be exaggerated and the term itself misused. Waltz, for example, states that globalization 'would mean that the world economy, or at least the globalized portion of it, would be integrated and not merely interdependent. The difference between [the two concepts] ... is a qualitative one ... With integration, the world would look like one big state'[19] – which in reality it is not.

For Ali Mazrui, although globalization is not a new phenomenon, in its current form it marks a more rapid pace of development. Globalization is 'all forces which are turning the world into a global village, compressing distance, homogenising culture, accelerating mobility and reducing the relevance of political borders ... globalization is the gradual villagisation of the world ... Four forces have been major engines of globalization: religion, technology, economy and empire. These ... have often reinforced each other'.[20] Mazrui's mix of hard and soft globalization – religion and technology – is particularly informative for exposing, in some of the analysis, the interdependent and multifaceted dimensions of the process. Held adds more flesh to this line of inquiry, noting that 'Globalization is neither a singular condition nor a linear process. Rather, it is best thought of as a multi-dimensional phenomenon involving diverse domains of activity and interaction including economic, political, technological, military, legal, cultural and environmental. Each of these spheres involves different patterns of relationships and activity – each with its distinctive forms of logic and implications for other domains'.[21]

Despite the scepticism, particularly among political scientists, there are others who see globalization as nothing short of 'a revolution [and as] with all revolutions, globalization is irreversible and uncheckable, transforming whole societies'.[22] But before one gets carried away, a prominent commentator on the phenomenon cautions that 'globalization does not necessarily imply homogenisation or integration. Globalization merely implies greater connectedness and de-territorialization'.[23] This is a valuable distinction, and is echoed by Waltz, Paolini,[24] and others. De-territorialization is a fundamental hang-up of many less-developed countries, of course, and in the GME at least it can imply national implosion and regime collapse, so to assume that globalization will threaten territoriality raises quite important questions about the MENA state in the context of this force. Furthermore, as integration and fragmentation are presented as the other related forces associated with globalization, the geopolitical context of its role in the Middle East will also have to be highlighted, particularly when one assumes that globalization is a dynamic force that applies pressure on several fronts and on multiple levels.

Sklair argued back in 1990 that globalization represented one dominant global system, which had emerged around the axes of the transnational corporations, a transnational capitalist class, and the culture-ideology of consumerism.[25] Note that at that time she was talking about globalization as a 'system', not a process. The agenda of globalization was said to be one of domination: 'the dominant forces of global capitalism are the dominant forces in the global system'.[26] But for Stiglitz, who might share some of Sklair's sentiments, and who is certainly a vocal critic of the 'Washington Consensus', globalization is in reality a 'force for good' which could 'enrich everyone'.[27]

Broadly speaking, therefore, globalization is said to be 'a set of economic and political structures and processes deriving from the changing character of the goods and assets that comprise the base of international political economy'.[28] But others have considered globalization to be more than this.[29] A 'set of processes leading to the lowering of borders to all forms of interaction, which challenges the way people communicate, interact and do business with each other around the globe. It signals the fact that one state can no longer be isolated from others, and it heralds the interlinking of human relations across space and time'.[30] The decline in the importance of distance is the essence of globalization, according to this view.[31] Shortening of distances, among other things, in turn creates opportunities for more interaction.[32] The shortening of distance also squeezes the space between actors, threatening confrontation – an 'interaction of differences', according to Cerny.[33] 'The essence of globalisation', states Paul Judge, 'is increased interconnectivity and like other forces it has an action and a reaction. More interconnectivity results in greater economic, political, religious and other flows across countries and cultures, but those affected often resist the impact of these global forces as their customs and incomes are changed'.[34] It is, at its heart, a dynamic 'process', according to this perspective, and therefore much less of a system.

In more concrete terms, three factors give substance to the meaning of globalization: the steady process of internationalization of capital and its related fields (production, transportation, standardization, communication, speed) since the late 1960s; the dominance since the early 1980s of a neo-liberal international economic agenda closely associated with the 'Chicago School' (or the Washington Consensus) of economists who consistently argue for the adoption of market-based and -oriented approaches to economics and economic development; and the end of the Cold War and the collapse of the Soviet Union in the late 1980s as the ending of the (competing) two-system international economic order, which lifted the lid on the globalization of capital as a commodity and capitalism as the only system *and* process of socio-economic change. 'Productive structures in each nation are reorganised reciprocal to a new international division of labour ... As each nation is restructured and subordinated to the global economy, new activities linked to globalisation come to dominate', according to Robinson.[35] Globalization describes a dynamic process whereby the world economy is becoming more integrated because of both technical advancement and a more liberal world trade system. It is mostly a process of change, notes Kugler, and 'not an already existing structure'.[36]

Furthermore it is, says Mittelman, 'about opportunities arising from reorganizing governance, the economy, and culture throughout the world'.[37] Gains and losses in such a world economy will be determined by such factors as technical knowledge, robust institutions and competition. It is, therefore, a highly uneven process as well. Marshall notes that 'structural features such as interstate competition, hegemonic rivalry, and centre–periphery configurations remain constants in what is becoming a tightly integrated global capitalist system'.[38] Levelling is not one of its attributes, according to this view.

As for its origins, most observers would probably agree with Stubbs that, for analytical purposes at least, globalization can be dated to 'the mid-1970s', that is, to when rapid economic growth in the newly industrialized countries went hand-in-hand with significant rises in foreign direct investment: 'this date marks the onset of industrialization as foreign direct investment began to flow into [the Southeast Asia] region in rapidly increasing amounts'.[39] But the world-system theorists make a strong case that globalization is merely a phase in the evolution of capitalism as a world system. Wallerstein has articulated this position most succinctly in the comment that 'though it is fashionable to speak of globalization today as a phenomenon that began at the earliest in the 1970s, in fact transnational commodity chains were extensive from the very beginning of the system, and globally since the second half of the nineteenth century ... I contend that there has not been any fundamental change in the structuring and operations of these commodity chains in the twentieth century, and that none is likely to occur because of the so-called information revolution'.[40] Arrighi endorses this analysis by adding that 'much of what goes under the catch-word 'globalization' has in fact been a recurrent tendency of world capitalism since early-modern times', and as such its outcome is more predictable than assumed.[41] As such, globalization is no more than a new feature of the dominance of the 'centre' (the West) over the 'periphery' (the less-developed World).[42] At its most basic level, Waters comments, globalization 'is the direct consequence of the expansion of European culture across the planet via settlement, colonization and cultural mimesis'.[43] Expansion of European culture has gone hand-in-hand with the expansion of Europe's mode of production, capitalism, Sartre would add.

But globalization of the late-twentieth century went much further than the mere export of capital. In effect, it localized foreign – Western – capital and its multitude of industrial, manufacturing and services enterprises. As such, McDonald's, the most prominent face of American socio-economic culture, had little choice but to emphasize its 'nativeness'. The company, according to its publicists, was no more than a 'confederation of local companies': 'we don't act local; we are local. It's localization not globalization'.[44] But this overwhelming local presence added to the sense of resentment felt by really local actors, be they political or economic. What the Western transnationals did not readily appreciate was that the more 'local' foreign capital tried to become, the more vulnerable it became.

Second, the more native they tended to become, the greater has been the sense of fear in the host country about the power of the incomer and its intentions. Not surprisingly, in a region such as the Middle East, in which conspiracy theories thrive, the American economic presence in the absence of a Soviet balancer has been seen as another arm of America's hegemonic ambitions. Globalization is thus seen in many quarters as the means through which the USA's hegemonic ambitions are being asserted. 'The international order that sustains globalization', notes Plattner, 'is underpinned by American military power'.[45] This view is readily shared by many in the Middle East, who can claim first-hand experience of the raw power of the USA in military terms, and the force through which it is able to apply its soft power as well.

It was noted above that globalization is seen by many commentators as a compressor of time and space, interaction at high speed, and proximity of societies without physical or spiritual closeness. In Giddens' words, globalization is 'the intensification of world wide social relations which link distant localities in such a way that local happenings are shaped by events occurring many miles away and vice versa'.[46] It is, as a process, open-ended and dynamic, and therefore highly destabilizing as the point of reference is constantly changing. While it is often said that globalization is a tide that brings people together, evidence suggests that it can just as easily divide people and communities into increasingly smaller groups or subsets. Globalization, therefore, also fragments. The example of multichannel satellite television that Micklethwait and Wooldridge give illustrates this point. Globalization has not only spawned the global networks of CNN, MTV and so on, but has facilitated the birth of dozens of other small, locally focused stations that are dedicated to serving specific community/ group interests.[47] If globalization gave us CNN at the beginning of the 1990s, by the end of the decade it had also given rise to the Qatar-based al-Jazeera satellite television. The Arab world's first intra-regional TV station, al-Jazeera used the tools, philosophy and techniques of its Western counterparts to revolutionize coverage of contemporary events and affairs, and to bring to many Arab homes across the world an articulation of their views combined with news in a manner that has forced most state-owned or government-controlled MENA media to professionalize their own communications media and to fine-tune their reporting of domestic and regional events.[48] Al-Jazeera challenged the conventional wisdom, spoke openly on regional issues, and brought a speedy end to the Soviet-style reportage of the media in the Arab world. The rest of the Arab world adopted the al-Jazeera model by capitalizing on the new technologies, with the result that today over a dozen such channels beam across the world, often from the region's tiniest territories. Al-Arabiya, for example, has sprung up in the UAE to compete with al-Jazeera, which in turn has forced the latter to diversity its activities, branch out into multilingual broadcasting, and add new features to its programming. In broadcasting across the political boundaries of the Arab world, such broadcasters have fragmented the Arab world, while also separating it from the rest of the world.

Critics of globalization have also argued strongly that the fruits of globalization are, in any case, too unevenly distributed to give it much credit as a life-changing phenomenon affecting the whole of humanity.[49] Gilpin is one of those who argues this, stating that, even in the twenty-first century, 'most of the world's population is excluded from a globalization associated primarily with the industrialized economies and the industrializing economies of East Asia and Latin America ... [E]conomic globalization is limited and cannot possibly possess either all the negative or all the positive consequences attributed to it'.[50] As the process still affects only a minority of humanity, it can hardly be said to be 'global'.[51] The often-repeated argument is that, with most of the world's population living on US$10 a day or less, and without access to telephone or television, globalization, if a reality at all, is being experienced only by those living in Europe, North America, Japan, and European outposts in Australia and New Zealand. Judge, who is not by any means an anti-globalist, illustrates the point by arguing that the fruits of the process are very unevenly distributed: Just 16 per cent of the world's population (around 950 million people) have enjoyed US$23 trillion of the $26 trillion increase in world GNP between 1960 and 2000 (from $8 trillion to $34 trillion), while the share of the other 84 per cent (5.1 billion people) was a mere $3 trillion. In terms of purchasing power parity, the high-income countries have 57 per cent of the world's wealth ($25 trillion) and the rest of humanity only 43 per cent ($19 trillion).[52] Of the Fortune 500 list of largest transnational corporations in 2001, only 6 per cent (just 32 corporations) were from the less-developed world, a figure that has never got above 11 per cent (55 corporations in 1985) since the list of the world's biggest companies began in the late 1950s.[53] The disparity in wealth between the high-income countries and the rest is wide, and getting wider: Globalization 'widened the gap in living conditions between most of the world's population and the relatively small segment integrated into global production and financial networks'.[54] It may have created a single global market, but from this perspective it has also widened the gap between those who ride the wave of the single global market, and those who slumber under it. In universalizing the capitalist system, it has further fragmented the world.

Even among the high-income countries, the majority of their citizens spend much of their business life interacting with each other, rather than globally. Petras and Veltmeyer, who argue that globalization is an ideologically rooted concept, presented as inevitable largely by the advocates of a single integrated global market, maintain that globalization serves only to tighten the grip of American capital and its transnational corporations on world markets. Although around one-third of the top transnational corporations draw more than 50 per cent of their profits from their overseas operations, the majority (which are largely US-owned in any case) still draw much of their profits from their domestic (US) market. The single global market, therefore, is still a differentiated one, and the core countries continue to provide the base and the host for much of the world's corporations.

There are also structural problems associated with globalization. Competition increases thanks to globalization, but as it does so, so then does innovation. So far so good – innovation is in itself a great driver of change. But at the same time as innovation increases opportunity, so it also creates more problems than it can resolve: 'innovation results in capital-intensive industry at the expense of labor-intensive industry. Innovators are increasingly highly educated and specialized. The greater the degree of growth, the more demand for educated and skilled elites, and the lesser demand for the unskilled, who by the same token are marginalized by the productive process to form a more or less permanent underclass'. This is bad enough, particularly as it is likely to be repeated across the planet. The additional cost, however, is incurred as gradual marginalization imposes high social overhead costs, which manifest themselves as taxes on the productive sectors of society. 'In order to pay for the ensemble of social pathologies associated with risk and prolonged poverty, programs in areas such as education, job training, and welfare are required ... To tax without losing market share requires greater productivity. This in turn, insofar as it is a function of innovation, intensifies polarization. It is a self-defeating proposition'.[55] Even though states and citizens may have become beholden to globalization, they suffer because it is almost impossible to break the negative cycles created by it.

A somewhat deterministic approach to the social impact of economic globalization is to be found in some recent studies of industrialization, in which modernization theory tools are readily applied to the analysis of globalization. In one case, Kerr *et al.* speak of the 'logic of industrialism' that follows the process of industrialization. Societies, Waters paraphrases, 'progressively seek the most effective technology of production [and] their social systems will also progressively adapt to that of technology'.[56] Where industrialism may not be deeply rooted, as in much of the GME, social systems are unlikely to find it easy to adapt to the new technologies of production without incurring a high cost. In practice, therefore, when push comes to shove, as it invariably does, they find it easier to resist globalization, or better still, find ways of by-passing it.

If we accept that globalization is simply capitalism gone global, then we must assume that it will continue to manifest at its core the basic characteristics of capitalism, which have been present since its inception. One such characteristic is uneven development. Globalization as a system encourages further vertical stratification of the international system. It will thus continue to generate uneven development (and uneven prosperity) within countries and across states in a regional system. As Castells puts it, 'There is polarization in the distribution of wealth at the global level'. A clear 'differential evolution of intra-country income inequality, and substantial growth of poverty and misery in the world at large, and in most countries, both developed and developing' is in evidence.[57] Globalization of capitalism deepens uneven distribution of wealth and income: 'the income gap between the fifth of the world's population living in the richest countries, and the fifth in the poorest, widened from 30 to 1 in 1960, to 74 to 1 in 1997'.[58] This differential, forming one of the basic elements of performance indicators, also encourages diversity of action, as it encourages the struggle among states to strive to a higher level of interaction with the international system. What this line of argument takes for granted, however, is the global nature of international trade and investment. Empirical observations do not endorse this view.[59] This is so despite huge increases in both the volume (magnitude) of trade since the mid-twentieth century, and its volume in relation to GDP growth. As Pelagidis and Papasotiriou show, international economic trends, which have certainly ballooned, in fact point in the opposite direction: 'International transactions are not truly global, but flourish in the advanced regions of the world and, in lesser degrees, in some of the former Warsaw Pact and Third World regions'.[60] In neo-Marxist parlance, globalization is about little more than the distributive power of the metropole countries and a select few locations of the semi-periphery. Hoogvelt works the same (structuralist) seam to argue that globalization does much more than reinforce the center–periphery relationship. It alters, Hoogvelt states, the whole inter-state relationship by altering the balance of social classes on a worldwide scale: 'the global division of labour is rendering a core–periphery relationship that cuts across national and geographic boundaries, bringing on board, within the core, segments of the Third World, and relegating segments and groups in both the traditional core of the system and in the Third World to peripheral status. Core–periphery is becoming a social relationship, no longer just a geographical one'.[61] And it is all-encompassing. 'What all this globalization is doing, instead of promoting understanding', notes Thomas Friedman, 'it's raising the world's blood pressure'. The mismatch between the rapid speed at which we now receive information and that which helps us understand each other means that 'it's now like we're sitting around the same dinner table. Americans, Arabs, Europeans, Muslims, Hindus and Jews, we're all around the same dinner table and everyone is shouting at each other and throwing food, and you can't go anywhere in the house anymore to escape the argument'.[62]

But it can be argued that globophobes measure globalization by the wrong yardsticks, and end up with the wrong assessment. For in reality 'globalization increases people's freedom to shape their own identities rather than assuming those of their ancestors'.[63] It is therefore a truly liberating phenomenon. But, in places where ancestral links are part of the fibre of an individual's identity – 'which family is he from?' is the often-asked question in the GME – and where people are still known by reference to their fathers, how can the severance of such identity chains help but cause social dislocation and an identity crisis?

Conclusions: System *and* Process?

As shown above, very few commentators on globalization draw a clear distinction between it being a system or a process, and some seem unaware of the difference. Where globalization is alluded to as a system, the focus tends to be on the workings and mechanics of capitalism as the world's most successful and powerful mode of production. Where it is presented as a process, then the emphasis tends to be on the 'liberating' side of globalization and its ongoing nature. It reduces time and space between people and regions, easing transportation and communications, and accelerating transnationalization.

To understand globalization one must adopt an eclectic approach, and in this book I shall treat this dynamic phenomenon as both system and process, for these I regard as the dialectics of globalization. Globalization is the latest, perhaps last, stage of capitalism, which is built on impressive advances in the realm of human interaction and means of exchange, but it is unlikely to have an end point to it. As such, it will continue to challenge existing norms and change established structures. Moreover, globalization has to be seen as both a system and a process, because it is in a theatre (the GME) contending, if not clashing, with other powerful forces that have massive geopolitical and geo-economic weight. It is the relationship between the two that provides the basis for a multifaceted explanation of globalization's impact on the Middle East, but this too has to be seen as an ongoing and changing relationship.

We could just as easily, *à la* Lenin, argue that globalization is about creating the conditions for the exploitation of the planet's resources and its people, domination of the planet by a small politico-economic elite, nations' cultural and economic emasculation, and the final division of the world into a handful of corporate empires. Yet an equally strong argument could be made about the constructive power of globalization, a means of providing a new dynamic agency for positive change (*à la* Bill Warren), as the ultimate leveller, the uncontrollable force that will, without prejudice, sweep across the world like a gigantic wave to change societies for the better. I would argue that both tendencies are ingrained in globalization – destroy and construct. These are no longer either/or; what needs to be explored in detail in the Middle East context is the 'where' and 'how' of the process of change in the globalized system of capitalism. If globalization is a universal force, its presence can be detected only on the ground within regions and territories marked out as countries. Ultimately, at every juncture, it will be local conditions that determine which side of globalization is operational.

Judging by the century-old controversies surrounding such concepts as imperialism and modernization, and the continuing debate about their contours internationally, the chances are that globalization as a twenty-first century socio-economic phenomenon will not acquire a universally acceptable definition either. As we delve deeper into the GME, the question of whether globalization really is the final stage of capitalism, which many on the left believe it to be, or the latest phase in its evolution, will be subjected to much closer examination.

2 Globalization and Strategic Interdependence

> The societies of the Middle East are caught in the throes of unprecedented transformation. History provides us with many dramatic examples of social change – the emergence of Islam in the seventh century, the Mogol conquest of Baghdad in 1258, the fall of Constantinople in 1453 ... None of these events, however, can match the contemporary era in terms of the depth and universality of change.
>
> James A. Bill and Rebecca Bill Chavez, 'The Politics of Incoherence:
> The United States and the Middle East',
> *Middle East Journal*, 56 (4), 2002, 562–75.

Globalization – The Way to Go?

As shown in the previous chapter, much debate continues to surround the phenomenon of globalization. Globalization, through its horizontal (levelling of the international economic field) and vertical (shifting production and related processes between a few global production and financial hot spots) slicing of the world, has generated significant strategic interdependencies across the planet, where fluctuations, force of events and developments in one part of the world leave an impression elsewhere. Globalization also digs deep grooves into the regional organization of states. As globalization has accelerated over the past 20 years, so it has become more and more reliant on the different geopolitical settings of the international system (regional systems and regional groupings) in order to sustain itself. In some parts of the world (the EU, North America, Pacific Asia) there has been a fairly smooth relationship between regionalist tendencies and globalization, which has often helped in ironing the path for the latter in providing appropriate policy frameworks within which to function. But in other parts of the world, most notably the GME (and much of sub-Sahara Africa), geopolitical complexities have come not only to disrupt the globalization process, but also hinder and challenge it.

In the GME, the reason lies largely in the geopolitical forces governing the region, and also elite fears of loss of control to extra-territorial powers.

From the elites' point of view, while globalization precipitates chaos, they crave 'order'. Voices from within the region provide ample evidence for this.[1] Scepticism, coupled with the perceived threat to Arab and Muslim social values 'through the export of American popular culture, leads the general Arab population to be fearful of further Western penetration of their Societies'.[2] A typical geopolitically rooted view is that globalization is little more than the invasion of a 'Satanic civilization', which is bent on corrupting Islamic values and destroying Islam's central unity.

> It seems that we have been invaded by a civilization whose characteristics are different from ours and which invaded us without our being aware of what was happening ... Madonna ... had a child from [her husband to be] three months before the marriage ... Catherine Zeta-Jones had her child two months before her wedding ... Woody Allen was involved in a relationship with his stepdaughter ... and let us not forget Bill Clinton's affair with Monica Lewinsky as well as with Paula Jones. She was so shameless as to appear nude in a magazine in order to boost her income! This is the civilization which now leads the world in science, technology and military might. We face the caravan of Satan with all its weapons and attractions. Its attack is against our society.[3]

Iran's former Foreign Minister Kamal Kharrazi, who served in President Khatami's two administrations and is known for his moderate views, stated at an international gathering in Rome in 2001 that 'neglect of cultural rights of the nations, disregard for cultural values, and efforts geared at the creation of a mono-culture rank among the negative consequences of globalization that presage whole new challenges for humanity at large ... A case worth mentioning is that the shaping of a monolithic culture ... runs counter to the ideal of cultural pluralism and could trigger violent reactions by its critics'.[4]

Under the title of 'Globalisation Yes, Americanization No', an influential English-language Iranian daily warned in 2000 of the dangers of blindly following advocates of globalization: 'Despite what simple-minded people may think, the American version of globalization has nothing to do with democracy, human rights, better standards of living or the fair distribution of world resources. Quite the contrary, it is all about establishing a global market for the products of industrialized nations at the cost of disregarding the rights of sovereign nations to protect their economic and financial interests'.[5] Iran's most authoritative and outspoken anti-globalist, Ayatollah Seyed Ali Khamenei, saw the phenomenon in a slightly different light. To him, it was the 'big powers led by the United States [forging] economic, political and cultural hegemony over the globe'. 'For some time now', he declared at a meeting with Iran's parliamentarians, 'a new movement has gained momentum at the international scene like a destructive flood and certain countries believe there is no way but to surrender to the "global flood", or globalization ... Iran believes that nations should neutralize globalization by strengthening their economic, political and cultural structure'.[6] In the Arab world, similar issues are peddled. For Arab intellectuals, it is also often the concerns about Arab/Islamic culture that dominate. Globalization, for them, will eventually extinguish the *khususiyyat* (specialities, peculiarities) of Arab culture.

At another extreme are the leading entrepreneurs of the region, figures such as Prince Walid bin Talal of Saudi Arabia, who have become uncompromising champions of globalization, which they see as a powerful energizing force. In a typical interview in December 1999, for instance, he argued that change must come to the Arab world if it is to keep up with the rest of the world. The Arab world, he said, is 'very backward at all levels', in which the 'adoption of the Western economic model, from capitalism to globalisation will force the (Arab) states into changing their way of thinking'.[7] Three years later, he was still insisting that the Middle East had to embrace globalization 'in order to shore up the region's economy'.[8]

The Dubai Strategy Forum, which has emerged as one of the key venues for undertaking strategic debate in the region, has been adopting a similar posture. In its deliberations in 2002, speaker after speaker endorsed the virtues of globalization, which was regarded as 'a fact of life' of the new economy. The 1000 or so influential delegates were reminded that ideas and knowledge, rather than capital, were the biggest sources of competitive advantage in the new era. Nemir Kirdar, president and chief executive officer at Investcorp, was not alone in declaring that 'Globalisation is a reality. It is here to stay. And my message is don't fight it, embrace it. But to best use the open routes that are available we, too, have to be open and work with a high degree of integrity ... The globalised economic environment has empowered creative minds to set up businesses with little capital. In this new environment, capital, raw material and distance are not the issues. It is talent, brainpower, ideas and software. In fact, trained talent is one of the most scarce resources in the new economy'. Having argued that capital was not the core prize of the new economy, he ended his remarks by urging a further globalization of MENA capital and further diversification of capital investments by the Cooperation Council for the Arab States of the Gulf (formerly Gulf Cooperation Council, GCC) and away from the region itself. He said: 'Regional countries with huge oil wealth should look more towards investment possibilities in the rest of the world since they cannot invest all their money within the region'.[9]

In January 2003, support for major reforms in the Arab world, as an acknowledgement and full embracing of globalization, came from a least expected quarter – the conservative Kingdom of Saudi Arabia. In its new 'Arab Charter', the Kingdom noted that 'full reform is needed in order to respond to the requirements for positive integration within the field of international competition, to achieve sustainable development, and to deal objectively and realistically with the myriad of novel changes in the economic sphere, especially with the emergence of huge economic blocs, the rise of globalization and what it provides in opportunities and imposes challenges, and accelerating development in the technological, communication and information areas'.[10] Saudi Arabia's new thinking on globalization had already been trailed by some of the Kingdom's most articulate officials. Dr Ghazi al-Qosaibi (until 2002 Saudi Arabia's Ambassador to Britain), for example, explained to officers of the Military Staff College in Riyadh that globalization was 'a crucial part of our historical development because it offers so many opportunities but is equally shrouded with risk ... To benefit from the opportunities and avoid the risks involved we need to tackle modern developments with both expertise and proficiency ... Time would wait for no-one and without these skills the race to compete in the globalised world market would be lost'.[11] Many voices in Saudi Arabia today echo similar sentiments. Note the comments of Saudi Arabia's most prominent businesswoman at the 2004 Jeddah Economic Forum, in which she urged the country's leaders to embrace change as a strategy: 'Our government, and I believe the private sector as well, needs to abandon its progress without change philosophy. A progress without change philosophy has a certain comfortable attraction and gained currency in much of the Middle East throughout the 1980s and 1990s. The idea was that we in the Arab world could adopt many of the trappings of the modern West, and in some sense modernize, but not really change, thus preserving our uniqueness and remaining somewhat separate and distinct. So, if we in Saudi Arabia want to progress, we have no choice but to embrace change ... The real value is in the changes that will strengthen us and make us more competitive so that we can overcome the challenges that face us both here in the kingdom and throughout the Arab world'.[12] Sheikh Mohammed bin Rashid al-Maktoum, the architect of Dubai's economic miracle, has spoken in a similar vein, giving unreserved support for the process of globalization. In boasting about Dubai's achievements, his message at the Dead Sea World Economic Forum meeting in May 2004 was to embrace the opportunities offered by globalization. The key factors of success, he said, were economic freedom, openness to the world, an inspiring vision, and efficiency in implementing the vision.[13] Such positive endorsements of globalization stand in sharp contrast to the more cautious and largely sceptical views prevailing across the region, particularly among its Islamist-leaning forces.

The State of the MENA State

As is evident from these positions, globalization keeps throwing the spotlight back on the domestic environment (in particular on the role of the state) as the most pertinent unit of analysis in the MENA region. More so in the era of globalization than at any other time in modern history, it is the local and the domestic that matters most in the Muslim Middle East. Kamrava notes in this regard that three 'structurally related' phenomena –

'authoritarian ruling bargains', the state trade policies, and 'economic semiformality' – come together to act as the main impediments to globalization of the Middle East. He goes on to argue that 'meaningful integration into the world economy would be exceedingly difficult, given the region's present overall political economy. With the exception of Turkey and Israel, states in the Middle East and North Africa do not have the popular legitimacy and electoral mandates to be able to undertake significant structural adjustments to their political systems and their economies'.[14] In other words, elite fears of loss of authority continue to encourage states to seek to manipulate globalization – to manage it, rather than enabling it to roam the national space unhindered.

Muslims line up against globalization for another reason too, for the process also impinges on the cultural space of the state, encouraging secularization, among other tendencies, which is referred to as a 'Western disease of the mind' by some Muslim clerics. The Iranian Supreme Leader epitomizes this line of thinking, for he has warned consistently against the 'spread of the poison of secularism' among the Muslim youth: 'clerics as well as young theological students shouldered the responsibility to find the best possible cultural counter-attack against that wave'.[15] He, and many others like him, believe and advocate that the counter-attack is rooted in Islam. For them, the fight is not just cultural, but at the same time political.

Even among those who believe there is no back-pedalling from globalization, voices of dissent are often heard. There are those who still maintain that the 'true story of globalisation [is that] the North has to make maximum benefits and the South is only entitled to a limited margin of development; if the margin is crossed, the Western speculators are there to take you down as quickly as possible'.[16] While, on occasion, these statements form part of an elaborate political dance designed to score points against the West in North–South debates, they nonetheless sketch a much deeper fear of globalization. Deeper fear of complete domination continues to inform opinion, where 'region-specific Pan-Arab and Islamic identities and norms carry powerful credibility ... [and feed the desire for] autonomy from Western domination'.[17]

Globalization 'involves complete economic liberalization ... with transnational corporations ... at the forefront', it is often argued. 'Governments create an environment that is as conducive as possible to its growth of business. Regional groupings like APEC, GATT and WTO are totally committed to the same goal. The nexus between big business, governments and regional and international institutions to create an environment for globalization is not an accident. It has historic roots in colonization, hence why the dominant forces are based in the West'.[18] More forcefully put is the view that globalization is, in essence, 'the corporate rape of poor nations' resources'. 'Globalization is primarily an affair with the dollar and not an affair with the mind, heart, and conscience of individual or collective humanity. Such rapid exchanges of good and services can only serve to undermine local businesses, customs, cultures, languages, ethics, and most importantly, the religious and community values so cherished in Islam'.[19] As such, it stands to reason why Muslims should fear globalization.

In Held's words, 'by creating new patterns of transformation and change, globalization can weaken old political and economic structures without necessarily leading to the establishment of new systems of regulation'.[20] As many of the political and economic structures in the Muslim world are already weak, one effect of globalization in this environment is to make the state more defensive, while acting as a rallying point for Islamist activists (among others) who resist globalization on the basis of its corrosive impact on Muslim systems of social regulations, to use Held's vocabulary. Henry and Springborg articulate the problem in political economy terms, arguing that the region draws a direct line between the pressures of globalization and those 'neo-colonial' ones exerted through such bodies as the International Monetary Fund and the World Bank. 'With the rise of the Washington Consensus in the 1980s and its overt extension into the political realm with "good governance" in the 1990s, governments in the developing world perceived IFIs [international financial institutions] as the shock troops of globalization. Structurally adjusted states in the Middle East have seen their economies opened up to international markets and multinational companies in return for the provision of much-needed loans. This has caused globalization to be perceived as a Western imposition forced on countries that have very little alternative'.[21]

Another important dimension is the perceived promotion of individualism and, even more crucially as far as the state is concerned, the emergence of links between individuals beyond the mediating role of the state. Marc Plattner's observation that 'globalization goes beyond more frequent and more intensive contact among peoples' has particular resonance in the community-driven Muslim world. In arguing that globalization 'is a process of integration that draws together *individuals* living in different countries ... making national differences less sharp',[22] Plattner is highlighting one of the main flashpoints of the relationship between Islam and globalization. While the liberal value system of globalization has become more universally acceptable today in eastern Europe, East Asia, Latin America, and in the industrializing parts of Africa, compared even with the decade following the fall of the Berlin Wall in 1989, in Islam's heartland there still exists a real fear that the promotion of the individual by globalization can corrupt the Muslim mind and cause tension between the value-driven Muslims and their non-Muslim counterparts.[23] The unfettered relationships between individuals that globalization facilitates, through the Internet and other mobile forms of communication, is seen as another aspect of the threat posed to Muslim societies.[24]

So we see that there is acute awareness of globalization at all levels of society in the GME, but this universal awareness does not yield common positions on the process. At both popular and elite levels, one is aware of the tensions and contradictory positions that have emerged in the area. While some Arab elites, particularly among the ranks of those in the internationalizing economies of the GCC states, have accepted the need to conform to the regime of globalization, other elites (notably the Islamist or nationalist-leaning ones) continue to resist its pressures.[25] Even in the former group, much dichotomy still exists in the formulation of policies towards a globalizing world and perceptions of globalization.

Geo-economics of Globalization

Added to the pressures on the state that globalization brings, we can name others that have a strong economic focus. Hook *et al.* identify three dimensions to the economics of globalization: 'as a world without borders in which TNCs [transnational corporations] act in the three core regions of the global political economy [USA, Europe and Far East]; as the spread of a US-led liberalist political project which forces the removal of protective national and regional barriers to global trade; or as the fragmentation of economic interests and growth of sites of resistance to global economic trends'.[26] With regard to the Middle East, these three elements converge to generate new pressures for the region to manage. With fairly small and underdeveloped markets outside the MENA oil economies, and as the transnational corporations are unlikely to divert resources from the three cores to expand their presence in this region, some parts of the region will present themselves as 'resistance sites'. However, as the GME area is likely to be increasingly sucked into the Eurasian economic space, some states may stand to benefit as close satellites of that part of the core. In geo-economic terms, the 'energy zone' of the GME – the Persian Gulf and the Caspian basin combined – stands to draw closer to the three core regions of the global economy identified above. This development will have major implications for the political economy of the region as a whole and its economic balance of power, further shifting it to the smaller, but oil-rich states.

On the issue of USA's liberalist strategy, the region has been a subject of the US liberalist political project from at least 1977 and President Carter's democratization drive. Some would say that the Shah of Iran was the first victim of this drive,[27] followed by President Marcos of the Philippines. But since 9/11, the US liberalist political project has acquired new life, great urgency, and a much hardened edge. To all intents and purposes, the US liberalist political project is now rooted in the Middle East, as President Bush's 'forward strategy for freedom' has continued to underline since early 2002. As we see in chapter 5, the new liberalist political project has left no Arab state immune to the associated pressures to open up the public space, which in itself is proving a destabilizing situation as far as Arab elites are concerned. But the process of controlled openness is allowing the emergence of political forces still hostile to the economic and political imperatives of globalization. In Palestine, in its parliamentary elections of January 2006, for example, we saw the rise of the anti-peace-process Hamas as the single most popular bloc, a force that is likely to resist the pressures of regional integration on what it perceives to be Israel's terms. In Egypt's parliamentary poll of November/ December 2005, the banned anti-Western Islamist Muslim Brotherhood managed to secure some 100 seats in the 454 seat parliament, again on a platform of resisting imposition from the USA. Even in post-war Iraq, the affairs of state are now increasingly being determined by Islamists of one type or another.

Finally, as Hook *et al.* suggest in fairly broad terms, there is an inevitable backlash from the pressure of economic globalization; in the GME, where resistance has been felt, it has largely originated in the Islamist rejection of open borders and low barriers. The fragmentation of the region itself, due to geopolitical pressures and the slow death of Arab nationalism as an enduring elite protective cloak, has meant that Islamist forces have emerged to provide the resistance to the open borders and low barriers that might threaten the realm of Islam. This is despite the fact that the militant Islamist groups, such as al-Qaeda and Hizbul Tahrir, have used the spaces created by globalization to carry out cross-border operations and networking in both the Arab world and on the eastern edges of the GME.

Politics of Globalization and its Fallout in the Middle East

Much of the debate about the politics of globalization has focused on the tensions between the territorial state as a sovereign actor and the boundary-busting thrust of globalization.[28] In his *Globalization and the Nation-State*,[29] Robert Holten argues that states have never enjoyed absolute sovereignty and, although economic globalization poses some new challenges for the state, it is by no means their ultimate harbinger. Krasner largely agrees, maintaining that 'regardless of how sovereignty is understood, it is difficult to make a case that contemporary developments, notably globalization, are transforming the nature of the system. There has never been a mythical past in which states were secure in the exercise of either their control or their authority. Globalization has raised some new and unique problems for sovereignty understood as control, but states have confronted comparable challenges in the past'.[30] Waltz's eloquent intervention in the debate has underlined the same point, arguing that the globalization of the international system is, at best, exaggerated. He challenges the notion that economic and technological forces impose 'near uniformity' of political and economic forms and functions on states, stating that 'what I found to be true in 1970 remains true today: The world is less interdependent than is usually supposed ... [and] footloose corporations in fact turn out to be firmly in their home bases'.[31] Nor has global or world politics taken over from national politics, he argues emphatically. He states: 'the twentieth century was the century of the nation-state. The twenty-first will be too. Trade and technology do not determine a single best way to organize a polity and its economy ... States still have a wide range of choice. Most states survive, and the units that survive in competitive systems are those with the ability to adapt. Some do it well, and they grow and prosper. Others just manage to get along'.[32] In all cases, it is national politics that determines international economic developments, and not international markets – or the so-called 'herd' of electronic–financial wizards who are engaged daily in the transfer of substantial sums around the world.[33] Nevertheless, some see a real challenge being posed to the world of states by the denationalization of money and credit, and the long transnational capitalist supply chains being created: 'there is no doubt that these operations today not only differ in many ways from those of national capitalism, but threaten it in vital respects. The most important of these threats is the capability of supranational capitalism to rearrange the global division and distribution of political and economic power'.[34] Shifting the economic geography of the world to the Pacific basin from the Atlantic is quoted as the most dramatic example of the power of 'modern supranational capital' to challenge the status quo.

Before any detailed analysis of the political dimensions of globalization in relation to the Middle East is undertaken, it is worth recalling that – unlike other regions whose leading members often acted in practice as the champions of globalization – due to a multitude of barriers imposed on several of its key actors from outside, the MENA region was virtually in a dysfunctional state when the forces of globalization encountered it. Geopolitical pressures were already at work to create strong disarticulating conditions. For much of the 1990s, Iran and Iraq were under 'dual containment', for example; Iraq and Libya were under UN sanctions; Sudan and Syria were forcibly marginalized; and Israel was never able to interact fully with, let alone function within, the regional political economy.[35] Under these circumstances, there was little hope of what could be classed as regional responses to the complexities introduced by globalization. The internal vulnerabilities of the region did weaken the state actor, but did little to prepare the way for globalization. Weakness here did not result in unchallenged penetration of globalization. Moreover, unlike other regions (such as Southeast Asia and Latin America), in which the dominant actors had set about charting responses, several of the powerful regional actors in the MENA region had effectively been so emasculated as to prevent the emergence of co-ordinated approaches to the process of globalization within a regional context.

With the region already exhausted by war and its own economic failings, and by the cumulative pressures of containment, sanctions and isolation imposed on several of its key actors, the fragmentary impact of globalization was manifested here more easily than in other regional systems. The ways in which the end of the Cold War deepened globalization-induced fragmentation is in need of some comment too, for until 1989 the region had largely been bound by the bipolar structures of the Cold War, and it was only after the demise of the Soviet state that the regional actors began to behave out of the mould of the Cold War. With no international alliance structures to provide regional stability any longer, key actors began to explore the prospect of independent action in a post-bipolar environment, sometimes with disastrous consequences.[36] State behaviour tended to be anachronistic, although still rational within its own narrow terms of reference. Actions by different governments undermined, instead of complementing, collective action.

Globalization and Geo-culture: Circling the Wagons?

Evidence suggests that even advanced countries remain very sensitive to the cultural impact on their national cultural identity of close economic ties with the USA. Patricia Goff shows that two of America's closest economic partners – Canada and the EU – have taken significant steps to protect their own cultural identity from American encroachment, while busily introducing measures that strengthened their economic ties.[37] But at the cultural level in the Middle East, globalization can cause serious new ruptures between society and the elite. Although, on the one hand, the elite is expected to protect society from the cultural encroachment of the West, on the other, largely in an effort to adjust society to the tempo of globalization, it feels compelled to encourage the adoption of international norms and as well as baggage loads of Western practices. Not unexpectedly, the resulting schizophrenia has been known to lead to policy muddles, U-turns at some critical junctures, and the rhetoricalization of key debates about the future direction of state policy in which the West tends to be targeted for 'imposing' its own will on honourable Muslim societies. Although the latter has served as a useful defensive mechanism for virtually all post-colonial leaders of less-developed countries, in the era of globalization it can backfire spectacularly and lead to unexpected tensions between the elite and international society. However, Pfaff's argument that the 'internationalization' of any non-Western economy 'automatically undermines [its] social practices and religious and cultural norms' also has much analytical merit.[38]

Evidence from the region does suggest, however, that globalization can encourage the re-Islamization of society, an effort to halt the undermining of its religious and cultural norms – the deeply rooted forces that give it its core identity. As Falk shows, where religion is challenged by what he calls the 'dominant motifs of globalisation', it can 're-emerge as a force for renewal that offers resistance to globalisation and provides alternative readings of reality'.[39] Bill and Chavez place the emphasis more squarely on Islam itself: 'As a powerful universal force, Islam finds itself in great demand by those trapped in incoherence'.[40] Roy holds that the Islamic 'neo-fundamentalists' preoccupation is with the cultural impact of Westernization (globalization). Their rejection of globalization and of the Western model is predicated on a return to the 'golden age of Islam' and to Islamic values and principles and a related set of codes for public and private life. While globalization privatizes (individualizes) the public sphere and, through new means of communication and association, renders it accessible to all, for neo-fundamentalists the campaign is about control of public space and 'shrinking the public space to the family and the mosque'.[41]

If Islam is seen by many as the solution, then the place of Islamic civilization in the global order would require examination. In the course of this debate, we also will have to tackle the issue of whether such a thing as an 'Islamic civilization' actually exists, who speaks for it today and, if it does exist, what are its dimensions? A related question is whether, when we talk of an Islamic civilization today, we actually mean a set of shared cultural values and symbols embedded in the practices of Islam as a religion and way of life, or indeed a civilization?[42]

Strategic Interdependence and Regional Politics

The Middle East and North Africa is a geopolitical system with strong political and cultural cross-border linkage and interdependencies. Here political events are intertwined with one another, and the effects of events in one part are quickly felt in its other parts. Globalization, while fracturing the region, has also deepened these linkages and accelerated the transmission and delivery of political developments to every corner of the regional system.

As noted in the Introduction, the regional debate about globalization has been finding expression in an altogether different and uncharted international context since September 2001. From that moment, the nature of the debate changed in the Middle East, as did the USA's relationship with the region. 11 September 2001 became a new defining moment of the relationship between the West and the Muslim world. It also formed a strong feature of the USA's position (as both victim and aggressor) in, and relations with, the Muslim world, as both cause and victim of violence.

One of the key strategic changes since 9/11 has been the transformation in US–Saudi relations, which for over 50 years had assisted both countries in dealing with their domestic and regional problems. The Kingdom had been a strong ally of the USA for years, assisting it in containing radicalism, Arab nationalism, and Soviet communism in the Arab world.[43] Saudi Arabia had been one of the USA's key partners in the fight against the Soviet occupation of Afghanistan in the 1980s; it had assisted the USA in its efforts to contain the Iranian revolution; and had been the main regional ally of the US-led, UN-sanctioned military coalition against Iraq in 1990/91. Indeed, it was a historical irony of the latter partnership that brought 500,000 American soldiers to the holiest Muslim land, and in the process sparked off bin Laden's campaign against the al-Sauds.

Even today, Saudi Arabia is still touted as an important ally in the war on terror. Yet it is hard to deny that after 9/11 something fundamental changed in this partnership. For one commentator, the partnership was now said to be 'in tatters'.[44] Not only was the image of Saudi Arabia in the USA tarnished, but in policy terms the Kingdom's role as a regional pillar of American power changed to that of a neo-pariah, where it was seen more as part of the problem for the USA in its war against terrorism, than a trusted ally. Victor Davis Hanson of California State University was not unique in publicly and vociferously questioning every aspect of Saudi Arabia's society and its partnership with the USA. In an article entitled, 'Our Enemies, the Saudis' in the influential and widely read *Commentary* magazine, he argued that Saudi Arabia was every bit part of the Islamist terror network.[45] Another commentator boldly stated that 'the roots of much terrorism lie in the intolerance and hatred preached in many mosques and taught in madrases, often supported by Saudi money'.[46] It was also being said in American circles that 'there can be little doubt that the key components of al-Qaeda derive direct support ... from the desert kingdom. The group's leader is himself a Saudi from one of the country's richest and most powerful families. Fifteen of the 19 [9/11] hijackers were allegedly Saudis, and though there is no direct evidence yet, logic suggests that much of al-Qaeda's financing comes from sympathizers there'.[47] The Washington Institute for Near East Policy, the Heritage Foundation, the RAND Corporation and the CATO Institute were among the key think-tanks peddling a similar argument and advocating a weakening of political and security ties with the Kingdom. Some even recommended regime change in Saudi Arabia as the ultimate solution to the problem of Islamic terrorism.[48]

A Strategic Shift?

The consequences of any strategic shift in the relationship between the USA and one of the world's key oil states is likely to be far-reaching, but already, as Niblock notes, since 9/11 both countries have found good reason to step back from the intimate partnership that had marked their relations since the middle of the previous century.[49] In the sub-regional environment of the Persian Gulf, where Washington has consistently relied on Saudi Arabia to contain Iran and Iraq, it will now act more unilaterally and distance itself from the largest Arab country on the Peninsula, relying more on weaker and smaller allies such as Kuwait, Bahrain and Qatar. This would have seemed hardly likely, or sensible, at the turn of the century. Yet that is exactly what has been happening since the military campaign which unseated the Iraqi dictator in March 2003. The neo-conservatives' regional agenda did not end in Baghdad, however: Iraq was just the beginning. In the words of a former Assistant Secretary of State for Near East Affairs (Edward Walker): 'they want to foment revolution in Iran and use that to isolate and possibly attack Syria in [Lebanon's] Bekaa Valley, and force Syria out ... They want to pressure ... Libya and they want to destabilize Saudi Arabia, because they believe instability there is better than continuing with the current situation. And out of this, they think, comes Pax Americana'.[50]

But the loosening of Saudi–US ties also affords Riyadh the chance to engage more forcefully with South and East Asia and consolidate the already strong energy partnerships into broader political and security ones. In this regard, the Saudis would be travelling down the road that another important Persian Gulf state (Iran) has already set off on, in terms of building solid ties with China, India, Japan, Pakistan and Southeast Asia, as well as with Central Asia. As discussed in chapter 4, a strategic shift could be taking place in the Middle East as the states of West Asia slowly but surely gravitate closer to their eastern Asian neighbours. The strategic shift is already influencing, and will further affect, the flow of globalization in the MENA region as it will increasingly penetrate the region with both a Western and an 'Oriental' face. It will be shown later that as China, India and their satellites rise in the coming years, so the geographical shift in the power of globalizing forces themselves will play into the strategic shift taking place in the GME.

For the USA, which today is depicted as a global hyper-power with overwhelming military and economic power – even as the New Rome – these strategic developments have macro-consequences.[51] This hyper-power looks around the world and identifies the 'unruly tribes' – the rogue states and actors – and goes out of its way to bring them into line. Where it can, it will also aim to punish them for challenging the New Rome's power and its unilateral pursuit of its interests. It also pursues them in order to make an example of them in front of other potential rivals. In the context of the post-9/11 international environment and the USA's new national security strategy, MENA regional actors must be seen to pose the most serious and direct challenge to this hegemonic actor.[52] The American strategy anticipates confronting them in an effort to 'roll them back'. In the context of globalization, the 'containment' strategy has surely been replaced by 'roll back', as exemplified in the treatment of Iraq in 2002/03. Globalization and the revolution in military affairs in the 1990s, as well as the USA's strategic responses to 9/11, have brought the New Rome and its regional rivals more directly into confrontation with each other. The posture the Middle East oil exporters' Asian partners adopt in this struggle will have direct and far-reaching consequences for the region, as well as for the USA's global strategy. If they resist the USA in West Asia, they will encourage the regional counter-hegemons to resist. But if they submit to the USA's grand strategy, will they not only help in strengthening Washington's grip on the region? They cannot afford to remain passive actors when the re-ordering of the region is being encouraged in the manner outlined by the Bush White House since 2002 and the publication of its two (2002 and 2006) national security documents.

But American imperial over-reach will also have huge implications in the MENA region. Over-reach can lead to deeper and more prolonged military engagements – a procession of rolling and costly wars with no end and no clear winners or losers.[53] This is already the state of affairs with regard to the wars led by the Bush administration in Afghanistan and Iraq. Under such conditions, the security aspects of globalization can very easily undo any economic fruits that liberalizing responses to globalization might have brought. In the long run, it is not inconceivable to expect the GME region to be exposed to further tensions, but more as a consequence of its security parameters than of its socio-economic failings, which globalization so forcefully unveils. As we will see, strategic interdependence of this nature will extract a higher price for globalization of the region.

3 The MENA Regional System in Crisis

> What is evolving around the world is ... economic alliances that promote development within regions, while making all borders more porous.
>
> John Naisbitt, *Global Paradox: The Bigger the World Economy, the More Powerful its Smallest Players* (London: Nicholas Brealey, 1994).

A Region without Regionalism

For over 50 years, the MENA region has been seen as a single unit of analysis. I have viewed it in these terms myself, making assumptions about the political, socio-economic and cultural aspects of MENA as a distinct subsystem of the international system. Its body was neither invented nor imagined, to apply Higgott's comment referring to East Asian regionalism.[1] But to argue that MENA is a regional system does not necessarily mean that its 'regionalization' is also pre-ordained.[2] As shown below, this is one of the least 'regionalized' regional systems of the world, when measured by economic integration criteria – market integration, freedom of mobility, unhindered trade and investment flows, an internal market for the subsystem's members, collective measures to standardize legal and financial management regimes, a truly region-wide technical secretariat for co-operation or establishment of a convergence criteria, etc. Many of these features are conspicuous by their absence in the MENA region, despite efforts in the early 2000s to reduce intra-country barriers.

To make MENA-related analytical frames even more complex, in the Arab political lexicon the so-called 'area' has historically referred to the Arab world as a whole. In this context, 'regions' mark the territorial divisions within the Arab world itself. In Ba'athist ideology, for example, the region is defined by reference to the territorial state within the greater Arab order. Ba'athist Iraq until 2003, and present-day Syria, have been known locally as 'regions' of the Arab nation. The MENA region thus has a complex political identity – 'national' in populist Arab discourse means the Arab nation as a whole, not the political identity of a particular nation-state.

Despite – indeed, some might argue in spite of – the strength of Arabism as a transnational force, states remain the strongest unit of political organization. State barriers to integration are strong, and national frontiers are far from porous in political or economic terms.

Beyond the security realm and externally imposed theatres of operation, such as that of the Bahrain-based US Central Command, it is hard to justify the MENA region as a fully fledged subsystem.[3] Indeed, as the security envelope widens, we have to include in our analysis an understanding of the GME, which incorporates Pakistan, Afghanistan, and the Asian republics of the former Soviet Union into one large, strategic realm. It thus becomes even more difficult to locate a core to the subsystem. By the same token, it will not be easy to identify the convergence criteria for the region.

As will be shown, subregions are much easier to define analytically in the MENA region than the boundaries of the MENA subsystem as a whole. Moreover, it has been at the subregional level that attempts at institutionalized co-operation have been most effective, although not necessarily particularly successfully.

At the heart of the MENA region is the Arab world, the states of which are 'joined at the hip' by a common language, religion, customs, roots, geography, and some shared history. With these strong links, virtually unmatched by other regions in the world, one would have expected the rise of a single unit regulating the affairs of the Arabs. Alas, since the mid-twentieth century Arab states have found it particularly difficult to use this 'material basis' for co-operation or as 'ready-mixed cement' for structure-building. They have also found that their common features do not necessarily lend themselves as platforms for common action in instances of strategic importance. Stretched in several directions due to external pressures, these states and the Arab peoples in general have found unity an unrealizable destiny. As Barakat has put it, this sense of Arab one-ness 'is constantly being formed and reformed, reflecting changing conditions and self-conceptions; together these exclude complete separation as well as complete integration'.[4]

Colonialist policies of the European powers, and then the 1945–89 Cold War, have had much to do with the creation of divisions in the Arab world. Sovereign Arab states have found it hard to create an effective Arab-wide platform to share, as manifested in the failures of the Arab League as a regional organization since its foundation in 1945. Arab states, since their foundation, have been divided, largely thanks to the machinations of such western European powers as France, Britain and Italy, and their own desire to carve for themselves national identities. Halliday argues that 'part of this involved the assertion and maintenance of claims with regard to other states, based on what were viewed as historic rights, or on denunciation of the partitions and divisions imposed by colonialism'.[5] However formed, these divisions enabled, indeed encouraged, the Cold War's superpowers to separate the Arab political units from each other, placing them in opposing camps. Even here, though, neither superpower was able to impose discipline on its regional allies, and co-operation between them was not always a common feature of such alliances at the regional level.

Early Arab attempts at co-operation, like the Egyptian–Syrian-forged United Arab Republic, were too narrowly based and ideologically motivated to act as a magnet for the rest. The United Arab Republic, even with Iraq's interest in it after its revolution in 1958, mounted to very little power in international terms. Indeed, one of its chief failings was to allow itself to become a weapon against the conservative bloc of Arab states. An 'Arab cold war' ensued,[6] which lasted until the 1970s and the rise to prominence of petrodollar diplomacy in the Arabian Peninsula states. Petrodollar power challenged and, within a decade of its rise, subdued the nationalists, changing for at least 200 years the geopolitical weight of the region in favour of the Arabian Peninsula states. Despite the presence of radical states among the oil exporters (Algeria, Iraq and Libya), petrodollar politics helped in taking the ideology out of inter-Arab politics, and seemed to offer the chance for a more pragmatic, or dare I suggest 'functionalist', interaction. On the basis of this, Korany has argued that the petrodollar–labour relationship could have provided the glue for integration of the Arab system. He notes that, once development projects were started in the Gulf Arab states, skilled and unskilled labour was going to be needed to build the various capital projects. 'This labor-import was not only feasible, but was also beneficial to the Arab system as a whole, for the problem of the majority of the Arab world has been the reverse: a labor surplus. What better prod could integration get than the complementarity between the different factors of production, labor and capital, and thus a higher resource exploitation and development for the benefit of all?'[7] In reality, the substantial transfers of labour to the Gulf Arab states, and the importance of remittances to the home country, did not provide sufficient momentum for further integration, and the opportunity proved to be short-lived.

As well as intra-Arab problems, other geopolitical factors were at work to prevent the Gulf Arab states from creating a wider Arab market. No sooner had the regional star of the Gulf Arab petrodollar states begun to rise, then the Iranians next door rose against their ruling monarch, and in one fell swoop in 1979 replaced his secular, pro-Western regime with a Shia-led theocratic anti-Western one. For some of the Gulf Arab states, such as Saudi Arabia, which had seen itself as the only true beacon of Islam, the emergence of a new revolutionary (Shia-based) Islamist state in the same neighbourhood was a challenge too far. Instead of focusing on the widening of the economic net to neighbouring Arab countries, at the height of the oil boom Saudi Arabia and the smaller Gulf Shaikhdoms were, instead, making haste to throw a defensive blanket around themselves, thus isolating themselves from the rest of the region. From 1981, these countries became inward-looking as far as the Arab world was concerned, and international as far as their economic relations were concerned.

By the by, Iran's propaganda in the heyday of its revolutionary phase also forced the return of ideology – this time in Islamist terms – to centre stage. Slowly but surely, Islamist discourse spread across the Arab world in the 1980s, directly affecting the domestic politics of Algeria, Palestine and Sudan, and indirectly doing so in Jordan, Egypt, Lebanon, Yemen, Morocco, Kuwait, Bahrain, and even secular Syria.

While the Arab states themselves must shoulder much of the blame for the failures of the Arab order, the role of the MENA region's non-Arab states in disrupting and distorting the flow of inter-Arab politics should not be overlooked. Iran, Israel, Turkey, and to a lesser extent Pakistan have directly influenced inter-Arab politics by playing a critical role in the shaping of the region's politics, its security parameters, and its alliance structures. The first three have been dominant in this role, and whether through war, revolution, or diplomacy, they have independently managed to weaken and ultimately fracture the Arab world. Iran's revolution accelerated the Islamist backlash in the Arab world, for instance, which was itself sustained in the first place by Israel's aggressive actions and its military policies in the region. Tel Aviv's ability to prise Egypt – the 'beating heart' of Arabism – away from the rest of the Arab world in 1979 left the Arab world leaderless. This in itself fragmented Arab strategy towards its most important security problem – Israel. But Egypt's separate peace with Israel in 1979 also opened up the field for other Arab states to bid for leadership. Iraq, on the one hand, and Syria, on the other, both did so, but with very different priorities and expectations.

The fragmentation of the Arab world was soon followed by its fracturing, thanks to Iraq's invasion of Iran in 1980. Iraq's next act of violence, the invasion of Kuwait a decade later, led to the atomization of an already weak and vulnerable Arab order. The 'Arab system' was no more. Hinnebusch provides crisp analysis of the consequences of the non-Arab states' actions for the Arab world: 'Its fragmentation made the Arab world exceptionally vulnerable to the powerful revisionist impulses that were being unleashed on its peripheries', he writes. 'Initially, the Iranian revolution snapped the Tehran–Tel Aviv axis against Arab nationalism and threatened to shift the power balance against Israel; but Iran's efforts to export revolution to its neighbours ... at a time when its own military capabilities had been decimated by revolution, precipitated the Iraqi invasion of its territory and the eight-year-long Iran–Iraq war. This immediately reshuffled the deck to Israel's advantage: Iraq's marginalisation combined Egypt's removal from the Arab–Israeli balance, freed Israel ... to project power in the Arab world with little restraint'.[8] Iraq's war, however, also allowed for the return of Egypt to the Arab fold and the further loss of ideology from Arab politics. In regional integration terms, incidentally, this process was to find manifestation in the Iraq-supported, Egypt-endorsed, Jordan-orchestrated and North Yemen-followed Arab Co-operation Council (ACC) in 1989. Each state chose to join the ACC for pragmatic reasons and in the context of some narrowly defined national interests. But they did so for largely politico-military reasons, not socio-economic ones.

In the exercise of fragmentation, the non-Arab states were assisted by the activities of some Arab states themselves: Iraq's war against Iran (1980–88) and its invasion of Kuwait (1990–91) did more harm to the Arab world than anything an outside power could have done at the time. Iraq's adventurism under Saddam Hussein also helped the West, particularly the USA, in consolidating its military and security grip on the region. By the same token, Libya's wild swings in the western Arab world between pan-Arabism and anti-Arabism helped in no small way to unbalance the Arab world and deepen Arab North Africa's internal divisions. Libya's regional mood swings, and its adventurist foreign acts from the mid-1980s through to the late 1990s, helped rob the Arab world of the focus needed to present a common, or united, response to European initiatives in the Mediterranean. Nor did Libya's regional policies allow for the consolidation of a uniquely Maghreb bloc, which the other three North African states had dreamed about even under French rule. In addition, conflict within Arab states – such as civil war in Sudan, Yemen and Algeria – created further fractures in an already fragile Arab 'system'.

There is a regional system here, with strong geopolitical characteristics – but what we do not have here is regionalism.[9] Such regionalist drivers as the North American Free Trade Agreement (NAFTA), the Association of Southeast Asian Nations (ASEAN), or *Mercado Común del Sur* (MERCOSUR in South America) have not been replicated here. The Arab Common Market plan remains just that, and even outside assistance from the USA, albeit modest in financial and technical terms, has not ignited the regionalist fire in the MENA region. It is ironic that as regionalism has taken hold of all the other continents bar Africa, the MENA region, for all its potential, has remained an unstructured regional system. While its Arab core has displayed a strong sense of 'regional awareness', 'regional identity' and even 'regional consciousness', this powerful combination of factors has not fostered trans-Arab or inter-Arab regionalist tendencies.[10] As we have seen, these critical factors came into play only as collective tools at the sub-regional level.

Economic regionalism, as a by-product of globalization, in terms of trade, investment and labour mobility, does not seem to be growing roots in the MENA region, despite regionalism's potential to underpin economic rejuvenation of the Muslim Middle East. It is therefore hard to associate John Naisbitt's analysis of the 'global paradox', quoted at the outset of this chapter, with the MENA region. Despite several attempts, no single regional trading bloc has come to exist, let alone endure.[11] In the Arab world, lack of economic diversity and factor endowment has left a negative mark on integration. In the western Arab world and the eastern Mediterranean, agriculture (mainly olives, citrus fruit and cash crops) dominates; and in the

Mashreq (largely the Gulf region) it is hydrocarbons that rule. Trade networks cannot be sustained through this narrow range of tradable goods. Furthermore, one often finds that the agricultural producers of the Maghreb are in competition with each other over market share and therefore unable to act collectively. In the GCC, in contrast, petrodollar income has enabled them to form global networks as their import strategies, displaying little dependence on regional markets or products. They are therefore missing a vital ingredient of integrationist tendencies: little or no dependence on local regional markets for survival or prosperity. As their trade patterns show, demand in the Persian Gulf subregion has for years been satisfied by extra-regional suppliers. A handful of European Union (EU) members, the USA and the key economies of Asia feed the GCC's economies. In other words, their aspiration to function within a global network has helped loosen their economic ties to their geo-economic hinterland. While movement of labour, from the rest to the oil-rich states, did help in some transfers and assist the development of mutually advantageous economic linkage in the Arab world, this was always going to be an insufficient force for forging wider economic co-operation or integration. *Thawra* (revolution) may have given way to *tharwa* (riches) in the Arab world, but *tharwa* did not carry within it sufficient force for integration of the region.[12]

From *Thawra* to *Tharwa*: Subregionalism in Full Flow

One of the MENA region's big problems has been that politics, rather than economic imperatives, has been driving inter-state relations.[13] In the end, Arabism in itself proved to be an insufficient force for cementing closer economic ties. Over time, with political problems mounting after the Arabs' defeat in the Six-Day War in 1967, the region began to slide towards subregionalism.[14] Egypt's waning influence after the death of President Nasser in 1970 helped in loosening Arab centralist forces, and as oil income grew to dominate the process of regional relations, so it was that the shift in the balance of power to the Gulf Arab states encouraged the subsystem's subregional tendencies. This same process inevitably also weakened the post-1940s Arab order that Nasser and other pan-Arabists had been so instrumental in founding.

The birth of the six-member GCC in 1981 as an organization of oil-rich Arab monarchies has symbolized the tendency towards subregionalization. But the GCC has been far from successful in creating a cohesive unit, or a dominant club, in this subregion. It has made little progress towards political union of its members (a specific goal of the organization as exemplified in its charter), nor has it managed to create an integrated market. A common market is certainly in operation today, but it is far from an integrated one. Nearly 20 years after its birth, one commentator noted: 'even today the nature of the GCC has yet to be clearly defined. It has clearly evolved into all things to all people. Each of the member states has its own perceptions and expectations. Some ... emphasize its economic integration function. Others vigorously advocate greater military cooperation. Still others remain exclusively fixated on internal security as the principal objective of the GCC'.[15] Vulnerable geographically, demographically and in security terms, its success can be measured only in terms of its ability to develop some unified structures for its members.

'Perhaps the single greatest constraint upon the GCC in terms of realizing its vision and mission is one it shares with numerous other international organizations, namely that it is not a supranational authority. Unlike the member-states, it has no sovereignty or political independence, and other than the complex of buildings in Riyadh, where it is headquartered, no territory either. As such, it lacks the authorization and power to demand the member countries' compliance on any matter. In addition, few outsiders are aware of how limited the GCC Secretariat's staff is relative to other, more established regional organizations. For example, the Brussels-based EU has more than 7,000 employees. The GCC's staff, by contrast, is slightly more than 300. Notwithstanding the fact that many EU employees are translators, unnecessary for the monolingual GCC, the organization still operates with a small number of employees'.[16]

Despite these drawbacks, on 1 January 2003 a customs union was established by the GCC to standardize customs duties among its members. In accordance with the customs union, Saudi Arabia approved the reduction to 5 per cent of customs for goods formerly charged between 7 and 12 per cent. In addition, the GCC agreed to the principle of a single port of entry. It was agreed by the members that most related laws and regulations be standardized by the end of 2005. The customs union was a landmark event by regional standards, but even this measure took over 20 years to mature, and followed slow progress on such agreements as labour mobility. Internal problems endure and hamper integration,[17] but so too do regional problems.[18]

A key reason for the GCC's slow evolution has been the complex geopolitics of this 'chronically conflict-oriented' subregion, to borrow Abdulla's phrase.[19] Marr notes that this is a subregion 'without cultural or political cohesion, the Persian Gulf comprises countries and societies at varying levels of development and with differing resource bases that share a common body of water of critical importance to all of them'.[20] Their diversity, in other words, helps to divide, rather than unite, the eight countries bordering the waterway. The northern shores of the waterway are dominated by Iran and Iraq, both of which have had their fair share of political anguish over the past half-century. Since 1979, though, their domestic politics have been particularly effective in spilling over their borders to destabilize the entire neighbourhood. As Iran's politics has settled down, Iraq's has since 2003 again entered a new period of instability. The fuller consequences for the Persian Gulf states of the fall of Baghdad in spring 2003 will take a decade or more to be manifested, as will the long-term impact of the al-Qaeda-led terror campaign against the ruling al-Sauds in oil-rich Saudi Arabia, who control over 250 billion barrels of the world's finite oil reserves. The wider impact of any attempts by the USA to weaken the GCC's hegemon (the Saudi state) as a means of checking the growth of al-Qaeda will also take time to emerge. Playing geopolitical dare with this critical country, or talk of threatening to dismember the world's most important oil state, or forcefully seizing its oil assets, if it fails to fully and transparently participate in the USA's war on terror – as has been done on several occasions in US circles since 9/11[21] – raises huge questions about the role of the USA in regional and subregional orders of the Middle East, as well as the long-term stability and freedom of such subregional organizations as the GCC to ignite wider integrationist fires in the subsystem. A combination of violence and political uncertainty in the Gulf region's largest Arab actors will more than likely further dampen the collaborative tendencies of the states of this strategic waterway – which will adversely affect the political economy relations of the wider MENA region.

Nearly a decade after the birth of the GCC, another all-Arab subregional organization, the Arab Maghreb Union (AMU), was founded (in February 1989) for creating a common market and for managing the economic affairs of the North African states with their more powerful northern neighbour, the EU. The five-member AMU was meant to forge a common market and act as a single unit in relations with its geographical peripheries. While looking northwards, the AMU was also to play a role in the Organization of African Unity (later renamed African Union), to which they all belonged. Its success, however, was limited due to Libya's continuing international isolation, the western Sahara dispute between Morocco and Algeria, and the threat of Islamic militancy arising from the bloody civil strife in Algeria in the 1990s.[22] The AMU, for all its collective agreements on the removal of trade barriers, investment guarantees, and the free movement of goods and services, had became moribund by the late 1990s, largely because it failed to move from diplomatic integration to the higher level of developmental integration.[23] As Zartman explains, the Union 'was in catalepsy as a political organization ... Integration in the Maghrib had fallen back to the diplomatic level, following the dynamics of the basic structural rivalries'.[24] The AMU's birth nonetheless marked the second breach in the wider pan-Arab wall, effectively reinforcing the tensions that the GCC had put on it.

To make matters even more complex, then there were three! The Arab Co-operation Council soon followed the AMU, in 1989. The ACC brought Iraq under the same umbrella with three of its most helpful allies in its war with Iran: Jordan, Egypt, and North Yemen. The ACC became the third all-Arab subregional organization to emerge from the ashes of pan-Arabism. With its birth, the Arab world was effectively segmented into three unequal subregional entities. The three organizations had encompassed 15 Arab states, from Morocco in the west to Yemen in the east. The failures of the AMU and the fate of the short-lived ACC speak volumes about the strategic vulnerabilities of the Arab order and its structural weaknesses. It is partly due to the weaknesses of the subregional organizations themselves, as well as the absence of an Arab hegemon to regulate inter-Arab relations since the early 1970s, that the Arabs have failed to impose a pan-Arab regional order on the MENA subsystem.

The birth of the ACC was enthusiastically engineered by the two Husseins: the ruling monarch of Jordan and the ruling president of republican Iraq. The ACC seemed very different from its neighbours. It was the first subregional organization not to enjoy geographical contiguity; it was also the most geographically diffuse, being the first to straddle the Arabian Peninsula, the Persian Gulf and the eastern edges of North Africa. With a combined population of over 100 million, it promised much in economic terms, but its short shelf-life – it was only around in 1989 as Iraq's invasion of Kuwait in 1990 pitted the ACC's most powerful members (Cairo and Baghdad) against each other – meant that it could not deliver on its promises. Indeed, as its untenable position in the 1990–91 Kuwait crisis illustrated, it was again politics and geopolitical complexities that forced the undoing of a promising subregional organization.

Post-Cold-War politics did, however, open one new window for regionalism in the area. The decision of the Economic Co-operation Organization (ECO) members (Iran, Pakistan, and Turkey) to incorporate the Muslim republics of the former Soviet Union and Afghanistan in the early 1990s created a regional body of over 300 million people. Blessed with mineral, agricultural and some significant industrial wealth, it was expected that the founding members of the ECO would push this organization as a new economic force in Asia. But weak political structures and lack of security (inter-state and domestic), combined with the dynamism of the Asian power balance, dampened the impact of the ECO. Today, this all-Muslim, non-Arab regional organization has little to show for its existence. While the existence of the ECO may have helped bilateral relations among some of its members, it has not, as a rule, created a functional regional bloc to straddle south, west and Central Asia.

As we have seen, subregionalism may have provided some tactical solutions to the region's economic and political dilemmas, but these organizations have also tended to deepen the 'balance of weakness' in the Arab world, to borrow Noble's phrase.[25] As a consequence, Arab states and peoples, who still share a common fear of globalization and a US–Israeli conspiracy to dominate their lands, have been exposed to even greater unhindered pressure from the outside. At the technical level, too, high tariffs and customs duties, red tape and other artificial barriers to free trade (such as quantitative import restrictions) hamper economic integration. So long as large Arab states are able to accrue substantial revenue – as much as 20 per cent of government revenue outside the GCC states[26] – from tariffs and import duties, they are unlikely to voluntarily negotiate reducing their protectionist practices. And if they do not do so, the environment for closer economic links cannot be enhanced.

Mounting pressure after 9/11 has added to the fragility of the region as a whole, and in the context of its existing vulnerabilities, has allowed for the penetration of the region's agenda by its most recent hegemonic power, the USA. This hegemonic power is unpopular and its presence enjoys little legitimacy in the Muslim-dominated MENA region. The inability of this hegemon consensually to manage the emergence of a new regional order has merely added to the subsystem's instability.[27] As we have seen in Iraq, the USA is able to impose its will on the region through the application of its military might, but because its policies towards Israel and the Arabs are seen as inequitable, and its pursuit of reforms as hypocritical, its behaviour constantly generates instability in the region, which in turn breeds Islamist and other opposition to its presence here.[28] The loss of control of Iraq by the Coalition in early to mid-2004 testifies to this reality. After waves of attacks on US forces, relative security for the coalition forces was finally restored through the application of massive force and huge casualties, but the military campaign helped fundamentally to undermine the Coalition's political agenda in Iraq, considerably worsened by the revelations about US and British abuse and humiliation of Iraqi citizens in their custody.

In the MENA region, then, Naisbitt's optimistic forecast about regional economic alliances creating the conditions for development have not, unfortunately, come true. Borders remain solid and economic alliances narrowly based. Moreover, there is now a real danger that these states could find themselves further down the ladder of economic prosperity as they fail to take advantage of European trade opportunities. They faced a similar problem in the 1980s, when the European Community was busy accommodating the addition of Greece, Spain and Portugal to the organization.[29] As the EU juggernaut turns its full attention to the absorption of its 10 new members from eastern Europe, it is possible that the poorer neighbours in the southern Mediterranean could find themselves further on the margins. These new EU members offer their western European cousins markets, skilled but relatively cheap labour, and unhindered access and investment opportunities. MENA economies will probably now have to go out of their way to find novel ways of attracting European capital outside their hydrocarbon sectors. Ironically, the record shows that while integration in Europe and the free trade in North America spurred the Far Eastern countries to try and emulate the same, in the MENA region such push factors have failed to ignite the same movement.[30]

Thirdly, MENA states will have to find ways of minimizing the 'metropolization' of economic activity within the region.[31] That is to say, once the regional states find creative ways of accommodating globalization, they would at the same time have to find economic and bureaucratic mechanisms for minimizing the core–periphery/rich–poor dichotomy of globalization and its over-urbanization of economic activity, by trying to spread the benefits of linking with the world economy to the remotest corners of each country. In freeing their economies, MENA states will have to try and manage the local needs of their populations against both regional and global pressures. Globalization's tendency of spatially concentrating vibrant economic sectors could affect employment patterns and opportunities, hasten rural-to-urban migration, and add a further burden on these overstretched economies.

Regionalism 'Lite'?

Evidence suggests that globalization fragments, and also encourages, the creation of larger regional trading blocs. In the MENA context, this means the weakening of the state-form, the further fragmentation of the Arab order, and a definite expansion in the influence of the more advanced economies of the region – most notably the GCC, Israel and Turkey – in the whole area. They would have to do for MENA what Japan, South Korea and China have done for the Far East, or the USA has done for NAFTA. But control of the regional economic train by two non-Arab MENA states is not likely to go down well in the Arab countries. Feeling even more beleaguered and under pressure from the West since 9/11, these countries will not welcome an already strong Israeli–Turkish security axis also gaining control of the economic agenda of the region. It is also far from clear that any of the MENA states are prepared to make concessions on their political sovereignty or national control of economic forces to friends, let alone contemplating this with regard to Israel or Turkey. Some countries, such as Jordan, Morocco, Bahrain, and Qatar, have welcomed greater US economic involvement in forging sustainable regional markets, but access to the US market does not come without strings attached, and cannot be the answer to all the region's economic problems. What, moreover, will come of the European leg of a 'MENA free-trade agreement'? Will the EU and US options overlap, or end up competing with each other? If the latter happens, then we are in for another round of MENA divisions and fragmentation. If the former is presumed, all MENA countries will need to be involved if the project is to work. Will Tehran, Damascus, or even Riyadh find it comfortable, if at all possible, to share economic destinies with Israel in the absence of a just peace in the Holy Land? I doubt it. Which means that we are back on the political track again, and the commitment of the parties themselves and the sponsors of the peace process, to agree a lasting solution to their historic differences. As we have seen since the 1991 Madrid Conference, without peace in Palestine/Israel, no regional integration agenda can proceed; without regional peace, the best that can be hoped for is further subregional development.

As globalization has not taken sufficient hold in the area, it is not surprising that regionalism has not flourished either. Under current circumstances, the best that could be hoped for in the medium term is 'regionalism lite', in which MENA states accept the need for wider co-operation, but begin to act on it only selectively.

The assumption that globalization fans regionalism could be true insofar as, in the MENA region, the weakness of globalization is mirrored in the absence of any move towards a larger trading bloc. A combination of the role of politics (as the continuing primary driver of inter-state relations) and security factors have stood as powerful obstacles in the way of both globalization and regionalization. It is worth repeating the broad conclusion of a major study on regionalism: 'the absence of a viable regional security environment in the Middle East has constituted the major impediment for economic cooperation in the Middle East'.[32] Yet, elsewhere in the international system, the same combination of security and politics has actually enhanced the prospects of regionalism, with ASEAN providing a good example of this. In the MENA subsystem, it appears that the absence of regional cohesion or concert has hindered the development of regionalism. The Arab world today may be trying to address the problem by initiating such economically driven programmes as the Greater Arab Free Trade Area, which was launched in 1998, but even here the disparities in wealth and economic prowess among the MENA states hinder progress, as does the continuing desire for total state sovereignty in terms of complete independence and autonomy of action.

For all its fragmentary tendencies, the 'Middle East remains a single unit from an international security point of view, just as it was a century ago', notes Roger Owen,[33] and this means that the region continues to harbour the capacity to disrupt international stability, on which rests the force of globalization. Herein lies much of outsiders' concerns about the MENA subsystem. Without strong political or socio-economic 'pan-Arab' regional structures to contain its volatility, or MENA-wide integrationist impetus to ignite an economic revival, the region is set to remain fragmented, and thus its economic potential will be partially captured by its most vibrant subregions – most notably in the strategically fragile Persian Gulf. But so long as the Persian Gulf subregion continues to dominate the political economy of the region and the Mashreq its geopolitics, the presence of outside actors such as the USA and the EU will remain a certainty, adding to the subsystem's complexities. As in the early formation of this regional system, so today the policy priorities of the extra-regional powers, most notably the USA, will play a significant part in determining the region's collaborative efforts. Today, Washington's instinct is that the MENA region needs to reform for the sake of US and international security, and this remains a big driver of US policy in the GME.[34] But the broader impact of US initiatives, in terms of more elections and a longer list of candidates, could mask the rise of deeper geopolitical barriers to globalizing forces in the region, as its drive for democratization invites to the power table political forces still resistant to globalization (as much as to US power itself). US hegemony has generated counter-hegemonic tendencies in the past in the region, but the limited success of these responses should not be interpreted in balance-of-power terms, or as a consequence of regional passivity.[35] This is a region in which collective political structures, notes Paul Aarts, tend to take the form of hegemonic regionalism.[36] Commentators agree that the region may be on the verge of another explosion, created by the interaction between US and autonomous local actors. In their volatility neither the force of regional explosions, nor their direction, can be predicted. Thus, despite the region's very real potential as a prosperous common market, it is likely that due to constant movement along its geopolitical fault lines, and the role played by outside powers, it will remain in a state of integration paralysis, which will, as ever, expose its members to pressures well beyond their control. Politics overriding economics remains a real barrier to regionalization.

How the unstructured GME is coping with the pressures of US unipolarity, on the one hand, and those emanating from the two powerful and dynamic territories to its north and east, on the other, will be discussed in the context of Eurasian power politics in the next chapter of this book.

4 Geopolitical Tectonics
The Greater Middle East on the Margins of Eurasia

> Our lack of the objective distance necessary to understand the current process of change [rise of the East] in our era has its roots in the fact that the contemporary Arab circle is an offshoot of the traditional global order that emerged in the West in the 16th century and that culminated with US global dominance following the collapse of the bipolar order. Perhaps this explains why many cling to the impression that the centrality of the West is a permanent, everlasting phenomenon, forgetting that history before the 16th century testifies to the rise of many other great empires from Egypt of the Pharaohs, to China, to the vast Islamic empire.
>
> Anwar Abdel-Malek, 'While We Were Sleeping',
> *Al-Ahram Weekly*, 13–19 October 2003.

Introduction: The Shaping of Eurasia

The MENA region forms the very heart of the GME, and is caught between the two most powerful regions in military, economic and political terms outside the Americas: Europe and the Far East. It cannot afford to neglect either, nor can it afford to become an exclusive periphery of one. Not for the first time in its long history, grand geopolitics is emerging as a powerful tool in the shaping of the MENA regional system. While it is true to say that the region's destiny in the twenty-first century is still in the grip of the all-powerful 'intrusive' power (the USA), the force of strategic changes taking place in post-communism Europe and post-Soviet Asia is likely to drive the region's agenda in the decades to come. As shown below, clear patterns are already emerging that demonstrate the tremendous pulling power of Eurasia for the GME. But, at the same time, Eurasia's own importance as the world's largest continent and its 'axial' geopolitical role, to use Brzezinski's term, is ensuring that the Middle East will find itself at the centre of the struggles for domination of this vast geopolitical entity. This is the chessboard, he argues, on which the game for global supremacy is played. 'A power that dominates Eurasia', Brzezinski states, 'would control two of the world's three most advanced and economically productive regions ... control over Eurasia would automatically entail Africa's subordination [as well] ... About 75 percent of the world's people live in Eurasia, and most of the world's physical wealth is there as well, both in its enterprises and underneath its soil. Eurasia accounts for about 60 percent of the world's GNP and about three-fourths of the world's known energy resources'.[1] It is not surprising, then, that the Middle East should inescapably be caught in the post-Cold-War geopolitical grand games of Eurasia.

With reference to Europe, the so-called democratic bridgehead of Eurasia, the issue facing MENA is how much further Europe-wide integration and the expansion of the European Union will go, and how this process will directly affect the workings of the region. With the 10 new members that joined the EU in 2004, its boundaries have shifted ever eastwards to reach the geographical boundaries of the Mashreq. And once Turkey joins the Union, the three MENA states of Iran, Iraq, and Syria will become direct neighbours of the EU. The EU's stake in regional stability and prosperity will therefore be that much greater, as demonstrated by its 'New Neighbourhood Policy'.

In the case of Asia, on the other hand, the problem is that great impact is being made in the absence of a solid and coherent regional structure – such as the EU – to moderate inter-state and intra-regional relations. The unco-ordinated expansion of links between the several Asian regions will, nonetheless, heavily influence the direction of MENA economies and their strategic links.

With MENA's two powerful neighbours remaining in a state of flux, however, the role that the USA might come to play in influencing the direction of change in the Middle East will remain crucial, even decisive in the long run, given its presence in the area and its active engagement. So, ironically, the USA's own strategic role in the Eurasian land mass is likely to leave a definite mark on MENA's relations with the regions pressing on it from the north-west and the east. Furthermore, as US preferences in Eurasia will have a distinct security undertone, for the foreseeable future its policies will keep engaged in 'out-of-area' operations both its own armed forces and those of its European NATO partners. NATO's role in Afghanistan can be seen as the precursor for other deployments in West Asia. In addition, a congruence of Asian security issues, coupled with the USA's broader strategic interests in East Asia, will also keep the remaining superpower heavily engaged in Asian matters. The USA thus provides the strategic link between the three geopolitical poles of the EU, post-Soviet Asia and North America, and the three are geopolitically tied together in the GME.

In concrete terms, the region is sandwiched between two continental forces. In Europe the matter of further integration around the EU is a direct challenge; while in Asia 'anarchy' and the absence of a regionally defined order beyond ASEAN brings a wide range of opportunities and security challenges to bear on the Middle East. Torn between being Mediterranean and Asian, the room for the MENA region to emerge as an autonomous regional system in its own right is likely to be more limited as time goes by, even though some pundits still believe that, as globalization takes hold in the MENA subsystem, so regionalism could emerge as an integrating force in its own right. Geopolitics and globalization become powerful countervailing forces in the MENA context.

Here we see that the region is being pressed in divergent directions. A discussion of why this is the case is important, because it highlights the importance of regionalism as part of the larger process of globalization. On the other hand, a focus on regionalism in the MENA context serves to underline some of the inherent tensions that exist between the need for regional co-operation, as a means of 'saddling' globalization; and the pressures that globalization brings to bear on MENA's larger neighbourhood as European and Asian powers respond to the profound changes that globalization, particularly in the wake of the end of the Cold War, is bringing – what Halliday has referred to as 'both fusion and fission'.[2]

The idea of fusion is particularly apposite, through which we see the western European democracies' attempts at integration as symbolizing the trend towards fusing their economies and some of their decision-making processes. The term fission, on the other hand, best summarizes the collapse of the Soviet Union, but it can also be used to explain the potentially explosive nature of European–Middle East relations in the post-Cold-War era, where Europe's own regionalist momentum could arguably be said to be disrupting the political, economic and social rhythm of its southern Mediterranean neighbours. Fission could also describe the turbulence of the crisis-ridden MENA subsystem itself, where political elites are finding it increasingly difficult to adjust to global forces, the challenges of the post-9/11 international order, and the deep-rooted economic and social difficulties facing their societies.

European Union–Middle East relations are being forged in a climate where globalization and regionalization are reshaping the international system. While relations between the two regions have been entering a new phase, the EU's regionalist enterprise, and its increasing assertiveness, have been clashing with the neighbouring MENA subsystem which, as we have seen, has been suffering from a long period of malaise, compounded in recent years by deep fragmentation and greater subregionalist tendencies. Nonetheless, MENA states do look forward to closer European–Mediterranean relations and to a more constructive European presence in the MENA region. Effects of a more determined European voice in international politics are sought in the two realms of the Arab–Israeli peace process and the Persian Gulf, which also inform the EU's Mediterranean policies more broadly.

The EU as Global Actor

The analysis begins with an assessment of the EU and its place in the international system, and continues with observations on the impact systemic changes have had on Europe and on the Middle East. Two dynamic, rapidly evolving and inter-related forces can be identified as the main engines driving the EU's development of its internal structures, as well as the redefinition of its role and behaviour in the international system. The first of these, which can be termed regionalization, is rapidly becoming a response to the second – globalization. As we saw in earlier chapters, globalization has been reshaping the international system in its entirety, imposing boundaries on the states' zone of influence, on the one hand, and opening up tremendous economic opportunities in every corner of the world, on the other. Regionalism, by contrast, is usually characterized by the inward movement of a fairly well defined geographical space, designed either to bolster the regional club against external pressures, or merely to strengthen the process of co-operation among neighbouring countries, which may have arisen from the convergence of one or more of the following: geopolitical factors, cultural likeness, political affinity, or territorial proximity.[3]

Taken together, regionalization and globalization have been forcing profound changes on state behaviour worldwide. We saw in earlier chapters that, whether in the realm of a country's foreign policy or that of its domestic social and economic environment, globalization is imposing limits on the autonomy of the state and forcing it to make compromises and sacrifices, in the interest of prosperity in the post-Cold-War economic order. One such compromise is finding itself manifested in regionalism – the worldwide trend of regional co-operation and integration by geographically and/or culturally proximate states in their collective interests. In regionalizing, states sacrifice some of their sovereign domain to the greater good of the club.

In addition to these global factors, other systemic changes have been helping to shape Europe's destiny. Two, in particular, are of great significance in the European context: the collapse of the Soviet Union (and its political and military departure from eastern Europe); and the unification of Germany. Together these developments, one centrifugal and the other 'convergenal', have helped in what one commentator has called the dismantling of the 'very structure of European stability'.[4] They have also been responsible for stretching the very fabric of the post-World War II European political and economic order. One western European response to these highly destabilizing developments has been to deepen the capitalist economic structures of Europe (the EU), and also to try and cocoon the Union from the global winds of change by surrounding it with a series of economic, political and security partnerships and alliances, of which the North Atlantic Treaty Organization is the most visible. Other initiatives in the 1990s, such as the EU's partnerships with its eastern and southern neighbours, the strengthening of the western EU, and support for such multilateral gatherings as the Euro–Mediterranean Dialogue, can be seen as forming key elements of the same security architecture. Much of this activity, it is fair to say, has been informed by European realization of its need in the post-bipolar world to find a collective, if not united, voice in response to regional crises, such as the 1990–91 and 2003 Persian Gulf crises around Iraq, and to major disruptions in the international system.[5] An example is 9/11: the event brought about a high degree of transatlantic unity, but Washington's policy responses – particularly in West Asia – created deep divisions in the Western alliance.

The success of multilateral and bilateral agreements with its peripheries, however, has always been conditional on further successful integration of the western European economic club. The most significant aspect of such moves in recent years has been the creation of a single economic space in the capitalist heartland of Europe.[6] Although the creation of a single market may not have been a new strategy – the decision to create a fully unified internal market was taken back in 1985 – the unification of Germany and the disintegration of the USSR caused a marked shift in focus within the EU and accelerated the rate of flow towards further European integration – and ultimately expansion eastwards. The vision of a single European entity was being pushed at the time by key continental powers (Germany and France, in particular) and was vehemently opposed by Prime Minister Thatcher of Britain, who found herself helpless in efforts to reverse the tide of what was depicted as creeping 'federationalism'.[7]

Within a few years, albeit tentatively at first, the core western European powers and their smaller European Community (as it was then known) partners started taking the first steps that were to mark the transitional process from the 'Common Market' to the 'Single Market' and finally towards the 'Union'.[8] Today, 'unionization' has led to the deepening of the single market and opening of a battle front between the Atlantic powers, between the EU's euro and the mighty dollar. As the euro strengthens against the dollar and the Japanese yen, its vitality raises serious financial considerations for all those countries whose primary trading currency is one of the latter two. In the MENA region, in particular, global currency battles have a dramatic impact on the trading posture of these countries. MENA countries constantly have to juggle their income from hydrocarbons (traded in dollars) against the euro, the currency of their major trading partners in Europe. Rapid shifts in the relative value of these two global currencies, as seen in the post-9/11 period, has a very direct and serious impact on the financial health of these states, whose export currency is the dollar and whose import currency is the euro.

Fear of the rise of the euro, moreover, has not only alarmed Japan, but may have moved the USA to try and strengthen the dollar's geopolitical grip in such a strategically important region as the Middle East. More than one commentator has mused that the 2003 Iraq war was partially rooted in US concerns about Baghdad's insistence from 2000 that its oil be valued in euros; and indeed it was claimed in 2004 that Washington's increasingly bellicose line against Iran was driven by a similar concern. The argument has been made that Iran's requirement since 2003 that EU importers pay for their Iranian oil in euros, coupled with its plan to start the region's first oil bourse in Tehran in 2006 (which will be able to trade in euros), may have underlined America's increasingly aggressive position with regard to Iran's regional role and its nuclear programme.[9] Although this argument is contestable, the fact that a global currency battle has been in full swing is beyond doubt. As this currency war is a symptom of a broader, global struggle for economic supremacy, it is again not surprising that globalization emerges as a key driver of the security dynamics of the MENA region.

For the MENA states, therefore, developments in Europe are of great significance, not only because the EU is a major global player[10] and their main trading partner, but more particularly because most of the EU's decisions tend to have a direct impact on the prosperity and security of the more vulnerable societies around it. Table 4.1 illustrates the relative power of the EU even before it expanded to 25 members. It is clear that the collapse of the Cold War coincided with the strengthening of the Union.

Additionally, as MENA economies have developed closer ties with the EU, so they have been increasingly exposed to the same winds of change that were blowing in the Union itself, which are embedded in EU economic policy in terms of making the single market sufficiently efficient and competitive to take on the USA and Japan, as well as the other export-oriented economies of Asia. To realize this aim, the European Commission has had to make the EU economic space 'leaner and meaner' but, as O'Hearn argues, the increase in 'the competitiveness of the largest and most technologically advanced firms, sectors, and regions [has threatened] to exacerbate uneven development among [EU] regions and, in particular, to marginalize the so-called European periphery'.[11] With much of the periphery now inside the EU, it can be argued that a similar fate might be awaiting the expanded '15+10' EU's external periphery, where the contradictions of the EU's competition policy might spill over and lead not only to the 'economic balkanization'[12] of the Arab system, but also to the 'uneven denationalization'[13] of the MENA countries. EU action is now more important than it has ever been and EU policies, such as its new 'Neighbourhood Policy' announced in November 2003, are likely to have profound implications for the region.[14]

Table 4.1 Main global economic players, mid-1990s

	Population (million)	Territory (1000 km²)	Economy (US$ billion)	Share in world national production (%)
EU (15)	369	3240	8420	32.1
USA	260	9372	6952	26.7
Japan	125	378	5110	19.5
Russian Federation	149	17,075	363	1.3
China	1205	9571	630	2.3

Sources: European Commission; Dresdner Bank (Frankfurt).

The horizontal and vertical evolution of the Union has put before the MENA states an entity of enormous economic and financial power, whose every political act is likely to reverberate around the region.

EU–MENA Relations in the Context of International Transformations

The international setting for EU–MENA relations in the post-Cold-War and post-9/11 orders can be viewed as the end of American hegemony in the economic realm and the emergence of a truly multi-centre economic order. In this post-Cold-War order, power may have become a more fluid commodity, slowly shifting from the post-1945 US–western Europe-dominated Atlantic international order, to a still-undefined, incoherent and evolving East Asian-dominated Asia–Pacific world in which Japan, China and the East Asian newly industrializing countries may be forming only the leading locomotive of a forward-moving Asian–Pacific economic train. While the growing power of the Asian economies is beyond dispute, it is interesting that 9/11 may have given the USA a renewed drive to attempt to play the role of the decisive actor across the power centres of Eurasia, freely flexing its economic muscle for strategic gain. In this new environment, industrial western Europe is caught between two powerful competing forces: to respond to the Asian challenge but containing the latter's power on its home turf and in its own markets; and to balance against US power in Europe's own southern backyard and also the Middle East.

In this rather uncertain strategic situation, the Middle East is once again at the crossroads of the struggle between Europe, Asia, and the USA. It is caught in the crossfire of a global economic battle between these three huge politico-economic spheres. For the USA, which has a strong military and economic presence in the other two regions, the 'Euro–Asian struggle' can be of great strategic value, a moment of rich pickings, as it were – as was the case in the decades following World War II. To take advantage of this strategic 'window of opportunity', the USA has had to maintain a presence in both, while also keeping its own economy lean and responsive to global changes. Half-way through the 1990s, it had already started to put in place the strategies that would allow it to exploit this window of opportunity fully.

A prolonged Euro–Asian struggle could also very easily sour the USA's carefully nurtured ties with either or both of these sets of economies, and thus compromise its post-9/11 strategic objective of establishing the transatlantic liberalist regime that the US champions as the Asian norm, in place of the international mercantilist traditions of Japan and the Asian tigers.[15] In this new landscape, the Middle East forms part of a vital link between the two Eurasian geo-economic spheres, and as such is a significant global beachhead. Not surprisingly, therefore, it is where the USA has been keenest to play a dominant, active and holding role: to hold the balance of power and thus influence the calculations of its European and Asian partners and competitors. For the remaining military superpower, dominating this strategically significant region is vital if it is to keep its European and Asian challengers at bay.[16] In geopolitical terms, the USA and its competitors fully realize that the MENA region – indeed the GME as a whole – is caught between two potential 'heartlands' of uneven power,[17] which are poised to control the 'world island'.

From another, complementary, perspective, the MENA region is caught between the marching force of the so-called Asian values-based economic organizational strategies (the 'Easternization' of the workplace) on the one hand, and the Westernization of the entire world (the adoption at global level of the capitalist mode of production and its Western-based cultural heritage) on the other. Against the pressures exerted by these forces, the MENA region and its new periphery in the shape of Central Asia (MENACA) is, to paraphrase Frederick Starr, a pivotal region and key to the security of the Eurasian land mass in the twenty-first century.[18] It is here that many global struggles are now being played out, and important international battles are being lost and won.

Without stability in the broader MENACA region, long-term development in Eurasia cannot be sustained, nor security obtained for its many billions of people and many dozens of states. This point is clearly underlined by a contemporary list of so-called pivotal states drawn up by a group of American scholars.[19] It is noteworthy that this list predates the strategic consequences of 9/11, and of the 10 less-developed countries listed, four (Algeria, Egypt, Turkey, and Pakistan) operate within the MENACA region, and a total of six belong to Asia. All four countries listed above are now the USA's partners in its war on terrorism, and Pakistan has emerged as a vital pawn in Washington's playing of the West and South Asian security maps.

Yet the MENA region itself is not only highly unstable, continuing to threaten in different ways the very stability of the post-Cold-War order, but has also been subject to many destabilizing external pressures as well.[20] The region's weak economic base adds to its fragility and vulnerability, and seems to deter substantial foreign investment commitments[21] which, in turn, merely reinforce the prevalent cycle of decline.

Table 4.2 focuses on the period of heightened investment activity before the Asian financial crisis of 1997, to show the prevalent global trends. It is self-evident that the MENA region was a very small player then, and it is of grave concern that, over 10 years on, the figure for the region has barely improved, standing at no more than 1 per cent of global foreign direct investment (FDI) today, while in the case of the Far East, the figure has continued to rocket. In 2004, for example, East Asia attracted some US$105 billion in inward direct investment (with China having the lion's share of the total with $65 billion worth of FDI), and Latin America a further US$68 billion. Brazil alone attracted US$18 billion in FDI in the same year, compared with just US$9.8 billion for the whole of West Asia. Of the latter,

Table 4.2 Foreign direct investment flows to developing countries by region, 1995

	Value (US$ million)	Percentage
Far East	65,033	65.2
Latin America/Caribbean	26,560	26.6
MENA	4230	4.3
Sub-Saharan Africa	2895	2.9
Other	952	1.0
Total	99,670	100.0

Source: UNCTAD, *World Investment Report 1995* (New York: UNCTAD, 1995).

more than 50 per cent was concentrated in just three countries – Saudi Arabia, Syria, and Turkey.[22]

In concrete terms, five key developments can be identified as having defined the pace and nature of EU involvement with the MENA region since the early 1990s. Two of the events earmarked for further analysis here accompanied the ending of the Cold War, and may have accelerated its eventual end, helping in the process to shape the order that followed. The first was the Iraqi invasion of Kuwait in 1990 and the Western/Soviet response to the Iraqi action. The second, and of more importance, was the implosion of the Soviet superpower. This event in itself has had a profound impact on the international system, particularly in the ways in which it has altered the very conduct of international relations and characterized the passing of bipolarity. It is no wonder that the implosion of the Soviet Union was dubbed as the 'big bang' of the international system.[23] The Soviet collapse also changed the geopolitical map of Asia (in particular in western and Central Asia), and with it the Cold-War pattern of alliances. The very balance of power in both Europe and West Asia changed as a consequence.

The third development of note was the coming into force in Europe of the Maastricht Treaty on 1 January 1993. As will be shown later, this treaty transformed the 12-member European Community into a 'European Union' and prepared the way for the emergence of a single western European politico-economic space. The rise of the EU had a direct impact on the MENA region.

The fourth development, of much importance to EU–Middle East relations, was the Arab–Israeli peace process and the EU's role and expectations in that regard. Particularly important were the EU's economic and security initiatives towards the Middle East (such as the call for a Conference on Security and Co-operation in the Middle East), and the ways in which it attempted to address post-Cold-War security concerns arising from its neighbouring MENA region. Until the Sharon–Bush agreement of April 2004, in which the USA gave Israel the green light to unilaterally settle the Palestinian–Israeli dispute, the EU prided itself on being one of the main pillars of the 'road map' and a key player of the peace process's quartet. Now it is again sidelined, and can only reiterate its long-held policy that the EU is unlikely to recognize 'any change to the pre-1967 borders other than those arrived at by agreement between the parties'.[24]

Finally, we need to ask what might be the implications for the Middle East of the numerical, and therefore spatial, expansion of the EU in 1995, 2004 and 2007. These developments will need attention, particularly with reference to the changing balance of power within the Union itself between the Mediterranean and the continental states, first moving southwards in the mid-1980s and then moving northwards, and also in relation to the eastward expansion of the EU in 2004 and 2007 and the Union's future direction.

Iraq and Persian Gulf Security

The Iraqi invasion of Kuwait in 1990 marked a major turning point in the history of the MENA region. First, it sounded the death knell of Arab unity, and with it the region's ability to contain and resolve conflicts with its own resources. Second, it marked a new phase in the subregionalization of the entire MENA territory, a process of fragmentation that has been spreading itself in the restructuring of the Middle East subsystem.[25] This subregionalization has been accompanied by an atomization of the region, whereby states no longer seek collective solutions to regional problems, and instead aim to maximize their own independence from regional powers in an effort to find 'independent' or external solutions to their domestic and foreign policy dilemmas.

Moreover, the end result of regional crises arising from the Kuwait war and the inter-state conflicts of the 1980s manifested itself in several ways. First, it led to the isolation of certain key regional powers, most notably Iraq and Iran in the Persian Gulf subregion. Second, it saw the pro-Western Arab regimes enter into comprehensive defence pacts with Western powers, most notably with the USA, Britain and France. Third, the western European powers capitalized on the vulnerabilities of the MENA states to strengthen their own presence in the MENA region and also, largely through the European Commission, to reach advantageous trade agreements with MENA states and MENA subregions. The process of regionalization that had accompanied globalization of the capitalist system, and had given birth to such subregional entities as the Gulf Co-operation Council (GCC), the Arab Maghreb Union and the short-lived Arab Cooperation Council, were further reinforced by the Commission's trade and investment agreements reached with MENA states after the Cold War.

Into this polarized and fractured MENA arena settled the Western powers, headed by the USA. In the absence of the Soviet Union, they began re-ordering the region, seeking in the process to make it more compatible with President George Bush senior's 'new world order'. The US-led Western alliance became the new power broker in the Middle East, with the USA acting as the region's new hegemonic power. Thus, well before 9/11, the region had been thoroughly penetrated and dominated by the USA. What 9/11 did was to provide the perfect pretext for absolute domination of the region and its agendas.

The Western powers' demands of the MENA regimes, since the 1990s, for compatibility have been based on the realization in the region of certain economic and political priorities: conformity in approaches to economic development (in the form of economic liberalization and structural adjustment); support for Western initiatives in the region (the Arab–Israeli peace process, Persian Gulf security, containment of anti-Western terrorism, suppression of Islamist movements and 'rogue' states, etc.); and the development of pluralist and democratic institutions and processes. As we will see in chapter 8, this agenda was adopted and strongly reinforced after 9/11, and its implementation accelerated through President George W. Bush's redefining of his father's 'new world order' to include the option of pre-emptive strike on America's enemies, and the policy of regime change where certain regional political elites attempted to resist, or failed to conform with, the above strategy. A manifestation of the rapid development of the USA's regional agenda was its 2004 Greater Middle East Initiative (to be discussed later in this books) and his administration's drive to seek EU support for Washington's proposed democratic and socio-cultural reforms. In return, the main Western powers agreed to underwrite the security of the most important Middle Eastern states, particularly where Western interests dictated a direct presence.[26] This policy brought overt US, British and French security guarantees for several Gulf Arab countries, which ironically later on unleashed the wrath of al-Qaeda on the most important of these states – Saudi Arabia. More specifically, US security initiatives towards the GCC countries included the reactivation and modernization of the US Fifth Fleet in the summer of 1995, combining access to naval bases in Bahrain and elsewhere with the pre-positioning of much military hardware in the Persian Gulf.[27] Indeed, a multi-billion dollar modernization and expansion of the Bahrain facilities was completed in early 2004, barely 9 months after the commencement of the war to unseat the Iraqi regime from power. At the same time, the USA quietly constructed one of its largest air bases in Qatar, which was used to great effect in the 2003 war to unseat Saddam Hussein's regime in Iraq.[28]

In the face of US military consolidations in the Persian Gulf, the EU has remained hopelessly divided over the legalities, causes, origins and outcome of the Iraq war. Despite the parliamentary elections in Iraq in January 2005, and efforts to form a national government of unity in 2006, the Iraq dispute between the two sides, and broader concerns about establishing Persian Gulf security, failed to go away. By 2005, an even greater security dilemma had come to dominate the transatlantic agenda: that of Iran's nuclear-related activities under an overtly anti-Western and populist neo-conservative president. Over this and several other Gulf-related security matters, the EU had a very fine line to tread, being fully overwhelmed in practical terms by the military and political might of the USA in this subregion. An example of the EU's strategic weakness was to be found in its final abandoning of nearly 2 years' intensive talks with Tehran over the suspension of some of the key aspects of its nuclear programme, and instead to lead the campaign for referral of Iran to the Security Council for failing to halt nuclear enrichment. By mid-2006, the EU was following the US line on Iran's nuclear activities.

The Implosion of the Soviet Union

The implosion of the Soviet superpower a year after the Iraqi invasion of Kuwait was of considerable significance in the shaping of Euro–MENA relations.[29] The end of the Soviet Union posed serious problems for many Middle Eastern countries, in particular for those that had developed a politico-military dependence on Moscow and the Warsaw Pact countries. In the first place, these countries (most notably Syria and Libya) had to readjust their foreign policies in such a way as to show some recognition of the US hegemony in this region. Syria's agreement to participate in the 1991 Madrid Arab–Israeli peace talks and meetings with Israeli representatives stemmed, in part, from an acceptance of such realities. Libya's willingness since the late 1990s to address its problems with the United Nations, the USA, France, and the International Atomic Energy Agency (IAEA) over its past 'rogue' behaviour is indicative of the same process. Its willingness to settle several international claims against it was capped only by its declared willingness to give up its activities relating to weapons of mass destruction in 2003. Prime Minister Tony Blair and President George W. Bush stated clear satisfaction with the latter, and the President declared that 'leaders who abandon the pursuit of chemical, biological and nuclear weapons, and the means to deliver them, will find an open path to better relations with the United States and other free nations. With [the] announcement by its leader, Libya has begun the process of rejoining the community of nations'.[30] The crowning moment of this strategy was the announcement in May 2006 that Libya had been removed from the USA's list of terrorist states, and that full diplomatic relations between Libya and the USA had finally been restored.

But, while the implosion of the Soviet Union strengthened the hand of the Western powers in this region, it also provided the old 'southern belt' countries and other MENA powers (such as Israel, Saudi Arabia, Syria, and Egypt) with the opportunity to extend their economic and political reach to new territories in the Caucasus and in Central Asia. The fact that many of the new states emerging from the former Soviet Union were largely comprised of Muslim peoples was an added bonus for Iran, Turkey, and Saudi Arabia, in particular. But over the 1990s, Israel also managed to develop close economic and security links with several of these states, most notably with Azerbaijan, Uzbekistan, Kazakhstan, and Turkmenistan, threatening to extend the MENA region's own Cold War to these territories.

On another level, the implosion of the Soviet Union acted as a catalyst for further subregionalization of MENA. The political fallout of the Soviet implosion for the MENA region resulted in strategic vulnerability for the remnants of the so-called radical Arab regimes. In broader strategic terms, however, the end of the Soviet system resulted in several fundamental changes in Eurasia.

As far as EU–Middle East relations were concerned, two developments were of particular importance. First, the Soviet collapse created a short-term power vacuum in the heart of Asia which, in turn, encouraged further regionalist tendencies in this area as neighbouring MENA countries scrambled to build new links to these new republics. This they did through extensive bilateral exchanges, as well as through multilateral agencies such as the revamped Tehran-based Economic Co-operation Organization (ECO). It allowed the non-Arab Muslim states of the Middle East (Iran, Turkey, and Pakistan) to consolidate their relative position in the region's post-Cold-War geo-economic order by expanding the ECO to include all the Muslim republics of the former Soviet Union and Afghanistan. This 13-member organization is unique, for not only is it one of Asia's largest subregional organizations, consisting solely of non-Arab Muslim states, but it also boasts huge territory and immense natural resources, with a potential market of over 300 million people. The ECO, furthermore, is only one of several regional organizations with a Middle Eastern dimension that have emerged from the ashes of the Soviet Union; other such notable subregional organizations now filling the former Soviet space include the Black Sea Grouping, the Caspian Sea States Organization, and the Shanghai Co-operation Organization.

Second, Moscow's weakened geopolitical position allowed the Western countries to use Europe-based institutions, such as the Organization for Security and Co-operation in Europe (OSCE) and Partnership for Peace, to extend their influence into the heart of Asia – even as far as the Pacific rim via Russia, and to the western borders of China via Central Asia. Thus, even before 9/11, Western powers were active here and, through such mechanisms as the OSCE and the Council of Europe, were already demonstrating their institutional capability to take an active part in shaping the post-Soviet regional order.

With regard to the role of the EU more specifically, both directly (through such frameworks as the '5+5', Euro–Mediterranean, Euro–Arab, and EU–GCC dialogues) and indirectly (largely through NATO and the OSCE), the EU was able to enhance its capability to shape the emerging regional order in MENA proper, in addition to being able to influence the shape of MENA's new periphery in the landlocked territories of Central Asia. Largely through economic (trade, investment, and aid) measures based on negotiations, and through its support for the establishment of one or more overarching regional bodies such as a (European-style) Organization for Security and Co-operation in the Middle East and the Organization for Security and Co-operation in the Mediterranean, the EU has been pressing its agenda.[31] European support for the establishment of NATO–Mediterranean dialogue in early 1995, in which Egypt, Israel, Mauritania, Morocco, and Tunisia were involved, was also part of this same strategy of engagement.[32]

These economic partnership/association arrangements have taken the form of bilateral trade and investment agreements, or multilateral pacts designed to tie the MENA countries (in particular the Mediterranean states) to collective co-operative structures. The EU's role in this regard can hardly have been exaggerated, particularly given that the Union is the main economic partner of the MENA countries, a region in which inter-regional trade barely reaches 10 per cent of these countries' total trade. See Table 4.3.[33]

Since the mid-1990s, the EU has been taking over 40 per cent of all Arab exports and providing as much as 45 per cent of their imports. For the Maghreb states, as much as 50 per cent of each of the countries' trade is with the EU, rising to over 60 per cent in the case of Egypt.[34] In terms of their export markets, the Arab states are even more beholden to the EU. In the cases of Tunisia, Algeria, and Morocco, between 70 and 75 per cent of their exports are destined for EU markets, and in the case of Egypt, the

Table 4.3 Inter-Arab trade relations in the mid-1990s (US$ million)

Country	Inter-Arab trade (A)	Total trade (B)	A as percentage of B
Algeria	202	9231	2
Bahrain	460	2656	17
Djibouti	54	89	61
Egypt	671	5562	11
Iraq	0	2	0
Jordan	226	1424	16
Kuwait	75	8445	1
Lebanon	435	737	59
Libya	404	7826	5
Morocco	376	4013	9
Mauritania	2	464	0
Oman	205	4831	4
Qatar	220	2913	8
Saudi Arabia	3674	45,630	8
Somalia	105	130	81
Sudan	118	515	23
Syria	762	3151	24
Tunisia	379	4657	8
UAE	1709	20,906	8
Yemen	45	1048	4
Total	10,122	124,285	8

Source: *OAPEC Monthly Bulletin*, August/September 1996.

most populous Arab state, the figure is about 60 per cent. Some 90 per cent of Libya's oil output is consumed in Europe. As far as Israel and Turkey are concerned, over 35 and nearly 60 per cent, respectively, of their exports are bound for the EU, and no less than 50 and 53 per cent, respectively, of their imports originate in the EU.[35] Israel is the EU's 20th export market. In Syria, the EU is its biggest trading partner, accounting for just over 40 per cent of its total trade in 2003.[36] For Iran, the EU is a 'strategic partner', acting as its main trading partner. The EU has 28 per cent of the Iranian market share, and by the same token, Iran imports 37 per cent of its needs from the EU.[37] In the GCC, the EU accounts for around 30 per cent of these countries' total imports.[38]

The problems such trade dependencies have generated have been compounded by the considerable trade surplus the EU enjoys with many MENA economies,[39] and the fact that the Mediterranean and the Persian Gulf account for no more than 4 and 2 per cent, respectively, of total European trade.[40] Table 4.4 looks back at the early 1990s to illustrate the depth of the existing imbalance in European–Mediterranean trade. As more recent data suggest, little has changed in this relationship over the years.[41]

As is evident, despite its heavy energy dependence on the Mediterranean region, the EU enjoys a considerable trade advantage in the vitally important manufacturing sector, and a small advantage in the agricultural goods sector, which forms the main economic activity of the southern states of the Mediterranean.

Maastricht and the MENA Region

Hugh Corbet surmised as long ago as 1977 that 'because of the economic differences between them, the countries of the European Community are affected differently by global problems, which means that their governments are bound to react in different ways. This provides a clue as to what must be done if the Community is to develop further'.[42] The Maastricht Treaty was the long-overdue response to the structural problems associated with the

Table 4.4 Euro–Mediterranean trade, 1992 (US$ billion)

	EU exports to Mediterranean	Mediterranean exports to EU	EU balance
Agricultural goods	4.1	3.8	+0.3
Manufactured goods	38.3	15.0	+23.3
Energy	0.7	12.4	−11.7
Minerals	0.4	0.6	−0.2
Total	43.5	32.9	+10.6

Source: Bichara Khader, *Le partenariat Euro-Mediterraneen*, Working Paper No. 9523 (Cairo: Economic Research Forum for the Arab Countries, Iran & Turkey, 1995).

deepening and extension of European co-operation. The real momentum for the treaty, however, came not from international economic pressures, but from within Europe itself, particularly from the federalist forces that German unification had unleashed in 1990.[43] Despite the problems associated with different European interpretations of the Maastricht Treaty, it was enforced on 1 January 1993.

The battle between the various European tendencies did absorb much of the member-states' energies in the 1990s which, in turn, delayed to a degree the final steps of integration. Prior to its negotiation, and in the aftermath of its implementation, Maastricht also caused an internalization of its contradictory tendencies by national political forces, thus helping to split further many national polities and European institutions. One result of these internal divisions in the post-Maastricht EU has been the Union's inability to advance the foreign policy and security aspects of the treaty. While the treaty established some of the structures for forging a common European foreign and security policy, evidence from European positions on the 2003 Iraq war clearly shows that the EU has not been able to create the conditions for its implementation. Put another way, although the treaty has rationalized the mechanisms that enable the EU to attack problems as a united force, it has not successfully driven the system to complete the essential conditions for adopting common action. Different and, at times, divergent national objectives have proved far harder to overcome than previously anticipated. Such problems will arguably continue to plague the Union after its expansion in 2004, and will further complicate the implementation of monetary union for all its members.

The problem of collective action, though, is not insoluble or absolute. The EU states are gradually responding to change, and show signs of collective action on some international issues. On some important external policy matters, for example at the World Trade Organization's multilateral trade liberalization negotiations, and fighting the USA's 1996 D'Amato Bill and its steel tariffs in early 2000s, the Commission has clearly spoken on behalf of the Union. And in discussions with Tehran between 2003 and 2006 over its reluctance to accept further and more intrusive IAEA inspections, the trio of European foreign ministers of France, Britain and Germany soon passed on to the EU as a whole the credit for their success in convincing Iran to open up to greater IAEA inspections of its nuclear facilities. The visit to Iran in January 2004 by the EU's External Commissioner (Mr Javiar Solana), to reinforce the achievements of the trio in October 2003, also signalled the collective nature of policy implementation over collectively agreed issues. This visit was followed up by the November 2004 'Paris agreement', in which Iran agreed to suspend all its enrichment activities. The EU's final failure to effect a permanent suspension should not detract from the above argument, and should in any case be seen in the context of major political developments in Iran itself, and the rise of its own unique kind of neo-conservatives to positions of legislative and executive power.

Nonetheless, Maastricht has had some direct, albeit subtle, effects on the MENA region. First, on the economic front, as George Joffé has noted, the single market immediately raised a series of non-tariff barriers against non-members' exports to Europe.[44] New economic pressures ranged from requiring the MENA countries to raise the quality of their manufactured exports to the EU to European standards; to accepting the imposition of European regulations on their products and exports; to competing with each other to find a secure toehold in what was increasingly being seen as 'fortress Europe'. The EU's round-table discussions with its MENA economic partners were a partial response to these problems, and a way of addressing some of the economic consequences of the creation of the EU single market.

Second, on the political front, the treaty introduced a series of new administrative structures and procedures of governance, which provided the opportunity for western European powers to develop a collective and co-ordinated voice in MENA regional affairs. The EU's ability to develop and implement a 'Mediterranean policy' is an example of this trend. But in other areas of policy too – the Arab–Israeli peace process, Persian Gulf security matters, political dialogue, and so on – the treaty enabled the EU to intervene with more confidence and assertiveness. This, of course, has largely been so because the Maastricht Treaty gave birth to a new 'pillar' of decision-making and allowed for at least the theoretical possibility at the centre of a 'common foreign and security policy'.[45]

The last word on the treaty has to be that, while it created the conditions for collective European action in foreign and security matters, it did not act to distil the external interests of the EU countries in such a fashion as to be able to formulate basic EU foreign policies. The EU remains largely reactive in this regard, and has not emerged as the proactive superpower many of its Commissioners had wished for. Where the Maastricht Treaty's presence has been felt in the MENA region, however, it has been more in the economic sphere: in their trade and investment policies (particularly where the EU is their main partner); on their economic units (firms and industries); on their legislation (from competition law to intellectual property rights); market reform strategies; and regional co-operation and integration schemes.[46] These are important areas of national activity – of a neighbouring region – whose workings the EU's own internal logic has been able to affect and shape directly.

The Arab–Israeli Arena

The renewed vigour and speed with which the USA pursued the resolution of the Arab–Israeli conflict after the 1991 Gulf War owed much to the long overdue recognition by the Western allies that, despite other tensions in the Middle East, this conflict had continued to destabilize the region. On this point there was complete agreement between Washington and its EU partners although, as we shall see below, consensus on how to resolve the issues was much harder to find.

The peace process was made possible because of the regional changes that followed the multi-national alliance's war in 1991 against Iraq.[47] Direct European involvement in the Kuwait war, and its long-standing commitment to a just and peaceful settlement of the Arab–Israeli dispute (as enshrined in the Venice Declaration of June 1980), brought the Community into the game as a full player, despite the fact that the USA and the USSR were identified as the sponsors of the historic Madrid peace talks. Typically, though, following the first round of talks, the geographical momentum of the bilateral talks shifted towards the US land mass, with the European countries being left in charge of some of the less overtly political multilateral talks.

This situation, in which Europe found itself playing second fiddle to the USA, began to change in September 1993 with the signing of the Palestinian–Israeli Accords, which ushered in a new era in contacts between Israel and its Arab neighbours. The direction of the new era was emphatically underlined by the Jordanian–Israeli peace treaty of October 1994. In these new contacts between Israel and its Arab neighbours, the USA continued to reserve for itself the role of supreme political master, while the Europeans were increasingly required to act as paymasters for the parties engaged in the peace process. While the role of paymaster was generally welcomed by the Community,[48] allowing the Europeans not to have to address the thorny issue of a united policy on an important regional matter, it soon transpired that some of the key European powers were beginning to show signs of displeasure at not having a political voice to match their economic clout in matters that were so important to European security, and to relations within the Mediterranean region in general. For the Europeans, it should be remembered, the process of reconciliation as a by-product of the post-Cold-War world had allowed the rebirth of a multilateral era, the 'UN era', in which they sought the opportunity to drive home their UN Security Council numerical advantage and, capitalizing on their two-member majority, to influence the resolution of regional conflicts around the world, including in the MENA region. The Middle East had become for the Europeans not just the test case for assessing the limits of a common European foreign policy (so badly exposed during the Kuwait and Iraq crises, about a decade apart), but the arena in which the EU should seek to apply its economic muscle to the resolution of thorny political problems.

The Palestinian and Jordanian peace accords with Israel provided the catalyst for a change of gear by Europe in formulating relations with the MENA region, also enabling it to emerge as the main economic sponsor of the evolving Palestinian entity.[49] First, Europe sought a more direct involvement in the peace process, both as mediator and as enforcer. Second, it increased its interest in enhancing European–MENA trade, investment and political agreements based on bilateral and multilateral arrangements. Here, paradoxically, while Europe's posture was encouraging regionalization, its actual policies were reinforcing fragmentation, as these were based on the finalization of bilaterally reached association agreements with MENA countries. The EU's action was also encouraging the creation of a new division in the MENA system between 'ins' and 'outs' – between those with access to EU markets and resources, and those without such preferential access.

Third, the Community introduced a series of Mediterranean initiatives that culminated in the introduction of the Euro–Mediterranean Partnership in 1994.[50] The idea of a partnership had emerged from the Lisbon European Council meeting of June 1992, which had proclaimed the Community's 'strong interests in terms of security and social stability' in the Mediterranean region,[51] and the December 1994 summit of the European Council in Essen, when the Mediterranean was declared 'a priority area of strategic importance for the European Union'. These new European initiatives towards the Mediterranean region stemmed from the concern, expressed in 1989, that the fall of the Berlin Wall had forced on the Commission a reassessment of the Community's periphery, south and east.[52] On the southern front, the Commission based its policy on economic co-operation,[53] which was increasingly contingent on Mediterranean non-member countries' efforts towards economic restructuring – the same principles as were applicable to its relations with the new democracies of Eastern Europe.

The EU's position on the Arab–Israeli peace process increasingly contradicted, and therefore complicated, its relations with the Clinton administration, whose policies were unashamedly pro-Israel. The Europeans were keen to increase direct pressure on Israel in order to encourage it to comply with the relevant UN resolutions on the conflict – or, failing that, at the very least to live by the agreements reached with the Palestinian Authority – while the USA appeared to be giving the Rabin-led, Labour-dominated Israeli Government a free hand in formulating its own policies towards its Arab neighbours – even at the expense of violating the spirit and letter of international norms and of the UN Charter. It was not lost on European powers, either, that both the USA and Israel were content to see the Europe marginalized in the negotiations. Both parties, to different degrees, regarded its stance in the conflict as Arab-leaning and biased in favour of the Palestinians in the peace process.[54]

The tensions between the USA and EU sides reached new heights in the second half of the 1990s. A few examples suffice to illustrate the point. In 1996, the Israeli bombardment of southern Lebanon in April, and the victory of the Likud-led coalition in Israel's May general election, acted as a double wedge in US–EU approaches towards the Arab–Israeli conflict; while both developments were received with open dismay by the Europeans, the USA was much more reserved in its assessment of the situation, post-Rabin. Their differences were further marked with the USA's failure to invite the EU's American representative to the Arafat–Netanyahu

Washington summit of October 1996, and the Palestinian leader's unscheduled stop-over in Europe and his meeting with several senior Europeans on his way to the American capital.[55]

Relations between the new Israeli Government and the EU, on the other hand, had also hit a new low by the middle of 1996.[56] These tensions flowed onto the streets, as it were, with President Chirac's high-profile visit to Israel and the Occupied Territories in October 1996, where he not only snubbed the Israeli Parliament and chose to become the first Western head of state to address the Palestinian legislative council, but also adopted the role of an EU peace-maker, ready to step in where Washington had failed. Relations between Israel and the EU had already been damaged by the EU foreign ministers' strongly worded statement on the Middle East in early October, in which they had pointedly criticized many aspects of the Likud Government's policies in the peace process.

Paris's position on the direction of the peace process was, by this time, being echoed by the EU over some of the most sensitive issues in the negotiations, the most central of which was East Jerusalem, where the European line – rejection of Israel's 'unilateral annexation of East Jerusalem' – was causing a further widening of the distance between the American and European positions on the one hand, and Israel and the EU on the other. In March 1997 relations took another turn for the worse when an EU-drafted Security Council resolution expressing 'deep concern' about Israel's proposed new housing project in East Jerusalem was vetoed by the USA.[57] This embarrassing episode, when the USA rejected a position statement proposed by several of its NATO partners, highlighted more clearly than ever the growing rift at that time between the Atlantic allies over conflict resolution in the Middle East, whereas their co-operation had been deemed essential at almost every G7 Summit since the end of the Cold War. The already imperfect US–EU relations over the peace process were mirrored in the deepening tensions in EU–Israeli relations, where EU institutions and high-level personnel increasingly expressed their dissatisfaction with Israeli policies, and acted on it. The European Parliament's resolution in March condemning Israel's settlement policy was one such action, as were the comments made around the same time by the European Commission's commissioner responsible for the Middle East, Manuel Marin, and the EU governments' Middle East envoy, Miguel Moratinos, on Israel's policies in relation to East Jerusalem.[58]

Until 9/11, the contrast between the European and American policies and approaches towards the peace process could not be sharper, but in the aftermath of suicide bombings and an acceleration of violence in the Occupied Territories from 2000, the election of the Likud Government in Israel under Ariel Sharon and that of George W. Bush to the White House forced the EU to seek accommodation with the USA and the adoption of the European-engineered 'road map' to peace, under the watchful eyes of the 'Quartet' (US, EU, UN, Russia). The USA was trusted with political progress in the Palestinian–Israeli talks, with Europe finally accepting a junior position in this arena.

The picture was also complicated by EU concerns over the USA's policies towards Iran, Libya and Cuba, with Washington being keen to isolate these three countries internationally through levying unilateral secondary sanctions against them. The main bone of contention in the 1990s was whether 'containment' of Iran was a superior strategy to the EU's declared policy of 'critical dialogue', later to become 'constructive engagement'. In the absence of an EU–US agreement on this issue, the Western alliance remained divided over its policy options towards Iran, a problem that came to haunt the West with a vengeance as Iran accelerated its nuclear programme early in the 21st century.

Despite the negative impact of the Mykonos trial on EU–Iranian relations,[59] the fact that the verdict of the trial was seen as a moral victory for Washington, the reality that the Iranian regime had been engaged in campaigns against its opponents overseas, and that 'critical dialogue' was suspended by the Europeans, neither the USA nor the EU was able to capitalize on this crisis to find a co-ordinated and common policy towards Iran. Disputes over the treatment of Iran continued to dog transatlantic relations, even after the regional changes following 9/11. The treatment of Iran has remained an intense policy dilemma for the NATO allies to this day, threatening the already fragile balance of forces in the region, and also strengthening the dangerous link that has grown between accelerating energy prices and the geopolitical tensions associated with a confrontation with Tehran.[60]

In sum, then, the EU has increasingly been seeking a political role in the MENA region to match its overwhelming economic position in Eurasia. It has calculated that an enhanced political profile in Eurasia is likely to allow the EU to expand and enhance its global economic standing in relation to its main competitor regional organizations, in particular the North American Free Trade Area and the Asia–Pacific Economic Cooperation. The political role the EU has been contemplating is a reflection not only of its importance as a major regional organization in the post-Cold-War international order, but also a recognition of the need for the Union to respond positively to the problems it identifies on its southern and eastern peripheries. Political empowerment of the Union, furthermore, is a manifestation of the desire of some of its members to develop the institutions of the EU in order for it to be able to act in unity in the interest of the collective. In the face of the post-9/11 American offensive in the region, this EU desire has been shared by some MENA countries. Egyptian writer Mahmoud Muawad has noted, for example, that 'if history will mention the name of Saddam Hussein for boosting the tyranny of the unilateral U.S. power, which has imposed a globalization that only serves rich nations at the expense of developing ones, then the history of the occult conflict between Europe and the United States over the division of power in the world will write new lines that will register the birth of a new moral alliance'.[61] This alliance was declared 'in the 40th anniversary of the Elysee treaty between France and united Germany, when ministers and representatives of the two peoples attended a big ceremony in Paris, where the rejection of war was announced, even if the matter were to lead to the use of the veto in the Security Council, and where the establishment of a European Union for defense and security was announced, giving priority to military armament'.

EU–MENA Strategic Dilemmas

More than ever before, European interest in the MENA region is being underwritten by security concerns,[62] many of which can be regarded as geopolitical[63] and therefore relatively constant. The territorial proximity of northern and southern Mediterranean countries, the boundaries of three of the world's important strategic choke-points, Black Sea maritime competition, etc. have been added to some unwelcome concerns emerging in the aftermath of the Cold War: Islamic terrorism, growing ethno-nationalism, particularism, sectarianism, human migration, and territorialism.

In concrete terms, European security concerns have been articulated in terms of the negative impact that inter-state conflict in the region could have on European interests, the destabilizing impact of the MENA region's continuing militarization and economic difficulties, a population explosion that could devastate southern Europe, and the possible fall-out from the march of al-Qaeda and the broader forces of political Islam in the southern Mediterranean countries and in Europe itself, with its own large (and largely of MENA origin) Muslim communities.[64] Geoffrey Kemp notes that Europe's estimated 15 million Muslims comprise one strong reason for the EU's sensitivities towards the region, but he also suggests that no single EU country faces the same issues with regard to its Muslim minority.[65] On most of these issues, and the potential threat posed by Mediterranean instabilities to Western interests, the US not only concurs with its European allies, but actively courts their support in countering them.[66]

Looking at the recent past, in the 1990s, just as the military threat had begun to recede on the European continent, reinforced by the prospects of NATO's expansion eastwards, the Mediterranean theatre emerged as a new area of instability. In the eastern Mediterranean, the Balkans had been on fire for the best part of the decade, Albania was in turmoil for some time, and Turkish and Greek horns were again locked over Cyprus and other bilateral problems. In the Mediterranean, the new military relations that have been emerging between Israel and Turkey have been threatening the post-Iraq-war regional balance of power, worrying Syria sufficiently for it to try and strengthen its strategic alliance with Iran, refusing to relinquish its grip on Lebanon, and also advancing its already established post-1990 politico-security ties with Egypt and Saudi Arabia. Before the fall of Baghdad in April 2003, Syria was pursuing the same tactical partnership with

Saddam Hussein, securing access to cheap oil and Iraq's markets in exchange for helping the regime out of the sanctions straightjacket.

Elsewhere, Libya's international isolation, the costly Algerian civil war, and inter-state tensions in the Red Sea subregion (between Egypt and Sudan, and between Yemen and Eritrea) all contributed to making the Mediterranean area a less safe place in the post-Cold-War period. All this was taking place against a backdrop of European concerns over the expanding armouries of MENA countries in general, in terms of sophisticated and lethal weapons acquisition, and continuing high military expenditure by the key Mediterranean countries. See Table 4.5

The need for a European Mediterranean initiative had therefore been well understood by the EU countries for some time,[67] but the crowning moment of these efforts did not come until the middle of the decade, with the Barcelona conference of November 1995 in which 27 countries participated, including eight Arab countries (Algeria, Egypt, Jordan, Lebanon, Morocco, Palestine, Tunisia, and Syria), Israel, Turkey, Cyprus, and Malta. The conference set about sketching the political and economic guidelines for future relations between the EU and its Mediterranean neighbours around three axes: (a) a common area of peace and security; (b) an area of shared prosperity; and (c) cultural ties and exchanges between civil societies.[68] With much optimism, the EU also announced the launch of a region-wide free trade zone to be established by 2010, covering 27 countries and up to 800 million people.[69] The conference's momentum was to be sustained through a series of '15+12' meetings to implement the agreed plan of action.[70]

It was also in the mid-1990s that the EU's political engagement began to show signs of deepening, with countries like France seeking a more active role for the Union in Middle Eastern affairs.[71] Using words reminiscent of the American superpower, the French articulated the EU's new assessment

Table 4.5 Military profile of main non-EU Mediterranean armed forces, 2003

Country	Defence expenditure (US$ billion)	Advanced aircraft	Advanced naval systems	Advanced surface-to-surface missiles	Non-conventional weapons
Algeria	2.2	Some	Yes	No	Chemical
Egypt	2.7	Yes	Yes	Yes	Chemical
Israel	10.7	Yes	Yes	Yes	Nuclear/chemical
Libya	0.7	Yes	Yes	Yes	Abandoned
Morocco	1.8	Some	No	No	No
Syria	1.5	Yes	Yes	Yes	Chemical
Turkey	11.6	Yes	Yes	No	n/a

Sources: IISS, *The Military Balance 2004–2005* (London: Oxford University Press for International Institute for Strategic Studies, 2004); Anthony H. Cordesman, *Perilous Prospects: The Peace Process and the Arab–Israeli Military Balance* (Boulder, CO: Westview Press, 1996).

of the situation in the following way: 'The Middle East is of essential, even vital, interest to us [the EU]'.[72]

Much of the European debate about the EU's future role in the MENA region, however, coincided with fairly public disputes between the USA and some of its European NATO partners over other issues: the command structures and future role of NATO in Europe, the desirability of its expansion eastwards, and NATO's peace-keeping operations on the European continent. For France, at least, strengthening of the European role in all the above was a given, a position that did not endear Paris to Washington, and that also threatened to open up a rift with France's own, less intervention-minded and pro-USA, European partners.

Implications of the 1995 and 2004 EU Expansions for the MENA Region

The EU's 'Atlantic–Alpine'[73] enlargement of 1995 (to include Finland, Sweden, and Austria) shifted the geographical balance of the EU away from the Mediterranean in the south and towards the centre/northern territories of the continent. The impact of this geographical shift, however, proved to be smaller than at first feared by the MENA states. First, the main threat to the security of Europe still comes from the south, so the focus did not shift. Second, within the EU the southern European countries exercise much power. They have been able to place the Mediterranean firmly on the EU's priority agenda and have gone so far as to form 'an effective lobby, often using their veto power to gain additional resources for specific regional projects'.[74] Third, the new EU members did not benefit from the political advantages that could be derived from the weight of a large population (a total of 24 million people between them) or economy. As such, they proved unable to influence the EU's strategic agenda. Fourth, while the new Atlantic–Alpine members may have had a greater interest in consolidating the EU's growing links with Eastern Europe, they showed little interest in blocking the Union's Mediterranean initiatives. As the 1995 Barcelona conference shows, the initiatives not only took place in the first year of their accession, but were allowed to become a powerful glue for keeping the Mediterranean arena attached to all EU agendas.

Over time, however, and as the Eastern European countries begin integrating with NATO and the EU in early twenty-first century, new alliances within the Union will emerge, which may encourage direction of EU funds in an eastward direction and could marginalize the Mediterranean as a priority EU area. Transfer of economic resources will be followed by some transfer of political power within the EU itself, which will inevitably have a knock-on effect on the EU's relations with the MENA countries. Second, eastward expansion will ensure that fewer resources will find their way to the MENA region, and it is very likely that the core energies of the Commission will be given over to the integration of the new members in the decade following their membership in 2004. Thus a prolonged period of internalization will follow the 1 May 2004 expansion of the Union, possibly resulting in a neglect of the MENA region at a most crucial time in its development. Furthermore, as few of the 10 new members of the Union have much legacy of contacts with the region, they will, over time, encourage the adoption of a more neutral, business-like line on such regional issues as the Arab–Israeli conflict. The diplomatic proximity to the USA of such newcomers as Poland will also act as a factor in the EU's relations with the region.

Third, the addition of Greek Cyprus to the Union will have a direct bearing on Greek–Turkish relations and on the prospects for Ankara's own relations with the EU. It will, in the medium term, encourage even closer links between Turkey and the Union – again with direct consequences for the GME, given Turkey's ties with Central Asia as well as its more immediate neighbours.

As we have seen, the EU has been engaged in a protracted campaign of dialogue with its eastern and southern neighbours. While initially it was distracted by the collapse of the Warsaw Pact, the EU did, from the mid-1990s, try hard to follow a two-track policy (one based on economics, the other on security structures) towards its neighbours. Much of the EU's recent efforts, however, have concentrated on finding a workable formula for absorbing the Eastern European countries, at the same time as formulating a new relationship with the non-member Mediterranean states and the GCC countries.

The prerequisite for this complex strategy is a cohesive Union. But divisions within the EU, which surface at virtually every summit meeting of its political leaders these days, have been hampering its efforts to found the broad Euro–Mediterranean environment which the Commission has been planning, and which is regarded as vital for the geo-economic supremacy of the EU in the new Eurasian hemisphere.[75] The issues the European leaders have been discussing into the new millennium are not new ones. They are to do with fusion, economic integration and political compatibility, which have been openly discussed at least since the early 1970s (when the European Economic Community expanded to nine). At that time, it was being argued by some that the convergence of the economic and the political in Europe was a 'functional inevitability'.[76] The launch of the EU constitutional debate in 2003, one can surmise, is a precursor to this 'inevitability'. But how can we explain the dismal failure of the pan-Europeanists to get the EU constitution accepted by the European electorate and public opinion?

Apart from its internal difficulties, several regional problems also continue to hamper the fulfilment of the EU's MENA strategy. Chief among these is what used to be known as the 'Eastern Question',[77] but is today seen in the dilemmas the EU faces in the southern Mediterranean countries' desire to join the European club. This is where the EU's relations with its Mediterranean neighbours could turn sour. Indicative of some of the problems that may lie ahead of the EU's integrative Mediterranean strategy are its turbulent relations with Turkey, whose 1987 application to join the Community was rejected in December 1989. The Commission stated that Turkey's application had raised 'very large questions'.[78] In a detailed response, it basically argued that apart from its domestic political problems (human rights violations, absence of pluralism and democratic government, etc.), as a poor, territorially separate and culturally distinct country Turkey was an unsuitable candidate for membership: 'Turkey covers an area exactly half that of the old 'Nine' and the population [that] ... by the end of century will be far larger than any Community state. There are obvious cultural differences which are far stronger than those between, say, Portugal and the Community; moreover, Turkey, apart from its small border with Greece, will never be contiguous with the rest of the EC. It is considerably poorer than any of the other Mediterranean EC members. The implications for the regional and social funds of the Community are literally unthinkable, unless membership is treated simply as part of a political bloc'.[79]

These issues have continued to dog the EU's relations with Turkey, which the EU recognizes as a strategically important country, providing bridges to the east (in the Crimea as well as the Caucasus and Central Asia) and the south (the Middle East). Unlike the southern Mediterranean countries, however, Turkey claims to be a fully fledged European country that has had a close association with the European entity as far back as 1963. Over a generation later, the EU still shows reluctance to entertain the idea of Turkish membership, and in March 1997 the German foreign minister stated the view of several EU members when he said: 'Turkey will not become a member of the European Union in the foreseeable future'.[80] To the dismay of Turkey, such views surfaced at the time when the EU had agreed to admit to its ranks eight Eastern European countries 'in the near future'.[81]

With virtually every other non-member Mediterranean country, similar problems are likely to arise, particularly where high population growth, economic incompatibility and underdevelopment are in evidence, and the footsteps of political Islam can be heard (as in Turkey itself). Ironically, the debate over the opening of the EU to Turkey and other Mediterranean countries is also causing tensions in the Atlantic alliance (between the USA and the EU) and among the Union partners themselves,[82] holding up uncomfortable decisions by the Europeans about their own future, as well as the future of their southern allies.

To avoid some of these inherent problems, the EU agreed to keep Turkey's membership file open while trying to check the Mediterranean countries' aspirations for membership through its Euro–Mediterranean initiatives, provision of easier access to EU markets, etc. Such initiatives have been designed to create zones of prosperity around the EU in such a way as to slow down to a crawl the pace of accession of these countries to the Union.

They are being looked at along with other proposals, which include giving preferential treatment on trade matters, or creating a 'two-tier' Union (which has already been proposed by some eurosceptic members of the EU about their own future role within the Union), in which some of the Mediterranean countries become full members of certain programmes and institutions but remain outside others – one foot in Europe and another not.

It should be clear from the discussion here that we can no longer speak comfortably of an exclusively 'European' space when, by virtue of the security questions arising from the collapse of the Soviet Union and the disappearance of the communist European bloc, such western European-dominated entities as the OSCE, NATO and the Western EU can now reach the shores of the non-European Mediterranean states as well as the very heart of Asia and, by definition, much of the region we call the greater Middle East. If geographical separation of territories is proving impossible in the post-Cold-War order, it is even more problematic to separate economies and economic processes. In today's interdependent, dynamic, and global economic system, power can be gained as swiftly as it can be lost. Regional bodies such as the EU have recognized the salient features of such a globalized economic environment, and are working hard to try and protect their own corner, and competitive niches, in this highly competitive system.[83] At the same time, though, the EU is unique among today's regional bodies in having to secure its interests and security through extended contacts with its peripheries. It has had to accommodate some of the aspirations of its neighbours in order to secure its own long-term interests and address many of the security concerns arising from its fragile and unstable southern periphery.

With these factors in mind, it can be argued that at least part of the EU's policy has been based on enlightened self-interest. The EU assumes that, if the economies on its periphery do well, not only will they become more stable polities, and therefore less of a threat to the EU, but the EU as their main trading partner could also benefit enormously from their economic prosperity. At heart, the EU's policy appears to be based on the notion that economic development offers the only real barrier to political instability and social decay in the MENA region. There is much truth in this view. Consider one fact: in order to be able to check just the negative economic impact of population growth, the Arab world would need to grow by as much as 6 per cent a year. To actually develop their economies, however, and prepare them for globalization, the highly populated Middle Eastern states would need to achieve sustainable growth rates well above this figure. They would need to make great strides in order to succeed, and can only do so on a scale reminiscent of the achievements of the tiger economies of Asia. It is therefore not surprising that, in the aftermath of its 2004 membership expansion, the EU has begun refining its partnership with its MENA periphery in terms of a new 'EU neighbourhood policy' for the non-accession countries, which would ultimately offer them 'a share in the internal market, including the free movement of goods, services, capital and people, though without representation in its institutions ... this represents a serious effort to design a pro-active EU strategy for those countries bordering the Union which will not be offered full membership for the foreseeable future'.[84]

In the last analysis, the dynamic energy the EU needs to harness if it is to guide developments in its MENA periphery, and to keep this region engaged, is that of the Mediterranean basin. It needs to engage the Mediterranean's human and capital assets, as well as its vast natural resources. But it also needs to find a way of accommodating the 2004 post-accession geometry of its relationship with its southern neighbours, in which (if we exclude Turkey) only eight Arab countries and Israel would remain. This much may be obvious. But, in the face of the immense weight that globalization places on EU economies, and the problems associated with NATO's and the EU's restructuring and expansion, the hardest conundrum for the EU is how to manage its alliance with the USA, consolidate its own vertical integration, and accommodate its massive horizontal expansion in the early twenty-first century, while at the same time keeping what Jacob Kol refers to as its 'pyramid of preferences'[85] – an architecture vital for EU's future relations with the MENA countries – from collapsing.

The real test for the EU will be how to define the parameters that would allow it to ensure its own solidarity without necessarily fragmenting the cohesion of its non-European neighbours. Its new European Neighbourhood Policy, issued in 2004, is part of the process of trying to maintain peripheral cohesion. The EU will also increasingly have to take stock of the impact that Asian strategic developments may be having on its MENA periphery. As the MENA region looks eastwards, so the control of its relations with the MENA region are no longer in its own hands. While the EU may try to keep the region from total collapse, it cannot in any meaningful way engineer full recovery without appreciating the impact of Asian geo-strategic realities on the Middle East. It is proper, then, that we now turn the focus of our attention to Asia as MENA's other important and increasingly vital territorial neighbour.

The Other Side of Eurasia: Asian Geo-strategic Dynamics

Much of the debate about the post-Cold-War order has rotated around the notion of unipolarity in the international system, in which the old bipolar world is said to have been replaced by a US-led unipolar international system. Robert Jervis's confident belief that the USA 'is a hegemon in today's unipolar world order' is widespread.[86] Brzezinski's three-point argument – that for the first time in history the world has seen a single state as a truly global power; that this non-Eurasian power is globally the pre-eminent state; and that the world's true central arena (Eurasia) is also dominated by the world's first global and non-Eurasian power – are all valid. But while there may be a great deal of truth in this argument, particularly with regard to the direction of the international political economy and the USA's overwhelming presence in its old regional haunts, it is far from clear that unipolarity at that level has also taken root in Asia. In this part of Eurasia, one of the key characteristics of the system is its dynamic multipolarity. Furthermore, because of its multiple regional system structure, Asia is also a multipolar security complex in which power is divided, albeit unevenly, between the three continental actors China, India and Russia, as well as shared with a number of smaller, but equally influential regional players – Iran in West Asia; Japan and South Korea in the east; and Indonesia in Southeast Asia.

These relationships show that Asia does not have, nor has it had in modern times, a stable balance-of-power structure or a dominant power capable of imposing order on the region. As a consequence of the unevenness of its power relations, Asia has been exposed to, and has tended to suffer from, the dynamic and exploding energies of its regional and subregional actors. Thus, while Russia has managed to remain an important Eurasian power into the twenty-first century, the depletion of its strategic assets is matched only by China's rapid rise. This has caused a flux which, in itself, is a destabilizing process, but if we add the impact it is having on the broader Asian structures and Asia's myriad of regional systems, we find that the imbalance in this equation is an even more dangerous one. Additional complicating factors relate to India's role. Although India has continued to attach itself to the falling star of Russia it has, in search of a bigger regional and international role, built up its military base, invested in both nuclear weapons and a blue-water navy, and sought to draw close to the USA. Post-9/11, both South Asian rivals have used the war on terror to draw closer to the USA which, in turn, has embraced both.

Just as in Europe, moreover, Asian power relations are further complicated by the overarching presence of the USA as Asia's dominant intrusive power. The US presence in Asia is felt through its economic muscle, which is very strong, and also through its global security structures straddling the continent. On the one hand there is NATO, now expanded not only to include several Soviet satellite countries on the western edge of Eurasia, but to have a presence in some of the former Soviet Asian countries as well. On the other, there is US Central Command (CENTCOM), whose remit includes much of the Middle East and all of Central Asia and the Caucasus region. Added to these are Washington's close military alliances in East Asia: Japan, South Korea, and Taiwan. These security structures are underpinned by the USA's own overwhelming military presence: the Fifth Fleet in the Persian Gulf, the Sixth Fleet in the Mediterranean, and the Seventh Fleet in the Pacific.

One must further consider the impact that geo-economic forces will have on Asia's security structures. The potential of the Caspian states to emerge as medium-to-large hydrocarbon producers and exporters of the twenty-first century will raise their strategic importance, while adding an inevitable competitive edge to the Caspian states' relations with the traditional hydrocarbon exporters of West Asia. Hydrocarbons will – as they have done in the Middle East, South America and Africa – introduce their own power hierarchies amongst the Caspian 'haves' and 'have-nots'. But they will also suck into the area a number of energy-hungry economies from Asia and Europe. The needs of the latter groups, and the ways in which they set about satisfying them, will act as a powerful tool in redrawing the strategic map of Asia. It is therefore highly likely that the presence of hydrocarbons will give birth to a new range of power relations in Asia, and directly affect their globalization efforts. Energy may also cause a shift in West Asia's strategic map, gradually moving the exclusive focus away from the Persian Gulf to a new Caspian–Gulf 'energy zone', which will be an eventual amalgamation of the two hydrocarbon centres of West Asia.

Finally, a broad glance at the core and periphery of the Asian continent suggests that the right conditions may be emerging for the rise of a 'pentarchical' Asian power structure, in which four or five large players could grow, in the next 25 years or so, to dominate the expansive Asian landscape. They will be able to play a predominant role in shaping the continent's regional systems within multilaterally reached agreements, as well as through unilateral action. Pentarchy may, for the first time, lead to the creation of a relatively stable and co-operative balance-of-power system in Asia, which could prove an effective means for mediating regional and subregional crises and also provide the necessary conditions for the development of a broad Eurasian economic community, stretching from Europe's westerly edge to Asia's eastern frontiers. Under this scenario, it is possible to foresee the EU and 'Chapan' (China plus Japan)[87] forming Eurasia's economic engines, while the Persian Gulf–Caspian energy zone functions as the energy plant of this vast, increasingly interdependent, economic space. Such economic interdependencies will inevitably deepen the continent's strategic interdependencies, and also increase the ease with which both good fortune and bad can be transmitted across Asian borders. Globalization will facilitate exchange with a vengeance!

Asian Geopolitics in Action

Much of the international security agenda since the end of the Cold War seems to have been shaped by developments and events in Asia. In the Asian context, the drama of 9/11 created a new backdrop for an already complex and dynamic situation, in which states have learned to regulate their relations with each other with an acute awareness of the volatility of the environment surrounding them. Before the events of 9/11, the formulation of the USA's 'war on terrorism' as a new foreign policy doctrine, and the dismantling of Taleban rule in Afghanistan, Asia had already undergone huge strategic changes. The last two decades of the twentieth century had seen the end of the Cold War and the collapse of the Soviet superpower, both causing major movements in regional relations. The final collapse of the Soviet superpower may have been linked to the regional developments in western Asia, which followed its military occupation of Afghanistan in December 1979. This act enabled the USA strategically to open new accounts with a number of Asian countries, and to draw closer to Moscow's main Asian rival, China, and to a number of Muslim countries bent on punishing Moscow for its invasion of Muslim Afghanistan.

The American covert support for the Afghan Mujahedeen fighters from the late 1970s to the late 1980s, which was made possible only by technical, financial and logistical support from such countries as Pakistan, Saudi Arabia and Egypt (among others), and the presence of a large number of Muslim volunteer fighters from the Arab world, kept the anti-Soviet alliance together until the collapse of the Soviet Union. This loose alliance not only facilitated the rise to power of the Mujahedeen factions in Afghanistan in 1990, but also created the conditions for the Taleban coming to power in 1996. Many Muslim actors, such as those linked to Islamic groups in Egypt, Sudan, Algeria, and Saudi Arabia, and those Sunni Muslim countries wedded to Salafi interpretations of Islam, positively supported the Taleban in its bid to act as a new pole for the disparate groups of anti-US and largely anti-Western Islamist militants.[88] With its strict interpretation of Islam, Islamic values and precepts, the Taleban set about changing social relations in its home country; but, as these 'ruler-students' grew in confidence, and as the level of support for them was increased by their three main backers (Pakistan, Saudi Arabia, and the United Arab Emirates), so they became emboldened to intervene in regional affairs as well. Thus in 1998 they nearly managed to provoke Iran into a war with their forces; they emerged as one of the key suppliers of arms and finance (money earned through the narcotics trade) for the Islamic groups in neighbouring Central Asia; they made efforts to provide weapons and personnel for the Muslim Yighurs fighting the Chinese government in the western Chinese Xinjiang Province; and committed themselves to supporting the 'jihad' of the Pakistani-backed Kashmiri Islamists against Indian rule in that province, and that of the Chechens against Russian rule in the Caucasus. These relationships had very much deepened after the Cold War and due to the collapse of the Soviet Union. The 9/11 attacks, however, disrupted these already destabilizing regional relationships and caused a more-or-less total revision of the balance-of-power equation in Asia.

In short, Asia was already in some strategic turmoil when al-Qaeda struck at the heart of the USA and invited the US superpower to revisit South Asia.

While some of these changes were stimulated by the demise of the Soviet Union as the dominant Eurasian empire, deeper Asian transformations were driven partly by economics, and partly by the presence of other forces. Chief among the economic factors has been the rise of China and the other Asia–Pacific economies. In other contexts, the growth of Islamic militancy as a pan-Asian phenomenon, and the growing economic and military links between West Asian states and Asia's new powerhouses, have played a crucial part in defining Asia's post-Cold War strategic map. An exploration of the intricate relations between the eastern and western edges of the Asian continent, and the way in which these have come to influence the shape of Asia's geopolitical mass, will provide a fascinating reference point for understanding the effects of recent events on the strategic map of Asia, and the ways in which President George W. Bush's regional strategy will have been understood in this most dynamic of regional systems.[89]

As already noted, it was the end of the Cold War that transformed Asia's strategic landscape, in one stroke giving birth to a new set of geostrategic realities. Previously, Asian affairs had been dominated by the power politics of the USSR, China and India as its main actors, and the security calculations of the USA and its core Asian allies (Japan, South Korea, Taiwan, Indonesia, the Philippines). But as the chain of events, which had begun in the late 1980s in central Europe, accelerated the end of superpower rivalries in Europe, the spectacular disintegration of Eurasia's only modern-day superpower created the conditions for a major shake-up of the Asian balance-of-power rubric. The old Asian power equation, between the USSR and China, began eroding in the early 1990s. In the first instance, the demise of the Soviet empire transformed Russia from an international or global power into a dominant but weakening regional power. In Michael Yahuda's graphic explanation, in a stroke Moscow's presence in Asia was reduced to that of a minor power: 'The once awesome Pacific Fleet now lay rusting in their Pacific waters bereft of fuel, maintenance and the capacity even to carry out exercises. The capacity to project power in the Indian Ocean and Western Pacific that had shaped the regional power balance in the 1970s and 1980s had suddenly ended. With it had ended much of Russia's significance in the Asia-Pacific as a whole ... Russia had declined absolutely as a power capable of shaping events throughout the Asia–Pacific region'.[90]

The rapid corrosion and disintegration of the Soviet Union, therefore, was a seminal development in Asia. Its true regional significance can only be appreciated if set against the resurgence of China, Asia's most populous country, as a global economic player and a growing Asian military force in its own right – a 'regionalizer', by sheer weight of economy if you will, operating in an increasingly multilateralist Asia.[91]

Throughout the 1990s China consolidated its position as continental Asia's economic powerhouse, absorbing well in excess of US$20 billion a year in foreign direct investment and with an economic growth rate of around 10 per cent per year. Inward investment had been so huge that at the end of the twentieth century, China's stock of foreign direct investment had stood at US$350 billion and its foreign trade at a massive US$475 billion, enabling the country to join the league of the world's top 10 exporters.[92] Its success has been so rapid that by 2005 the Chinese economy had overtaken those of France and Britain.

Such growing economic muscle also allowed for the acceleration in the pace of the modernization of its military structures and systems. With such eye-catching income figures, it was only a matter of time before the military would be given the opportunity to accelerate the pace of the armed forces' modernization. Thus a general restructuring, re-equipping and modernizing of the armed forces was proposed in 2000 in the context of China's *National Defence in 2000* document. As a consequence, in pursuit of a stronger military force, military expenditure for 2000/01 was increased at a faster pace, by 17.7 per cent, taking defence expenditure to a new high of US$17.2 billion,[93] although reliable sources report that the real figure for its military expenditures might be as high as US$42 billion.[94] The refitting of the People's Liberation Army has included massive purchases of weaponry from Russia, from equipment for tactical forces to such big-ticket purchases as strike and bomber aircraft (Su-27s and Su-30MK2s), some eight Kilo-class submarines, missile systems, and Sovremenny-class destroyers (an order for two of which, in January 2002, will have cost China some US$1.5 billion).

Although the rise in China's military-related commitments in the 1990s has been explained by its growing fear of US military superiority and the resurgence of 'Japanese militarism' (whose annual defence budget has hovered around the US$50 billion mark since the early 1990s), China's renewed interest in defence since the end of the Cold War has created the opportunity for extended security links with many of Asia's regional powers. China's steady rise from the ranks of Asia's powerhouses in the 1990s has inevitably encouraged the establishment of closer economic, diplomatic and political links with a number of other Asian countries and subregions, including several of those in West Asia and the Middle East. Indeed, some of these countries have been the main customers for China's arms exports, which stood at US$2.2 billion for the 1995–99 period.[95]

After over a century of Russian supremacy in Sino–Russian relations, in the 1990s the Moscow–Beijing pendulum had slowly but surely begun swinging in China's direction. As we shall see, the shift in this bilateral balance of power has had quite serious consequences for the Asian balance of power as a whole.

The collapse of the Soviet Union also created the conditions for the (re-)birth of a number of landlocked countries in the heart of Asia. But, unlike the USSR's European republics, which managed to attach themselves to the EU, the five newly created Muslim republics were disadvantaged from the start by their relative geographical isolation, and also in having rather weak political, economic and social structures.[96] These states also found themselves among a number of fairly powerful regional competitors and in the fast stream of changing regional structures. While, in reality, they were the entities that would eventually fully fill the geopolitical vacuum in Asia's heartland, at the time of their birth in 1991/92 they seemed to have neither strong political institutions, nor the foundations on which to build strong socio-economic systems. Although some were believed to have potentially strong lifelines, such as commercially viable quantities of hydrocarbon deposits, their remoteness, combined with broader regional instabilities, seemed to suggest that the key to the very survival of the Central Asian states, let alone their prosperity, would remain firmly in the hands of their neighbours, rather than their own political elites.[97]

Further south, in one of Asia's oldest subregions (the Indian subcontinent), stability has apparently been steadily eroded as India has been able to establish itself as the subcontinent's premier power since the early 1990s.[98] With a stockpile of tactical and strategic nuclear weapons and a growing blue-water navy, India has been able to widen its circle of influence in Asia. But as Pakistan has always been viewed as its closest rival, New Delhi's efforts in this regard were, until recently, mirrored in Pakistan's own nuclear weapons development and in its attempts to challenge New Delhi's self-evident military superiority through support for radical Islamic groups in Indian Kashmir and Afghanistan. Bad relations between India and Pakistan added to regional tensions that, thanks to the presence of nuclear weapons, in turn deepened pan-Asian strategic interdependencies first evident in the 1980s.[99] Instability in South Asia has been further compounded by the weakening of Pakistan as a state, a coherent polity, and an effective socio-economic entity. The depreciation of the balance-of-power equation between India and Pakistan, and the presence of nuclear weapons in such an unstable environment, has continued to be a major cause for concern, despite improvements in bilateral relations in the period following the fall of the Taleban in Afghanistan, and America's desire to make India and Pakistan strong allies in the war on terror.

Another important strategic development since the end of the Cold War has been the steadily growing military links between Russia and continental Asia's big three – China, India, and Iran. These links not only provide Russia with effective access to Asia's main power-brokers, but also engender closer links between Iran in West Asia, and China and India further east Table 4.6.[100]

Table 4.6 The conventional domains of power (late 1990s)

	Territory (thousand km²)	Population (millions)	GDP (US$ billion)	Strategic weapons NBC/SSM*	Military expenditure (US$ billion)	Armed forces (thousands)
China	9561	1190.92	630	NBC + SSM	55.9	2935
India	3287	913.60	279	N + SSM	15.5	1145
Iran	1648	65.76	60	C + SSM	3.3	513
Russia	17,075	148.37	392	NBC + SSM	65.5	1270

Sources: World Bank; International Institute for Strategic Studies. *NBC, non-conventional (nuclear, biological, chemical) weapons; SSM, surface-to-surface missiles.

The growth of such relationships has also helped to deepen Asian strategic interdependencies and create new opportunities for both co-operation and competition between the major continental Asian powers. In terms of co-operation, one can point to the efforts that the three have been making in order to identify new ways of extending cross-border trade opportunities to the countries of Central Asia. But where competition is most transparent, what really matters is that between the big two Asian neighbours, China and India – who, to be fair, have been trying to ensure that geopolitical competition does not lead to a rise in inter-state tensions. The opening of the ancient Himalayan pass between the two countries in July 2006 was another sign of the growing economic and trade links between the giant neighbours, and the importance that each now attaches to the broadening of relations. Although the competitive relations between India and China has a long history, India's deployment of nuclear weapons has disrupted the old uneven stalemate between New Delhi and Beijing, and has created the conditions for the birth of a new strategic relationship between the two. Now, not only do the two parties find themselves on a new (nuclear) strategic threshold, but they have to factor into their calculations the role of China's close ally and India's main regional rival (Pakistan) as a nuclear weapon state in its own right. With a chain of nuclear states now stretching across Asia, from the Yellow to the Arabian Seas, it is not hard to see that a more dangerous balance now marks the relations between the world's two most populous countries.

Added to the complications that have resulted from the broader post-Cold-War transformations and the more specific security developments, is the absence of any concrete security co-operation agreements in Asia and the paucity of any recognizable balance-of-power structure that could provide the framework for the establishment of inter-state regional or sub-regional security organizations.[101] To be sure, ASEAN and its South Asian equivalent have slowly developed into broad subregional bodies, as has the Asia–Pacific Forum, but these work largely at the economic level of exchanges. Yet, in the absence of proper security skeletons, it is hard to envisage the emergence of security structures that could accommodate Asia's complex strategic landscape. Indeed, it is perhaps because of such complexities that, until China's recent efforts to found an 'Inner Asia' regional organization around the Moscow–Beijing axis, an overarching security structure has proved difficult to build in Asia, where bilateral agreements have largely been more durable. It is also around such bilateral arrangements that Middle East–Far East relations can be determined.

East meets West: Relations across Asia

As already noted, the transformation of Eurasia into a large geostrategic web of interlocking subregions has generated a number of cultural, economic and security threads that have tended gradually to tie the fortunes of the Middle East area more closely with those of the other Asian regions – giving real substance to the idea of a greater Middle East. Of these threads, several can be said to be strategic in nature. As we will see, broadly speaking, energy, Islam as a transnational political force, labour and financial movements, military links and arms trade (including weapons of mass destruction), and Central Asian geopolitics keep Asia's regional systems joined at the hip, making each increasingly dependent on the others.

Energy

Asia's insatiable appetite for oil and gas is one of the key elements in the cementing of West and East Asian economic links. As fast and as surely as the Persian Gulf states produce oil, the Far Eastern economies consume it. Data show that, by the end of the twentieth century, the Asia–Pacific accounted for nearly 60 per cent of oil movements from the Middle East, compared with just 13 per cent to the USA and 21 per cent to western Europe. Asia–Pacific countries (excluding Japan and Australasia) were consuming the same amount of oil as the combined imports of western Europe and the USA. The trend is irrefutable. In the mid-1980s, the region accounted for 10 per cent of world oil production and 18 per cent of crude oil consumption; at the end of the century its share of production had hardly moved, while its share of oil consumption had risen by about 27 per cent.[102] The main oil-consuming countries, China, India, Japan, and South Korea, will continue to lead the Asia–Pacific hydrocarbon consumption table well into the twenty-first century.[103] As a leading Japanese commentator has said, 'we all will struggle for Middle Eastern oil among the three of us – China, India and Japan'.[104] The thirst of these countries can only realistically be quenched by other Asian hydrocarbon producers, despite China's efforts to diversify its sources and compete with the USA for access to hydrocarbon deposits of western and eastern Africa.

On current patterns, by 2010 around 65 per cent of the Middle East's oil will be heading for the Asia–Pacific region, a total reversal of the previous 100-year trend in which much of Middle East oil exports had headed westwards. This structural shift is compounded by the behaviour of the traditional consumers of Middle Eastern oil. The biggest global consumer, the USA, has based its energy strategy on securing the bulk of its hydrocarbon imports from the Americas and Africa, and Europe has been deepening its energy links with North Africa and some Gulf suppliers, while also tapping into Europe's own significant deposits. As a consequence of these changes to the patterns of consumption and Asia's rising demand, it is likely that in less than a decade's time, as much as 95 per cent of Asia–Pacific needs will be met by the Middle East. The Saudis, who until not too long ago were America's main oil partner, are already setting in place strategies for developing their Asian partnerships: 'Asia has become our number one customer. Today, we ship more than 4.5 million barrels per day (bpd) to Asia, about

60 per cent of our exports. This is about 20 per cent of Asia's current petroleum consumption ... the world's biggest crude exporter is keeping spare capacity to meet the needs of Asia's fast-growing economies'.[105] Iran's relationships have followed a similar pattern: its trade with China alone had jumped to US$9.5 billion in 2005, with the latter importing as much as 13 per cent of its oil needs from Iran.[106] Relations are likely to become even tighter when one factors in the key role natural gas is likely to play in the coming decades. As Asian economies, from China right around the Asian coast to India, switch from coal to gas (in its liquefied form, LNG), so will they look to countries nearer home (Australia, Indonesia, Malaysia, and Russia) as well as to the Middle Eastern and Caspian producers to meet this growing demand.[107] In the Middle East, Iran, Iraq, Qatar and Saudi Arabia will be the key exporters of LNG to Asia; and in the Caspian, Kazakhstan and Turkmenistan.

The Asian energy partnerships will create broader relationships, resulting in deeper interdependencies. For example, as the Middle East exporters increase their exposure to the Asian economies, so also they will leave themselves more vulnerable to the ups and downs of Asian mercantilist economic cycles. This was the case during the late 1990s economic downturn in Southeast Asia, for example, in which the Middle East's oil-exporting economies bore the brunt of the crisis emanating from Asia. The economic pressures would have been much greater and more intense if both Japanese and Chinese economies had also nose-dived.

On the other hand, the deepening of hydrocarbons relations will facilitate a substantial capital transfer from the eastern to the western edges of Asia, and encourage the eastward orientation of the hydrocarbon producers of West Asia. If we assume that Asia–Pacific imports of Middle East oil reach 25 million bpd by 2020, at US$25 per barrel (a very conservative estimate these days), then Middle East oil exporters' coffers will be boosted by an annual income of some US$250 billion from their eastern Asian neighbours. Today, oil prices of over US$60 per barrel mean that capital transfer westwards is already reaching such levels. As already noted, such substantial sums will encourage the oil exporters to intensify their eastward expansion, thus reducing their exposure to the traditional OECD markets of Europe and North America. At the same time, their eastward orientation will deepen the geopolitical gap between the Persian Gulf countries and the other members of the MENA regional system in the Levant and the Maghreb, which, as shown, are already locked into the European orbit.

Economic shifts of the magnitude discussed above will cause political movement as well, loosing the Western grip all the time that the link with the east becomes greater. America's erstwhile Arab ally, Saudi Arabia, is a case in point: by 2006, its trade with China had grown to over US$15 billion a year (growing by 43 per cent per year since 1999), and Saudi Arabia was now responsible for providing some 17 per cent of China's oil import needs.[108]

The growing hydrocarbons relations will also increase the economic vulnerability of the Asian economies to oil-price fluctuations and related crises emanating from the Middle East, even though some Far Eastern producers (such as Indonesia and Malaysia) stand to gain from such price increases. As the *Far Eastern Economic Review* notes, 'At Morgan Stanley Dean Witter, economist Andy Xie calculates that if oil prices average $29 ... annual growth in East Asia, excluding Japan, could drop by 0.6 percentage points ... in dollar terms, it could still cost the region between $15 billion and $20 billion [in 2000]'.[109] Indeed, it is estimated that for every US$1 rise in the price of oil, East Asia's trade surplus shrinks by over US$2 billion a year. Asia, therefore, is extremely vulnerable to oil-price fluctuations, and feels the pain of price increases almost immediately.

Such price increases hit Asian consumers in several ways. First, they cause a deteriorating trade position; second, they increase inflationary pressures in the economy; and third, they place a severe strain on government budgets. The financial balance is complicated further by the peculiarities of the petroleum pricing structures for Asian importers, where the Asian importers in fact pay much more for their Middle Eastern oil imports than do their western OECD counterparts.[110]

The intricate future energy picture of Asia would not be complete without a sketch of the strategic impact that the pipelines network and energy routes out of the Caspian may have on Middle East–Asia relations. Although proven Caspian oil reserves may not be too impressive (around 29 billion barrels, as opposed to the North Sea's 17 billion barrels and the Persian Gulf's 600+ billion), the US Department of Energy and several oil companies continue to calculate that the Caspian's potential oil reserves could be as great as 160 billion barrels, which would turn the Caspian into a leading source of energy in this century.[111] It is based on these estimates that experts calculate the Caspian's locked hydrocarbons to be worth in the region of US$4 trillion in total.[112] And it is this kind of sum that drives the oil majors' interest in the Caspian's strategic reserves, despite the fact that the cost of extracting a barrel of oil here is many times that in the Persian Gulf.[113]

Despite the reservations about Caspian oil deposits, it is estimated that by 2015 the Caspian will be producing up to 4 million barrels of oil per day, more than Iran's output in 2001. Such a level of output, if sustained, can bring significant riches to the producer countries, generating well in excess of US$20 billion in annual income for the countries. But, as the Caspian's reserves are much smaller than the Persian Gulf's, the Caspian oil states and the oil majors will be looking to optimize the return on their huge investments by maximizing output, possibly hurting the position of the established producers.

The estimates of the Caspian's natural gas reserves, set to become one of the main energy sources of the twenty-first century, are quite impressive. According to the US Department of Energy, the Caspian may be harbouring some 650 trillion cubic feet of this valuable resource. In comparison, Iranian and Russian natural gas reserves (outside the Caspian) stand at

1700 trillion and 810 trillion cubic feet, respectively.[114] The figures for the three new Caspian states therefore support the contention that they are likely to emerge as key players in the Asian energy market of this century, despite worries about their oil reserves. To find and develop the Caspian's hydrocarbon resources is a big enough task in itself, requiring considerable technical skill and experience. But in the Caspian, this problem is overshadowed by the difficulties associated with establishing viable transport routes. The Caspian's hydrocarbon deposits are located largely offshore: over 80 per cent of Azerbaijan's, around 40 per cent of Kazakhstan's and around 35 per cent of Turkmenistan's are under the Caspian Sea. The discussion about Caspian hydrocarbon transport routes, however, has been highly politicized. On the one hand, the USA has attempted to bypass Iranian and Russian territories by strengthening its ties with Azerbaijan and encouraging the building of the trans-Caspian and the Baku–Ceyhan pipeline, which opened for business in July 2006.[115] On the other hand, Iran and Russia have been busy making the business case for building and strengthening existing north–south transportation routes. The fact that the US$3.5 billion Baku–Ceyhan pipeline was even being discussed is testimony to the strength of the USA's position, and its ability to convince local actors in the Caucasus that on this occasion politico-security considerations should override financial calculations. But now it is built, neither Iran nor Russia is willing to abandon the Caspian's strategic prizes to the USA; both have been engaged in their diplomatic battles for the transport routes out of the Caspian.[116]

Apart from the hype about the potential of Caspian oil and natural gas reserves, the key attraction of the Caspian to the international oil companies has been the new states' preparedness to offer fairly generous concessions to the oil majors, particularly at a time when the oil business itself was consolidating, and very few new business opportunities in upstream investment were forthcoming. Here was a potential bonanza situation with few political strings attached, and no-one was apparently prepared to spoil the party by factoring in such substantial problems as security, geography, law, or supply routes. Few even questioned the authenticity of the data on Caspian reserves.[117] By and large, the relationship between these states and the West, and the USA in particular, has been based on one simple calculation: 'the Caspian region will hopefully save [the USA and its allies] from total dependence on Middle East oil'.[118] The chief US concern being that 'stable and assured energy supplied from the Caspian [will reduce American] vulnerability to disruption in world energy supplies'.[119] It was vital, therefore, that this oil should not flow southwards and out of the Straits of Hormuz (which would defeat the object of diversification of supplies by giving countries such as Iran an even greater lever in relation to the Caspian–Persian Gulf energy zone and effective control over both Persian Gulf and Caspian oil flows), or northwards (thus reinforcing Russia's position in the Caspian), but rather westwards and eastwards.

Encouraged by its mineral wealth, and now no longer hampered by the pressures of the Cold War and the presence of powerful Asian rivals, the USA set about creating new levers of influence in the heart of Asia, slowly nestling the Caspian countries into an increasingly pro-West orbit. If US actions were to be seen as displaying neo-hegemonic tendencies, they do signal a long-term commitment to the Caspian. Regional powers in the shape of Iran, India, China, Pakistan, and Russia are already taking stock of this reality. While some of these states are looking for ways of accommodating the USA, others are actively seeking ways of rendering the American presence limited and ineffectual in the long run. For all, however, the pursuit of energy security will be an overriding consideration.

Military Partnerships and Arms Trade

Another binding fibre of Asia–Middle East relations is the arms trade-supported military relationships that have been consolidated since the end of the Cold War. First, there is the role Russia plays. Since the late 1980s, Russia has been able to consolidate its position as Eurasia's largest arms manufacturer and exporter by becoming the leading supplier of arms and military technologies to Asia's big two (China and India), as well as to Iran and a number of other smaller Asian countries. Moscow, moreover, acts as the main nuclear technology supplier of both China and Iran, having earned in excess of US$6.5 billion from this trade alone since the mid-1990s. Russia is building Iran's only nuclear power plant in Bushehr and is also negotiating with China for the introduction of more advanced power plants, while bringing on-stream a large nuclear power station in China's Lianyungang area.

Russia, therefore, is at the centre of an arms-trade web that brings together Asia's largest countries with some of its biggest energy providers. This relationship gives Moscow considerable influence in Asia, and also binds it inextricably to the Asian power balance, as demonstrated in the unprecedented Russian–Chinese military exercises held in August 2005. The air, sea and land force drills of some 10,000 troops, dubbed 'Peace Mission 2005', were launched in Vladivostok and took place in China's Shandong region. Significantly, the Shanghai Co-operation Organization members and observers (India, Iran, and Pakistan) were also invited to watch the exercises, which saw in action Russia's Su-30 interceptor and its nuclear capable Tu-95 and Tu-22M3 long-range bombers.[120] The three 'observer states' either were already buying Russian military hardware, or were looking to do so.

This military relationship, however, is only one part of the picture. Another crucial dimension of the arms trade is China's extensive military ties with the countries of the Middle East. China is one of Iran's main military partners, for example, and has also had a fruitful military relationship with Iraq (until 1990), Saudi Arabia, and Yemen. There is every indication that China will continue to foster military links with the countries of West Asia, particularly with those that have oil and those that have the hard currency to pay for China's military hardware. China, therefore, is able to underwrite its strategic energy needs through bilateral arms agreements with the hydrocarbon exporters of the Gulf region. In this manner, it is therefore also able to affect the West Asian balance of power.

The arms trade has created other, less obvious east–west Asian relationships as well. There is an increasingly intimate military partnership between Israel on one side and China and India on the other, where Tel Aviv is known to have supplied (or be supplying) the former partner with a wide range of military software and related technologies, and the latter with as much as US$15 billion worth of military hardware, software and upgrade know-how for its Soviet-built hardware.[121] Today, India is probably Israel's most important defence market. All the while, Israel has also been a close military partner of Taiwan, China's main security concern in East Asia. Israel is also actively deepening its recently acquired military partnership with Turkey, through which Ankara has been able to hold major military exercises, buy a wide range of advanced military hardware, and use Israel's expertise in upgrading its older weapons systems. This relationship has created some tension, not only in Turkish–Iranian relations, but also in Ankara's relations with the Arab world – which feels that this partnership is largely forged against it. Russia, too, is concerned and remains suspicious of Turkey's ambitions in the Caucasus, the Balkans and Central Asia. Both Moscow and Tehran are also worried that Tel Aviv will use its warm ties with Turkey as a means of developing closer links with Azerbaijan and the Central Asian republics. The Israeli prime minister's comments in Turkey that 'I will say in Ankara that we are willing to enhance the relationship with Azerbaijan against Iran, Russia and Armenia', will have done little to allay these fears.[122] Robert Olson notes that, with Israeli armed forces now stationed in eastern Turkey, and with Israeli access to Turkish military facilities (where 12 per cent of the Israeli air force's formidable strength is now said to be stationed), it is perhaps only a matter of time before the other parties react to this security challenge.[123]

These are significant military relationships in their own right, but the point to underline is that while Israel is busy developing close security-related links with China and India, the latter countries, and to a lesser extent Turkey, are increasingly tied into an energy web that has at its heart Israel's Middle East regional rivals, most notably Iran. In strategic terms, the dynamics of the energy and military axes are such that they seem to be leading the countries involved in opposite directions, creating the conditions for future polarization and possible conflict. One example of the latter was seen in July 2001 when, for the first time, Iran used its rather small Caspian naval forces in anger in order to assert its interests against Azerbaijan, embroiling in the process the oil giant BP in the tensions between Baku and Tehran.

A further disturbing dimension is the role that weapons of mass destruction are playing in the shaping of Asia's regional security equation. Today, not only do we have two powerful South Asian countries as established nuclear-weapon states (India and Pakistan), but we are also witnessing the emergence of the economically weak and politically totalitarian state of North Korea as a nuclear-weapon state. In the course of just half a century, Asia has emerged as the most intensive nuclear theatre in the world, in which the number of nuclear-weapon states has risen from zero to five (Russia, China, India, Pakistan, and North Korea). But Asian geostrategic conditions are such that we cannot rule out significant additions to the list: Iran, Japan, and South Korea have the potential and the geopolitical incentive to develop an independent nuclear-weapons capability, and if they do so, the pressures on other actors in the Middle East or continental Asia to follow suit would be enormous. Also, the nuclear-weapons technological assistance that North Korea has received from Pakistan in exchange for missile technology has set a bad precedent for other nuclear exchanges arising, to destabilize further what is an already extremely fragile set of Asian regional (dis)orders.[124]

Investment and Trade

At least since the 1970s, East Asian countries have been significant investors in the oil economies of the Middle East. The trade and investment relationship has grown partly out of the Asian energy importers' needs to compensate for the high cost of their oil imports by exporting to the oil-producing countries. But the leading Asia–Pacific countries are also interested in participating in the liberalizing economies of the Middle East, where their firms are often beating their Western counterparts to lucrative management or investment contracts. Japanese and South Korean success is now being emulated by China, which is winning infrastructure projects across the region – in Algeria, Egypt, Iran, Oman, Saudi Arabia, Sudan, and Yemen, China is emerging as a serious player.

It is the oil-exporting states, however – the only Middle Eastern countries with any 'surplus capital' – that have accelerated investment of their petro-dollars in the Asian markets. For some time now, Gulf Arab private investment has been finding its way into the Japanese downstream oil industry, for instance, and Gulf investment capital has entered the Korean, Taiwanese and Chinese markets as well.[125] China's Sinopec (its state-owned oil company) has already signed an agreement for gas exploration in Saudi Arabia's largely untouched Empty Quarter, and Saudi Aramco has signed a US$3.6 billion deal with Sinopec (and Exxon Mobil) to build chemical and refining plants in China's Fujian Province. With Iran, on the other hand, China's Sinopec has signed a massive 30-year US$70 billion gas deal to import gas from Iran's South Pars offshore field, and also to develop Iran's Yadavaran field.[126] India was a part of this deal (taking 20 per cent), and within weeks of this agreement, Iran was finalizing a US$7 billion pipeline deal with India and Pakistan to carry its gas to South Asia.[127] Iran and Saudi Arabia are leading where the UAE, Qatar, Kuwait and Oman are following, each looking to strengthen its own trade and investment ties with Asia's growing giants.[128]

These trade and investment ties have given the two sides of the energy equation a large and equal stake in the economic stability and security of the other. Even where oil is not involved, the Gulf Arabs are increasingly engaged with Asian economies. The case of Dubai's announcement in June 2006 of its intention to invest as much US$30 billion in Pakistan, in property, financial services and infrastructure projects, is a case in point. The Pakistan Government has identified Dubai's commitment as the largest investment of its kind in this country of over 120 million people.[129]

One can therefore add the impact that political economy has been having on the strategic interdependencies straddling Asia: it acts very much as a reinforcing factor, bringing some of Asia's subregions together as partners in a hydrocarbon-driven exchange. But as India joins the race for energy sources and for strategic advantage in Asia, so it is likely to compete with China for these. A clear example of such rivalries taking hold was evident in 2005, in the struggle between India and China to buy PetroKazakhstan (which owns one oilfield and half-owns two others in Kazakhstan). The China National Petroleum Corporation's initial bid of US$3.2 billion was trumped by India's state-owned Oil and Natural Gas Corporation, which offered US$3.6 billion for the buy-out. In the end, China raised its bid to US$3.6 billion and was successful in securing the Canadian-based company, and encouraging it to divert its exploration and marketing activities towards satisfying China's own large market.[130] This was played out as a zero-sum game between Asia's giants.

The growing interest in Islamic economics (finance and banking in particular) is another important economic link between the Middle and Far East, where Islamic banking is now a fully fledged sector, and in which the Muslim countries of Southeast Asia (Brunei, Indonesia, and Malaysia) have a large commercial sector of their own. In Pakistan, too, the popularity of Islamic banking has brought Gulf Arab interest, and the Dubai Islamic Bank is likely to become the first GCC bank to be able to open (as many as 50 to 70) branches across Pakistan, making it the largest foreign bank operating in that country. Billions of dollars of assets from West and Southeast Asian customers are now managed by Islamic finance houses in the Persian Gulf or Malaysia.[131] These banks work closely with each other, as do the Islamic banking branches of the Western banks, facilitating globalization on the one hand, and reinforcing economic links between these subregions of Asia on the other.

Labour and Migration

Labour is another link reinforcing relations between the Far and Middle East. Since the 1970s, labour from such countries as Pakistan, India,

Bangladesh, Sri Lanka, Thailand, South Korea, the Philippines, and Indonesia has been providing the backbone for the Gulf Arab countries' building industry and a wide range of service industries. The rapid, large-scale construction expansion of the 1970s and 1980s was possible largely due to the cheap and plentiful Asian labour that the oil-producing countries were able to import. Some Asian countries, such as Korea and Taiwan, actually provided the labour force for most of their building contracts won by their corporations. So significant has this trade become that, in the 1990s, non-nationals made up nearly 72 per cent of the total GCC workforce of 7.5 million. Of non-nationals, some 58 per cent were from East and Southeast Asia, and the remainder largely from the Arab world.[132] Sustained high oil prices since 2002 have meant that construction and capital investment projects are again boom industries in the GCC states, attracting large numbers of labourers from the rest of Asia. Today, around 50 per cent of the 7 million expatriate labour force in the GCC is from India, for example, making this subregion of vital importance to this fast-growing Asian economy. The 3.5–3.7 million Indian workers generate an estimated US$5–8 billion a year in income for India, adding significantly to the over US$30 billion worth of trade between India and the GCC.[133] Similarly, bilateral relations with Pakistan are dominated by labour. Labour remittances from the Gulf are the second largest source of income for the South Asian country, generating some US$4.2 billion a year in income for this resource-poor state. Kuwait hosts 3000 Chinese workers, and their number in the Iranian capital is now so great that local traders have begun catering (in terms of specialist shops and restaurants) for the dietary requirements of this largely specialized labour force.

Collectively, these workers have emerged as major earners of hard currency for their home countries, while also servicing the most basic needs of the Gulf oil monarchies – from domestic servants, cleaners and drivers, to shop-keepers, municipality workers and attendants.

At another level, migration across Asian borders could create severe tensions between states. First, there is the issue of cross-border ethnic groups and their influence on inter-state relations. The presence of such groups is not in itself a problem, but in times of crisis, for example when tensions run high between India and Pakistan, their movements can make borders more porous and make the host countries more vulnerable to the export of political violence from other parts of Asia.

In another geographical setting, the presence of Igurs in both China and the neighbouring Central Asian countries has complicated China's relations with its new Muslim neighbours. On one hand, it has had to step up its own border security structures on its western borders, and on the other hand it has had to forge closer links with its western neighbours. Beijing has done the latter through closer bilateral (and multilateral, like the 'Shanghai 6') relations with such countries as Kazakhstan, over cross-border movement of militant groups, smugglers and so on. Since 9/11, the management of their mutual border has emerged as a very important factor in their bilateral relations. This had already been underlined by China as it had begun to assess the importance of Kazakhstan as a potential solution to China's energy needs and the securest route for the passage of its hydrocarbon imports from Central Asia.

Second, the flow of refugees, as from Afghanistan to the neighbouring countries, can have a direct impact on the socio-economic stability of the weak states of West and Central Asia, as well as the wider region. The presence of large numbers of refugees creates tensions with the local inhabitants, increases the pressure on what are often quite limited resources, and causes difficulties in diplomatic relations between states if refugees are deemed to be badly treated, or indeed if the host country came to view them as a threat to its internal security and prosperity. The rather tense relationship between the millions of Afghan refugees and their Iranian, Pakistani and Tajik hosts very much fits this pattern.

Religion

Political Islam has been a thorn in the side of many Asian countries. Even before the rise to prominence of al-Qaeda, Islamic militants had been active in the Central Asian republics as well as in China, India, and Russia. Moscow has been scarred by bombs said to have been planted by Islamist groups associated with the Chechen struggle for independence from Russia; western China has seen several attacks by militants in Xinjiang Province, who have managed successfully to combine Islamic militancy with the local people's sense of ethno-nationalism; while in India the Kashmir issue, attacks on its national symbols, as well as clashes between Islamists and Hindu nationalists have raised the spectre of internal instability in the world's largest democracy.

In the Eurasian context, militant Islam is an important element of interactions between the Middle East and the rest of Asia. Each of Iran, Saudi Arabia, Pakistan, and Afghanistan has, at one time or another, advocated a particular brand of political Islam, and each has harboured a particular type of Islamic fundamentalist. As we have seen in relation to the Taleban in Afghanistan and Osama bin Laden's al-Qaeda network, many of these militants have international links, which allows them to operate easily in more than one country, and gives them the capability of carrying out terrorist acts across any frontier. For these reasons, sub-trans-state militant Islam, as exists between the Caucasus to the west, Xinjiang to the east, and the Arabian Sea to the south, poses a direct threat to the stability of the Eurasian heartland. This threat is seen to be sustained either by some Middle Eastern states or by elements based on their soil.

Concerns about militant Islam, and the open disputes between the Islamist states themselves, have generated a number of responses from the regional countries. The 'Shanghai 6' of the Shanghai Co-operation Organization

(China, Russia, Kazakhstan, Kirgyzstan, Tajikistan, and Uzbekistan), which was crafted by China, is an example of one such response. This organization was created to frame a regional response to the threats of 'terrorism, separatism and extremism', representing the concerns of a diverse group of Asian countries. For the big two in the Shanghai group, the three dangers listed all have an Islamic dimension, concerns about which are shared in equal measure by their Central Asian counterparts. China and Russia are both grappling with ethno-Islamic militants on the edges of the trans-Caspian region, and are anxious to stem the flow of fighters, financial and military resources from Afghanistan and elsewhere to their own separatist movements. Thus Afghanistan, and South Asia in general, has also entered the frontline of the struggles between militant Islam and the ruling regimes in the heart of Asia.

Indeed, only weeks before the 9/11 terrorist attacks on the USA, Moscow and Beijing had consolidated their bilateral security links by signing a wide-ranging 20-year security pact. The pact, signed in August 2001, adopted a shared responsibility for what the parties referred to as the security of 'Inner Asia' (Central Asia and Afghanistan). Parties had expressed the hope that the organization would be able to expand into an overarching security pact in which some Middle Eastern states will have a major role. Iran, one of the three countries on President George W. Bush's infamous 'axis of evil', has been mentioned in this context, where it would join an expanded Shanghai 6 structure to form a Eurasian security alliance.[134] How Iran's presence in such an overarching Asian security structure might affect US relations with China and Russia remains to be seen, however. Nonetheless, it is fair to say that it is likely to add to the list of differences between the USA on side and China and Russia on the other over military support for Iran (which the latter two countries provide in abundance), and the positive role that an increasingly pluralist Islamic state such as Iran can play in the wider Asian security environment. At least since the late 1980s, Moscow and Beijing have systematically breached the USA's 'containment' net around Iran. The leaders of Russia and China often remind Washington that they stand to lose much more in economic and security terms, as well as in terms of geopolitical advantage, from an isolated Iran than they do from engaging with this important West Asian power. To the chagrin of the White House, since the terror attacks in September 2001 their argument with regard to Iran virtually mirrors that of the other key Eurasian actor, the EU.

The USA's strategy towards the geopolitically important country of Iran will, however, have a lasting effect on the Asian balance-of-power equation. While it vacillates between the two contradictory positions of regarding Iran as a potential anti-terror target for its opposition to the Arab–Israeli peace process and support for Islamic militants, and one of a force for stability in West Asia due to its chain of relationships stretching from Afghanistan, Iraq, Lebanon and the GCC countries, it cannot meaningfully participate in the emerging security architecture of Eurasia without stepping on the toes of Asia's main power-brokers.

Conclusions

Unquestionably, the attacks on the USA in September 2001 are slowly redrawing the emerging post-Cold-War strategic map of Asia, straining some alliances, creating new ones, and forcing a restructuring of the remainder. Within weeks of the attacks, some dramatic changes began to occur. In the course of the crisis, Iran nearly found itself allied to the USA; Pakistan emerged as a close security partner of the West; India and Pakistan co-operated to counter the corroding influence of the Taleban in their countries, but they also profited by having their nuclear weapons status accepted; Russia moved closer to the USA in an effort to remove the thorn of Islamic fundamentalism from its 'near abroad' and the Caucasus; the Arabian Peninsula states extended their support for the West's international anti-terrorism campaign – which resulted in the severing of the Taleban's lucrative financial and broader politico-religious links with the UAE and Saudi Arabia; and the USA itself fully rediscovered the importance of Central Asia, in geostrategic terms, to its Eurasian interests.

The USA's Central Asia strategy in the aftermath of the crisis, and the role that the USA may assign itself, will have a dramatic effect on the strategic map of greater Asia. Disengagement is no longer a viable option for the USA, and analysts in that country are considering the contours of the US medium- to long-term presence in Russia and Iran's backyard. It may be years and several other crises before we have the final picture, but there are those who believe the USA is presented with an extraordinary opportunity to 'project power for the long term in Central Asia by setting up a pro-Western government in Afghanistan'. This would then provide the basis for the USA to 'oversee a pipeline across [Afghanistan] from the rich Caspian oil fields to ports in Pakistan, and would be perched to react to political changes in volatile Iran. An outpost in Afghanistan would also give America added leverage with Europe and with Russia, which has always had a heavy hand in the region'.[135]

The spread of American influence to this region, and on the doorstep of so many of its competitors in Asia, could be a costly venture to pull off, but any real gains by the USA will more than likely accelerate the pace of security co-operation between China, Russia and Iran, and also stir the radical Islamists into a more intensified targeting of US interests and regional allies in the Middle East and Asia. If one throws into the hat the regional impact that the Turkish–Israeli alliance has been having, and India's not inconsiderable weight, it can safely be concluded that new and unexpected trans-Asian alliances can yet emerge to totally upset the apple cart.[136]

With the twentieth century now behind us, and the Cold War increasingly a distant memory, only now is a fuller understanding emerging of the impact it had on the strategic map of the Middle East and the vast Asian continent and its other dynamic peripheries. A new era has already begun in Asia, which is slowly unfolding in the context of the much-changed rules of the game in international relations. The shift from a bipolar international system to one that is fractured and multilayered – between multipolarity in economic terms and unipolarity in military power and international influence terms – is having a telling effect on the Asian continent, and ultimately on its inherently unstable power relations.[137] The prospects of multiple groupings congregating around two or more of the more powerful states in the system cannot be ruled out.[138] In the Asian context, the argument that a multipolar system is likely to be more stable today than a bipolar one is particularly relevant. But if one is considering overlapping power relations, perhaps Rosecrane's arguments might be more appropriate. His argument that a 'bipolar–multipolar system' may be able to avoid the extremes of both bipolar and multipolar systems is quite enlightening in the Asian setting. This model is based on the assumption that 'enough bipolar control of multipolar realms would take place to prevent extremes of conflict', thus minimizing the conflict as it dissociates 'bipolar interests from outcomes in the area'.[139] Kenneth Waltz, though, would argue that in a multipolar environment, the making and breaking of alliances is more possible, thus making the entire system quite unstable.[140] Such an outcome, where we would see a system of rapidly shifting alliances, could be quite disastrous for Asia. In Waltz's model it is the 'swing powers', which may not necessarily be the most powerful states in the system, that could end up holding the balance of power, perhaps indefinitely. Such swing powers could use their privileged position to break alliances, and also to charge 'rent' for their assistance in forging new partnerships. The USA as the non-resident dominant military power could call on the services of such states in its hour of need, but probably at a price. Asia, unfortunately, is replete with states that have the potential to act as swing powers – Iran, Israel, Kazakhstan, Pakistan, Turkey at one geographical end, and Indonesia, the Philippines, South Korea at the other end of the spectrum – but also have the potential to often end up disrupting the balance. It should be self-evident that more than one of these powers would be able to place itself in a position to exploit its comparative advantage, and profit handsomely from acting opportunistically. In the last analysis, it will probably be the extent of daring demonstrated by one or more of these powers in trying to shape the Asian regional environment, and the US perception of their actions, that will influence the direction of Middle East–Asia relations, and with it the EU–MENA ties. After 9/11 we can be sure of one thing – the Asian race for pre-eminence has already begun. In this race, China's role cannot be underestimated. As Ernest Bower, President of the US–ASEAN Business Council, has observed, 'I have never seen a time when Southeast Asia is so much in transition and open to ideas, and never seen a time when the US is so distracted from the region. In contrast, China is focused on the region like a laser beam. I do feel the Chinese Monroe Doctrine is being built here in the region. As the Chinese get their act together and play on the world stage, this region is the first of a series of concentric circles'.[141] The destiny of Eurasia, and also of globalization's reach in greater Asia, we can conclude, is in the hands of China and its economic and energy partners. But these partners do not share the same vision of the future, nor the direction of change in the geostrategic space increasingly referred to as the Asian super-region. For the GME, the development of the Asian super-region that is being accommodated within Eurasia is still a work in progress, but it could still spill disaster were it to threaten or disrupt the stability of the deep-rooted links with the West that have grown since early last century to form the region's core partnerships. The region will have to balance the globalization of economic activity with the geopolitics of the vast Eurasian space if it is to find a path to prosperity from the opportunities and fluidities that the collapse of the Soviet Union has brought. It is not at all certain that it can do so, given its own geopolitical uncertainties and instabilities.

5 Government and Governance in the Era of Globalization

> Westerners are killed not for any political reason but simply because they are part of a civilisation that militant Islam now sees as the enemy. Striking at the West, in any form, is therefore justified ... as part of the struggle against a culture and way of life that it sees enveloping the world, suffocating Islam and inexorably changing the face and attitudes of the Muslim world.
>
> Editorial, *The Times*, 15 October 2002.

The State

More than 190 states are now occupying the international space, with over a dozen new ones having burst on the scene just in the years since the end of the Cold War in 1989. It seems hardly the time, therefore, to be discussing the tensions globalization has generated for the nation-states of the Middle East. Yet this does seem to be the correct starting point for my discussion of the politics of globalization in the MENA region. In this region we are far from an 'eclipse' of the state, even though there a number of weak and vulnerable states operating on its terrain.

The challenge of de-territorialization that globalization harbours can easily translate into a security threat when considered in the historical context of state-building in the Middle East, and of the existence of several strategically placed 'quasi-states' in this region. Yet it can also be argued that capital travelling the world with globalization needs a strong state to see through the fundamental changes needed at the economic and social levels for its growth in the MENA region. So while globalization does weaken the barriers raised against its effects, because of economic interaction, at the same time it demands a strong state role, so that order can be maintained and the political system kept on an even keel during the period of transition. The state needs to be there to keep economic reform on course, but also to prevent the rejection of globalism at the popular level, and to contain those forces (largely Islamist in nature in the Middle East) that articulate alternatives to wholesale integration with the West/the rest of the world. Under these circumstances, not only do state elites take advantage of their custodian role of the state for private gain (thus reducing the revolutionary impact of economic reform on existing socio-economic structures), but at the same time seek support from within and without for maintaining the strong state as a barrier against instability. This is the essential contradiction of globalization in the MENA region. The picture is therefore somewhat more complicated that the – still true – assertion of globalists that, in the Middle East, the 'fundamental problem is a lack of economic and political freedom'.[1]

Despite its general fears of globalization, largely thanks to its hydrocarbon deposits and the insatiable thirst for this raw material, the region has formed one of the main supporting pillars of the international economic system since the early 1920s. In the post-War era, oil became such a significant factor in the operation of the international economic system that it came to dominate the security strategy of the superpowers towards the Persian Gulf and the surrounding area.[2]

Ironically, over the years, largely through oil exports, significant enough economic resources were transferred to the region to create strong mutual dependencies between the oil-producing states and their main consumers, the Western economies. Oil income also forged a link between the labour-rich and the labour-poor (but petrodollar-rich) MENA economies. Due to the oil trade, the region was already well exposed to unstable market conditions arising from recession in the leading economies. Such interdependencies existed well before globalization had made an appearance as a new regulator of international trade and financial flows. Oil, in effect, had created organic links between the oil-producing states and the international economic system. But the linkages went even further, for at the same time oil income also provided the lifeline for several resource-poor countries in the region – Jordan, Palestine, Egypt, Sudan, Syria, and both Yemens. These secondary-rentier states were gradually sucked into the same international financial currents to the extent that their economies, too, were increasingly exposed to international conditions.

This begs the question, if it is the case that the region is highly penetrated economically, why do so many people in the Middle East believe that they are not as yet 'globalized' and, as a corollary, express an instinctive fear of economic globalization?

These questions can be answered in the following manner. First, the oil sector has traditionally been largely isolated from the rest of the economy, so the tentacles of the international system did not easily reach the entire domestic market. Second, oil has traditionally cushioned the MENA oil exporters' populations from international economic pressures. The date of the first big 'oil shock' is remembered for the dramatic rise in oil prices in the early 1970s, not a fall. The shock, as a trauma to the system, occurred only in 1986, when oil prices finally collapsed to no more than US$7 per barrel. As argued in chapter 6, until then most oil exporters were reaping the benefits of this export commodity, and enjoying the premium and relatively high revenues that an uncertain politico-security situation in the Persian Gulf had brought about.

Furthermore, oil has carved the peculiar rentier state form, in which the elite has been able to take charge of the commanding heights of the economy and take responsibility for distributing largesse to the population in terms of jobs, housing, healthcare, education, subsidized goods and services, and a modern infrastructure. The state also emerged as a more autonomous actor in MENA societies, largely thanks to the grip that the flow of oil provided for the ruling elites. Few states in the region have been willing to stand by and see this autonomy eroded and replaced by a more accountable system of governance. The same pattern is also in evidence in the largely non-oil Arab states: Egypt, Syria, and Jordan all have an active and largely unaccountable state at the helm, itself guided by a powerful elite. In Egypt, Syria, and even Libya, we see the emergence of a peculiar political hybrid of 'bonapartism', or republican monarchism. Hereditary republicanism has already succeeded in Syria, putting into the presidential palace the son of President Hafez al-Assad after his death, and was also infecting Saddam's Iraq before the regime's abrupt end in March 2003. To the dismay of his political allies, in the same way as President Hafez al-Assad had done in Syria in the 1990s, and in the same time frame, the Iraqi president had begun devolving more and more political authority to his two sons, Ouday and Qusay, grooming them for succession. While Bashar al-Assad did inherit his father's republican throne, Saddam Hussein's sons met a violent death at the hands of the occupying Coalition powers within a few months of the fall of their father's regime.

The Egyptian president and the Libyan leader have the same strategy of succession in mind, as they too extend important public platforms to their sons, but they have to ensure their sons' status does not destabilize the regime, and that they themselves are able to strike a balance between continuity in the system, and change/reform being demanded by the population.

More broadly, even where political reforms have been introduced more widely, until recently these have been rather cosmetic and structurally shallow. Perhaps the pattern of political liberalization in the Middle East provides support for the Petras and Veltmeyer argument that, far from encouraging democratization, the best form of political reform that globalization can lead to is a new kind of 'neo-authoritarianism' in which even the introduction of competitive elections will not affect the elite decision-makers. A 'hybrid political system' is born that 'combines elite decision-making and electoral processes, elected legislators and non-elected corporate decision-makers and electoral campaigns and decrees, undermining the notion of a civic culture'.[3] The Arab world's republican and royal monarchies seem best adjusted to the work of this hybrid political system. Broadly speaking, elections in the MENA region, which are often seen as a positive political by-product of globalization, provide no more than a veneer of democratization.

Globalization cannot countenance power changing hands as a consequence of elections in this region, nor see ruling elites lose control of the instruments of decision-making. That is why 'political actors who play the democratic rules suddenly kick over the table when they lose elections and become or embrace dictatorial regimes'.[4]

'Marketization' of the State

Globalization encourages the opening up of domestic markets to local and foreign capital; reform of market structures; liberalization of economic activity; and the dismantling of state monopolies. In practice, however, in developing-country settings such as the Middle East, the state rarely withdraws from the economic arena. While, in an ironic fashion, this could be one of the desirable outcomes of globalization for neo-liberal economists, in practice the process forces a reshaping of the relationship between market and state, not always to the advantage of the market. It does not end state intervention, or even its dominance in many places. What happens in reality, in regional settings such as the MENA region, is that corporatism mutates and capitalism is repackaged.[5] Out of state monopolies emerge large, dominant, private firms, which are then spun into more than one entity when offered on the local stock exchange. As privatization unfolds, so elements of the political elites transform themselves into economic elites, but do so without relinquishing many of the levers of power. Whether populist, left-leaning or rentier in nature, the state's response in the Middle East to the economic pressures of globalization has more-or-less uniformly been the same: to try and rig the market to ensure the state does not come off worst in the changed relationship between market and the state.

But the private new monopolies are exposed from birth to unpalatable pressures. First, the state's marketization strategy must include liberalization of trade and investment in order for its efforts to be seen as credible by global regulators such as the International Monetary Fund and the World Trade Organization. The opening up of domestic markets to foreign capital and international firms often puts unbearable pressures on the private-sector monopolies, which have to either face loss of market share and therefore profitability, or form uneven partnerships with the dominant foreign firms. In the latter mode, they become little more than comprador agents of foreign capital.

Second, in the absence of protectionism, which globalization discourages, innovation and development of nascent industries become a virtual impossibility for developing countries. While, among the MENA countries, some of the capital-rich oil states have shown the ability to capitalize on the communication and transportation revolutions to skip some stages of economic development, and emerge as regional actors in finance and related service and tourism industries, the bulk of the region's economies will not have the capacity to compete with their East Asian, let alone Western, counterparts in terms of innovation, product development, research and development, and efficient production. On one hand, local firms become much more dependent on transnational corporations' product development, and ultimately become reduced to outposts for the transnational corporations. At the same time, the development of market niche or 'national' economic sectors become an impossibility when the state is forced to maintain open borders in order to keep a place for itself in the global market game.

Under such pressures, before too long relations between the son (the new private monopoly) and its father (the state) become sufficiently strained to create real tensions between a liberalizing government and its homespun entrepreneurial economic champions. The mutually beneficial relationship (which is a fundamental assumption of market reformers) between the state and the private sector evaporates into recriminations and tense political battles between elements of the elite for control of the state. Inter-elite rivalries mount, in turn leading to more corruption and cronyism, thus deligitimizing the elite as a whole and broadening the rift between the rulers and the ruled.

With such developments taking place, assumptions about the state benefiting from economic restructuring come under scrutiny. Tax revenues from individuals (employees), for example, are often an insufficient source of revenue for the state to meet its multitude of infrastructural, welfare, civic and civil, and public policy obligations. These commitments, although great, are nothing compared with the commitment of the state to quench the thirst of the military sector for personnel, facilities and sophisticated military hardware.[6] On average, Arab states devoted 27.5 per cent of their current annual spending to defence during 1997 and 2002. This represents nearly one-third of their annual expenditure. The highest 2002 figure was Oman's, standing at 41 per cent, which had already been substantially reduced from a high of 54 per cent in 1997. As Table 5.1 shows, in relative terms Oman's high military expenditure over this period was not the exception. According to one estimate, with an average GDP of around US$650 billion by the early 2000s, the defence expenditure of the Arab states accounted for around 6.3 per cent of the total GDP of the Arab world, or equivalent to over US$40 billion a year. In the 1997–2002 period, the Arab states may have spent as much US$247 billion on defence.[7] Saudi Arabia alone accounted for around 50 per cent of the combined Arab defence expenditure in the 6-year period to 2002.

Defence takes the bulk of income, yet the badly needed tax revenues from private sector corporations are either evaded or remain uncollected. States are even more reticent to lose the little tax that they do manage to collect through market liberalization and industry privatization. Were it to lose its monopoly control of national finances, the state could easily find itself having to borrow even more, in order to afford to provide the rudimentary and basic needs of a fast-growing population.

The long-term consequences of marketization, of capitalist development in a borderless economic system, should not be overlooked. So long as

Table 5.1 Selected Arab defence and security spending as percentage of current expenditure, 1997–2002

	1997	2000	2002
Algeria	22.4	22.2	22.2
Bahrain	32.2	34.9	34.4
Egypt	18.8	18.9	18.7
Jordan	44.8	35.7	28.2
Kuwait	30.7	33.2	29.5
Oman	54.3	47.4	40.6
Qatar	34.5	32.2	32.6
Saudi Arabia	31.8	30.9	30.6
Syria	41.9	34.3	32.1
UAE	30.4	29.9	29.9
Yemen	43.9	29.5	28.8
Total	27.8	27.8	26.7

Source: The Arab League.

capitalism relies on the state for protection and regulation of the 'bazaar', which it blatantly does, then it cannot easily come to terms with the erosion and corrosion of state power brought in the wake of globalization.[8] In the MENA region, the state remains such a dominant actor that, as MENA states rush to open up their economies to global forces, as they transfer some of their powers to corporate agencies, so they contribute to the democratic deficit brought about by economic globalization. That is, as private actors and private regimes take control of big chunks of the economy, and as the territory of economic activity is redrawn to suit the needs of the giant corporate actors, the global money markets, and their legal regimes, so the state will find that it is 'willingly' relinquishing key areas of decision-making about the national economy to globalized forces.[9] As it does so, it also loosens its grip on the polity.

But in the MENA region, while the state can easily further deliberalize politically, it cannot forgo political control of the national economy and not risk losing power. Thus the MENA state finds it hard to adapt to what Sassen calls the new 'geography of power' arising from economic globalization. There is one simple explanation for this, and that is to be found in the powerful and influential nature of the MENA state itself. In Tripp's words, 'the politics of the countries of the Middle East and North Africa bear testimony not to the enfeeblement or the crisis of the state, but rather to its resilience as a form of organization and as an imaginative field. Particular regimes and elites may face challenges, but the state retains a powerful hold on the imagination of those who might challenge them, as well as remaining for many the chief instrument of power'.[10]

Globalization therefore exposes the contradictions of capitalism as a world system of private capital flows across the bureaucratically controlled territorial boundaries, but it does not, by itself, transform the role of the state. Globalization exposes the tension between state and capital without providing the necessary tools for the state to manage its impact.

The Challenge to Elite Legitimacy

In the post-9/11world, and the subsequent ambiguities brought about in the USA's relations with several of its trusted Arab allies, the position of Middle Eastern authoritarianism has become ever more precarious. This is largely so because the vital link between the external pillar of legitimacy for these regimes has been severely strained by changing American attitudes towards the reliability of its regional allies, as well as its publicly stated concerns about Arab societies being the 'breeding ground' for ruthless, ideologically driven, international terrorists. As one Western diplomat has put it: 'People didn't worry about the peculiarities of Saudi Arabia because they did not affect them. Now the peculiarities are seen as creating a threat for the west. They are no longer acceptable'.[11] Washington's preparedness to put some distance between itself and several of these Arab elites provided a public spectacle for those forces in the region that had campaigned for the 'domestication' of their national affairs and the removal of the USA as a factor in their internal affairs. For the elites, however, the new American attitude after 9/11 provided a new source of anxiety. Why this should be the case has a simple political economy answer: dependency.

The erosion of the external pillar can become an existential problem for many a ruling comprador elite, whose very livelihood is dependent on global capitalism. This proposition in relation to less-developed countries is explained succinctly by Gowher Rezvi, who observes that: 'since authoritarian regimes lack popular legitimacy, they seek to compensate for their vulnerability and insecurity ... through external alliances and assistance. The external 'props' – economic assistance and military support – become integral to the survival of these regimes'.[12] Earlier, in the late 1980s, the left-leaning MENA states, such as Algeria, Iraq, Libya, Syria, and South Yemen (People's Democratic Republic of Yemen), had already tried to cope with the loss of the Soviet Union as their external prop, and if their experiences are any guide, then any significant changes in the internal–external balance of power for America's allies could be disastrous. It is noteworthy that all five regimes took radical steps to manage their affairs in the absence of the Soviet umbrella. Algeria embarked on a controlled political liberalization strategy that resulted in a bloody and destructive civil war (1991–2000); Libya finally (in the late 1990s) abandoned political violence and covert politics as tools of its diplomacy; Iraq's response was typically military (the invasion of Kuwait in 1990); Syria sought to manage its alliance deficit by opening up domestically while also drawing closer to the West; and Yemen found (in the 1990s) an uneasy path towards unification of North and South and a more open political system. For these states, loss of the external prop produced dramatic and traumatic results. In the case of their pro-Western counterparts, where political economy plays an equal part in the relationship, there is no telling what could ensue.

Other legitimacy challenges posed by the spread of globalization relate to the flow of information, control of the sources of information, the rapidity and the stealth nature of information and communication flows. On another level, the preconditions for economic reform – in terms of transparency, the rule of law, and accountable functionaries – bite into the hitherto exclusive domains of the state. In the absence of pluralization of the political system, the elites' loss of control of information flows, coupled with the need to reform the structures and institutions of governance, provide a double challenge to their legitimacy as rulers and guardians of the nation.

Political Reform: A Double-edged Sword?

Yet, in the face of their deep socio-economic difficulties, MENA regimes seem to, albeit reluctantly, agree that they have little option but to persevere with liberalization. Such paradoxes of globalization are well understood in the region, and several ruling elites have begun to respond to them seriously. In the Arab part of the Muslim world, democracy, as understood in the West, is still a rather scarce commodity.[13] However, in many corners of this community of 22 states, pluralism has been a fast-rooting concept. Popular elections, a necessary but insufficient condition for democracy, have grown hugely in number since the late 1980s. They are now frequent and regular and form a common feature of the regional landscape, and as such are indicative of a slow but perceptible process of change. In the 10 years between 1989 and 1999, for example, over 80 elections took place in the region, more than the entire number in the previous half-century (Table 5.2).[14] In the twenty-first century, Algeria, Afghanistan, Bahrain, Egypt, Iran, Kuwait, Lebanon, Palestine, Qatar, Saudi Arabia, and Turkey have all held major elections. In some instances, elections have been held for the first time in their history.

Significant elections now take place regularly in more than half the Arab countries, affecting the political lives of more than 150 million people from Morocco to Oman. If we add Iran and Turkey to the equation, then the total number of citizens affected by electoral politics will increase by another 130 million. Today, elections regulate the political life of more than a dozen Muslim Middle Eastern countries and their 280 million citizens.

Table 5.2 Number of elections in the MENA region, 1989–99

1989	1990	1991	1992	1993	1994	1995	1996	1997	1998	1999
6	4	3	10	6	4	7	12	9	5	15

Source: data from A. Ehteshami, 'Is the Middle East Democratizing?', *British Journal of Middle Eastern Studies*, 26 (2), 1999, 199–217.

Although many of these elections have had conditions placed on them, and not been 'free' elections as understood in the West, nonetheless they have become a welcome fixture of the political landscape. Elections have come to play such a role in shaping the context of the debate for 'democracy promoters' that these pundits have come to believe that 'elections will serve to broaden and deepen political participation and the democratic accountability of the state to its citizens ... it has been assumed that in attempted transitions to democracy, elections will be not just a foundation stone, but a key generator over time of further democratic reforms'.[15]

Party politics has also spread roots, and political parties increasingly act as vehicles for mobilization of the masses by both liberal and Islamist actors in the Arab world. In Morocco, some 22 political parties participated in its 2002 parliamentary elections; in Algeria's in the same year, 11 registered parties participated; and in Jordan's June 2003 parliamentary poll, key figures formed electoral 'fronts' as surrogate parties in order to organize their electoral campaigns. In Morocco and Jordan Islamists were able to compete, but the regulatory system prevented them from becoming dominant partners, leaving the space open for other forces to emerge as well. In Palestine, however, in its parliamentary poll in January 2006, the rejectionist Islamist Hamas party won a major victory, forming the Authority's first Islamist government.

Political dynamism is also in evidence in some unexpected quarters. In the traditional monarchies of the Arabian Peninsula today, for example, one encounters a growing momentum for political and social reform and a gradual opening up of the political space. Indeed, the extent of change has been so great in these societies that John Peterson has begun referring to them as 'post-traditional'.[16] In political terms, in Bahrain, Qatar, Oman, and Kuwait, we now have active participation in a deepening and broadening parliamentary environment, and the leadership of all four states talks openly of the need for broadening the political base through pluralism.[17] In the two states of Bahrain and Qatar, the talk is of full democratization, although obviously under the control of the rulers. Kuwait's national assembly is now a fully functional political institution in its own right, charging ahead with liberalization of both private and public space in the country. Indeed, the assembly is so active and effective that, in the succession process subsequent to the death of Sheikh Jaber al-Sabah in January 2006, for the first time it intervened in what had for the previous two centuries been a family affair, to force the abdication of the crown prince and emir-designate, Sheikh Saad al-Sabah. 'For virtually the first time, an Arab parliament', noted Mai Yamani, 'had voted a head of state out of office and asserted its will on choosing a successor'.[18] This bold intervention proved to be the precursor to a much greater set of demands being placed on the ruling family, who needed the assembly's formal endorsement of the alternative emir-designate in order to legitimize the continuing rule of the al-Sabah. The parliamentarians' demands included the legalization of political parties, the separation of the posts of prime minister and crown prince (which had traditionally been held by the same person to ensure the political authority of the ruling family), and the consideration of appointing the prime minister from outside the al-Sabah family. Rightly, Yamani has called the situation in Kuwait 'revolutionary'. The 'revolutionary' process has continued thanks to the voting behaviour of the Kuwaitis in the country's parliamentary elections of June 2006. Of the 249 candidates competing for the assembly's 50 contested seats (out of 65) 28 were women, and the 65 per cent voter turnout delivered a largely reformist parliament.

Saudi Arabia is also openly debating the introduction of broad, but incremental, reforms.[19] Significantly, as a major first step, it announced the introduction of direct municipal elections to take place by late 2004 in order to increase 'the people's participation in the administration of local affairs through direct elections and activating the municipal council'.[20] This is after the same monarch's comments a decade earlier that, in his view, elections were incompatible with an Islamic system. On 29 November 2003, the late King Fahd had already approved another major reform initiative, which is enhancing the legislative role of the 120-member Consultative Council. King Fahd had spoken of following a path of political and administrative reform: 'we will broaden the scope of popular participation and open new horizons for women in the workplace', he declared in May 2003.[21] More telling still, in the context of this discussion, is his declaration that not even Saudi Arabia – '[which is] at heart of the Muslim world and ... the cradle of Arab identity' – can develop in isolation, 'we are part of this world. We cannot be disconnected from it'.

The position of the Emir of Qatar (Sheikh Hamad bin Khalifa al-Thani) is another case in point. Since the late 1990s, he has been pulling his country towards pluralism and has staked the future of his entire regime on the successful introduction of political and economic reforms. He told his country's Advisory Council at its 31st session that 'excellence and creativity demand a healthy climate of freedom of expression and the sense of belonging which can only come with popular participation in decision-making'.[22] In other words, economic development and pluralism can only work in a transparent and open political environment.

Clearly, while he has been keen to keep the external prop intact, which he has largely managed to do through forging much closer military and security ties with the USA, he has also been adding a much stronger internal pillar to his regime. This pillar is being built around the base of participatory politics, in which Qatari citizens will eventually enjoy the protection of the law as well as the right to speak freely and elect their representatives in a fully elected national parliament. These reforms were being introduced in the context of a much-heralded new constitution, which promised 'separation of powers and the creation of an elected parliament',[23] and the securing of 'freedom of expression as well as the freedom of economic and money markets'.[24] That globalization can create organic links between the political and economic realms is clearly understood and is being acted upon.

Qatar, along with Bahrain, Kuwait, Oman, Morocco, and Jordan, represent some cases of successful preservation of the external prop, along with a managed change in the relationship between the elite and the populace in ways that strengthen the internal pillar of legitimacy. All six countries have close security ties with the USA and also partnerships with some of its European allies.

Although the Qatari and Bahraini concerted responses to the paradox of globalization are by no means unique in the MENA region, nonetheless their progressive packages of reform proposals do place them among a small group of MENA countries whose responses to globalization have resulted in broad-brush domestic reforms. But the impetus for reform is growing with every passing year, fed by the domestic imperatives of MENA countries, as well as the external pressures since 9/11 for the region to catch up with the democratizing wave of the 1990s. What is of particular interest in the context of institution-building and Islamic practices, however, is that these Gulf Arab states deliberately use traditional platforms of consultation as vehicles for the introduction of institutional reform. As we have seen, while Kuwait enjoys the benefits of a well established national assembly, in Bahrain, Qatar, Oman, and Saudi Arabia the old practice of consultation has become formalized in substantive consultative councils (Majlis al-Shura), which act as the main vehicle for the introduction of political reforms. In Bahrain and Qatar, constitutional changes have accompanied the reform package, which in practice has produced a complementary framework between the traditional and Western forms of political organization and association. In Kuwait, moreover, the extension of voting rights to its 200,000 eligible voters, who exercised this right for the first time in the country's April 2006 municipal elections, is symptomatic of the further erosion of traditional boundaries and the empowerment of nationals, irrespective of gender. But as Nonneman notes, reform and liberalization are not synonymous with democratization, 'nor do they necessarily lead to it'.[25]

But as elections and party politics broaden, so political forces in the Arab world learn to play by the given rules of the game, and when irregularities arise – as was the case in Egypt's 2006 legislative poll – they increasingly rely on the judicial system to investigate their grievances. All parties seem to want to avoid a repeat of the Algerian case, in which 'electoral irregularities' triggered a bloody and protracted civil war between Islamist forces and the regime. Recourse to the judiciary, in turn, encourages recognition and application of the rule of law, no matter how imperfect the laws may be, or how badly they may be applied in practice. However, elites and ruling regimes, who ultimately devise the national rules of party and electoral politics, also learn to manipulate the system to their own advantage.[26] They apply the law to regulate access to levers of power, and to control participation of political forces. In effect, they use the civil law to exert control over the political process. Unchecked, such practices can easily transform a transitional step towards democracy into an 'elected authoritarian' regime in which elections become no more than a hollow shell for disguising deliberalization.[27] The regimes also use the same mechanisms to balance the competing political forces in the political arena. Their differences in legislative bodies can assist the regime effectively to implement a policy of 'divide and rule', and when parliamentary political groups manage to work more closely together, the regime can take advantage of their pragmatism, demonstrated by their ability to compromise, to push through its own reform agenda. Jordan, a small but important country in the heart of the Middle East, provides a classic example of this process.

The Bush Factor

While the internal context for such reforms is self-evident, the external dimension has acquired a life of its own since President George W. Bush's administration made democratization of the Middle East an important feature of the war on terrorism: 'as long as the Middle East remains a place where freedom does not flourish, it will remain a place of stagnation, resentment and violence ready for export'.[28] No other American administration, notes Brumberg, 'has talked more about democracy in the Middle East than the Bush administration'.[29] Secretary of State Colin Powell's placing of political reforms on the agenda of the USA's Middle East Partnership Initiative in November 2002 was the first stage of the policy commitment to follow the publication of the USA's new national security document. A year later, President Bush's address at the National Endowment of Democracy, followed by his speech at the Mansion House in London soon after, reinforced the thrust of the new democratization strategy: 'a forward strategy for freedom in the Middle East', the president called it. At its heart, the strategy believes that, in the words of President Bush, 'in the long run stability cannot be purchased at the expense of liberty'. Turning a blind eye to autocrats' repression of basic human rights was a wrong policy in the past, and today is counter-productive and can only ferment more radicalism. As globalization facilitates the export of such radicalism to all corners of the planet, the USA has to act to contain this threat at source. So the USA will support countries such as Bahrain, Morocco, Qatar, Oman and Jordan to spearhead the democratization drive in the region. Secondly, America's strategic allies (Egypt and Saudi Arabia) will be encouraged to walk faster and further down the political reform path. Thirdly, it would be expected that 'the establishment of a free Iraq at the heart of the Middle East will be a watershed event in the global democratic revolution'.[30] Iraq will create a democratic wave in the region, in this estimation. Fourthly, states such as Iran and Syria will be pressured to introduce meaningful reforms. Finally, the strategy will look to countries like Turkey and Afghanistan for guidance on how to mix Islam with a pluralistic (and largely secular) political system.

This vision of the future for the Middle East stands in sharp contrast to that of President George Bush senior. Hadar noted in 1992 that 'Washington's concern about the rise of democracy in the Middle East stems from the fear that free elections in Iraq, the Arab gulf states, Jordan, and North Africa will threaten the Arab regimes that help maintain strategic interests of the United States and its access to oil in the region as well as endanger American support for Israel'.[31] Today, the other President Bush is shaking the apple cart and is actively seeking democratization as the only long-term guarantor of stability in the region and the security of America's interests therein. He is, in this regard, going in the exactly opposite direction to that of some recent Republican presidents. He has criticized his predecessors for being 'willing to make a bargain, to tolerate oppression for the sake of stability ... [overlooking] the faults of local elites'. He has talked bluntly about the problems associated with the Arab 'democratic deficit', arguing that 'we cannot turn a blind eye to oppression just because the oppression is not in our own backyard'.[32] This vision will effect a very different geopolitical environment from that of the Cold War era, or indeed the first post-Cold War new world order ushered in by President Bush senior. The new American vision, as documented in the 2004 Greater Middle East Initiative, for example, presupposes the need for a massive political and socio-economic shake-up in the Middle East as the precondition for long-term stability in the region, and the only underwriter of security internationally.

This bold strategy will, of course, be resisted by the Westernizing elites who may stand to lose, as well as those radical Islamist forces that are bent on pursuing the violent jihad against the West and its local allies in the Muslim world. These forces will not take the American challenge lying down, as the responses to the Bush speeches in late 2003 have shown. One pro-government source in Egypt, echoing feelings across the Arab world, noted that 'Bush has forgotten that the Arab and Islamic peoples prefer to be ruled by a dictator such as Saddam Hussein than by a democratic president of the likes of Bush, who lies to the world every day, deceives his people, sows hatred towards it in the souls of all the peoples of the world, and annihilates the lives of his people in battles that do not concern them at all. Oh Mr. Bush, if you were a democratic president as you claim to be, you would abandon your post immediately and disperse all your Zionist aides and advisors, since your lies, your fraud, and the fact that you do not respect Iraqi and Afghan human rights have been exposed to the eyes of the entire world'.[33] An editorial in *Al-Ahram* newspaper stated that 'Recently, voices have arisen in the American government demanding direct intervention in order to impose democracy on peoples and governments, as if the people were minors or mentally retarded and needed their hands held! These demands ... are in themselves a violation of the rules of democracy. This intervention is reminiscent of the abhorrent idea of previous centuries regarding the white man's responsibility for the other peoples, for liberating them from ignorance and backwardness. The result was that this white man maintained colonialism of these peoples for centuries, and this caused the backwardness from which they [the Americans] want to rescue us today!'[34] Ahmad Alwan, a member of the supreme council of Al-Wafd, Egypt's biggest opposition party, wrote in the party daily *Al-Wafd*: 'We will never accept a message from a tyrant who understands only force and whose use of weapons is the only way of spreading his message. In contrast, we live on the land of the Arabs who understand the truth regarding [Bush's] greedy aspirations in our region ... It is not our rulers' oppression of us that planted our hatred [for the US], but American support for the Zionist state and, in particular, the current Bushist–Sharonist era, may Allah remove them from our path'.[35] In Syria, in the meanwhile, Nasser Shamali wrote in the government daily *Teshreen*: '[Bush's] speechwriters are [members] of the Zionist gang that wrote the speeches of the war on Iraq and on the Arabs and Muslims. This is the same gang of usurers and bloodsuckers whose discourse on US-style democracy refers to expanding its dictatorship all over the world, killing anyone it wants to, and robbing anyone it wants to'.[36]

A powerful official response to President Bush's pronouncements came from Syria's Minister for Immigrant Affairs, Buthaina Sha'aban. In a direct response to President Bush, Minister Sha'aban stated: 'The first thing that worried me in your speech was the statement that your adherence to democracy will be tested in the Middle East. Whether this hinted at Iraq or at the Arab–Israeli conflict, I say that what you are doing in both cases has created a real schism between the U.S. and millions of Arabs and Muslims ... The second thing that worried me ... is your statement that the advance of freedom leads to peace. How can people taste the taste of freedom when they are occupied? There is no doubt that freedom and security are the natural fruits of peace, but the child cannot be born before his mother ... The last and most important point ... is your statement that democracy is the path to honour. The subject of honour is the most important factor in the misunderstanding between the US and the Arab and Islamic world. If honour is the essence of democracy, why does the democracy of the US not take into account the honour of the Arabs?'[37] The American call for democratization was not well received.

Furthermore, it is also increasingly apparent that the US preoccupation with the Middle East post-9/11 has had an impact on its wider international strategy. Détente with North Korea, for example, could be sacrificed in the short term so that the axis of evil does not degenerate into a battle between Washington and the Middle East. A senior South Korean official made the argument rather well in 2002, when he confided that: 'I think the talks [scheduled at the time to talk place between North Korea and Japan] will come to a deadlock. The United States will tell Japan not to go ahead. The United States does not want the talks to proceed. It is inconvenient for the U.S. if North Korea is dropped from the 'axis of evil' category. If they are dropped, the war on terrorism will become a war between America and Islam'.[38]

The Challenge of Globalist Jihad: Terrorism, Globalization and the State

The 9/11 attacks, according to Griffel, were a result of the 'globalization of several civil wars and political conflicts between Islamists, military governments, like Syria and Algeria, or monarchical governments ... The attacks were the terrible consequence of a strategic decision on the part of the most radical Islamist movements stemming from their defeat in many Muslim countries'.[39] Taking advantage of the tools of globalization, they attempted truly to globalize their struggle by striking at the anchor of globalization and its spearhead in the Middle East. They used globalization to jump the barrier of the state in their home countries, as both survival and offensive strategies.

What are the issues? First, let us not lose sight of the fact that Islamists saw globalization as a cause for a new jihad.[40] For such committed groups, the chances of living in peace with the West were, by the late twentieth century, pretty non-existent. The West, through providing logistical and financial support for its cronies, was instrumental in defeating Islamist challenges in Algeria, Tunisia, Morocco, Egypt, Jordan and even Saudi Arabia. For many Islamists, through its two-pronged attack – the spread of material corruption through globalization; and extensive military/security assistance to Arab ruling elites in their struggle against Islamists – the West had declared war on Islam and a global jihad was the appropriate response to these challenges.[41] Abu Bakar Baaysir (leader of the Indonesian Jemaah Islamiyah) has stated that: 'It is the United States and not Islam that is responsible for the terror in the world today. They want to blame us Muslims for attacks like the one in Bali but we had nothing to do with it ... It is the United States and its allies that have strong motive. They want to show Indonesia is full of terrorists and so gain sympathy for their attack on Iraq'.[42] He declared on 17 October that the Bali bombing was 'engineered by infidels in order to launch war against Islam'.[43]

Secondly, 'globalist jihadis' are comfortable in using and applying the modern means of communication, transportation and warfare in their campaigns. So, as the MENA state liberalizes the communications space, these forces take advantage of the new public spaces to broaden their network and appeal. They also use the same technologies in their efforts to rely on the element of surprise and to seek to inflict maximum damage on their targets. Their use of a wide variety of communications systems, fast means of transportation, and modern, mobile and lethal tools of warfare are new features of this new breed of Islamist campaigners. Lest the qualitative leap is underestimated, it is worth recalling that as recently as 1979, Ayatollah Khomeini's use of taped messages to his followers inside Iran was being regarded as a novel and innovative use of communications tools for political campaigning.

Thirdly, like the transnational corporations, the globalist jihadis see the world as a single theatre of operations. They, too, have become 'footloose' and increasingly less tied to, or reliant on, a solid territorial base for their international operations. While a home like Afghanistan, Iraq, Sudan, Somalia, Yemen and Pakistan may be handy for management of operations and personnel, constant presence in one country seems less of a requirement than (even) compared with the mid-1990s.

Fourthly, the globalist jihadis tend increasingly to move their battles out of the MENA and Muslim arenas and engage their enemies on their own turf, or on neutral territories where a strong Western presence may already exist. They have managed to spread the insecurity net far and wide, and have forced the West to rethink its own security parameters in truly post-Cold War terms where set-piece bloc warfare is giving way to increasingly small-scale, insurgency-type conflicts around the globe. For example, a terror alert from London, Paris, Berlin, Madrid, Rome or Washington these days has a global ring to it, and the routine threat assessments of Western countries today necessarily include an analysis of the activities of small organizations, monitoring of key individuals dotted around the world, monitoring of suspicious financial transactions, and the deployment of stealth technologies, human and sophisticated sensors in remote monitoring.

Finally, where globalization inadvertently weakens the grip of the elite on the territorial state, globalist jihadis double their efforts in order to take advantage of the exposed physical and bureaucratic borders between states to spread their tentacles and ensure their cross-border effectiveness. They thrive on the lowering of boundaries, of whatever type, even though their ultimate aim is to isolate and separate the Muslim world from the West.

On another level, the globalist jihad is a challenge to the understanding reached between Arab elites and the West. Their transnational challenges have undermined an already weakening but long-standing understanding between Arab regimes and the West about, for instance, the role of Islam in politics. It is worth remembering that during the Cold War, and more emphatically during the Soviet occupation of Afghanistan in the 1980s, political Islam (of the non-Iranian variety) was, as a whole, welcomed as a partner in the anti-Communist crusade of the USA. The Islamists' depiction of the Warsaw Pact as godless served not only US geopolitical interests, but also the domestic struggle of its Arab allies with their leftist and anti-imperialist nationalist counterparts. The Islamists had, by and large, become a legitimate force so long as they did not challenge the status quo in the MENA regional system. But as the globalist jihadis have over-run these boundaries and have undone the implicit understanding between Arab rulers and the USA, so they have removed the most convenient lever of control from the Arab rulers. They have also made a more obvious bedfellow of the elites and the West, and have forced a re-examination in Washington of the virtues of close relations with those Muslim elites whose domestic arena is dysfunctional, or worse still is a breeding ground for radical Islam.

Looking back, it is now clear that events of 9/11 were the biggest salvos in a much wider international terror campaign to engulf many countries of the region. In Afghanistan, Jordan, Pakistan, Morocco, Tunisia, Turkey, post-Saddam Iraq, and Saudi Arabia, al-Qaeda activists started attacking civilian targets at will, forcing the state to intensify its security measures. Using the tools of the IT revolution, al-Qaeda networks developed safe command-and-control structures in several MENA countries, and used their members in those countries to target and execute acts of terror. In Saudi Arabia's case they clearly intended to destabilize the al-Saud regime; in other instances, by attacking soft targets (synagogues, residential complexes for expatriates, hotels), their intention seems to have been to drive a wedge between Muslims and non-Muslims, between elites and their popular base, and between Muslim states and the West. One commentator has noted that the November 2003 suicide bombings in Istanbul were a deliberate 'political message that Jews and Muslims should not mix. [It was retribution for the fact] that Turkey and Israel have a close military alliance and that Turkey had been considering sending troops to help Iraq'.[44] This analysis was eerily consistent with the message put out by bin Laden himself: 'God says', he had warned, 'O ye who believe! "Take not the Jews and the Christians for your friends and protectors: they are but friends and protectors to each other". And he amongst you that turns to them [for friendship] is of them'.[45]

So, in an interesting twist of history, precisely at the moment that MENA governments were beginning to consider opening up the state, lowering their many rigid barriers to global flows of commerce, people and information, just as they were yielding some of their powers to national and globalizing forces, regional governments such as Saudi Arabia's were being pressed by their international allies as well as their violent opponents to raise the barriers, protect the state, and make its presence in society even more intrusive. Globalist jihadis have thus, possibly inadvertently, forced MENA countries again to put the state in the way of globalization. Their projection of a transnational Muslim presence beyond the boundaries of the individual nation-states has directly challenged the already fragile political contract in the region, dangerously forcing the regimes to balance what are essentially their technical requirements for survival against such significant legitimizing pillars as identity.

The Saudi slogan 'you are either with the country [the state] or with terrorism [transnational Muslim forces that emerged in the aftermath of the Riyadh bombing of 9 November 2003]' exemplifies the problem rather well.[46] The Saudi establishment has to maintain its interests in, and perceived responsibilities towards, the Muslim world while at the same time focusing on the imperatives of protecting its national security from direct attack by transnational Islamist forces. Ultimately, by resisting Western power in the region, what they regard as the political machinery of globalization, globalist jihadis have also targeted the modern Muslim state itself. Their personification of this resistance, through their suicide missions and other violent acts in Muslim countries, singles them out as martyrs to a wider Muslim cause. By their ability to reach the *ummah* (the whole Islamic world) – through cyberspace, and both over the heads of the regimes and beneath their feet (beneath the security radar of the state) – they have conveniently positioned themselves as bridgeheads in the fight for preservation of the zone of piety in the face of attacks on Islam by the West. The MENA state is hopelessly exposed to the full force of the political winds blowing with globalization. The unwelcome war on terror, now imposed on Arab elites in particular, helps in widening an already large gap between Westernizing masters of the state and their largely religious and traditionalist societies.

Furthermore, by pitching their message at the *ummah* level, the globalist jihadis are reweaving similar tensions in state–society relations in the Arab world to those that existed at the height of the Arab nationalist struggles between Arab nation and Arab state. What ensued then was divided loyalties among the Arab peoples and a weak, fractured and fragmented Arab state system. Ultimately, that battle was won by the state, and Iraq's invasion of neighbouring Kuwait in August 1990 was perhaps the last nail in the coffin of pan-Arabism as an intra-state political force. Since then, an already exposed region has been more systematically dominated by outside powers. In the twenty-first century we may well be witnessing a more emphatic redrawing of the same battlefield between the MENA state and a transnational force. But this time the lines are being put between the state and globalization, and between the state and radical pan-Islamism, the latter being an inordinately more resourceful force than pan-Arabism. The state itself, this time around, is also in a more vulnerable position. On one hand it is facing a serious 'demographic crisis' at home, while on the other it is attempting to mediate the intrusive aspects of globalization on society.

The geopolitics of pan-Islamism is another factor to bear in mind. Inter-Arab rivalries from the 1950s to the 1990s were largely played out in the Arab arena itself. By contrast, today's globalist jihadis feel free to take their campaign to every corner of the Muslim world, and are thus able to manipulate the geopolitical map of the conflict with the West and the ruling Muslim regimes to suit their agenda. They can apply pressure where needed, confident in the fact that wherever they act, the consequences of their actions will be felt in the Middle East region. A classic example of this was 9/11 and its fall-out in the Middle East. But the US–UK invasion of Iraq in March 2003, invasion of a powerful Arab actor and the eastern gateway to the Arab world, has provided another example of the ways in which new twists can surface in an already difficult relationship. Iraq's occupation took place under the pretext of disarmament and the need to prevent Saddam Hussein from arming al-Qaeda and other terrorists with deadly weapons of mass destruction. The fact that no significant links were found between the Iraqi regime and al-Qaeda seemed hardly to matter, nor indeed the reality that Iraq was no longer in a position to develop, let alone stockpile, weapons of mass destruction.

However, as a consequence of the Iraq war, the arc of crisis from Palestine to the Euphrates deepened and the Western presence in the Middle East substantially broadened. The war, ostensibly fought on behalf of Iraqis and the civilized world, added more weight to the Islamists' assertion that America was actively conspiring to destroy powerful Muslim countries for Israel's benefit. The war then played straight into the hands of al-Qaeda, helping them in opening yet another front in their jihad. A typical proponent of the view that the USA is forcing changes in the geopolitics of the region is bin Laden himself, who analysed the (impending) war in these terms: 'We are following up with great interest and extreme concern the crusaders' preparations for war to occupy a former capital of Islam, loot Muslims' wealth, and install an agent government, which would be a satellite for its masters in Washington and Tel Aviv, just like all the other treasonous and agent Arab governments. This would be in preparation for establishing the Greater Israel'.[47] The fact that their other perceived foe, the Shia people, would benefit from the war was another unexpressed concern of al-Qaeda.

As already noted, the war has helped in yet another redrawing of the geopolitical map of the region, and it is likely that in the course of the next decade inter-state relations will begin to conform more closely with the region's new power realities. This pattern is already evident in the way that Bahrain, Jordan, Morocco and Qatar are realigning to take advantage of the opportunities presented by a deeper engagement with the USA. On the other side of the equation, it is also noteworthy that Turkey, Egypt, Syria and Iran – the big hitters in the region – have, in one way or another, found themselves more on the margins of these new alignments, with Iran and Syria deliberately being singled out by the USA as destabilizing actors. The relationship between the USA and these two neighbours of Iraq could become even more tense if Baghdad was to emerge in the course of the next decade as a strong state, a stable friend of the West, and one of its main Arab economic and security partners. But, looking at the deep crisis in Iraq in the early twenty-first century, this must be a big 'if'. Things can easily spin out of control in rather unexpected ways.

Consider a not altogether implausible situation, for example, in which Iraq in the twenty-first century is dismembered as a solution to its inherent geopolitical problems, to again resemble Mesopotamia at the beginning of the twentieth century: a division into three 'districts' of Mosul, Baghdad and Basra. This alternative did not reach the planners' drawing board in the immediate aftermath of the fall of Baghdad, but one can envisage a situation in which Iraq's continuing problems make disaggregation an acceptable scheme. The unravelling of such a pivotal Arab state as Iraq into two (one Kurdish, one Arab) or three (Kurdish, Sunni, Shia) statelets will have consequences of historic magnitude. Not only would it shift power in the region and reshape the geography of the area, but it would also leave the door open for further territorial revisions in the Middle East at a time when the state is under siege from internal pressures and those of globalization. Other multi-ethnic and multi-national countries of the Middle East and West Asia, of which there are many, will have little choice but to erect defensive barriers around themselves and reinforce their authority through further centralization of power. This outcome will be diametrically opposed to the flow of globalization and its barrier-erasing tendencies. As the twenty-first century unfolds, we could inherit the wind in the Middle East in terms of more wars, inter-state conflicts and social violence, rather than the democracy wave out of Baghdad that was so eagerly promoted by the Bush White House in 2003.

But if the region experiences dissolution of its existing territorial states into smaller units, into a numerically larger group of states that are qualitatively more fragile, this will not help in the consolidation of globalization in the Middle East. This kind of downsizing cannot provide for the basic minimum requirements of capitalist expansion, or indeed for the immediate needs of the people. Dysfunctional states, as these dismembered countries will inevitably be, cannot advance the cause of stability. What happens in Iraq, therefore, and the probable destruction of the 'artificial' state of Iraq, will have huge implications for the countries of the region – Arab and non-Arab alike – and will redefine a wide range of relationships in the region, renegotiating the identity, culture, security, economics, religion and politics of nations encompassing a vast population base. The intra-Islamic dimension of the question, moreover, cannot be underestimated. With the fall of Baghdad, the Shia factor has now developed into a full-blown political force to challenge Sunni supremacy in the heart of the Arab world. The Shia factor also threatens further to generate an even stronger anti-Shia Sunni backlash, stretching from Indonesia to North and West Africa. Al-Qaeda violence will be joined by other Salafi and militant Sunni forces in efforts to contain the Shii. The Sunni–Shia struggles will directly affect Iran's relations with its Sunni neighbours, possibly straining its good relations with such powerful neighbours as Saudi Arabia, Pakistan and Turkey. The rise of the Shia in Iraq will also complicate US relations with the Arab world, for – rightly or wrongly – it is seen as the sponsor of Shiism in the Arab world. For some Arab Islamists, the USA's violent removal of the Ba'ath regime in Iraq is part of the same strategy of domination that seeks to strengthen the 'heretical' Shia and the 'Zionist-crusaders' of Israel against the Sunni (and Arab) majority.

MENA states, therefore, will inevitably find themselves caught up in the tailwind of al-Qaeda's operations in Muslim lands. The consequences for the MENA states of al-Qaeda's ability to capitalize on globalization's time–space compression, and the West's security-orientated reactions to al-Qaeda actions, will assure a high degree of uncertainty in inter-state relations in the Middle East, which will in turn cause serious unease about further opening up of the politico-economic space in every capital in the region.

Al-Qaeda's strategy also influences the geometry of the region. When bin Laden declares that 'the most qualified regions for liberation are Jordan,

Morocco, Nigeria, Pakistan, the land of the two holy mosques [Saudi Arabia], and Yemen'.[48] one should be fairly sure that is where the fire of his troopers will be directed. Such statements reflect an open-ended and extensive conflict, broad in scope as well as geography. What al-Qaeda promises is not dissimilar in process to the dynamics of globalization itself. Without protection, the MENA state can easily become a victim of the explosive mix of these two forces.

6 Economic Internationalization and the Changing Balance of Economic Power in the Middle East

> Like most of the Arab world, we in Saudi Arabia had adopted the attitude that the government will always provide for, take care of and shield us, sometimes even from normal market forces. In fact, it did too good a job in the 1970s and early 1980s and even insulated us from taking on certain jobs by allowing foreign laborers to be brought in, in numbers that grew over the years.
>
> Lubna Olayan, Jeddah Economic Forum, 17 January 2004.

Figures Speak for Themselves

The undeclared big fear of globalization in the Middle East is of international economic marginalization on the one hand, and economic domination and subjugation on the other.[1] These are sentiments shared by countless others across the continents: globalization 'evokes much anger and anxiety in the South and tends to be experienced as yet another round of northern domination and concentration of power and wealth. In the slipstream of hundreds of years of weary experience, the common metaphor for globalization in the South is imperialism or neo-colonialism revisited'.[2] It is in the sense of powerlessness accompanying globalization that the real fear of many millions of communities in the developing world rests. Where some countries and regions seem able to overcome the fear, and forge ahead and accept the risks of riding the tide of globalization, others either fall by the wayside or, worse still, are crushed by the weight and volume of the tide. Despite concerted attempts at accommodation with globalization by some countries in the region (Bahrain, Israel, Tunisia, Jordan, Morocco, Turkey, UAE), the bulk of the MENA region remains firmly in the timid camp of countries, fearing change that could lead to loss of control.[3] The reason for this is simple – globalization is perceived as a negative economic force. Globalization in the MENA context implies 'reduced public assistance, reduced oil revenues, and even reduced arms subsidies. It means opening most domestic markets to foreign competition that is usually better equipped in skills, capital, and marketing power than local producers. Just as the

European imports of the nineteenth and early twentieth centuries had destroyed much of the MENA's handicraft industries, so a new wave of competition could annihilate years of independent state-led capitalist development in much of the region, including Israel'.[4] But much MENA economic data suggest that without fundamental and rapid change, the region is probably heading for a far less palatable outcome than even submission to globalization might suggest.[5] If one were to consider political, market and economic factors as the defining features of the region's global standing, then in global rankings the region's top six economies stack up as follows: Turkey is number 41, Saudi Arabia is 42, Egypt is 43, Algeria is number 55, and Iran and Iraq are 59 and 60, respectively.[6] Furthermore, according to the Heritage Foundation's 2005 Index of Economic Freedom, the MENA region was the only part of the world to experience a decline in economic freedom. The region's least economically free were Iran, Libya and Syria, with scores of 4.40, 4.16 and 3.90, respectively; and Bahrain, Israel and the UAE were seen as the region's most economically free. The region's freest economy was ranked only 20th in the world, however, and the UAE 48th.[7] In terms of 'good governance' indicators, the region does equally badly: the highest-ranked in the 2005 world governance competence table was the UAE at 29, followed by Israel at 40. Saudi Arabia stood at 92. Three other large economies: Algeria, Iran and Syria, were ranked as 129, 145 and 149, respectively, in the world rankings.[8] These data hardly paint a promising picture, despite the rapid oil price rises of the post-2002 period.

It is therefore prudent to begin our discussion of economic globalization and the Middle East with a brief survey of the prevailing economic conditions in the area. This is to be expected, given that per capita gross domestic product in the MENA region actually fell by 2.7 per cent in the 1980s, and real per capita export earnings for the region dropped by more than 4 per cent a year in the 1980–93 period.[9] Kamrava has demonstrated that the MENA region's role in terms of share in world trade, technology exports and direct foreign investment is actually rather poor, arguing that the region accounts for just 8 per cent of total merchandise exports from the developing world, and only 16 per cent of its manufactured exports.[10] For a region so close to the rich markets of Europe and not far from the emerging markets of Asia and Africa, which is well endowed in natural resources and abundant labour, the data present a startling picture.

Speaking at the Dubai Strategy Forum's second annual meeting in 2002, Prince Walid bin Talal al-Saud articulated the predicament of the regional economies with the observation that Africa and the Middle East in general, and the 'Arab world in particular has been afflicted with an economic malaise that can best generate anaemic growth'.[11] The chief architect of the acclaimed UNDP reports, Rima Khalaf Hunaidi, started her own interventions at the 2004 World Economic Summit in Jordan with a reference to the plight of the Arabs, noting that one out of every two women in the Arab world are illiterate, 10 million children do not attend school, and per capita income in the Arab world is the second slowest-growing in the world.[12] Numerous economic studies of the region have drawn similar conclusions. The 2002 *Arab Human Development Report* (AHDR), for example, has noted that 'GDP in all Arab countries combined stood at $531.2 billion in 1999 – less than that of a single European country'.[13] The report also noted that one in five Arabs live on less than US$2 per day, and the Arab unemployment rate of 15 per cent is the highest in the developing world. It is estimated that over 80 million new jobs will have to be created between 2004 and 2014 if the tide is to be turned.[14] The region's 3.6 per cent average growth rate in the early twenty-first century was barely faster than the 3 per cent gain in population levels, providing hardly any real room for growth and expansion.

Such economic stagnation has brought with it social tensions and political instability. Even in searching for the reasons for the violence unleashed by radical Islamism, great emphasis has been placed on the problems associated with the political economy of the region. Alan Richards, for example, has argued forcefully that the regional socio-economic crisis is to blame for much that is wrong with the region today. The crisis is simultaneously internal and external, he argues. It is a crisis of the domestic realm compounded by the pressures of the external. He states:

> it is internal because of population growth, failed economic policies, local authoritarianism, and cultural issues. It is external because wider forces of globalization play a critical role in stimulating growth and spread of radicalism. Much of the region's economic stagnation derives from its weak and distorted integration into the global economy ... failure of local regimes stems from a failure to manage and engage successfully the wider process of globalization.[15]

As Richards notes, the region's unique geopolitical condition, in terms of over-reliance on oil income and the domination of the area by European colonial powers, has had a largely negative impact on its ability to respond to the economic challenges facing it today.

Oil and the Shifting Balance of Economic Power

As noted above, the region's economic performance since the end of the big nationalizations of the 1960s and 1970s has been poor. But it is worth emphasizing that the region, until recently, was anything but stagnant. 'Backwardness' is not how the MENA economies were being characterized in the second half of the 1960s and 1970s. Remba stated in 1966, for example, that the '155 million people of the [MENA] region – nearly 100 million in Arab countries and 56 million in non-Arab countries – are considerably better off than a billion other people in Asia and Africa. Average per capita income more than doubled from less than $100 at the end of

World War II to $200–250 by the mid-1960's'.[16] Dramatic transformations were already under way in the 1950s. However, it was not until the advent of high oil income, coupled with the rapid expansion in the state-led capitalist economies, that a period of sustained vibrancy was noticeable. Through large investment projects, the state pushed the boundaries of economic growth to new heights. As Table 6.1 illustrates, both large and small countries in the region recorded historically high growth rates.

The region was seen in a positive light by international organizations as well, and some countries (Iran, Israel, Turkey) were being identified as fast-growing potential newly industrializing countries, which could also lead the way for others, such as Egypt, Saudi Arabia and possibly Algeria, to follow.

The World Bank notes that in the 1960–85 period the MENA region 'outperformed all other regions except East Asia' in both income growth per head and the equality of income distribution.[17] By 1990, 'only 5.6% of the population in MENA lived on less than $1 a day, compared with 14.7% in East Asia and 28.8% in Latin America'.[18] The World Bank is not known for unfounded praise, and these statements are indeed a reflection of the high level of development that the MENA countries have managed to attain, albeit as a result of the étatist phases of its development in the second half of the twentieth century.

High oil income from the late 1960s added a new dimension to this trend. Indeed, as a consequence of the enormous capital generated by oil exports, in the course of the 1970s a new category of countries began appearing in the World Bank tables – that of the 'capital-surplus' countries. Their development indicators established the Gulf Arab states as a new group of high-income countries. Their rise fundamentally transformed the political economy of the MENA region. El Azhary makes the point that the combined gross domestic product of the six Gulf Arab states had increased to around US$211 billion in 1981, which was a 19-fold increase from the US$11 billion figure recorded in 1971. This growth had been achieved in a very short period. Massive increase in oil revenues 'was accompanied by a very rapid

Table 6.1 Average annual GDP growth in selected MENA countries, 1965–80

Country	Growth rate
Algeria	6.8
Egypt	6.8
Iran	6.2
Morocco	5.6
Oman	13.0
Saudi Arabia	11.3
Syria	8.7
Tunisia	6.6
Turkey	6.3

Source: World Bank.

expansion in the economies of these countries which can be seen in a 14-fold increase in the value of manufacturing production between 1971 and 1981, a 15-fold increase in the service producing sector, and a 42-fold increase in construction'.[19]

Alnasrawi has also noted that, as recently as 1962, the combined GNP of the Arab world was only US$19 billion, and the gap between the oil-producing and non-oil-producing states was relatively small: for the oil states their per capita GNP stood at US$270 and for the non-oil states it was US$162. The oil states received 36 per cent of the total Arab national income, while the non-oil states received 64 per cent of the same in the early 1960s. 'It is worth noting', remarks Alnasrawi, that before the oil boom 'Egypt was the country with the highest level of GNP [in the Arab world], more than twice that of Saudi Arabia'.[20] In the next 10 years the picture was to change rather dramatically. Between 1962 and the early 1980s, the non-oil-producing Arab states' share of Arab GNP had declined to 30 per cent in 1974 and 25 per cent in 1981: 'at the same time there occurred an increase in the relative share of the oil-producing states in Arab GNP from 38% to 75%'.[21] Higher oil exports and the dramatically higher price for oil increased the national income of the Arab oil producers from US$26.2 billion in 1972 to US$78.6 billion in 1974. By contrast, the national income of the non-oil Arab states only increased 'from $24.7 billion in 1972 to $33.5 billion in 1974'.[22] This massive geopolitical transformation of the region following the oil-price rises of the 1970s is all the more remarkable when set against the historical record of income generated from oil exports (Table 6.2). In any of the years after 1974, the Middle East members of OPEC generated many times more income from oil exports than they had done in the entire 1946–64 period. In geopolitical terms, oil shifted the economic weight of the region, most notably in the Arab world, from the large étatist economies of the Levant to a small group of largely free-market economies in and around the Arabian Peninsula.

Oil therefore changed the economic balance of the MENA region, creating new dependencies between the oil producers themselves and the West, and between the oil exporters and their Arab hinterland. As the oil boom took effect, the latter became increasingly dependent on aid and expatriate labour income from the 'capital surplus' Gulf Arab countries.[23] Thus, less

Table 6.2 MENA oil income, 1946–64 (US$ million)

Persian Gulf States	Oil income	Other States	Oil income
Iran	3020	Jordan	35
Iraq	3040	Algeria	190
Kuwait	4615	Libya	230
Saudi Arabia	4842	Syria	215

Source: Oded I. Remba (1966), p. 84.

than 10 years into the 'oil boom', labour remittances had emerged as a major source of income for the Arab non-oil-producers:

> Remittances to Jordan, Lebanon, the two Yemens exceeded total commodity exports from these four countries [in 1980] ... remittances contributed 22% of the GNP of Jordan, 25% of Lebanon's GNP, 40% of the GNP of North Yemen and 44% of the GNP of South Yemen. Even for a country like Egypt, foreign remittances constituted 11% of its GNP and contributed to the equivalent of 87% of its total commodity export earnings.[24]

From the 1970s, oil became a major source of income for both oil-producing and non-oil-producing states in the Middle East and beyond, and allowed the traditional Arab states to overtake their 'revolutionary' counterparts in development and modernization. And there was apparently no end to the prosperity generated by the oil income. 'The result was that it became all too easy for us to give jobs at all levels to foreign labor rather than taking on the task of training our own young people. At the present time, there are between 3.5 million and 3.7 million foreign workers [in Saudi Arabia]', noted Lubna Olayan at the 2004 Jeddah Economic Forum meeting, 'who last year sent more than SR60,000 million [US$16,000 million] out of the economy. And over the past 10 years collectively, they have sent home SR586,000 million [US$156,267 million]. We could have domesticated some of those jobs and retained some of those funds in our economy'.

But as oil income became cyclical again and manifested a decline from the mid-1980s, and as the limits of ISI began to surface more rapidly across the region, so the economic ills of the region that oil income had partially covered, and had also partially deepened, began to surface.[25] Beyond this, the impact of the Six Day War in June 1967 on the political economy of the Arab region should not be overlooked. Until that point, Boudroua argues, there was every chance that 'reconstruction of Arab industry, which, if it had been sustained, would have led to real industrial development'.[26]

Malaise Amidst Opportunity

Yet, recent data suggests that the region had begun its slow decline amidst the bounty of oil revenues. The situation was worsened because of the restrictive practices, inflexible labour force and bureaucracies, and other inefficiencies (like subsidies) resulting from years of entrenched corporatism. In other respects, such factors as rapid population growth also certainly took their toll, reducing much of the economic gains accrued in the 1960s and 70s. The continuing dependence on natural resources for economic development has also been a problem for many MENA economies. Petroleum now dominates the economies of over half of MENA countries, and where it is not the main economic engine other minerals take its place. Thus, in the second half of the 1990s natural resources made up 53 per cent of Syria's GNP (and 62 per cent of its exports), 36 per cent of Egypt's (and 65 per cent of its exports), 32 per cent of Tunisia's (and 27 per cent of its exports), 29 per cent of Morocco's (and 45 per cent of its exports), and 20 per cent of Jordan's (and 50 per cent of its exports).[27]

Despite its internationalized political economy, in terms of international competitiveness and absorption of foreign capital the region has lagged behind all other regions bar sub-Sahara Africa. As has been noted by economists specializing in the region, foreign investment inflows (foreign direct investment, FDI), which acts as a measure of economic prowess, are pathetically small at present to make a serious impact on the region's debilitating economic difficulties. Hisham al-Razzuqi (chief executive of Gulf Investment Corporation) notes that in 2001 'the total FDIs inflow into the six [GCC] countries stood at $38.7 billion, including $26 billion in [Saudi Arabia] alone, while the total FDI flow to the Asian Tigers (South Korea, Taiwan, Hong Kong, Singapore, Malaysia, Thailand and Indonesia) during the same period was $774 billion. Hong Kong alone attracted $451 billion, over 11 times higher than the total FDI inflow of the GCC'.[28] In Iran, according to an IMF report, between 1993 and 1997 '50 [foreign investment] projects, totalling US$722 millions, were approved; however, actual investment inflows amounted to a total of US$40 millions'.[29] The stark difference between these figures and those of the Far East is quite shocking, symptomatic of the bigger problems facing the region, even though Egypt's prime minister of the day tried to portray a more positive image of his country's FDI. The officially announced FDI figure for 2002–3 of $600–800 million was 'not accurate', explained Atef Ebeid, at a major conference in Egypt, as it did not include the FDI in both the inland and free zone areas together with investment in the petroleum sector, real estate and capital market, the FDI figure would be closer to $2 billion.[30]

One of the direct consequences of low investment of course is under-employment and under-utilization of factors of production. Of all factors of production the condition of labour is the most sensitive and in the MENA region this means high unemployment and underemployment.[31] An International Labour Organization report in 2002 estimated that of a total global unemployment figure of 180 million people some 18 per cent were in the Middle East and North Africa, followed by Sub-Sahara Africa (14.3 per cent).[32] Not only does this represent waste of an important resource, but also underlines the point made by Alan Richards noted earlier that the political consequences of the 'internal crises' in the region poses a very serious challenge to stability of the entire area, and indeed a challenge for the globalization of its economies.

A key problem of the region in the second half of the twentieth century was the way in which state-led economic activity helped isolate the region from international developments.[33] As a consequence, the region today has the second highest level of trade barriers in the world, and one of the highest levels of government intervention in the economy.[34] Autocratic economic systems, accompanied by an import substitution industrialization (ISI) strategy, compounded the region's problems in the aftermath of declining oil incomes and the failure of ISI to deliver productivity, income growth and an efficient and responsive economic system.[35] Despite long association with the world economy through the oil trade and financial flows, economic autocracy-imposed isolation stored up deep structural problems, which were severely tested by globalization. As already mentioned, the evidence for the decline was to be found within several macroeconomic indicators: in the slowing growth rate figures from the 1980s, low investment rates, weak trade profiles, high unemployment and underemployment rates, high population growth rates against low productivity and national output levels, and the extensive relative poverty gripping the region.

From the Periphery to the Global: The Geo-economics of Oil

Yet much internationalization – leading to economic globalization – had already begun to take place in the 1970s, creating a critical socio-economic group in the Middle East region which was structurally linked to global capitalism. These were essentially the comprador-type classes spoken of by the dependency school. Ajami's graphic description of the structural relationship cannot be surpassed: 'If the Sadat diplomacy [towards Israel in the late 1970s] was a revolt, an exit by a poor society, the wealthy Arab states had exited in their own way. Great wealth had practically northernized some Arab states – in material standards but not culture, to be sure ... Their wealth had knit them in the Western-based international economic system'.[36]

Mohammad Ja'far has further clarified the dynamism of the relationship as it evolved: 'Arab ruling classes, which were composed of comprador bourgeoisies and big landowners up to the first half of the twentieth century, are today [in the 1970s] in the process of transforming themselves. The accumulation of vast financial reserves in the oil-producing countries is now creating a bourgeoisie of a cosmopolitan character whose arena for investment is the world capitalist market. At the same time, powerful local bourgeoisies have been or are being greatly strengthened by the experiences of state capitalism that countries like Egypt, Algeria and Iraq have been going through'.[37] Iran was another actor here, whose political economy combined a strong comprador class with a powerful bonapartist state. Before the revolution, Iran was well on its way to joining the newly industrializing countries, and its economic performance was often compared with some of the leading less-developed economies, most notably South Korea and Brazil. The oil boom then, and the economics of petrodollar recycling, created an advance guard for international capitalism in the Middle East, which was instinctively and organically attached to the circulation of capital at the global level. This was the region's 'cosmopolitan bourgeoisie'.[38] Ja'far has argued that this globalist bourgeoisie, by its very existence, is tied to the fortunes of the capitalist centres of power in the world. Ruling classes who were marked and damned by radical socialists for their extrovert tendencies, rather than introverted, region-based leanings, were slowly but surely changing the political economy of the region, opening it up to global capitalism. Powerful elites were being created from the traditional and conservative societies of the Arabian Peninsula whose prosperity was based on their relationship with the world capitalist system. In the course of the 1970s and 1980s, the Arab cosmopolitan bourgeoisie developed intricate links with foreign capital, rapidly opening up the domestic economy to international economic forces. Thus the Gulf economies were already 'globalizing' before the 1990s, when the movement is supposed to have taken hold internationally.

By extension, the rentier-dependent economies of the Arab world (Egypt, Sudan, Yemen, Palestine and Jordan) also became more vulnerable to the global winds of change. Egypt's open-door policy of the early 1970s is, in part, a reflection of these developments. But even beyond the Arab world, such large economies as Turkey and Iran were also consciously moving away from the ISI strategy towards an export-led approach to economic development. Iran in the mid-1970s and Turkey in the late 1970s had opted for the export-led model of growth, putting in place the infrastructure for this change in strategy. In Iran's case the pace of change proved to be too rapid, and led to the fall of the monarchy and with it the comprador bourgeoisie. In Turkey, the military government took charge of the economy in 1980 and pushed through many of the essential reforms for making the economy more externally oriented. Despite a series of crises in the 1980s and the 1990s – associated with high inflation (50–60 per cent between 1980 and 1990), a major financial sector crisis, the massive devaluation of the Lira in 1994, and high unemployment (reaching nearly 12 per cent in 2002) – Turkey today is characterized as 'a highly dynamic economy'.[39]

It is therefore fair to say that, just as the oil boom of the 1970s strengthened the role of the state and the corporatist elites of the Middle East, it also deepened and accelerated the pace of internationalization of MENA economies.[40] Internationalization of the region's oil-exporting economies was in evidence even before the oil boom, but from the early 1970s the rate of integration of these economies with the capitalist world accelerated quite rapidly. This is reflected in their trade figures, and the prominent role of petroleum exports in their overall export figures. Even in the less-known oil states such as Syria, some US$2.9 billion a year is now earned from oil exports; around US$900 million in Sudan, and a similar amount by Yemen.

Table 6.4 highlights the rapid rise in the 1970s and 1980s of the value of exports from the Gulf states, the bulk of which is accounted for by oil exports. In all six cases noted, oil exports and related products made up the largest proportion of their exports. The income generated by oil exports tied the oil states more tightly to the West, as their investments were made largely in the West and as their imports from the West also increased quite rapidly.

The same trade pattern was in evidence in the case of the region's other major oil exporters (Table 6.5). In North Africa, Algeria and Libya both showed a high dependency on oil exports. In the former, the proportion of oil exports to total exports hardly changed in the decade following the oil boom, and in Libya's case petroleum exports dominated its trade profile from the very beginning of the oil boom in the newly established revolutionary regime of Colonel Muammer Qaddafi.

External debt, which further tied the region to external forces, had emerged as a major problem by the late 1980s, compounded as it was by soft oil prices and mounting economic problems in both the oil-exporting and the non-oil MENA countries.[41] Table 6.6 postulates some of the possible political consequences to have followed the debt crisis in the region. It shows that as debt increased, it slowly eroded the political stability of several

Table 6.3 Oil dependence in trade and GDP (late 1990s) (%)

	As percentage of:	
	Exports	GDP
Algeria	97	52
Kuwait	99	52
Oman	95	52
Saudi Arabia	99	52
UAE	96	49
Iran	96	37

Source: World Bank Data Base.

Table 6.4 Selected Persian Gulf States – value of total and petroleum exports, 1973–90 (US$ billion)

		1973	1975	1977	1979	1980	1982	1984	1986	1988	1990
Iran	A	6.2	20.2	24.3	19.8	12.3	20.5	17.1	7.2	10.7	19.3
	B	5.6	19.6	23.6	19.2	11.7	20.2	16.7	6.3	9.7	18.0
Iraq	A	1.9	8.3	9.6	21.6	26.4	10.0	9.3	7.5	9.6	10.3
	B	1.8	8.2	9.2	21.4	26.1	9.9	8.9	7.0	9.3	9.6
Kuwait	A	3.8	9.2	9.7	18.4	19.7	10.9	11.6	7.4	7.6	7.1
	B	3.5	8.6	8.9	17.3	19.0	9.1	11.0	6.4	6.8	6.4
Qatar	A	0.6	1.8	2.1	3.8	5.8	4.4	4.5	1.8	2.2	3.9
	B	0.6	1.8	2.1	3.7	5.4	4.2	4.4	1.7	1.7	3.3
S.Ar.	A	8.9	29.7	43.5	63.4	109.1	79.1	37.5	20.1	24.4	44.4
	B	8.9	29.4	43.3	62.9	108.2	78.2	36.3	18.1	20.2	40.1
UAE	A	2.2	7.4	10.1	14.8	22.0	18.2	16.0	10.1	12.3	23.5
	B	2.0	7.0	9.3	12.8	19.4	16.0	12.1	7.0	7.6	15.0

Source: OPEC, *Annual Statistical Bulletin* (various years). Figures have been rounded up for convenience. A = value of total exports; B = value of petroleum exports.

Table 6.5 Value of total and petroleum exports in OPEC North Africa, 1973–90 (US$ billion)

		1973	1975	1977	1979	1980	1982	1984	1986	1988	1990
Algeria	A	1.9	4.7	6.0	9.5	14.0	13.2	13.0	7.8	7.8	9.6
	B	1.5	4.3	5.7	8.7	13.0	11.2	9.8	5.2	5.7	9.6
Libya	A	4.1	6.8	11.4	16.1	22.0	14.0	11.1	8.2	6.7	13.2
	B	3.9	6.7	11.4	16.0	22.0	13.7	11.0	8.2	6.0	10.1

Source: OPEC, *Annual Statistical Bulletin* (various years). Figures have been rounded up for convenience. A = value of total exports; B = value of petroleum exports.

Table 6.6 External debt of main Arab debtors, 1970 and 1988 (percentage of GDP)

	1970	1988	*Comment*
Sudan	14.8	74.6	Regime change in 1989
Yemen AR	–	41.7	Regime change in 1990
Egypt	22.5	126.7	Camp David accords in 1979
Morocco	18.6	89.8	
Tunisia	38.6	64.2	Regime change in 1987
Jordan	22.9	94.0	Severance of link with World Bank in 1988
Syria	10.8	25.0	
Algeria	19.8	46.6	Pressure for regime change in 1991
Yemen PDR	–	199.4	Regime change in 1990

Source: *World Development Report 1990*.

key states. Debt also undermined the MENA states' ability to cope with the pressures of globalization, as a higher proportion than normal of national income had to be assigned to debt repayment, thus restricting the availability of resources for domestic expansion.

Although, as compensation, relatively large amounts of petrodollars were recycled to the non-oil states through aid, soft loans and grants,[42] the difficulties of absorbing the high oil prices weakened their already fragile structures, hastening the pace of reform and structural adjustment in several MENA countries. As Table 6.7 shows, the better-off, middle-income countries had to find an extra US$14 billion for just the 2 years between 1973 and 1975 to finance 4.5 million barrels per day of oil imports. Many of these middle-income countries were themselves in the MENA region, and suffering from serious budget deficits.

More recently, the case of Jordan has shown that even fairly secure solutions to the problem of 'oil deficit' can be blown off course. In January 2004, some 10 months after the fall of the Ba'ath regime in Iraq, Amman was informed of the termination of the 13-year agreement with Iraq that had brought Jordan virtually all of the country's oil needs from Iraq (half at discount prices and half as a gift from the Iraqi dictator). Jordan immediately acknowledged that the disappearance of this arrangement would bring

Table 6.7 Oil imports of oil-importing developing countries, 1972–75

	Volume (million barrels per day)		Price per barrel (US$)	
	Low-income countries	Middle-income countries	Low-income countries	Middle-income countries
1972	0.4	3.3	0.4	3.6
1973	0.4	4.0	0.6	6.1
1974	0.4	4.2	1.8	19.2
1975	0.4	4.5	1.8	20.3

Source: World Bank Database.

chaos to the economy and much hardship to the Jordanians. Despite efforts to secure 'cheap' oil from the Gulf Arab states, it was expected that the inevitable increase in fuel prices would not only hurt the fragile economy, but also severely expose the nearly 2 million people who live below the poverty line to more hardship.[43]

Geopolitics and Globalization: The Visible Facets of Change

In terms of trade openness, indicating a measure of integration in the world economy and a feature of globalization, it would be wrong to classify any part of the MENA region as closed. Quite the opposite is true. As data from the Egypt-based Economic Research Forum demonstrate, the region is quite open when the share of trade to its GDP is considered. As the ERF notes, 'in 1996 trade/GDP ratios for the MENA region averaged 93 per cent (compared to 96 per cent for East Asia)'. Indeed, the paradox is that 'despite relatively high protection levels, most MENA countries have a medium to high propensity to trade (trade/GDP ratios ranged from 32 per cent in Iran to 207 per cent in Bahrain)'.[44]

In Turkey's case, as the country began dismantling its ISI system in the 1970s, so it began to re-link with the international trade system. Trade and investment followed Turkey's outward-looking economic policies. At the same time, however, Turkey was perhaps the first MENA country to show that the same policies of openness also exposed the economy to debt, a weak trade balance, and an even weaker currency (Table 6.8).[45]

If anything, the data illustrate very well the deleterious impact of sanctions, war and revolution on global integration of MENA economies (Table 6.9), highlighting one of the ways in which political problems have tended to distance the region from such potentially globalizing forces as direct foreign investment. In the case of Iran, which suffered both a revolution and a destructive war along with sanctions, it took over 20 years for the country to even begin to approach the trade/GDP ratios of the 1970s. Continuing US sanctions and political hostility between the two countries impose a heavy economic cost on Iran, weakening not only this oil giant's economic power, but also its ability to integrate more fully internationally and regionally. It is instructive that, in the light of the USA's hardening political line on Iran in early 2005, a number of major European companies chose to distance themselves from doing lucrative business with Iran. *The Wall Street Journal* commented that such decisions 'follow President George W. Bush's recent refusal to rule out using military force against Iran and Vice President Dick Cheney's assertion that Iran is 'at the top of the list' of global trouble spots'.[46]

In the case of Kuwait, the negative impact of the 1990/91 war lasted for over half a decade. The economic consequences of political turmoil cannot be overemphasized either, when we look at the plight of Iraq. These problems combined to inflict considerable damage on the region, even though certain countries may have temporarily benefited from the difficulties of their vulnerable neighbours. Geopolitical tensions that led to the marginalization of the region's key actors took their toll on the globalizing momentum of oil. In the words of the prominent businessman Prince Walid bin Talal al-Saud: 'My own view is that having lost our linkages and networks with others was one of the major contributory factors to our economic decline'.[47]

Globalization severely affects the state's ability to cater for the three realms of public good: the establishment and protection of public and private property rights, a stable currency, a regulatory system for economic activities, a system of trade protection and one of market failure protection;

Table 6.8 MENA trade openness: selected countries (percentage of GDP)

	1975	1980	1985	1990	1992	1994	1996
Algeria	76.5	6 4.7	43.9	48.6	47.2	52.1	56.8
Bahrain	–	239.3	191.6	221.7	223.7	191.0	206.9
Egypt	61.5	73.4	52.0	75.5	70.0	55.0	65.3
Iran	76.0	29.7	16.0	45.5	40.9	52.6	32.4
Kuwait	106.5	112.6	96.4	103.0	94.7	93.6	101.5
Saudi Arabia	99.2	101.0	80.0	82.4	84.5	69.8	73.5
Tunisia	64.0	85.5	70.2	94.2	86.0	92.3	88.6
Turkey	15.0	17.1	34.8	30.8	31.7	41.7	53.3
MENA	75.6	86.3	74.8	88.4	89.2	86.5	93.2

Sources: World Bank; Economic Research Forum.

Table 6.9 MENA economies in transition, 1960–81 (percentage of GDP).

	1960	1970	1981
Agriculture	24.1	19.8	11.6
Manufacturing	13.4	15.4	15.0
Other industry	18.0	19.6	28.9

Source: World Bank Database.

state-sponsored (or controlled) production and distribution (provision of infrastructure, subsidies); and the provision of redistributive public goods such as health and welfare services, employment policies, environmental protection and corporatist bargaining processes.[48] In the MENA region, all three realms have been under pressure since the 1980s and globalization has compounded the crisis.

The Last Chance to Join the Future

It was Muhammad Hassanain Haikal who said of the AHDR 2002 that it signalled the region's 'last chance to join the trip to the future'. How to acquire the ticket for the 'trip to the future' was the subject of the AHDR in 2003. The report has observed that knowledge, its collection, percolation and distribution, is the way of the future. A knowledge society, it states, means, 'instituting knowledge as the organizing principle of human life', something 'that Arab countries are far removed from'.[49] In terms of production of knowledge, the report notes that between 1980 and 1999/2000, Arab countries as a group registered 370 patents. In contrast, in the same period South Korea registered 16,328 patents and Israel 7,652. What might explain this deficiency in knowledge production? One reason is to be found in the rate of expenditure as a percentage of GNP for research and development funding, which is weak in the Arab world. In the Arab states as a group, the figure is a meagre 0.2 per cent of GNP, while in the USA the average expenditure is 3.1 per cent of GNP, and in a number of major European economies it is around 2.4 per cent. This is a fundamental problem in the region, which worsens the 'knowledge deficit' and its ability to increase productivity and creativity at home. In the era of knowledge economies and the Internet, the region has little choice but to introduce the rules being drawn up by the globalizing forces of the West, yet its authoritarian instinct is to try and control these forces. At the same time, the constant preoccupation with political crisis and conflict does not appear to provide the space for MENA states to address these fundamental deficiencies, even if the will may exist.

Critics of globalization argue, on the other hand, that if its shortcomings – it is a market-driven phenomenon that does not have adequate safety nets to deal with problems such as poverty, the environment, the inherent instability of global finance and other aspects of market failure – are not rectified, then globalization will only exacerbate the existing economic disparities between the industrial and developing countries. This represents an important objection to globalization, but the reality is that states can find ways of containing many of globalization's adverse effects. The more serious problem seems to be: can they face paying the high domestic price for doing so?

If we accept the argument that globalization has been driven by the two major forces of technological change and liberalization of trade and investment, then we need to ask, can the MENA countries take advantage of these related processes to profit from globalization? And secondly, how can they create the conditions for responding to the opportunities presented by globalization? It is clear that the force that has sustained globalization is the steady removal of both tariff and non-tariff barriers to trade and the reduction of restrictions on capital mobility between states. Figures from the General Agreement on Tariffs and Trade and its successor (the World Trade Organization) show that trade tariffs were reduced to less than 10 per cent in the early 1970s, and then again to as little as 5 per cent in the early twenty-first century. Tariffs on imports from the developing countries, imposed by the industrial countries, have fallen quite dramatically. In the USA in particular the average tariff has fallen from 11.4 per cent in recent decades to 8.7 per cent today; and in the European Union tariffs had fallen to 6.7 per cent in the 1980s.[50] However, the MENA region as a whole has not benefited from these tariff reductions, for two main reasons. Firstly, as crude oil (the mainstay of the region's economies) was not covered by the international trade negotiations, no reduction in the taxes imposed by the developed countries on their oil imports has been introduced. Thus oil exports continue to be heavily taxed by the industrial countries, with no tariff reduction benefits being introduced or passed on to the oil producers themselves. The trade in oil therefore remains subject to severe market imperfections.

Secondly, the region's own efforts to encourage intra-regional trade through the introduction of lower tariffs and the removal of other barriers to cross-border trade have been weak, excepting of course the GCC's efforts since 2003. The tragedy is that, for all the region's size, MENA states have not been able to compensate for their vulnerabilities at the international level through expanded intra-regional trade. Figures from the Economic and Social Commission for Western Asia (ESCWA) show that, despite 302 million inhabitants in the Arab world, its GDP of US$718 billion in 2003 (before the rapid rise in oil prices) was merely 2 per cent of the world's total GDP for that year. Arab intra-regional trade by the middle of the decade had stood at around 8 per cent of total international trade of the Arab world, despite the introduction of the Greater Arab Free Trade Area, according to ESCWA.[51] Intra-Arab direct investment stood at US$3.7 billion in 2003, a fraction of the estimated overseas Arab assets of some US$1.2 trillion.

To join the trade-and-investment train, the regional economies will therefore need to open up their markets and also find ways of reducing the cost of inter-regional trade as a means of increasing cross-border trade and investment within the MENA region. Apart from the association agreements being developed between the EU and the southern Mediterranean countries, and the USA's free-trade initiatives with Jordan, Bahrain, Qatar and Kuwait, the only other trade engine in the region is the GCC. Although small in terms of population base, nonetheless due to the sophistication of its economies and its size, as it gradually lowers tariffs and customs duties between its members, so the GCC will not only energize these vital economies themselves, but will actually encourage trade (and eventually investment) flows across the region. It can be argued, therefore, that a strong GCC is good for the future health of the Middle East region as a whole.[52] They are already the region's main investors and their corporations are heavily investing in infrastructure, construction, services and telecommunication sectors of other Arab countries.

A related point is that, as the GCC countries are already considered to be active participants in the world economy, theoretically their deeper engagement with the international system will pull the more sluggish MENA economies up with this group of countries.[53] The Far Eastern case provides a classic example of what is possible, despite the 1997 Southeast Asian crisis, which inflicted some short-term damage on the economies of that region. Gangnes and Naya demonstrate the 'cascading' effect of the follow-the-leader model: 'Japan's phenomenal growth in the early post-war period was an early signal to other countries in the region of the potential benefits of export-led growth. The message was reinforced by the success of Hong Kong and Singapore ... Korea and Taiwan ... took a cue from their success and that of Japan and began to move towards an export-led strategy in the 1960s'.[54] What is particularly interesting about these observations is that the Far East's geopolitical landscape of the time was as insecure as the Middle East's, and yet economic prosperity managed to take hold because of the presence and active involvement of regional role models such as Japan. Secondly, it is interesting that these huge economic shifts in the Far East were taking place at the height of the MENA region's étatist drive in the 1960s. In terms of timeline analysis, therefore, it could be argued that the MENA region was already being left behind the fast-developing Asian powerhouses.

Foreign investment and open trade have acted as the primary stimuli of economic growth over the past 30 years in the cases of Taiwan, Hong Kong, Singapore, South Korea, Japan, Thailand, Malaysia and Indonesia. As a group, these countries increased their share in world exports from just 8 per cent in 1965 to 13 per cent in 1980, and 18 per cent in 1990. The major source of this growth was manufactured exports. In the 1970s and 1980s, the four Asian 'tigers' increased their manufactured exports at a rate four times that of Japan.[55] China's economy since the 1970s has been built on foreign trade and investment flows, turning it into one of the largest economies of the world by the end of the twentieth century. By 2006 it had replaced France as the fifth largest economy in the world, and was poised to replace Britain as the fourth largest.

Nonetheless, for MENA states there are lessons to be learned from this Asian crisis in terms of the costs associated with an unfettered embrace of globalization.[56] The fear that global economic instabilities can be imported with fully open economic systems means that the state is reluctant to fully forego its controls over the domestic economy, despite the fact that, thanks to the oil trade, economic instabilities can already very easily enter the domestic arena of both oil exporters and aid importers. Also, the elites tend to shy away from radical decisions that could increase the social cost of economic reform, whether in terms of reductions to food and basic needs subsidies, or privatization of assets which could increase short- to medium-term unemployment.

Related to trade is the flow of investment. Internationally, the flow of capital has seen even faster growth than trade since the late 1980s. Foreign direct investment, portfolio investment and bank loans, have all grown in recent years. Capital flow achieves mutual gains for the parties concerned. In basic terms, to the investor, it is a way of diversifying and earning a higher return than in the home market. The host country, on the other hand, uses foreign investment for raising the level of investment capital in the economy and thus stimulating higher rates of economic growth – and extra revenue for the state through direct and indirect taxation. Transnational corporations tend to benefit the host country by bringing in new management skills and expertise, educational and training programmes, and by creating new and profitable links with outside suppliers and, even more importantly, with international markets.[57] Evidence from East Asia suggests that, for all its perceived faults, foreign direct investment can contribute directly to the expansion of output and exports from the host country. So it would seem obvious that the region needs to encourage foreign investment from established international corporations if it is to close the investment gap, expand the knowledge base, encourage research and development, generate new employment opportunities, penetrate new markets, and learn to adopt modern production techniques and processes. But this cannot happen if local capital retains the habit of taking flight. As Halliday suggests, focusing on the absence of FDI inflows distracts attention from another very real problem, that of 'massive flows of FDI *out* of the Middle East and into the OECD capital and property markets'.[58] With well over US$700 billion worth of Gulf Arab capital alone stashed overseas, it is not surprising that mechanisms for foreign capital absorption do not seem to have helped to generate inflows.[59] Such mechanisms remain weak across the region. Duke Anthony notes that 'just as constraining in its overall negative impact on economic growth has been the low level of private domestic investment in the GCC region in comparison to the extent of citizen money that exists. The latter has long exceeded what is known to be the amount of private financial largesse in any grouping of six contiguous developing countries elsewhere'. The effect of this problem, he states, needs underscoring, for: 'it has lessened substantially the overall financial wherewithal that the member-states need in order to grow their economies. It has constrained the degree to which they have been able to maintain and expand their commercial, industrial and service infrastructures. And, it has lowered the extent to which the GCC countries have been able to provide adequate meaningful employment for their burgeoning populations, the majority of which is youthful'.[60]

This picture may have changed somewhat since 9/11 and with the rapid rise in oil prices from 2003/4 onwards. The former encouraged GCC capital flight out of the USA and back to the region; the latter has generated huge amounts of cash for domestic investment and speculation.[61] Interestingly, GCC stock markets more than quadrupled in value between 2001 and 2005 (before their mini-crash in 2006), and Gulf capital has been exploiting opportunities at home as well as elsewhere in the region – notably in Egypt, Syria, Lebanon, Jordan, Tunisia and Morocco.[62] The cash injection has occurred at a rapid pace and at a high level across the oil-rich region, generating huge petrodollar surpluses in the region.[63] In the Gulf Arab countries, for example, net gains from oil exports stood at US$305 billion in 2005, compared with just US$60 billion in 1998. In Algeria, Iran and Libya, a similar picture of petrodollar plenty has been in evidence: OPEC data illustrate that in 2005 Algeria earned some US$40 billion from oil exports, Iran US$49 billion and Libya nearer US$30 billion. The biggest earner by far was Saudi Arabia, which pocketed some US$170 billion in oil-export income.

These figures reinforce the historic shift of economic power that began in the early 1970s in the Middle East, away from the larger actors. Since then, the small GCC states have played the prominent role in shaping the region's political economy. So long as hydrocarbons drive the global economy, they will add enormous economic and geopolitical weight to the smaller states of the region, and thus deepen the uneven balance of power in the area. The consequences of this for economic globalization of the region are great. It will encourage a multi-speed integration of the region into global processes (which could well accelerate with the introduction of a single currency in the GCC in 2010[64]), discourage the flow of investment capital into the less-endowed countries, widen the gap between the rich MENA states and their counterparts, and lead to further separation of the economies of the area, weakening the basis for regional integration. If in just one month – December 2005 – the six GCC states can manage to earn US$20 billion from their oil exports, what hope is there for the non-oil Arab economies to be able to compete with the powerhouses of the Gulf?[65] The problem can also be looked at from a different perspective and in macroeconomic terms. The UAE, with a population of just 4.3 million, today has a GDP greater than that of Egypt with 73 million people (US$98 billion compared with US$90 billion); Qatar's GDP of US$33.6 billion (with just 700,000 people) is today greater than that of Tunisia (US$30.5 billion) with 10 million people; and Saudi Arabia (26 million people) has a GDP (US$270 billion) greater than that of all its Arab neighbours combined.[66] The Kingdom's role as the dominant economic actor in the region is such that within the Greater Arab Free Trade Area (comprising 17 member states) it single-handedly accounts for 92.3 per cent of the total volume of trade of GAFTA members.[67]

The non-oil states can, of course, pursue their own course of economic liberalization, which may enable them to take better advantage of economic globalization, and also try and absorb some of the petrodollar windfall (through increased tourism, investment and labour remittances), but foreign corporate interests will always follow where spending power is the greatest, and that is still in the small states of the Arabian Peninsula.

Economic prosperity through globalization will come at a price, however: loss of sovereignty over economic policy and planning; danger of cross contamination if crisis hits other regions, and cultural vulnerability – the latter being a main concern of the oil-rich states Iran and Saudi Arabia in particular. But can the MENA countries absorb the possible negative effects of trade and investment liberalization in the short term, for bigger gains in the long run? Will the elites be able to absorb possible adverse consequences such as a rise in the number of unemployed, a shrinking bureaucracy (which, as it stands, is responsible for keeping millions of families above the poverty line), the exacerbation of poverty, a fall in government revenue, and reduction in subsidies? Evidence from across the region suggests that most still regard the price to be too high to pay for the promise of future prosperity.[68] There is good reason: this is an environment in which the distinctions between state and economy are still blurred, and the state (comprising a well established elite) is the dominant political and economic actor. As it is the agent that shapes the very 'terrain on which any ... reform is to be enacted ... the state's dominant role means that any reform process will be shaped by the logic of regime policy'.[69] In other words, the elite's calculations about regime survival override any technocratic plans for liberalization, or the introduction of broader reforms to meet the challenges and opportunities of economic globalization. Nazih Ayubi has cynically, but correctly, observed that if 'the private sector is gaining, it is not because of its initiatives, drive and organization, nor is it because the ruling elites have decided sincerely to hand the economy over to it. Rather, it is mainly because the state is no longer able ... to uphold its étatist and welfare policies at the same time'.[70] There is a political logic to liberalization, which has been highlighted by detailed studies of several MENA countries, and that logic is regime survival. In the last analysis, globalization is a powerful agent that can challenge the very basis of the ruling elites' survival strategies, and as such is resisted as much as it is accepted.

7 Culture Clash
Globalization and the Geopolitics of Identity in the Middle East

> The great divisions among mankind and the dominating source of conflict will be cultural.
> Samuel P. Huntington, 'The Clash of Civilizations?',
> *Foreign Affairs*, 72 (3), 1993, 22–49.

Culture Clash

As noted in chapter 1, the issue of identity cannot be separated from that of culture in relation to debates about globalization. In the Islamic greater Middle East, Islam is both a religion and a way of life, and this is daily reinforced and made routine by the education systems and the large army of religious advocates. Islam is a religion with its own legal code, traditions that provide the basis for order in society, and rules of social engagement. Islam provides a strong identity and order for an individual's life from birth to death.[1] Tibi says that Islam is a distinct cultural system in which the collective lies at the heart of its worldview and not the individual.[2] Indeed, 'the very size and cohesion of an Islamic community', Rubin notes, 'builds a religious, and hence cultural, wall against many aspects of globalization'.[3]

Islam also purports to have a legal basis for an 'Islamic' economic system, which it deems superior to both communism and capitalism.[4] This economic system is based on the notion of the Ideal Man, which itself is rooted in the social construct of Muslim community. Indeed, Islam is the only religion to provide such a comprehensive, albeit incomplete, set of principles that feed the belief and political economy systems of Muslim society. And it believes it has the best system for fair and just distribution of resources among the community. Islam is, ultimately, the answer to all the people's problems, to repeat the cry of many Islamist groups in the Muslim world.

With this kind of cultural infrastructure in place, it is not hard to find reasons for the ambivalent response to globalization in the MENA region, in ways not often associated with other regions of the world.[5] As a result, 'Latin America might worry about being overwhelmed by music and food items, but the Islamic Middle East is likely to look at the entire list of globalization products and ideas as dangerous'.[6] Globalization is not only seen as a rival of Islamic ways, but also as an alien force divorced from Muslim realities. Stressing the negative impact of the loose morals of Western life is a daily feature of airwaves in the Middle East. Such is the impact of the debate that a concerned Saudi citizen wrote to a local newspaper with the complaint that: 'We face the caravan of Satan with all its weapons and attractions. Its attack is against our society'.[7] The fears this man articulates are heard on Arab satellite television stations from all corners of the region, from Pakistan and Afghanistan to Egypt and Libya.

In addition, some Muslim forces wish to defend their realm against what they regard as the rapid import, through globalization, of Western consumerism and its throw-away culture.[8] This is a key characteristic of globalization, and its culture–ideology of consumerism, to paraphrase Sklair,[9] is something apparently incompatible with Islamic norms. Cultural synchronization, as an unprecedented new level of global domination of Western culture through globalization and modernization, has left a deep mark on Muslim societies.[10] Such leading Islamic scholars as Salim al-Awwa testify to this by depicting globalization as an invasion. He has emphasized that globalization, at its heart, is in fact a cultural construct and its meaning (*mahfoum*) is the Western discourse. Thus promoting globalization and engaging with it, he has argued, is like promoting Western cultural values and their dominance.[11] Other Islamic scholars with a prominent public face, such as Yusuf al-Qaradawi, have peddled a similar line, arguing that globalization is the imperialism of our age, and its mission is not only to encourage consumerism and 'looseness' of mores among the community of believers, but also to destroy Muslims' values and beliefs.[12] These Islamic thinkers and scholars represent the most public face of concerns among Muslims. Across the region, Friday prayer leaders, newspaper commentators and traditional intellectuals enter the discourse about globalization from a similar vantage point. They do not represent the fringes of Muslim communities – far from it, they tend to articulate the widely held fears of ordinary Muslims of the impact of the West and of globalization on their lives and societies.

Perhaps they may have good cause for their fears, for the level of penetration of Western ways is deep, demonstrated by the use even of religion as a marketing tool and for widening market share.[13] But beyond this, there is concern that globalization is challenging Muslim peoples' deeply felt personal values and practices, even their dress code. The dress code, particularly for women, is a deeply symbolic feature of Muslim values. In the UAE, which in many ways is the great gateway of globalization into the region, Muslim women have been complaining to the Ministry of Labour and Social Affairs in increasing numbers recently that they may have been discriminated against in the job market, or even dismissed by private-sector firms, for wearing the *hijab* in the workplace. Some are continually asked by their employers to justify wearing a headscarf at work, it is reported, which these Muslim women find objectionable. A recruitment firm had explicitly stated to a potential employee that its clients preferred to deal with women who displayed a 'Western outlook'.[14] This example is used because, in recent years, the UAE has emerged as the most cosmopolitan of all Mashreq states, and in the UAE nationals have been 'encouraged' by local authorities to wear the traditional (normally black) long robes as their public garb; in virtually every public-sector office where Emirati women are at work, they are seen wearing their traditional long robes. Not wearing a headscarf or the long robe is frowned upon.

At the other extreme, the most effective Western marketing tool, sex, is now used blatantly in Arab television adverts for consumer products. In a culture in which relations between the genders are still highly regulated and formalized, the use of sex in advertising offends the sensibilities of most Muslims, even liberal ones. Yet responses from within the Muslim world to these perceived threats demonstrate that Muslims are no longer able to resist Western consumer patterns, nor Western products. Products such as 'Mecca-Cola', 'Qibla-Cola', 'Macburger', or Iran's modestly dressed doll in reply to America's highly popular Barbie doll, only offer alternative products. These are not instruments for changing the material basis of the Western-dominated global culture manifested in Barbie, Coca Cola and McDonald's.[15] In some parts of the region even the holy month of Ramadan is increasingly commercialized, although this is not necessarily a new development, for exchange has always been a feature of Ramadan. What is interesting is the discomfort that blatant commercialization of the holy month is causing and the huge amount of debate it has generated. For a Saudi professional working in Dubai, the commercial capital of the Middle East, Ramadan is said to be 'changing from a religious month to a cultural or social event. You're using faith to commercialize something else. It doesn't feel right'. 'You're supposed to exercise abstinence, and the opposite happens', he says.[16] Alas, complains the grand mufti of Dubai (Sheikh Ahmed Abdelaziz Haddah): 'it's that people have taken this month to be a month of shopping'. Such adverts as 'Welcome Ramadan with a visit to Gargash Enterprises and you'll soon be feeling over the moon' are typical of the trend, which many find disturbing. What Dubai does, others follow, so in Cairo – the biggest Arab metropolis – the faithful are encouraged to read all 30 days of advertising and enter widely publicized sweepstakes to win prizes at the end of the holy month.

The principles of consumerism are fully established therefore; the battle is more over the product range and the types of commercial activity, not the deep-rooted presence of consumerism. Muslims may resist buying American brands in protest against its state policies, but they still spend in order to be happy. They continue to drink Cola.[17]

Such Middle Eastern foods as the donor kebab, shawarma and falafel are widely consumed in the West, but in the region they have to compete with their heavily branded Western fast-food counterparts. In Egypt, even the humble falafel is not safe, for the famous golden arches chain has started successfully to serve 'McFalafel' in its local outlets. None of the local foods has been able to champion a counter-food culture, at home or in overseas markets. In the absence of viable local brands and corporations with strong identities of their own, one is left only with the state-run or managed oil sector and the religious establishment as organizations capable of presenting uniquely national or Muslim icons. Thus the only option available to the capitalist moguls of the MENA region is to try and find 'authentic' substitutes for the most popular of Western consumer products. Ironically, in doing so they are merely reinforcing the very pattern of production and product relations that their citizens openly object to: Western-style capitalism (with its emphasis on individualism and private gain), materialism and rampant consumerism. There is strong tension in many parts of the greater Middle East between consumerism and the local cultural values as perceived by the traditional and still dominant forces in society.

The *Arab Human Development Report 2002* alludes to this problem by stating that the 'traditional culture and values, including Arab [read: Islamic] culture and values, can be at odds with those of the globalizing world'.[18] Being 'at odds' with the globalizing world, the report concludes, is not a healthy state of affairs for the region to be in. Its authors suggest that a way out of the impasse would be for the region to be more receptive to other ideas and to move away from the traditional division of the world between Muslims and infidels. A strategy of 'openness and constructive engagement, whereby [MENA] countries both contribute to and benefit from globalization' is the report's recommended way forward.[19] For all its virtues, and its rather brave criticism of xenophobia among Muslims, it still fails to grapple with the key problem that in the MENA region, where Islam plays such a dominant cultural role, globalization in the realm of culture is seen less as an opportunity for exchange than an effective tool for Western – Judeo–Christian – domination. Keith Griffin's optimism in 2000 that globalization could make cultural interchange a mutually advantageous process has not come to pass.[20] Sadly, his rather optimistic prognosis in the post-9/11 global environment appears to be almost completely out of place. In the cultural realm, at least, we are still some way from fulfilment of the above aspirations, as the 2006 Pew Global Attitudes Project (in a long line of such surveys) demonstrates. It notes that 'pluralities in all of the predominantly Muslim countries surveyed associate Westerners with being greedy, arrogant, immoral, selfish and violent'.[21] This is an astonishing statement to make, by any measure, but it is – sadly – supported by the wealth of data accumulated for this report. The arrival of al-Qaeda and the fallout from terrorist acts since 9/11 have merely compounded the problem.

Despite the ongoing debate about the impact of globalization on cultural values, and on Islam-based values and traditions and globalization in particular,[22] few of these many words have been as encapsulating as the image presented in a short news agency wire transmitting a story on Saudi Arabia. The piece, about the views of Prince Walid bin Talal on development, started with the provocative image of 'Western culture crash[ing] into the everyday lives of Saudis'.[23] This image sets the backdrop for how countless Muslims around the world receive globalization, and perceive its nature – as a crushing and overwhelming wave. For many millions it is a relentless 'cultural onslaught', to borrow the phrase from the commander of Iran's Islamic Revolution Guards Corps, Yahya Rahim-Safavi.[24] Indeed, in Iran there is a tendency to analyse the whole US strategy in the Middle East in terms of a sinister plot against Islam. Iran's then-Ministry of Intelligence and Security chief Hojjatoleslam Ali Yunesi told a gathering of political-party leaders in January 2003, for example, that the USA has started a 'political, economic, and cultural war against Islam'. And in an 21 October meeting with Lebanese Hizbollah Secretary-General Hassan Nasrallah in Damascus, Yunesi is reported to have said that the 'United States is trying to sow discord among Muslims' for its own political and cultural objectives.[25] Iranian clerics are not alone in expressing this view; in the Sunni world – from bin Laden to Tunisia's Islamist leader in exile, al-Ghannuchi – one hears similar sentiments being stated about the West and global economic forces. Friday prayer leaders across the Muslim world never miss the opportunity to chastise the West for unleashing its economic (alongside its political and military) power on Muslims.

In some parts of the Arab world, people are being told that 'by learning English we stand to lose our own language and cultural traditions. Can any of those who promote this idea cite even one instance of people losing their language and traditions by learning English or any other language?'.[26] In many ways, reflecting the same tensions as those over the commercialization of Ramadan, celebrating Valentine's Day is another recent arena of confrontation between the traditionalists and modernizers in the Muslim world. In Iran and Saudi Arabia, in particular, the practice of celebrating love in such a public – and Western – way is pounced on by the authorities as capitulation to Western cultural values and norms. Valentine's Day celebrations are regarded by local authorities as corruption of Islam. But these responses are not isolated incidents of discontent by Muslim elites. The cultural opposition of traditional and radical Muslim forces to globalization can be demonstrated further by their attitude towards the state's efforts at income generation through such service industries as tourism. Given that tourism is now one of the region's main industries and employers, set to generate some US$220 billion by 2015 according to the World Travel and Tourism Council (on the basis of US$33 billion worth of investment between 2006 and 2015),[27] and given that from Dubai to Turkey and the rest of the Mediterranean it now forms a major source of revenue and foreign exchange for these countries, resistance to it has acquired both a cultural and political economy dimension, directly challenging the imperatives of globalization in the region and also damaging the basis of legitimacy of ruling elites. Elites are often seen as selling short national cultures and values in return for a quick buck.

The Egyptian Gema'a al-Islamiya's attitude is typical of the opposition trends. The view is that as 'many tourist activities are forbidden, so this source of income for the state is [also] forbidden'. But worse than that, '[tourism spreads] prostitution and AIDS ... by Jewish women tourists, and it is a source of all manner of depravities, not to mention being a means of collecting information on the Islamic movement'.[28] Tourism, which is riding the wave of globalization and one of the beneficiaries of ease of access, is therefore little more than a foreign conspiracy perpetrated by the infidels and their lackeys through the local state. Furthermore, as tourism is the cause of sexual depravity as well – for it encourages sexual activity by Muslim men who are the main protectors of Muslim societies – it also weakens the very foundations of Muslim societies. Tourism, billed to become a real and strong source of income and employment for the next generation in the region, is, in this light, a corrupting activity which should be stopped. But it is impossible to expect any MENA government willingly to forego the revenues and opportunities tourism can generate on the basis of conservative opposition. In a globalized world where foreign travel is cheap and easy, and where the hard-pressed governments have little choice but to play to their comparative advantage and use tourism (sun, sand, sea and history) as one of their main sources of income, it is almost impossible to ban it on religious grounds, or for its 'corrupting' influence. The cultural clash between Muslim values and worldview and globalizing forces is set to continue, inspiring periodic acts of violence by the radical Islamists. Encouraging tourism also has a direct political cost attached to it, as it raises challenging questions about regime legitimacy in a region that tends to look at cultural penetration of Islamic lands with great mistrust. Given the region's patrimonial governance systems, the expansion of tourism and extension of tourist rights is seen by the people as, at best, the political masters' wilful neglect of the state's cultural sovereignty. Where 'domestic order is aligned with a claimed continuity of local values, to be celebrated and defended', the margin for error by the ruler is small.[29]

Nevertheless, globalization of culture has meant that the region's youth, in particular, are far more in tune with the world around them than traditionalists acknowledge. Rap and rave are common phrases on the Arab street, and access to satellite television ensures the latest Western fashions, music, fads and ideas are consumed and replicated on a vast scale. The receptivity of Muslim youth to Western cultural trends is not uniform, however, and it is often the more affluent classes and societies that are more directly engaged, often using the tools of globalization for this engagement.[30] In Jordan, for instance, where the urban population is highly cosmopolitan, 'Arabizi' (derived from the word *Inglizi* – English – meaning a deliberate mixing of Arabic and English words) is enabling young people to talk about taboo subjects without apparently compromising mores. 'It is easier to express yourself in English about topics considered taboo, like sex. I can't speak about sex with my friends in Arabic. The words are too heavy and culturally loaded. It all sounds *haram* (sinful). I feel more free in English. Arabizi is a way to escape taboos', explains a documentary maker about the prevalence and role of Arabizi in Jordanian society. In Lebanon, Arabic, English and French are all mixed up to create a unique blend of youth language in that country, reflecting deep infiltration of global networks in many parts of the region.

These trends represent not only globalization's cultural reach, but also its economic penetration. These linguistic changes manifest themselves in the cultural sphere, but tend to reflect a deepening of class differences as economies in traditional and formally Bedouin countries such as Jordan liberalize, putting further pressure on these increasingly stratified societies. Culturally, too, the rise of phenomena such as Arabizi have a large impact, the roots of which can be traced to globalization. For all its liberalizing virtues from the youths' perspective, one expert maintains that this phenomenon represents a means of 'putting a cultural distance between you and the pastoral and Bedouin world of traditional Jordan'.[31] Another commentator has blamed the prevalence of American popular culture for the increasing use of English as the language of choice by urban youths: 'some young people look down on Arabic language. They think that it is old and that English represents life and desires'. 'If the trend continues', notes Haitham Sarhan (a linguist at Jordan University), 'Arabic could be in danger. [For] young people think Arabic is boring'.[32]

In the UAE, the humble mobile phone is emerging as the tool of choice for cultural assimilation. In the realm of dating between Emirati boys and girls, for example, where contact between the sexes is discouraged, mobile telephone technology facilitates access.[33] Globalization of communications and its efficient networks and extensive tools (such as bluetooth technology) has given UAE males the opportunity to reach girls nearby (up to a 10-metre radius normally) with messages and even images through their mobile telephones. Boys use this technology to talk to girls they encounter in the UAE's American-style shopping malls without even approaching them for face-to-face contact. This technology allows high-mobility (unlike instant messaging, which requires a networked PC), immediate and easy access to the opposite sex, without ever damaging the reputation of the local girls whose chastity is paramount to the family's reputation in such societies.

But the cultural traffic is not one-way by any means, and the same tools of globalization facilitate export of Arab and Asian culture to the rest of the world, including the West. The relationship is perhaps most visible at the entertainment and media levels, where one finds that Arab pop music and cinema is openly and heavily consumed in Europe, and not just by the EU's immigrant communities. Western musicians, such as Sting, revel in weaving Arabic tempo with their own music, and Turkish tunes are readily adapted in Germany and elsewhere in Europe.

Media outlets themselves are also not solely in the hands of Western corporations intent on pumping their own values into the region. The broadcasts of the Lebanese Broadcasting Corporation are no less saucy than those of MTV, and the Saudi-owned Middle East Broadcasting Centre is a great disseminator of Arab music, game shows (although largely based on Western counterparts), popular chat shows and other frivolous programmes. These Arab-owned broadcasters have a massive customer base, and are equalled in their reach and influence by the current affairs satellite channels of al-Jazeera, al-Arabiya, al-Manar and others. It is partly a consequence of the latter channels' success that the BBC, CNN and Voice of America have found it prudent to invest large sums of money creating Arabic channels of their own. The Arab channels may give an alternative view of the world, may even act as defenders of some core values, but they do not in any way represent cultural authenticity. In general terms, they too consume and transmit a diet of Western programmes and the cultural baggage that goes with it. They, if you like, localize Western-dominated global cultural trends.

Finally, in debates about cultural transmissions and globalization, one must always be careful not to overplay the power of Islam in cultural terms, or use it as a tool to justify Middle East exceptionalism. The region's unique relationship with globalization is partly due to the influence and nature of Islam as a socio-cultural force; it is when culture acquires a geopolitical and political economy edge that real problems arise.

Patrimony and Globalization: *Rujula*, *Namous* and Honour

The issues of manhood (*rujula* in Arabic) and honour/chastity (*namous* in Persian) mark perhaps some of the most potent dividing lines between Islam and globalization. In manhood and honour, the average Muslim man finds his identity, core values and valour. The bedrock of his identity is the opposite sex, and his social point of reference the relationship between the two genders. Women here symbolize virtue, continuity, sacred love and social chastity. Their role in society, as mothers and therefore the 'incubators' of the next generation of Muslims, places them in a hugely controversial position in times of social tension.

On one hand, the heart of the problem is the challenges globalization poses for such gender-segregated societies, their male-dominated division of labour, and family control exercised by men. The gender dimension of the problem has been well illustrated by research conducted on the specific theme of women and globalization in the Arab Middle East.[34] It is found that globalization not only poses a direct challenge, in a generic sense, to male control of public spaces, but also, in a foundational sense, questions Islamic underpinnings of social relations. And it is with regard to the second dimension that Islamist forces (which are male-dominated) enter the fray as defenders of Muslim values. What are the values that Islamists feel need protecting? These can, by and large, be placed in three baskets: motherhood, family, and employment. Even in relatively prosperous Arab societies, such as Kuwait, pressures of globalization and economic restructuring have found one of their first victims in women's rights. Mary Ann Tétreault has argued that, as a consequence, 'women already working became targets of intense propaganda efforts to get them to quit their jobs. Working mothers were accused of neglecting their children and contributing to poor Arabic language skills among Kuwaiti youth, allegedly for handing over responsibility for child-rearing to Asian maids ... Delinquency, divorce, rising alcohol consumption, and even disunity in Kuwaiti society as a whole were blamed on women leaving their homes for paid employment ... These allegations resonated with the slogans of an ongoing campaign to promote national unity by "Islamizing" the state ... calling directly on patriarchal images and values deeply embedded in local religion and culture'.[35] This pattern of behaviour has not been unique to the so-called traditional societies of the Persian Gulf. At the western end of the Arab world, for instance in Tunisia, an Arab country known for its relatively open society, Islamists have targeted gender relations as the most important battle zone in their critique of state responses to globalization.[36] The country's most prominent Islamist movement, al-Nahda, preaches a message almost identical in nature and content to that heard elsewhere in the greater Middle East: 'women properly belong in the home, raising children and safeguarding the family. Nahda does distinguish between what is permissible and what is desirable, being careful to specify that it is the conditions of employment and the effect of absent mothers that are objectionable ... it envisages a society that would restrict, rather than expand, opportunities for women to work outside the home'.[37] Yet women do make up an important and active component of the workforce in virtually every country of the region. Even in Saudi Arabia, where women are often said to suffer from extreme discrimination, they now have an important social function. In the words of a senior member of the Saudi royal family, Prince Turki al-Faisal: 'the most prized woman today in our country is a woman who has a job. This marks a major turnaround from even 20 years ago when a husband would not accept his wife going out to work'.[38]

On the other hand, globalization is seen by urban Muslim women as providing the perfect bulldozer for breaking down barriers to training and education, employment and investment opportunities, entrepreneurship, informal contacts with the opposite sex, unsupervised pleasure, and individual choice – all things, in other words, that Islamist activists and traditionalists find abhorrent about Western lifestyles and norms. Such activists prefer a hierarchical ethical order in which 'Muslim women, veiled and obedient, are everywhere subordinate to men and are confined to roles dictated by their biological constitution. Their most natural and essential role is that of mother. The family is their natural domain, where they are maintained and protected by their husbands'.[39]

It would, however, be misleading to suggest that the region's feminists fit the Western mould – far from it.[40] Although there are undoubtedly very strong secularist feminist voices and forces in the region struggling for equal rights, alongside them one also finds an equally strong Islamic-leaning feminist current, so-called Islamist feminists, who argue for women's liberation from within the paradigm and teachings of Islam and Islamic values. In Iran, as in Saudi Arabia, Malaysia and Indonesia, one finds that 'women who break through the established paradigm [one dominated by men] are also carefully dressed in full hijab, claiming fealty to Islamic values, and invoking models of liberated women from an Islamic past in order to justify asking for what they want for their future'.[41] That even these boundaries are now being challenged, even in the most conservative of settings, was illustrated during the Jeddah Economic Forum meeting in January 2004. At this meeting several taboos were broken: the keynote speaker of the forum was a businesswoman (Lubna Olayan), and women played an unusually prominent role in the proceedings. Women were so visible at the gathering that the Grand Mufti Sheikh Abdul Aziz Al-Asheikh issued a condemnation of Saudi women who showed up unveiled and had mixed with men: 'We followed up what happened at the forum and which should be denounced ... namely, the mixing of men and women and the latter's appearance without wearing the hijab [as] ordered by God', the mufti is reported to have said.[42]

In this battle of sexes, globalization poses a direct challenge to the male-driven notions of cultural values and identity, and enters the region at the hugely value-laden intersection between universal rights and the 'Islamic/cultural-specific duties', between the socially proscribed boundaries for the sexes, and their social roles. Across Asia, and more uniquely in the Muslim world, by encouraging different work patterns, skills acquisition, earning opportunities and institutional organization, globalization threatens the male-dominated socio-cultural systems that have evolved to protect the position of men as defenders of the faith and of society, as well as to perpetuate a division of labour which is, at its most basic level, based on gender segregation.

Continuing male monopoly and domination of the socio-public realm is at the heart of the problem. And, in much of the Muslim world, the issue of social values is tied up with rights within Islam, and also sexuality. Two examples illustrate these points. The first is articulated by the founder of Iran's Islamic revolution and a source of emulation for the Shia communities of the world, Ayatollah Ruhollah Khomeini, who had effectively argued that, in social relations, women must live a different life from men, although in today's Iran this can hardly be said to be the case any longer. Like their counterparts in Turkey, Tunisia, Lebanon, Jordan and Morocco, Iranian women are now actively seeking public office and employment in the professions. They are, to coin a phrase, thoroughly modern. In most of these cases, they dare to enter the public arena largely independently of their menfolk's 'permission', which traditionally has been the Muslim way.

Returning to Ayatollah Khomeini's pronouncements, he had said that once a woman is 'a permanent wife' of a man, she 'must not leave the house without her husband's permission, and must submit herself for whatever pleasure he wants ... In this case her maintenance is incumbent upon her husband. If she does not obey him, she is a sinner and has no rights to clothing, housing, or sleeping [in the house]'. Maulana Maududi, one of the founders of Pakistan's militant Islamist movement, has gone a step further, suggesting that 'when a woman steps out of her house against the will of her husband, she is cursed by every angel in the heavens', while a prominent member of Pakistan's Jamaat-i Islami party has said that 'a man's primary duty is to "provide" (or "protect") for his family, and that of the wife is to raise children, take care of her husband, and be obedient to him at all times'.[43] This socio-cultural division between the genders is at the heart of Islamic cultural practices, and is being threatened very directly by globalization.

Muslim patterns of social organization therefore appear irrational to the regional globalizers. The latter are perceived by their anti-globalist counterparts in the Muslim world as peddlers of moral corruption. More fundamentally, as we have seen, where family law, inheritance regulations, and personal status codes are set to draw boundaries between genders, globalization sets out to remove them. It charts a path apparently directly opposed to these Arab–Islamic traditions which, over time, have acquired legal justification, broadly being enshrined in different aspects of constitutional law in Muslim countries.

Preservation of cultural norms as part of a transnational, transferable 'Muslim identity' and set of values is one of the main crossroads on which Islamists confront globalization. Where globalization requires standardization, Islamists instead see assimilation; where globalization requires transparency, Islamists see nakedness; where globalization encourages social intercourse, Islamists find adultery; and where globalization demands equality of opportunity, Islamists see sexual depravity. It should therefore not be surprising that a major battleground for the MENA anti-globalists is that of culture, and within that that of gender differences. Where, as in large parts of the Muslim world, religious and state structures have become mixed, it was only a matter of time before a secular force such as globalization would come to pose serious challenges to social cohesion, and also to social organization. The challenge is not only at the level of social class, laying bare patriarchal privilege structures, but also at the institutional level, where women can no longer be held back for reasons of tradition from fully engaging in all facets of modern existence. Globalization, in short, fundamentally challenges the old Arabic dictum 'mothers build homes and sons build countries', for its pressures drive both the mother and son to service a much larger economic unit, the world market. In challenging the traditional social divisions of labour described by the above proverb, globalization presses social groups to pass on the costs of home and nation-building to what is, essentially, an ill-equipped state outside the Gulf Arab oil monarchies. Even in the latter, it can be argued that globalization of information and knowledge has come too soon. As Frauke Heard-Bey observes; 'the education offered during the past few decades has not adequately prepared today's users of knowledge-highways with an understanding of the society's traditional values so that they may be equipped with the tools to deal with the many other influences. In the Gulf, these influences were accompanied by alien values transmitted by expatriate teachers, the global information market, and the Internet ... [it is now] very much up to the individual how to harmonize what comes from the outside with the traditional values of family, society, and religion. Many of the elders have their own problems of how to combine modernity with their traditional way of life'.[44] Similar, although not identical, problems exist elsewhere in the region, but the common problem remains that of the family unit's inability to mediate between economic pressures generated by globalization and cultural regeneration embedded in Muslim family values. We may have a more globalized world in economic and political terms, but along with it we also have an increasingly fragmented one in cultural terms.[45] It is in the world of fragmented cultures that many of the MENA region's battles with globalization are being fought. Culture is the realm deemed to be most in need of protection from global forces, and at the same time is also seen to be the key realm badly in need of modernization in Muslim societies.

It has been argued in this book that, as globalization transcends borders, so it also intensifies the quest for security, but the definition of security has widened quite substantially since the end of the Cold War and the march of globalization, to encompass the realm of culture (identity) as well. The crumbling of the Cold War's walls sharpened and also exposed the tensions that had characterized Muslim–Western relations in previous decades, at least in the greater Middle East. The threat of the so-called 'green peril' soon became a feature of the post-Cold War security debates, also feeding into the growing geopolitical tensions surfacing to mark the end of superpower rivalries in this part of the world. As early as 1990, identity had emerged as a feature of the global–local tensions and an element of the real or imagined geopolitical battle lines being drawn.

The Green Peril? The Geopolitics of Identity in the Greater Middle East

It was not long after the end of the Cold War that circles in the West began articulating a fear of the 'green peril'. The 'fundies', as *The Economist* dubbed radical Islamist movements/regimes, were everywhere threatening the security of the West.[46] Although many commentators did provide a thorough critique of the methodology of this message and, by extension, its content, the view slowly emerged that radical Islamists were the West's main enemy: armed with non-conventional weapons, they were intent on launching a violent jihad against Western civilization. From the early 1990s there was an 'urge to identify Islam as an inherently anti-democratic force [and as] America's new global enemy now that the Cold War [was] over'.[47] Amos Perlmutter was one of those who argued that Islamic fundamentalism represented an 'authoritarian, anti-democratic, anti-secular' phenomenon, an 'aggressive revolutionary movement as militant and violent as the Bolshevik, Fascist, and Nazi movements of the past', and violently opposed to the 'Christian–secular universe'.[48]

It was then, nearly 10 years before the September 2001 attacks on the US by militant Islamists linked to a global Islamist terror network, that Leon Hadar had warned of the dangers associated with applying the old Cold War jargon and mentality as a means of carving out of the body-politic of Islam a new enemy: 'there are dangerous signs', he wrote, 'that the process of creating a monolithic threat out of isolated events and trends in the Moslim world is already beginning. The Green Peril thesis is now being used to explain diverse and unrelated events in that region … of Islam substituting for the spiritual energy of communism'.[49]

The reasons for this were complex, but included the fact that the Islamists actually fitted this bill rather well, and that the West needed a new enemy after the collapse of the Soviet empire.[50] For the American right in particular, the 'yellow' and 'green' perils posed equally significant threats to the US and the Western civilization, albeit somewhat differently. The growth and increasing adventurism of Islamist movements and states in the Middle East universalized the perception of Islam as radical and raised its profile as the dominant threat to the West. No longer seen as a 'circumstantial phenomenon',[51] Islamic radicalism was depicted by Bernard Lewis as the 'rising tide of rebellion against … Western paramouncy'.[52] It is worth noting that these words were published in September 1990, barely a month into the Kuwait crisis of that year, and over a decade before the al-Qaeda had unleashed itself on American soil. In an otherwise informative and balanced article, Lewis's analysis could be seen to have left the door open for Islamophobia to take root in US policy circles. It was in Lewis's analysis, after all, where generosity of spirit towards Islam was balanced against fears of a 'clash of civilizations' between the two great traditions of Islam and Judeo–Christianity – in which Islam was depicted as the 'ancient rival' caught in an 'irrational' rage against the West. The purported clash between Islam and the West was forecast by Lewis well before Huntington's infamous article in *Foreign Affairs*, but at the same time Lewis did warn the West that, in order to defeat Islamic terrorism, 'it would surely be useful to understand the forces that drive them'. These words were published in late 1998, just a few months after bin Laden's declaration of jihad against the West had been widely distributed in February of that year.[53]

This theme, alas, was resurrected in the aftermath of 9/11. Margaret Thatcher, for example, who is regarded as an intellectual mentor of the

American neo-conservatives, rounded on 'Islamic fanatics' in early 2002, equating Islamism with 'early communism' and Bolshevism. She depicted Islamism as an 'aggressive ideology promoted by fanatical, well-armed devotees'. The USA and its allies, she argued, should engage in a long-term and all-embracing campaign to defeat this enemy. Seemingly blind to the contradiction that American troops fighting Islamists on Muslim soil could generate even more hostility towards the West, and in a manner reminiscent of a neo-imperialist grand strategy, she advocated that the USA should strike at the centres of 'Islamic terror that have taken root in Africa, Southeast Asia and elsewhere ... and to deal with those hostile states that support terrorism and seek to acquire or trade in weapons of mass destruction'.[54] As already stated, her words should not be taken lightly, for her views do – still – reflect the most powerful strand of modern conservatism in the West, and are taken seriously by neo-conservatives in the USA.

So, when Saudi Arabia becomes an open target of Capitol Hill and many faceless officials close to the White House, and Margaret Thatcher's analysis paints such dissimilar countries as Iran and Syria as 'enemies of western values and interests' and points to anti-Islamist Libya as 'a menace' which 'hates the west', one could be forgiven for thinking that, in more ways than one, Islam and Muslim countries in general are emerging as the main enemies of the West in the twenty-first century.[55] al-Qaeda's role in forcing a wedge between Muslim countries and the West should not be underestimated here, nor its ability to deliver pain to the West. But it is a fact of life that, even after 9/11, it was the Muslims who felt harmed by the West and under siege by it, despite al-Qaeda's attacks on Western targets.

The suspicions of the Muslims were aroused further when, in the autumn of 2002, several Western countries adopted policies seemingly hostile to Muslims. From 1 October 2002, the USA introduced a policy of blanket 'registration' on entry to and departure from the USA, for all men born in a dozen Muslim countries. The Australian prime minister announced in early December that his country reserved the right to engage in pre-emptive strikes against its (largely) Muslim neighbours if its security was threatened. Shortly before this announcement, a former president of France had just declared that Turkey should forever be barred from entry into the European club for being 'different', culturally and geopolitically. Turkey, Valéry Giscard d'Estaing said in November 2002, was actually in Asia and not an European country, and it had, in any case, 'a different culture, a different approach, and a different way of life'.[56] Difference was to be punished, from where the Turks stood, and not celebrated as a virtue in a diverse European Union.

As these comments were made barely a month after the introduction in the USA of fingerprinting and photographing of 'registered aliens' visiting the USA, so again Muslims might be forgiven for thinking that the West, in the aftermath of 9/11 and other atrocities committed by Islamic extremists, was pursuing a co-ordinated policy of containment and rollback of Islam, and embedded within its planning a 'forward strategy of democratization' of the greater Middle East, to use words used by President Bush and Vice-President Cheney in late 2003 and early 2004, respectively. The fact that the USA was, in fact, an advocate of Turkish membership of the EU passed many people by in the Muslim world. In the Middle East, in particular, where conspiracies tend to form at least one angle of policy debates, these actions were seen as further evidence of an emerging clash of civilizations with the West, a clash that seemed possible but not inevitable back in 1990, when the 'green peril' was being presented as a source of threat to the West.

But even before that, to broaden our horizons – from the late-1970s, and through the Islamic revolution in Iran and the take-over of the Grand Mosque in Mecca by religious militants in 1979, the rise of anti-Western Islamic militancy in Lebanon, and the fierce Afghani Jihad against the Soviet armed forces – political Islam's course was set to cross with that of the West in more ways than one. In geopolitical terms, the removal of the Soviet Union merely brought the two opposing camps face-to-face more easily.

Yet, ironically, in historical terms, the new Western strategy of containment and rollback is not too dissimilar to that pursued against the Soviet Union from 1949, the difference being that in this new cold war the West is prepared actively to use force and deploy troops to first contain and then defeat its Islamist enemies. This new war has no 'iron curtain' to mark the territory of the two sides and draw boundaries; nor is it based on the importance of spheres of influence. As it has taken shape, it has shown itself to be global and extra-territorial, able to be waged on the turf of all parties concerned, even those not directly linked to the campaign. It has ignited many local fires, set people against each other, and also ultimately driven further wedges spiritually between the USA and the Muslim world.

Examples abound of an already strained relationship between both traditional and radical Islam and US globalization. A respected post-9/11 briefing on the Middle East highlights the additional burden 9/11 has placed on relations between Muslims and the West, and those between the USA and the Arab world in particular: 'On a short visit to Egypt and Saudi Arabia, December 12–19, 2002, the Middle East Institute's Chairman and President found gloom and deep concern about the [US] Administration's policy toward the region. Popular opinion, as interpreted by Egyptian, Lebanese and Kuwaiti political analysts, was more antagonistic toward the United States than at any time in recent memory and was increasingly driven by stereotypes which bear little relationship to the reality of our policy or intentions. The perception is that we are driven by the 'Six C's' – cowboys; colonialism; conspiracy; Coca-Cola; cowardice; and clientist. The 'client' is Israel. The 'cowardice' is the perception that we are the school yard bully. Coca-Cola is the symbol of an alien consumer society; 'conspiracy' is based on unrealistic expectations of US capabilities; 'colonialism' is premised on a US drive to control oil; and 'cowboys' is drawn from a Hollywood style perception that the Administration shoots from the hip.

The reality is that when Arabs think of the United States they think of Israel – and when Americans think of the Arabs they think terrorism'.[57] This, in essence, is the core of the tensions in cultural terms that now underline relations between the USA (and its Western allies) and the greater Middle East, which could ultimately make the Muslim heartland more insular and inward-looking.

In cultural terms, these developments mean more violent confrontations, based on deep suspicions of the West's motives in Muslim lands. To a large degree, Fukuyama is correct to observe that 'modern economics – the process of industrialization determined by modern natural science – is forcing the homogenization of mankind, and is destroying a wide variety of traditional cultures in the process'.[58] It is precisely this fear that drives the opposition of radical, traditionalist and conservative Muslims alike to globalization. For them, homogenization under the American banner of globalization means the end of the uniqueness of Islam.[59]

8 Globalization and International Politics of the Greater Middle East

> The problems of the Middle East will be with us for the foreseeable future. They are primarily the responsibility of the peoples of the area, but they also affect us closely, for the Middle East provides 80 per cent of the oil required by the European economy, is crossed by the major trade routes between Asia-Africa and Europe, and could be the seedbed of a war.
>
> William R. Polk, 'The Lesson of Iraq',
> *The Atlantic Monthly*, December 1958.

Regional Politics in a Global Context

We have already established that, in the aftermath of the Cold War and 9/11, regional MENA politics have changed substantially, and at one level have widened the strategic arena of the traditional Middle East and Arab regions to incorporate the Caspian region as well as Afghanistan and Pakistan. This greater Middle East will remain at the heart of global strategy for some decades yet – this is indisputable, for a 'new strategic map' is said to be emerging 'that assures that the Middle East will remain a prize in an emerging international system whose future contours are not yet clear'.[1]

Developments and events in this wider region will therefore continue to cast a long shadow over much of the global order in the twenty-first century, disrupting and challenging it in equal measure. In this, at least, little has changed since the previous century, judging by Polk's pithy observation (quoted above) made over 50 years ago. In terms of its geopolitical worth and the vast hydrocarbon deposits it harbours, the GME will leave a direct mark on the workings of the international order and, by the same token, on the progress and effects of globalization. It is for these reasons that the region will form a core area of the international system. Add to this the geopolitical effects of the region's own political and security idiosyncrasies – from the strategic consequences of a nuclear Iran, competing interests of the Arab and non-Arab actors of the area, the rise of Islam in the political process, to the spread of inter-religious strife from Iraq – and one is faced with an intricate set of potential problems emanating from these Eurasian crossroads.

This is partly due to the ways in which insecurity is so easily transmitted across the region, and is internalized by outside actors as a consequence of strategic interdependence. Thus, says Cohen, the Middle East forms a primary 'shatterbelt' region, crushed 'between outside interests' while also lacking unity of action.[2] It is thus also highly penetrated. Brown noted in 1984 that the 'diplomacy of the region is characterized by an exaggerated conflation of seemingly minor issues and major international concerns. The boundaries dividing local, national, regional and international are blurred'.[3] The blurring of these boundaries creates direct links between seemingly minor issues (such as the victory of Hamas in Palestinian parliamentary elections in January 2006) and larger issues (such as the impact of this victory on regional politics and on the West's ability to manage the implementation of the 2003 'road map' as the only viable plan for the resolution of the Arab–Israeli conflict). But it is also partly because of the impact the region has had on the smooth operation of the international system, in a geopolitical 'heartland–rimland' face-off fashion. We must note the ways in which its internal dynamics have come to play an important or even pivotal role in determining global power relations, whether at crucial junctures in the period 1900 to 1945, during the Cold War itself,[4] or in the context of post-Cold War developments in which the new era's first inter-state conflict (that of occupation of Kuwait by Iraq in August 1990) marked its first watershed and led directly to the largest American military action since World War II and the arrival of what President George Bush referred to in March 1991 as a 'New World Order of justice and fair play'. Far from the region losing its strategic shine after the Cold War, as was anticipated by some commentators, it can be argued that the reverse has happened: developments associated with the region have in fact enhanced its strategic significance, centralizing its importance since 9/11.

As strategic interdependence takes hold and globalization deepens, the boundaries between local, regional and international are becoming harder to separate. Even where they are identifiable, these are no longer separate strategic realms. As Bahgat Korany notes, 'in the globalisation era, MENA's international relations cannot any longer be separated from type of regime and society's good governance'.[5] Nowhere is the problem of interdependencies and their strategic costs more clearly illustrated than in the USA's two recent National Security Strategy documents (2002 and 2006), which attempt to chart America's way in an unstable world. But, more specifically, the CIA's recent comprehensive strategic calculations about the medium term provide concrete and ample examples of the policy-makers' dilemmas with regard to the Middle East. The latter, the CIA's National Intelligence Council 2003 Discussion Paper on the Middle East, which is one of the most authoritative assessments of long-term trends in the region, has acknowledged that globalization will not only continue to have a steady impact on the region, but will actively destabilize its existing systems and structures. It has noted that 'the major influences, or "drivers", that were identified in *Global Trends 2015* have been affecting Middle Eastern events for some time and will continue to do so, to varying degrees, over the next decade and a half. In addition to sharing with other regions the effects of these worldwide influences, Middle Eastern affairs between now and 2020 will be shaped by the heavy hand of the region's own history and the peculiar legacy of conflicts, suspicions, and attitudes this history has left'.[6] The CIA's discussion paper provides a suitable backdrop for the debate about the inevitability as well as the dimensions of change in the region, and about the extent to which regional and external drivers are capable of crystallizing the future direction of events and processes in this strategically important subsystem.

The authors of the National Intelligence Council discussion paper identify a number of factors that they regard as influential in shaping the region between now and 2020. Of a long list of factors, the most significant appear to be as follows:

Demography (the pressures created by 'youth bulges') from Morocco to Iran will directly affect the region.

A struggle for natural resources allocation is inevitable: 'By 2020 the different consequences for economics and economic policy of the country-by-country differences in energy reserves and depletion rates will be more apparent than now. The interests of those with more rapidly depleting reserves ... will diverge increasingly from those with longer-lasting resources (such as Saudi oil and Qatari gas). Increased consumption of water as a result of population growth will make conflict over that resource increasingly acute between those who share aquifers (e.g. Israel and the Palestinians) or river basins (e.g. Turkey, Syria, and Iraq)'.

Information technology will provide an environment in which 'the spread of news, information, and ideas will ... affect political trends and political volatility in several ways, including popular reactions to emotion-laden events and the diffusion of ideologies, including extremist ones'.

The 'increased cross-cultural contacts accompanying globalization will engender a potentially destabilizing mix of emulation and resentment'.

In most MENA states 'a centralized state apparatus will remain the dominant actor in public affairs, with tribe and family retaining significant influence at the local level. A civil society worthy of the name will be more apparent in some Middle Eastern states in 2020 than it is now, but overall it will continue to be overshadowed by the state above and the village below'.

Conflict could become more intensive and harmful: 'the region's abundance of energy resources ... will provide the wherewithal for states to arm themselves with more advanced weapons as military technology progresses. Such weapons may include weapons of mass destruction, the proliferation of which will be a problem involving the Middle East at least as much as any other region. Enhancement in the arsenals of regional states will threaten to intensify conflicts between states in the region as well as conflicts involving the United States'.

The acknowledgement that the USA will be largely responsible for shaping Middle Eastern events between now and 2020.

The USA is 'the dominant military power in the region and it is the forger of a new political and economic system in Iraq. It is the principal security guarantor of several Middle Eastern states and the principal *bete noire* of several others. And it is the main source of an alien culture that is admired by many Middle Easterners but disdained by others'.[7]

The National Intelligence Council paper provides a strategic survey of the region, and an assessment of the risks associated with the changing political economy of the GME and the geopolitical consequences of its possible further militarization. By the very nature of the region itself and its interdependencies, which mark its links with the rest of the international system, some responses to these trends have been planned, at no point in recent times more fully than in the US National Security Strategy documents. The 2002 and 2006 documents stand as monuments to the USA's continuing concerns with the GME and also to its vision of its position in the international system. The 2006 National Security Strategy, published on 16 March 2006 (shortly before the third anniversary of the Iraq war), paints a geopolitical mess of Eurasia in which Iran, China and Russia take centre stage. In the context of the GME, the National Security Strategy states, the USA 'faces no greater challenge from a single country than from Iran'.[8] The document echoes themes of American supremacy and policy of first strike detailed in 2002, but it goes further by presenting a powerful set of reasons for the sole superpower's continuing engagement with the GME, and for striving to shape it.

In its analysis of the impact of globalization, the National Security Strategy returns to familiar themes (that globalization expands the marketplace of ideas and room for freedom of expression), apparently rejecting the CIA's analysis (noted above) that greater negative and paralysing political consequences may follow globalization of regions such as the GME. As an informed observer of the Middle East has pointed out, 'politics in the Arab world has long been consumed by two fears. First, the fear of the status quo, maintained by regimes that lack vision yet dominate endlessly. Second, the fear of the alternative: a puritanical opposition and its potential for revolutionary or even nihilistic takeover. Between these two poles, the Arab world has had no middle ground. Choose the present authoritarian governments with all their shortcomings, bad economic policies and limited measures of social and personal freedom. Or choose upheaval and the extremists whose theocracy would be draped in strict codes of behavior governing such things as dress, social interaction and the role of women in public life. Faced with these alternatives during the past two decades, the

Middle East opted for stagnation'.⁹ This stagnation has taken a heavy toll over the years, leading to a paralysis in decision-making as well.

Globalization itself articulates the areas in which the Muslim Middle East needs to reform if it is not to fall further behind the rest of the world in industrial, technological and human development terms. But this is not a linear relationship. The dynamism of globalization daily crashes into the dynamic and volatile MENA regional system, and as the foundations of both are political as well as economic, they are far from stable. Instability at both ends of the equation merely helps to reinforce the sense of crisis in the Middle East.

On the basis of the aforementioned dynamism, it is possible to argue that the region is facing several futures at present, arising from the relationship it finally develops with globalization, and the manner of its engagement with the West in the aftermath of 9/11. We saw earlier how several economic elites in the region, particularly in the oil-rich Arabian Peninsula area, are keen to accelerate the pace of reform in order to be better placed to take advantage of the opportunities presented by globalization. Many, although by no means all, of the region's political and religious elites, on the other hand, are fearful of losing control, and with it their identity, traditions and customs, and legitimacy. Here we should again remind ourselves that globalization 'involves consciously opening national borders to foreign influences. The explosion in cross-border links is as much a result of government decisions to remove restrictions on trade, foreign investment and capital flows as it is of better transport and communication'.¹⁰ Large sections of elites in the Middle East are not yet ready consciously to open their national borders to external political, socio-economic and cultural influences. Judging by the bemoaning that goes on, they recognize that such influences have already jumped the barriers and are active on the inside, but the elites have put their hope in their ability to contain the Westernizing trends.

It is in this context that, in the Middle East, the religious elites want to protect the cultural realm from globalization, while the political elite want to ensure their grip on the levers of power is not loosened by globalization. The complexities of the globalization process itself have resulted in the region's 'power elite' (political, economic and religious) developing divergent views of the process and impact of this force. On the same basis, their responses to it also have been diverging on both national and international issues. As Michael Scott Doran has shown with reference to Saudi Arabia, for example, the dichotomy of the various factions of that country's power elite have, in recent years, fed directly into perceptions of, and relations with, the West, most notably the USA. He has shown that, as the Wahhabi establishment openly views the USA as a hostile power – seen as the 'idol of the age' and one of Islam's greatest enemies since its birth – the domestic power struggle is largely couched in polemics about the Middle East policies of the USA, and the relationship of the al-Saud political elite with the sole superpower. With the considerable influence of the anti-US camp in the Kingdom – which today may consist of the heart of the Wahhabi religious establishment and a powerful group of the al-Saud princes gathered around Prince Nayef – the religious elite's role becomes critical in the process of reform, as well as its content and direction, in this most important of Arab and Muslim countries.[11] These competing forces can play out their competing worldviews and attitudes towards the USA on their home turf, in one of the region's most important economic and political players.[12] The rejectionists can show their displeasure against the USA and play out their opposition to it through attacking the power base of the reformers in the political establishment, such as that of King Abdullah. The reformers can, in kind, attack the power base of the conservatives, religious endowments and cultural organizations. This rather futile rivalry will, in the end, actually weaken the Kingdom's power elite as a whole, ultimately pitting faction against faction, prince against prince, *alam* against *alam*. With mounting internal and external pressures, one could find the principal groups of the elite locked in a perpetual confrontation over control of the country's national agenda. Globalization will undoubtedly have played an influential part in the coming crisis of the Saudi state, but the real harbinger will have been the targeting of the Kingdom by the American neo-conservatives for the role several of its citizens played in 9/11.

Although not unique, the Saudi case illustrates well the socio-political contradictions, in policy terms, constantly generated by the divergent views of members of the power elites in Muslim Middle East. The political elite has declared total war against al-Qaeda and joined the West's war on terrorism, while the religious elite continuously attack the USA for its regional policies. The contradictions, in policy terms, that the Saudi case highlights are played out daily, affecting the daily lives of millions of ordinary citizens across the region, permanently shaking the ground under their feet. The same also tests the nerve of those who seek to introduce substantive reforms into the region: can they take risks in introducing reforms without destroying the fabric of society and its delicate social balance?

The tensions between the USA's perception of its role in the Middle East, on the one hand, and the existing political process in the region, on the other, have been identified here as major causes of instability in the post-9/11 regional environment. While this tension is partly a product of the process of globalization, it is also a key feature of the post-9/11 regional order, in which the war on terror has come to play a major part. As noted in relation to Saudi Arabia, the nature of US engagements in the region today plays a significant part in the domestic politics of most MENA states – from the Mashreq to the Maghreb. The role of the US factor has been in evidence in the political processes of an ally such as Saudi Arabia, as well as in those of an adversary such as Iran. In Iran's February 2004 parliamentary elections, in which Iran's conservative forces manipulated the electoral roll in order to ensure the defeat of the reformist camp in the poll for the Seventh Majlis, one could feel the ghost of US power present in every debate. In the end, a real fear of the US policy agenda in the Persian Gulf subregion encouraged the success of the conservative factions in the parliamentary elections, and from there in the 2005 presidential elections as well. The irony of the impact of the US factor in the parliamentary elections has been captured by an editorial in Britain's *Guardian* newspaper: 'Tension between the secular and religious in Iran is nothing new. What has changed is the external context. Iran feels tremendous pressure, principally from the US, over nuclear arms, terrorism, human rights and the occupation of neighbouring Iraq and Afghanistan ... Alive to these threats and exploiting them, anti-western mullahs seem to be circling the wagons. Thus has George Bush's grandiose bid to democratise the Middle East helped produce in Iran the exact opposite; a democratic derailment'.[13] Is the USA's democratization drive for a pluralist future in the Middle East in fact further de-democratizing the region? Are its double standards and contradictory policies in fact emboldening the conservative and radical forces in the Muslim Middle East, while undermining the position of the very progressive reformists it desperately needs to see in power in order to push through the roots-and-braches reforms it wants to see introduced? With the region now regarding the USA as part of the problem, it is hard to predict how Washington intends to nurture the rise of democratic forces in the region and see democracy introduced, when one of the first acts of such democrats (as much in response to the demands of their constituents as their own conscience) will be to condemn the superpower for its occupation of Iraq, for the behaviour of its troops and political agents there, for its unconditional support for Israel and blatant disregard for international law and norms in the Palestinian–Israeli conflict, and for its continuing support for many of the region's authoritarian regimes. Emma Murphy has drawn insightful comparisons between the USA's current policies with regard to Iraq and democracy in general, and an earlier time, to suggest that the American initiatives are likely to be as damaging to the region as those undertaken by Britain just under a century ago: 'Britain occupied Iraq during World War I and, subsequently, gained international endorsement [for its occupation] ... Nominally, the mandate was supposed to prepare Iraq for independence ... In fact Britain used its occupation as a way to build up networks of military bases ... to consolidate its access to oil on preferable terms and to enlarge the British mercantile empire. British control was exerted increasingly through indirect means ... British military personnel remained alongside the emerging Iraqi army and security forces and implemented a harsh reign of terror over elements of opposition. Sounds familiar? ... The end result was a tide of Iraqi and Arab nationalism which saw the expulsion of foreign influence as the primary concern of the population. Movements pressing for national unity in the face of external sponsorship of puppet regimes rejected political pluralism and liberal values as divisive'.[14] Is the birth of an illiberal democracy to become the norm that the peoples of the region will have to endure in the twenty-first century? It is still too early to tell, but much of the outcome will depend on what kind of Iraq emerges from the ashes of war and decades of destruction, and what kind of peace follows from the eventual implementation of the Palestinian–Israeli road map.

Capitalism Rules OK

Another issue facing this region, as others, is the absence of any real political economy alternatives to market capitalism. In the post-Soviet era, the socialist and central planning development models have been so badly discredited that few forces in the Middle East today can seriously articulate the dream of a socialist utopia, or a 'managed' economy.[15] The regimes' bankrupt policies of the recent past have today made them hostages of the market economy. On the other hand, the 1997 East Asian crisis has provided a 'reality check' for those seeking rapid and complete submission to globalization. Even though the economic downturn in East Asia cost MENA exporters many billions of dollars, most governments were relieved that their economies were not exposed to such harsh and powerful global forces as those that challenged the economic integrity of several of the Far East's powerhouses. Yet the region also looks at China with marvel and envy. To them, not only have the Chinese managed to ride the wave of globalization and turn their economy into a leading force in the global system, but have done so while keeping their political structures intact and their cultural norms supreme. It is therefore not surprising that some MENA countries dream of implementing the 'Chinese model' in the Middle East – rapid economic development without political liberalization. Alas, while the West may have stood by and watched the rise of a more culturally authentic Asian economic model in the 1960s to 1990s, or was helpless to force the Chinese to reform their highly authoritarian development 'model', in the MENA region it has no interest in allowing the evolution of such alternative models. In the MENA region, the power of the Washington Consensus is unchallenged, and its prescriptions for prosperity (as enshrined in economic restructuring and liberalization) have been adopted across the board – from revolutionary Islamic Iran to nationalist Syria and Algeria; from conservative Yemen to post-Islamist Sudan; and from modernist republican Tunisia to modernist monarchical Jordan.

An important element of the alternative futures debate, in the context of adoption of the Washington Consensus model of reform, is the place of good governance in the institutional and organizational structures of the region. If nothing else, good governance practices and procedures would be a necessary first step in realizing any gains from a global economic system. MENA states must re-tool their governance structures so as to be able to respond to the opportunities globalization presents, and also absorb the pressures associated with it.[16] Because it is governments that determine public policies and the way society's resources are allocated, their integrity, methods of management, decision-making and administration play a crucial mediating role in the relationship between national economies and global forces. It is now widely recognized in the region that, for a country to be able to take full advantage of globalization, it would have to enjoy 'good governance'. To quote from the March 2004 'Alexandria Declaration':

> A democratic system is closely linked to the presence of strong institutions incorporating the three recognized branches of government: the executive, the legislative and the judiciary, in addition to the press, the media and civil society associations. These institutions should be reviewed to guarantee their sound democratic practices. Consequently, this requires full transparency, the selection of effective leadership, a defined term of office, and the effective enforcement of the principle of "rule of the law" with no exception, irrespective of any justification ... the need for the abolition of extra-judicial and emergency laws and extraordinary courts in any form and under any name, currently in effect in many Arab countries, since these undermine the democratic nature of political systems.[17]

The conditions for good governance, however, are not universally met in the MENA region. Are people free and able to elect their governments and hold them accountable? Is the press free from all forms of censorship except by the rule of law? Does there exist high quality of public services and efficient policy-making with a minimum of red tape and bureaucratic delays? Is the rule of law preserved through the creation of an independent judiciary, the protection of private property, and the fight against all forms of corruption? Unfortunately, only a small number of these conditions for good governance can be said to exist in the MENA countries, and none of the above questions can be answered in the affirmative. Furthermore, if Freedom House data (www.freedomhouse.org) are to be believed, on the basis of the average rating of political rights and civil liberties, few MENA countries can be classified as 'free'. Indeed, almost all Muslim MENA states are classed as 'not free' by the Freedom House measure. The best result is that of a handful of countries – Bahrain, Jordan, Kuwait, Morocco, Turkey and Yemen – which in this classification achieve the status of 'partly free'. This is hardly promising, but in addition the *Arab Human Development Report 2002* (AHDR) notes that the Arab world as a region has the lowest freedom score among the seven regions of the world.[18]

It is thus not surprising that a learned report such as the AHDR should call explicitly for the broadening of freedoms in the region as a precondition of socio-economic reforms. The AHDR 2003 report says that human development, in its broadest sense, is urgently required if the Arab world is not to 'remain in a marginal position in the next phase of human history ... as passive consumers of other countries' proprietary knowledge, technology and services'. Human development in the region, it states, is currently being impeded by 'the political exploitation of religion', which penalizes original thought and encourages irrationality and superstition. The analysis offered indicates that modernization has remained incomplete in many parts of the Arab world, with the result that 'a sub-culture that encourages superstition has remained to the present day and will certainly thrive in popular environments'. The way out, the report suggests, lies in encouraging interaction with other cultures, including through increasing the number and quality of translations of quality texts, among other things. Internet access should be promoted, publishing overhauled, and censorship and other controls removed from the press and media. Only in this way, the authors state, can the new challenges of globalization be met: 'The only historical possibility for Arab culture is to go through this new global experience. For it cannot exile itself, feeding only on its past, its history and its intellectual heritage in the new world of overwhelming powers that dominate knowledge, products, technology and global culture. There is nothing that can justify Arab culture, in light of its rich historical experience and heritage, seeking to escape from the new conditions ... Withdrawal, even if it were feasible, would only lead to the weakening, decline, and fading away of the structures of Arab culture, rather than their flowering and further development'.[19]

A further dimension to note is the international context. In the current international environment, any discussion of the region's international politics must take account of the consequences of the 9/11 attacks on the political economy and cultural cohesion of the region. The AHDR 2003 makes the argument that 'A new historical era is rapidly unfolding ... not only because of the high human toll ... but also because of the political and security consequences of that cataclysm'.[20] The war on terror, and the security and politico-legal measures taken by the West, most notably the USA, to protect itself against terrorism, have pushed authoritarianism on the defensive – but these measures have also provided an excuse for repressive regimes in the Arab world to use the war on terror to tighten the grip on the their populations. This has been happening at the very moment that Washington has been trying to pepper the region with democracy as the main element of its 'forward strategy of freedom in the Middle East'.

The AHDR 2003 report suggests that Arab states, acting within the 'Arab Charter for Anti-Terrorism', which 'neither explicitly prohibits detention or torture, nor provides for questioning the legality of detentions', have tended to curb freedoms through an expanded definition of terrorism.[21] The report equally criticizes the proclivity of the Arab regimes to use the pretext of Israeli domination to defer political and economic reforms. As a result, while the general trend saw 'freedom rise worldwide, in Arab countries it fell'. Arab countries have 'continued to evince the lowest levels of freedom among the world regions'.[22]

Since the 9/11 attacks, there has also been a renewed emphasis on the role of the state in international politics. Ironically, as shown below, while some political scientists were quick to see in globalization a decline in the importance and role of the state in mediating at the international level and managing at the national level, Islamist international terrorism in the twenty-first century has again made fashionable the emphasis on the security role that the MENA state, or some derivative of the existing state, can play as a fire-break in the war on terror. Democratic reform and the war on terrorism do not appear to be compatible in the Middle East, where Islamic terrorism and religion-driven political violence is a home-grown phenomenon that is rife across the region.

Regional Barriers to Assimilation: Economics, Politics and Culture

As has been illustrated in this book, the MENA region, as part of a so-called 'greater Middle East' (stretching from Morocco to Kashmir), has had more than its fair share of problems in trying to adapt itself to the forces of globalization. It is finding it difficult to assimilate and to avoid the fate assigned to it by the globalist jihadis on the one hand, and the civilizational jihadis on the other. At the political, economic and cultural levels, the region faces serious structural barriers to further integration into the global political economy. It is apparently unable to accommodate globalization, despite its rich human and natural resources, large markets, geopolitical advantage and great energy deposits. Here we revisit some of the reasons for this.

The Economic Level

Rodney Wilson has argued that, unlike East and Southeast Asia, the MENA region does not enjoy the benefits accrued from a 'flying geese' formation. He notes that, in the increasingly interdependent economies of the Far East, Japan, closely followed by Singapore, Hong Kong, South Korea and Taiwan, has led the region to rapid economic development. That process resulted in China emerging as a new economic engine for the entire region, fed by investment from its neighbours as well as the traditional OECD countries. China's rapid rise also provided a second boost for the process, which had begun in Japan in the 1950s and spread to other East Asian economies from the 1960s. In the MENA region, on the other hand, the most likely leading 'goose' (Israel) is not leading a regional formation,[23] and its closest rival for that role (Turkey) is too focused on the EU and Central Asia to pay much attention to the opportunities presented by the 'geese formation' in the Middle East. Even if Israel were to rise to this role, its isolation in the region, the size of its economy, and 'its lack of purchasing power to transmit substantial multiplier effects to other Middle Eastern economies' are likely to inhibit its ability to ignite rapid growth and development in its hinterland.[24] But even at the best of times this 'goose' would not have been able to find the way out of regional malaise, for time and again the Israeli economy has shown itself unable to shake off the effects of war and occupation in order to register sustained periods of prosperity. As recently as 2003, some 20 per cent of the Israeli population were living below the poverty line, and its GDP per capita growth rate had been reduced to just −0.5 per cent.[25]

We should further consider whether post-Saddam Iraq could act as a unique Arab 'goose' and pull the region towards a better economic future in the next two decades. At first glance, this looks highly unlikely. While Iraq is undoubtedly rich in terms of natural resources, the concern is whether the conditions for the profitable exploitation of these riches will be fulfilled in the first decade of the twenty-first century. With its infrastructure almost completely destroyed, it is likely that the cost of reconstruction will, in the medium term at least, impede the opportunities for capital accumulation and take-off. Membership of the World Trade Organization, rapid privatization of what remains of its industries, and open borders in trade and investment terms will all help. But they will not, in and by themselves, change the overall condition of Iraq's political economy.[26] For reform to take root, the all-important political and security conditions will need to be met. Iraqis themselves are of the view that Iraq will probably continue to be part of the regional problem, rather than the solution most people desperately want it to be.[27] The American neo-conservative dream of turning Iraq into a pro-Western base for the export of democracy, as well as a reliabl source of hydrocarbons, could be faltering at the first hurdle: the creation of a self-sustaining stable Iraqi political architecture in place of Saddam Hussein's corrupt and anti-democratic system.

None of the alternatives – an Islamist Iraq (of either Shii or Sunni varieties); a decomposed Iraq; an Iraq ruled by another 'strongman'; or, worse still, a 'Lebanonization' of Iraq (a long-running civil war providing the stage for proxy war in the region) – bodes well for the neighbourhood. For the moment, the forces for democratization remain weak and fragmented and the centripetal ones strong. But an Iraq at peace with all its Arab and non-Arab neighbours could, in the long run, rise to the challenge and, along with a group of its neighbours, play a major role in the development of the region, or at the very least contribute to the stability of the Persian Gulf subregion as a precondition of region-wide prosperity.

The Political Level

At this level, too, we have to watch developments in Iraq (and also Iran) with great care. Regime change in Iraq has opened up huge possibilities for reform in the entire region, but it has also destabilized the basis of inter-regional relations in both political and diplomatic terms.[28] In post-Saddam Iraq itself, we still need to find a secure voice for the Kurdish and Sunni minorities while making sure the Shii majority can play a significant, though non-dominant, role. The deep suspicions between these communities and the steady rise of Shia factionalism, however, have acted as constant drags on the rebuilding drive of Iraq. Yet it is not easy to see how the mix of inter-ethnic and inter-religious tensions can be overcome to the satisfaction of all parties. Contrary to the expectations of the White House and the Pentagon, the spirit of compromise has proved hard to forge among the much-abused Iraqis, where even political change for the better had, in the end, to be imposed on them through intense violence and from outside the Arab and Muslim worlds. Nonetheless, once Iraqis take control of their own destiny the situation will improve dramatically, but the external factor will probably remain critical for the foreseeable future.[29]

More generally, the state is now being pushed in contradictory directions across the region. On one hand, the Muslim states are being told by the USA that they need to reform their socio-economic and politico-legal systems, and open up their political systems by broadening their base and indulging in democratic politics.[30] At the same time, however, they are also being told that their state machinery and its fierce coercive arm must be strengthened in the interest of the global war on international terrorism. 'Increasingly, the state system has been eroding', noted former Secretary of State George P. Shultz in early 2004; 'Terrorists have exploited this weakness. But no replacement system is in sight that can perform the essential functions of establishing an orderly and lawful society, protecting essential freedoms, providing a framework for fruitful economic activity, and providing for the common defense. Our great task is restoring the vitality of the state system. All established states should stand up to their responsibilities in the fight against our common enemy, terror; be a helpful partner in economic and political development, and take care that international organizations work for their member states. When they do, they deserve respect and help to make them work successfully'.[31] Adding the political and economic dimensions of what is being asked of the MENA state, one cannot help but feel the gloom over having to square the circle it is being confronted with.

Moreover, there is a mixed message being sent to the region. On one hand, we have the message being sent by the forces of 'economization'; on the other hand, another being sent by the forces of counter-violence. The first requires the state to be nimble and light, open and welcoming, in order to be able respond to global economic trends. The second demands the state to be fierce, intrusive, inflexible and all-encompassing, in order to be able to combat terrorism. The message from the West reads in the region like this: those states that are able to apply their strong and centralized coercive arms should be rewarded for their efforts in the war on terrorism. States in desperate search of economic rewards can end up tightening the political screws on an already agitated society. At the height of their crisis, in search of economic support from the outside, some MENA regimes may actually end up undermining their position on the inside. This rather mixed and distorted signal being transmitted to the region by the globalists and the counter-terrorists is causing further confusion and instability in an already volatile and fragile environment. Such confusion further delays decisive action and positive engagement with globalization.

The Cultural Level

At this level, too, the region has much to do. The AHDR 2003 has identified a number of factors that block the dissemination of knowledge, for example with several of the knowledge factors the report identifies as being cultural in nature: authoritarian and over-protective child-rearing, the deteriorating quality of education in many countries in the region, curricula in schools that encourage submission, obedience, subordination and compliance rather than free critical thinking, lack of autonomy at universities, and the poor state of university libraries.[32] A knowledge deficit of this magnitude casts a long shadow over the region, preventing cultural renewal. The report estimates that by 1976, 23 per cent of Arab engineers, 50 per cent of Arab doctors and 15 per cent of Arab science degree-holders had migrated outside the Arab world. Approximately 25 per cent of 300,000 first-degree graduates from Arab universities in 1995–96 emigrated. Between 1998 and 2000, more than 15,000 Arab doctors had migrated overseas.[33] A similar pattern is in evidence in Iran and Pakistan. In Iran's case, one report notes that 'as of 1990 ... an estimated 637,000 of academicians, physicians, artists, writers, entrepreneurs, managers, capitalists, and their families ... [had emigrated], legally or otherwise, to other countries'.[34] Furthermore, on a yearly basis, the equivalent of US$11 billion in human capital continues to leave Iran – greater than Iran's total non-oil exports of some US$10 billion.[35]

In contrast, the only country that has enjoyed a net influx of skilled labour is Israel, which, since the collapse of the Soviet Union, has been able to absorb in excess of 500,000 trained professionals into its workforce.

In the wider context of globalization, the place and role of the media, and communications networks in general, knowledge transfer and education also need attention. With regard to access to mass media, the AHRD 2003 report says: 'Arab countries have lower information media to population ratios [number of newspapers, radio and television sets per 1,000] compared to the world average and to the average of middle-income countries'. In the Arab world, the figure is 53 newspapers per 1000 people, compared with 285 in the developed countries. This, the report argues, is due to the high rates of illiteracy in the region and a low standard of professionalism dictated by various instruments of control and coercion. According to the report, 'legalized restrictions on freedom of the press and freedom of expression in Arab countries curtail the independence and vitality of the mass media. In practice, the harassment of the press under the law is an all-too-frequent violation of freedom of expression, with newspapers sometimes facing closure, seizure, confiscation and sequestration'.[36] Again, a similar pattern has been in evidence in Iran, where in a short period after the victory of the reformist Khatami camp in the 1997 presidential and 2000 parliamentary elections, the blossoming media were quashed through the conservative-dominated judiciary. In a few weeks in 1999 and 2000, more than a dozen pro-reform newspapers were closed down, never to appear again in their original form.[37] The only countries in the region that at present enjoy free-flowing debate through their newspapers appear to be Israel and Turkey.

The absence of a free media has curtailed public expression of dissent and diversity, the influence of public opinion in decision-making, and the general public's sense of belonging to any given policy. Yet, under the conditions of globalization, the media often take centre stage in transmitting ideas and even in defending existing value systems. In the Arab world, much of the latter job is being undertaken by such widely watched satellite television stations as Qatar-based al-Jazeera, Abu Dhabi-based al-Arabiya, and others.[38] By capitalizing on the technological opportunities presented by globalization, these stations are now capable of rising above the nation-state in the Arab world to reinforce and distil Arab and Muslim transnational values across the region. They are able to do this for their own small populations as well as the many hundreds of thousands of expatriate Arab and Muslim communities, and the growing presence of 'native' Muslims in the West and elsewhere. Where national governments have failed, al-Jazeera and its vibrant competitors have stepped in to articulate the political and cultural regional responses to globalization, while themselves gaining technological and spatial oxygen.

The Geopolitical Context

The geopolitical context of the MENA region today provides another backdrop for the pace and nature of change. Broadly speaking, five countries in the GME region have the ability actively to shape the geopolitical setting of the area. The first two are Iraq and its non-Arab Shia neighbour Iran; the third is Israel; the fourth is Libya; and the fifth is Pakistan. With regard to Iraq, the geopolitical context is being shaped by a dangerous conflict between the country's Shia majority and militant Sunnis, including al-Qaeda.[39] The primary focus of the guerrilla operations in Iraq began to shift in the second half of 2003 towards the Shia community. It has been noted by Sunnis in general, and al-Qaeda and the Wahhabis in particular, that large sections of Iraq's Shia community not only did not rise against the US occupation, but has worked with the USA to facilitate a transfer of power that will make them the dominant political and socio-economic force in Iraq. In Iraq, the al-Qaeda and Sunni militants believe, the Shia, with the connivance of the USA, are busy implementing their plan for domination of the important Arab state of Iraq, and intend to use Iraq's territory to target Sunni Islam's heartland in Saudi Arabia. The terror campaign in Iraq, therefore, has acquired a dangerous geocultural slant, perilously threatening the stability of Shia–Sunni relations, non-Arab Iran's ties with its Sunni neighbours in the Arab world, and also Iran's and Iraq's relations with Sunni-dominated Pakistan, Turkey and Afghanistan.

The militant Sunnis' perception of the growing political role of the Shia in Iraq has increased the frequency and intensity of terror attacks on the

Shia communities there. These attacks reached a high point on Ashura (Shia Islam's major religious occasion) in early March 2004 (Islamic month of Muharram) with the deadly synchronized attacks on the main Shia shrines in Baghdad and Karbala, which killed at least 170 people and injured hundreds more.[40] The anti-Shia terror campaign in Iraq will probably resonate in Iraq's Sunni hinterland as well, and will stir greater hostilities between the Shia minorities of the Arabian peninsula states and their governments, as well as between the Shia-dominated states of Iran and Iraq and their neighbours. As a direct consequence of these developments, a clash of religious factions, if not 'civilizations', could eventually ensue to engulf the entire region.

Were this to happen, the Muslim world could again be set on a course of self-inflicted pain, with inter-factional collisions over ideology and identity. The USA will probably not be an innocent bystander in this situation. Having occupied Iraq and 'liberated' its Shia community, voices in Washington have begun to speak of the need to 'free the eastern province of Saudi Arabia' where the majority of Saudi Shii reside. Max Singer, the co-founder of the Hudson Institute, is among those who have suggested that Saudi Arabia's strategic oil region, its eastern al-Hasa province, should be separated from the rest of the country in an effort to curb Wahhabi extremism.[41] Other Washington insiders, such as Richard Perle, David Frum (President George W. Bush's former speech writer) and Senator Sam Brownback, have also recommended that the fight against terror be taken to Saudi Arabia. The Saudis need to be told to follow the US lead in its anti-terror campaign or watch the US encourage separatist tendencies of the Saudi Shia in al-Hasa.[42] By denying access to oil, the argument goes, Riyadh can be 'tamed' and Saudi fundamentalists deprived of the necessary funds to support al-Qaeda.

It is the rather sudden shift of focus in US circles to the geocultural overlap between Persian Gulf oil and Shia communities that alarms the (largely Sunni-dominated) Arab regional actors, as King Abdullah of Jordan, President Mubarak of Egypt and several Saudi princes have already articulated. The West, suggests Mai Yamani, has 'woken up to the accident of geography that has placed the world's major oil supplies in areas where the Shi'ites form the majority'.[43] It is the awareness of this geocultural cross-section in Western policy terms that petrifies the Arab leaders and fuels their suspicions of the USA's end-game strategy in the region. In the tense post-Saddam environment of the Persian Gulf subregion, even faint suspicion of US-backed sectarian power struggles between the Sunni and the Shia can ignite a much bigger fire to engulf the entire Arab world. Gulf Arab leaders, therefore, may be forgiven for not fully buying into the USA's Iraq mission; nor its grand democratization drive. If both these initiatives are to result in the empowerment of the Shia communities of the Arab world, it is hardly likely that Sunni leaders will embrace them with any warmth. Where Arab regime survival is at stake, the USA could be fanning flames of antagonism that could keep warm the fires of many decades of trench warfare between militant and jihadist Islamists and the West. The Shia, of course, will not uniformly welcome the USA's intervention on their behalf. US backing, short of delivering a defensible Shia protectorate, could threaten their efforts at co-existence with their Sunni brethren. As a minority in a sea of Sunnis in the Muslim world, the Shia are very careful not to fan the sectarian flames that could lead to their further marginalization or, worse, annihilation. The USA's grand designs could be creating new, unpredictable and uncontrollable instabilities in the region.

It is into this grave situation that neighbouring Iran treads. As the world's only Shia, and expressly Islamist, state, Iran in its post-revolutionary mode has been careful not to stray too far from the wider Arab region in its policy pronouncements. It has remained loyal to the Palestinian cause, has developed co-operative relations with virtually every Arab state, and has ensured that it keeps in close touch with its Gulf Arab neighbours. Yet the tempo of its domestic politics is hopelessly out of synchronization with its Arab neighbours. One commentator has speculated that 'In 20 years, perhaps less, Iran will be a powerful democracy and a solid US ally. Having rejected its own western stooge and endured an indigenous, orthodox replacement, the Iranians realize there is no alternative to liberal democracy. If the Arab world is entering a pre-revolutionary phase, Iran is in a post-revolutionary one. The Iranian polity is already more dynamic than many of its Arab counterparts. Its demographics – a growing population of young, secular reformers and a dwindling pool of ageing clerics – are working in favour of stability'.[44] On the basis of this scenario, Iran will have as much to fear from the tide of Sunni–Arab Islamism as its Western counterparts. Yet Islamist Iran finds itself in a geopolitical struggle with the USA and its main regional ally, Israel, and cannot act as a natural ally of the West in the war on al-Qaeda. Although both Tehran and Washington fear al-Qaeda, largely because of their own bilateral problems, they have been unable to form a Western–Islamic front against al-Qaeda and Salafi Islam. Irrespective of the Iran–US problems, however, Iran is destined to play a critical role in the unfolding drama of the region. Susser notes that in the Persian Gulf, 'Iran is the only regional power of consequence. Iraq is out for the count, and the Saudis are a broken reed'.[45] Such an assessment would have seemed hardly credible a decade ago. Thus the combination of Iran's fast-moving dynamic political system, its relations with the Arab and non-Arab Shias (in Iraq, Kuwait, Bahrain, Saudi Arabia, Lebanon, Afghanistan, Pakistan, India and Azerbaijan), and its geopolitical advantages will continue to give the leaders of this country a powerful voice in the region.

To the west of Iraq we have to consider the geopolitics of the Arab–Israeli conflict, which is increasingly defined by the policies of the one dominant actor, Israel. Since its foundation in 1948, Israel has never shied from using its considerable capacity to affect the geopolitics of the region to its own advantage. In the era of globalization, which Israel has utilized to great effect in order to advance economically, it can also now count on the security fallout from 9/11 and the war on terror campaign to advance further its own interests in the region. It has been able to do this much more easily with the fall of Baghdad in April 2003 than at any time since the signing of the Israeli–Egyptian Camp David accords in 1978–79. Compounded by the collapse of the Soviet Union and Iraq's foreign policy debacles since 1980, the Arab world has been unable to find an appropriate response to Israel's supremacy, having to watch from the sidelines Tel Aviv's manipulation of the Arab–Israeli agenda and its ever closer strategic partnership with non-Arab Turkey. Israel, therefore, has managed to secure for itself a key role in the balancing of forces in the Arab world.[46]

Libya's emergence from the late 1990s as a non-confrontational state was completed in 2003–04. By late 2004, virtually all sanctions on the country had been lifted and, with its denunciation of terrorism, support for the anti-al-Qaeda war on terror, and abandonment of all its weapons of mass destruction programmes, it was set to emerge as a key North African partner of the West, mostly the EU, in economic and political terms. Its geopolitical position and its hydrocarbon resources will place Libya at the heart of developments on the western side of the Arab world in this century. Its choice of regional partners, as it frees itself from the shackles of sanctions, will help in redrawing North Africa's economic and geopolitical map. Due to its strategic location, certainly in the war on terrorism, it could overshadow the services of Algeria, Tunisia and Morocco combined. It can also help in the development of closer economic links between the Maghreb countries or, conversely, choose to ignore its neighbours by cutting a vertical axis with Europe on the one hand and Africa on the other. If it were to follow the latter option, the dream of an Arab common market would be in tatters if the market were to lose Libya as a territorially and financially facilitating actor.[47]

Finally, Pakistan's role on the eastern fringes of the MENA region has grown immeasurably since it joined the US war on terror and assisted the West in its overthrow of the Taleban in Afghanistan and the military campaign against al-Qaeda. For the Gulf Arab states, Pakistan has been a steady supplier of cheap Muslim labour, cheap manufactured and processed goods, and military support. In the 1980s, Pakistan provided a great deal of logistical and personnel support for Saudi Arabia as the Kingdom tried to incorporate its massive weapons purchases in its rapidly modernizing armed forces. It has kept this military partnership alive ever since. But as the Muslim world's only nuclear-weapon state with close trade and cultural links with the Persian Gulf states, Afghanistan and some Central Asian countries, the impact of its foreign policy orientation at this crucial juncture in the history of the MENA region cannot be underestimated. Pakistan is not known for its political stability, however. 'During the past half century', notes Muhammad Ahsan, 'this Islamic Republic has had twenty-four heads of state and has adopted three constitutions. Half of its period of existence has been under three periods of martial law, and it has gone to war three times'.⁴⁸ This cauldron of instability is now a close US ally in the war on terror. How the US–Pakistani partnership develops will affect Pakistani politics in the years to come, possibly weakening the secular-leaning and pragmatic forces in this large Muslim country. Radicalization of nuclear-armed Pakistan, however, will destabilize the partnership not only with the USA, but with all Pakistan's neighbours. More so now than at any time in its history, any radical shift in Pakistan will therefore directly affect the GME.

Its partnership with the USA, its relationship with India and China, and its potential role as a permanent base for the war on terrorism in West Asia, raise serious questions about the policies Pakistan pursues with regard to the Middle East. Persian Gulf states are alive to the possibility that the positioning of Pakistan as a close US ally could have serious domestic consequences in that country. Any instability there, or a further consolidation of Salafi Islamist forces in Pakistan, can easily spill over into Afghanistan (and even Iran), and the Gulf Arab allies of the West. Pakistan's closeness to the USA, therefore, could worsen the political tensions between regimes and Islamist forces in the eastern Arab world, causing further instability in the region and possible delays in the implementation of badly needed political, economic and social reforms. Yet this anti-terror alliance is here to stay, despite American concerns about Pakistan's long-term stability.⁴⁹

The Middle East, concludes Clement Henry in a fascinating article about globalization and the region, 'may yet prove to be the battlefield that reverses the tendencies of most states to open themselves up to the benefits of commerce and investment associated with globalisation'.⁵⁰ Such policy initiatives as regime change as a strategy, the war in Iraq, and the war on terror campaign are some of the key factors that could determine the impact of globalization in the region, he notes. With this conclusion, few commentators who know the region can disagree. Added to these geopolitical developments are other forces at play that can fundamentally alter the direction of the region. The five states identified in this chapter for further scrutiny are uniquely placed to shape the geopolitical landscape of the GME – and what they do will also directly affect the economic environment of the region, inasmuch as they can set the tempo for engagement or disruption. The five will not work in concert, and will in all probability pursue contradictory policies. Some will compete for geopolitical advantage and some will seek outside support for advancing their own regional agendas, but ultimately it will be the policies of these states that will decide the nature of the interactions. Other key actors – Algeria, Egypt, Saudi Arabia, Syria – will play their role as well, and such countries as resource-rich Saudi Arabia or strategically placed Syria will become more heavily involved in geopolitical power plays as the fabric of the Arab order erodes further, but they will, by and large, be reacting to developments rather than setting the agenda.

In the last analysis – in a region where the shapes of post-modernist states are still blurred, and the state remains supreme – the tenor of the

GME's engagement with global capitalism will be set by the role perceptions and behavioural patterns of its pivotal states. They will not control the agenda in the era of globalization – far from it. Today, where communication and interaction flow ever more freely, even small actors (states or NGOs) will be able to exercise their autonomy and strike partnerships or ignite hostilities with near or far players. It is, rather, the role of these pivotal states in setting the conditions for such interactions that is significant.

9 Globalization and the Middle East in Perspective

> Closing the Greater Middle East region's prosperity gap will require an economic transformation similar in magnitude to that undertaken by the formerly communist countries of Central and Eastern Europe.
>
> Greater Middle East Initiative.

When the End is Near

It was argued at the outset of this study that globalization has a much more limited meaning when taken outside its OECD context. While every state is vulnerable to it, and while every community and individual can feel its force, the presence that globalization has in any given setting is still determined by local, domestic conditions. While in the areas of telecommunications and international finance the full force of globalization is omnipresent, its broader domestic effects are still determined largely by state actors. States certainly do feel the pressures globalization brings to bear, but their responses are conditioned by national political and political economy realities and, in the case of the Middle East, regional geopolitical factors as well.

Nonetheless, globalization has been seen as a powerful force that is bringing with it the momentum for change in the MENA region. This force may usher in some radical and destabilizing transformations – it may even undo the state structures developed since the end of the Ottoman empire. It may weaken the grip of ruling elites on political levers of power, or even brush some aside if their feeble resistance fails to mount a constructive challenge. States can prolong some battles, but there will be some key ones that they will have to lose on the path of progress, which itself can be packaged in terms of reforms in the socio-economic, political and macro-economic realms.

Throughout this book, globalization has been seen as a dynamic and ongoing process of rapid change; a leveller at the same time as a differentiator; a reducer of time and space, and yet a fragmenter of regions, nation-states and communities; a global force that can, at the same time, touch every individual on the planet; a powerful trans-border force in the face of the territorial state; and a 'villagizer' of the world without a predetermined agenda – a force that can be ridden but not necessarily controlled. Bearing in mind the earlier discussions about globalization and its many facets in the Middle East, it is instructive to draw some overall conclusions with a political economy perspective in mind. The MENA region, it has been argued, has many deep socio-economic and political problems, which are being compounded by the force of globalization and the region's geopolitical vulnerabilities in terms of penetration and domination by outside powers. To remember Brown: the 'entire world has been shaken and shaped by the West in modern times, but nowhere has the political dimension of that been more thorough and more consistent than in the Middle East'.[1] The region's relationship with the outside world has been further complicated by 9/11 and the USA's new security paradigms of democratization and the war on terror.

Globalization has exposed the region's economic weaknesses, posing serious challenges to its leaders in terms of finding workable strategies for effective competition in today's globalized market.[2] Globalization has also exposed the distance they have to travel in order to be able to climb up the international ladder of economic success and prosperity. But, at the same time, globalization has challenged the very roots of their societies, shaking to their foundations the region's dominant socio-economic structures and cultural norms. In one respect, globalization has challenged the patriarchal foundations of the MENA region's Muslim societies, questioning, as just one example, the legal–judicial subordination of women in society. In doing so, cultural norms are being threatened, but so too are the very economic frameworks of social and labour organization.

In another, perhaps more fundamental way, globalization has also challenged the étatist, rent-driven states of the region. Sharabi has made a persuasive argument to the effect that all MENA regime types – republican, monarchical, 'progressive' or conservative – have in one way or another embodied a peculiar form of political economy in which the state has become 'the central controlling force in society, not just by virtue of its monopoly of coercion but also by its vastly increased economic power – as owner of the basic industries, source of all major investments, only international borrower, and provider of essential services'.[3] As it did so, the MENA state took upon itself the role that the bourgeoisie in Europe had played in the early industrialization of these economies. Thanks to the rapid accumulation of rent from the 1960s onwards, the state began closely to mimic the bourgeoisie – indeed, slowly replacing the traditional bourgeois forces in many Muslim societies – thus becoming the largest employer in more than a dozen MENA countries, the main player in the political arena, and also the monopole of political power. A 'state bourgeoisie' came into being, tightening its grip on power through the bureaucracy and the armed forces. In Barakat's words, 'instead of protecting the big traditional bourgeoisie, modern armies [i.e. the state] became the instruments of its elimination in several Arab countries'.⁴ In the same process, the state became the new dominant social force, also acquiring independent powers over civil society. The balance had been tipped in favour of the corporatist state.

Globalization, helped along by the Bush administration's reform agenda, thus challenged the state's grip over civil society in very direct ways. If globalization's presence can be argued to be one of 'benign presence', President Bush's agenda can hardly be seen as anything but active intervention. The US push for the introduction of reforms in the Muslim Middle East, even more heavily trailed in President Bush's second term than in the first, is consistent with the globalization agenda, and is as destabilizing. Since 2002 President Bush has been consistent in his message, which was again spelt out in his presentation at the National Defense University in Washington, DC in the final few months of his first term in office:

> Our strategy to keep the peace in the longer term is to help change the conditions that give rise to extremism and terror, especially in the broader Middle East. Parts of that region have been caught for generations in a cycle of tyranny and despair and radicalism. When a dictatorship controls the political life of a country, responsible opposition cannot develop, and dissent is driven underground and toward the extreme. And to draw attention away from their social and economic failures, dictators place blame on other countries and other races, and stir the hatred that leads to violence. This status quo of despotism and anger cannot be ignored or appeased, kept in a box or bought off, because we have witnessed how the violence in that region can reach easily across borders and oceans. The entire world has an urgent interest in the progress, and hope, and freedom in the broader Middle East. The advance of hope in the Middle East requires new thinking in the region. By now it should be clear that authoritarian rule is not the wave of the future; it is the last gasp of a discredited past ... It should be clear that economic progress requires political modernization, including honest representative government and the rule of law. And it should be clear that no society can advance with only half of its talent and energy – and that demands the full participation of women. The advance of hope in the Middle East also requires new thinking in the capitals of great democracies – including Washington, D.C. By now it should be clear that decades of excusing and accommodating tyranny, in the pursuit of stability, have only led to injustice and instability and tragedy ... It should be clear that the best antidote to radicalism and terror is the tolerance and hope kindled in free societies.⁵

In pursuing reform, the US president appears to be wishing to cure exactly what intellectuals and activists in the region have been diagnosing for some time as the region's grave disease, namely that 'Arab citizens have been rendered powerless because they have been excluded from the political process. Marginalized, and isolated from the human and material resources civil society should place at their disposal, the people of the area suffer from state tyranny over society ... the affairs of the community and society have ceased to be their own'.[6] The Bush administration has tried to undo the very étatist and corporatist structures and systems that Barakat, Sharabi (and many others) have identified as the key causes of the MENA region's problems.

Globalization, for all its dangers, can offer a way through the rather bleak picture gleaned from a political economy study of the region. Instead of reinforcing the impasse in the Arab and Muslim Middle East, globalization can be the crossroads of opportunity for the region insofar as it does encourage empowerment of the individual in society. Women can become full partners in the social contract, and civil society can be helped to grow. But a precondition would have to be for the region's articulated modes of production – a mixture of pre-capitalist and capitalist structures – to become more capitalist, sufficiently to enable independent socio-economic actors (women, a bourgeoisie free of state control) to forge the expansion of civil society. This could happen with more globalization of the region. The late Nazih Ayubi has cautiously noted that 'what has tilted the balance towards more democracy in recent years [in the Middle East] has been the growing globalisation and undisputed ideological hegemony of the "West" following the collapse of socialist regimes in Eastern Europe'.[7] But he also warns that democratization through globalization is not inevitable in the Middle East, and that it will be difficult, to say the least, to remove the clientalization of society to the 'producer–distributor' state.[8]

An independent bourgeoisie, which grows in the shadow of the state, could prove to be less than a championing class for civil society. Any independent MENA bourgeoisie will remain dependent on the state for prosperity and for protection against foreign competition, even if offered in a limited form. Thus, while the comprador bourgeoisie, aligned to the state, may seek ways of using globalization and American pressure to prize open the state sector, so long as its commercial operations remain located in the international orbit it will be unable to act as midwife to new political economy. Ironically, the social force ready and waiting to undertake this role is the Islamists, which is closely associated with the besieged traditional middle classes across the Muslim Middle East. In Iran, the alliance between them and the radical section of the religious establishment generated an unstoppable revolutionary force in 1979. Elsewhere, this alliance may be more opaque but equally real, its power visible just beneath the veneer of the state. Although not anti-capitalist, they are largely anti-globalization by persuasion. How this force may face up to the challenge of the 'modern woman' in a more liberalized social and political environment marks another of the unique challenges facing the Middle East.

To sum up, it has been argued in this book that, based on its historical legacies, the MENA region should not find interaction with other cultures and polities difficult, or even threatening. The region has a long history of engagement with the outside world – from China to the heart of Europe, from southern Africa to the Iberian Peninsula. Before Islam, its empires ruled the modern world; after the rise of Islam, it assimilated other peoples and cultures to build monumental towers of knowledge and science. The arts and literature, as symbols of a confident social order, flourished.

From the sixteenth century the Europeans arrived in force, slowly taking control of the region's destiny. Despite the Middle East's rejection of colonialism, the region did adapt to European ways: Mohammed Ali in Egypt, Kamal Attaturk in Turkey, Reza Khan in Iran and Habib Bourgiba in Tunisia were pioneers of the assimilation process.

The Europeans also located and provided the means for extracting the region's most valuable and sought-after commodity, oil. In more recent times, thanks to oil, the region has had intensive interaction with the outside world, and the geopolitics of oil put the Persian Gulf at the forefront of this interaction.

The region has adopted modern ways in politics, economic relations, planning and the fundamental systems of social renewal. In education, training, public administration, public policy, public health, etc., the MENA states have scored notable successes, often easily mirroring developments in the OECD countries. Yet today, the region is weak on the inside and exposed on the outside. Its economies are in urgent need of rapid and comprehensive reform, its public organizations need overhaul, its political systems need to become more open and transparent, and its leaders more accountable and receptive. It needs to find employment for its army of many unemployed, it needs to keep its many hundreds of thousands of young people engaged, it needs to relearn the art of scientific inquiry, it needs to replenish its cultural reservoirs – it needs to give its people hope and a brighter future. In the midst of these fundamental problems has appeared globalization as a powerful, corrosive, destabilizing and imposing force, challenging the region's political orders, its economic foundations and its cultural underpinnings. As a dam-busting force, globalization is showing its ability to threaten the jealously guarded territorial state – 'having ... come to terms with the modern territorial state ... Muslims now must readjust to the decentralizing pressures of globalization'[9] – which can unwittingly loosen the grip of the power elite on the polity. The elite is feeling the chill, and is apparently grappling to respond to the challenges as creatively as it possibly can. But what it feels comfortable attempting may be too limited in terms of the depth and dimensions of the problems it faces.

This will be due partly to the role that security matters continue to play in this region. As we have seen, post-9/11 (in)security, defined in a geopolitical context, may override the implementation of the many urgent reforms needed for riding the globalization tiger. Yet without the reforms, the ability to achieve long-term and durable security, in its social as well as political contexts, may prove impossible to achieve. The vicious circle of crisis management will not, unfortunately, be broken. Whether the region's failures will, in the end, be judged as the realization of a self-fulfilling prophecy, or a historic opportunity missed, can be determined only by the next generation.

There is, nevertheless, widespread recognition of the task ahead – as we will see, even the original 2004 Greater Middle East Initiative (GMEI) acknowledged the difficulties to overcome. Yet the region itself apparently remains too paralysed to deal with its many problems. While its leaders object to what they regard as outside interference, they consistently fail – as a group – to articulate a coherent response to the political, socio-economic and security dilemmas facing the region and, by extension, virtually every member of the subsystem. Ironically, in their collective paralysis they leave the door wide open for outside forces to pile on the pressure.

Old Games, New Rules

One result of the problems is that MENA elites will probably find it increasingly difficult to provide economic (and physical) security nets for their citizens in return for their acceptance of political apathy, tolerance of corrupt practices, and the exercise of economic power by ruling circles. This is so despite the rapid rises in oil prices. As Cordesman notes with reference to one of the richest oil states of the past 100 years, 'Saudi Arabia is no longer "oil wealthy" in the sense that its present economy can provide for its people. The doubling of Saudi Arabia's population and worldwide cuts in real oil prices have reduced its per capita earnings from petroleum exports from $24,000 in 1980 to $2,300 in 2002 ... Saudi Arabia ... has faced nearly two decades of major budget and trade deficits, and its government debt is nearly 100% of its GNP. It no longer can provide social services, modernize and expand its infrastructure, and diversify its economy without major economic reform and foreign investment. Such reform and investment is critical to Saudi internal stability, but it requires US support'.[10] Despite relatively high prices, to a large extent the picture Cordesman has painted still holds true, for, as Malik and Niblock note, reforms and high oil prices will not remove the need for a new 'social contract ... between the state and the population, encompassing political and economic dimensions' of the Saudi state's role in society.[11]

The same story can be repeated for four other oil-rich MENA states: Algeria, Iran, Iraq and Libya. In Iran's case, the conservative Heritage Foundation's 2003 'economic freedom' index pointed out that, among 155 countries, Iran came in at 148th for its economic standing in the world.[12] Algeria, Iraq and Libya, alongside many other Arab states, are either beginning the long process of transition, or contemplating it. All four countries, however, need a massive injection of foreign capital and know-how if they are to remain big players in the oil market in the twenty-first century, despite the heady oil prices of over US$60 per barrel mid-decade.

Socio-economic and political problems will be compounded as population growth begins to outstrip economic performance and overrun each country's plans to generate the millions of new jobs needed each year.[13] This is not a passing problem – new data suggest that the region's population is exploding beyond the states' ability to manage its impact. By 2050, Saudi Arabia is set to have a population of 50 million (doubling between 2005 and 2050); Yemen's is set to grow to 71 million (rising by 243 per cent); Egypt's is to grow to 126 million (from 74 million in 2005); and Iraq's is projected to reach 64 million (rising by 121 per cent between 2005 and 2050).[14] The three small Gulf Arab states of Bahrain, Kuwait and the UAE are to see their populations grow from 7.9 million in 2005 to 17.5 million in 2050. The Arab world needs to generate some 100 million new jobs over the next two decades to cope with the current population bulge, let alone with the numbers that are to come through by mid-century. As a consequence, and in the course of the predictable tensions, some countries will close up, adopting a defensive posture; while in others reforming elites will break rank and openly pursue a more liberal and forward-looking approach. But, as was asked indirectly earlier, can such schemes as the USA's 2004 GMEI help in advancing the cause of reform, or do they hinder it? The initiative, first brought to light by Vice-President Dick Cheney at the World Economic Forum meeting in Davos in January 2004, was called 'the most ambitious U.S. democracy effort since the end of the Cold War'.[15] Its existence was made public a year after the Arab world's own 'Arab Charter', which Saudi Arabia tabled in January 2003. The charter, seen as a revolution of sorts in its own right, had called for 'internal reform and enhanced political participation in the Arab states'.[16] The later US plan, in contrast, had encompassed a wide range of diplomatic, cultural and economic measures. The GMEI had deliberately moved the agenda on by calling for the USA and its European allies and partners (in the G8 Group, NATO and the EU) to press for and assist free elections in the Middle East (through support for civic education, the creation of independent election commissions in MENA countries, and comprehensive voter registers), foster the growth of new independent media there, press for judicial reforms, help create a 'literate generation' by helping to cut regional illiteracy rates in half by 2010, train 'literacy corps' of around 100,000 female teachers by 2008, finance the translation of Western classical texts into Arabic to foster better understanding of the West among Muslims, establish a European-style GME Development Bank, an International Finance Corporation-style GME Finance Corporation to assist the development of larger enterprises, and give US$500 million in micro-loans to small entrepreneurs, especially women, in order to assist 1.2 million small entrepreneurs out of poverty.

Since 9/11, reform of the region has become a high US priority, and the launch of the GMEI should be seen in the context of developing and accelerating the reform process. The concern from the region, however, has been that the 2004 US initiative, like its predecessor in 2003, tried to explain its logic in purely Western security terms – as its early 2004 draft states: 'So long as the region's pool of politically and economically disenfranchised individuals grows, we will witness an increase in extremism, terrorism, international crime and illegal migration'.[17] Furthermore, there was concern that the initiative perceived the region in largely Cold War terms – for example speaking of creating MENA security structures based on the 1975-launched Helsinki process and NATO's Partnership for Peace programme. It anticipated that a complex set of security structures could bring six Middle East countries, including Egypt, Morocco, Tunisia, Qatar and Israel, into partnership with NATO. But leaving such prominent regional players as Iran, Syria and Saudi Arabia out of such regional security arrangements was always likely to fuel discontent, creating new divisions and breeding further instability across national boundaries. In the context of globalization and MENA fears of a political–cultural and economic invasion of the region, drawing parallels with the East–West Helsinki process has done nothing to assuage fears; indeed, it has accomplished the opposite. On more than one occasion, regional policy-makers have stated that the Helsinki process first ended the alternative power bloc to the West and then caused an internal collapse of the Soviet Union. 'Is that what's in store for the Muslim world as well with this initiative?', several leading Arab (and Iranian) policy-makers have asked.[18]

Another important concern was how much notice the initiative would take of the situation on the ground in the Middle East, and how much attention it would give to the legitimate concerns of the region's ruling regimes.[19] It was precisely because of the ambiguities attached to the original proposal that President Husni Mubarak of Egypt 'denounced with force the ready-for-use prescriptions proposed abroad under cover of what are called reforms'.[20] As he headed home from a meeting with the late King Fahd and Crown Prince Abdullah of Saudi Arabia, President Mubarak told Egyptian journalists, 'we hear about these initiatives as if the region and its states do not exist, as if they had no sovereignty over their land ... these kinds of initiatives do not deserve a comment, [but] need to be confronted by scientific and convincing answers from thinkers, so as not to leave people to fall prey to misleading impressions and misconceptions disseminated by such initiatives'. In Riyadh, an official Egyptian–Saudi statement noted that 'imposing a certain model of reform on Arab and Islamic states from the outside is unacceptable ... [Arab countries are] progressing on the road to development, modernisation and reform, but in a way that is compatible with the needs, interests, values and identities of their peoples'.[21]

The voices of some other Arab leaders, including those from Jordan, Morocco and Syria, were added to this objection, all rejecting the plan as an external imposition, as the news of it began to filter out in February 2004. 'No matter how well-intended the Americans and Europeans say their initiatives are, it will take more than words to comfort skeptical Arab rulers and a worried Arab public. The regimes see many signs suggesting that the

United States is determined to enforce change or "reforms," while the public – initially desperate for real reforms – suspect that the foreign calls for democracy are only an excuse to interfere in the region and redraw it in accordance with the West's own interests. The occupation of Iraq and the disinterest in Palestinian suffering have reinforced those fears', noted the *Cairo Times*.[22] Former National Security Advisor Zbigniew Brzezinkski added that: 'There is no question that the administration has its work cut out for it. For starters, the democracy initiative was unveiled by the president in a patronizing way: before an enthusiastic audience at the American Enterprise Institute, a Washington policy institution enamored of the war in Iraq and not particularly sympathetic toward the Arab world. The notion that America, with Europe's support and Israel's endorsement, will teach the Arab world how to become modern and democratic elicits, at the very least, ambivalent reactions. (This, after all, is a region where memory of French and British control is still fresh.)'[23]

Yet, as the initiative provided the first indication of a concerted drive to reform the region, many civil society groups and liberal voices in the region came (albeit quietly at first) to welcome the GMEI, with the proviso that it must enjoy 'high local content'. According to *Al-Ahram*, at least one opposition leader welcomed the initiative, noting that 'sadly enough, it was only this kind of pressure that forced [Egypt's ruling party] to finally relinquish its 22 years of stubborn refusal to embrace any kind of political reform, establish a human rights council and allow a remarkable amount of press freedom'.[24] The German partner of the GMEI had this factor in mind when he presented its content to the Egyptians in terms of the two highly critical Arab Human Development Reports.[25] It is said that 'by 12 February, German ambassador to Cairo Martin Cobler had given Osama El-Baz, President Mubarak's chief political adviser, a copy of the new US–EU transatlantic initiative'. He had told officials that the initiative aimed at securing a full partnership between the transatlantic coalition and the greater Middle East, 'in the light of US and European consensus that reforming the Middle East must be a top priority'. He is reported to have said this is so 'because reform is the basic measure required for uprooting terrorism, which is a danger to both the West and the Arab world'. Cobler had also explained that, in order to achieve the objective of reforms, the GMEI would attempt to adopt recommendations made by the two Arab Human Development Reports which, he said, 'discuss educational reform programmes, democratisation and human rights schemes, as well as the need to strengthen the region's entrepreneurial and economic capabilities'.[26] But a sceptical commentator soon questioned the integrity of the link being drawn with the Arab Human Development Reports, stating that 'any honest reading of the report(s) would show that [they] ... said that the Israeli occupation is the greatest obstacle to human development in Arab countries', and using the UN reports in this context is 'like a drunkard leaning on a lamppost, to save himself from falling, and not for enlightenment'.[27] Not surprisingly, the GMEI initiative in its 'American format' was soon shelved, to be replaced with a much more 'region-friendly' package adopted at the Sea Island (Georgia, USA) G8 summit in June 2004, which was again endorsed at the NATO summit in Turkey later that year. The title shift from the 'greater' to the 'broader' Middle East was the signal that the new initiative was not as sweeping and geographically encompassing as first envisaged.[28] The focus shifted rather dramatically towards building regional structures, more in keeping with the EU's outlook, from the USA's initial re-ordering agenda outlined above.

Despite the dramatically milder initiative, and the Arab League's endorsement of the calls for region-wide reforms at its Tunis summit in May 2004, Washington has continued to press on with its own democratization agenda for the region, openly pressing ally and foe alike to open up or accelerate the pace of reform. This again featured heavily in 2006, forming a main plank of the State of the Union address in January: 'Ultimately, the only way to defeat the terrorists is to defeat their dark vision of hatred and fear by offering the hopeful alternative of political freedom and peaceful change. So the United States of America supports democratic reform across the broader Middle East. Elections are vital, but they are only the beginning. Raising up democracy requires the rule of law, and protection of minorities, and strong, accountable institutions that last longer than a single vote'.[29]

Bush's vision is consistent with earlier US attempts to change the world in America's image. Soon after the start of the Cold War, and well before President Reagan's 'evil empire' typology of the 1980s, the right had begun a wide-ranging assault on Marxism. By adopting a Marxian lexicon for referring to the expansionist zeal of the Soviet Union (calling it imperialist, for example), these forces slowly but surely made of the Soviet state and its successor states their own allies in the globalization process. As Stephen Ambrose noted, those Americans who 'wanted to bring the blessings of democracy, capitalism, and stability to everyone [advocated that] the whole world ... should be a reflection of the United States'.[30]

Political Peace as a Prefix of Globalization

A main fear in the region has been that the West's plans for the region are half-baked at best. The case in point has been developments in the Arab–Israeli arena. The EU–US plans appear to put the cart before the horse, particularly as they seem to correspond with the long-held neo-conservative view that reforming the Arab world would somehow create a magical solution to the Arab–Israeli conflict. Yet, within the region, the reverse argument is the one that holds true. As a senior member of Egypt's ruling National Democratic Party (Mohamed Abdellah) put it, 'The Bush administration's talk of peace, democracy and freedom in the Arab world will be pointless as long as Israelis and Palestinians remain committed to slaughtering each other every day'.[31] The same view has been expressed in European capitals. The French Foreign Minister of the time (later Prime Minister of the Republic), Dominique de Villepin, echoed the same concern when he said: 'If we want to be credible, we can't ignore the Israeli–Palestinian conflict. Re-creating a dynamic for peace is an indispensable condition for any initiative in the region'.[32] Although the G8 and NATO summits of 2004 did mention the need to resolve the Israeli–Palestinian conflict, it was not until the death of the Palestinian leader Yasser Arafat in November 2004 that real momentum in their bilateral relations was felt. But without outside (in particular US) commitment, the 'road map' did not by itself lead to the establishment of the State of Palestine or final peace. Indeed, within 14 months of the Palestinian leader's death, the reverse seemed to be in progress: the rejectionist Islamist group Hamas had entered the Palestinian Parliament as its largest bloc, formed the authority's new government, and fundamentally challenged the very basis of the road map, and also the foundations on which the whole peace process had been built since the Madrid discussions of 1991.

Thus, without durable peace in this arena, the realization of alternative and better futures for the Middle East remain distant, and the Middle East crisis can objectively be reduced to this geopolitical logjam.

Back to the Future

We can discuss at length the many alternative futures awaiting the Middle East, and those dreamed up by the West, but the one initiative – over all others – that can surely unlock the region's energies and help in releasing its tremendous spirit of enterprise is the resolution of the century-old Arab–Israeli conflict and, at its heart, the creation of two secure and viable states in territories formerly known as Mandate Palestine. For all the forward surges that globalization generates, in the MENA subsystem the past continues to haunt the future. Local and dominant outside powers alike must share responsibility for the region's current predicament, and also bear the burden of freeing the region from decades of violence and insecurity.

The historical irony is that, without a 'democratic peace' in the Arab–Israeli conflict, and the other political fundamentals in place, the impact of globalization will probably continue to remain peripheral to the main forces shaping the region. As we have seen, globalization is certainly already felt across the region, but its force has not changed the region. Deglobalization could come to define the region's exceptionalism if that debate continues into the twenty-first century.

Many observers would regard globalization's inability to fundamentally change the subsystem as the ultimate nightmare scenario to be avoided in the region, even if this were to be achieved at the cost of retaining American forces in the area. For them, neglect by the global forces of change is worse than engagement through force. Looking at the options, all the MENA states have to do, it seems, is to find a mechanism for balancing the destabilizing force of globalization against the destabilizing impact of US domination. This is an act that few of them have mastered, or are likely to be able to master in the foreseeable future. In the meantime, globalization marches on, and on, and on.

Returning to the National Intelligence Council's 2003 assessment (discussed in chapter 8) – its conclusions that globalization will destabilize the region, that channels of communications and information transfer will ease the spread and adoption of extremist ideas, that war will remain a main feature of the region, and that the USA will remain a cause of tension in the area do not, as a whole, bode well for those seeking to deepen the influence of the more extrovert, peaceful and integrative tendencies in the region. Instead of playing a dangerous game by old rules, as Carl Brown suggested, it is perhaps more appropriate today to suggest that, when it comes to this region, arguably many of the old games are being played by new rules.

In the context of such a gloomy diagnosis, while the inevitability of change and dynamism cannot be questioned, its direction and end product certainly ought to be. In a globalized world of perpetual motion and uncertainty, the greater Middle East, and within it the MENA regional system, more than any other part of the world will be exposed to the dangers of stagnation at home and the frictions arising from a shrunken global time–space continuum. Against all the odds and despite the huge opportunities, the patterns of the previous 200 years could well be repeated, stifling the region and setting back the clock for another generation or more.[33] An interdependent and vulnerable world may not be able to contain the fallout from the discontent of the next generation of disgruntled warriors as easily.

Notes

Introduction: Globalization and Geopolitics in the Middle East

1. See Saul B. Cohen, 'Geopolitics in the New World Era: A New Perspective on an Old Discipline', in George J. Demko and William B. Wood (eds) *Reordering the World: Geopolitical Perspectives on the 21st Century* (Boulder, CO: Westview Press, 1994).
2. Alan Bullock and Oliver Stallybrass (eds) *The Fontana Dictionary of Modern Thought* (London: Fontana Books, 1977), p. 263.
3. L. Carl Brown, *International Politics and the Middle East: Old Rules, Dangerous Game* (Princeton, NJ: Princeton University Press, 1984).
4. Mohamed El-Shibiny, *The Threat of Globalization to Arab Islamic Culture: The Dynamics of World Peace* (Pittsburgh, PA: Dorrance, 2005).
5. Robert J. Holton, *Globalization and the Nation-State* (London: Macmillan, 1998), pp. 80–81.
6. See Holton's discussion, *ibid.*, chapter 4.
7. Richard Falk, 'The Monotheistic Religions in the Era of Globalization', *Global Dialogue*, 1 (1), 1999, 143.
8. Katja Füllberg-Stolberg, Petra Heidrich and Ellinor Schöne (eds) *Dissociation and Appropriation: Responses to Globalization in Asia and Africa* (Berlin: Das Arabische Buch, 1999).
9. Raymond Hinnebusch, 'Globalization and Generational Change: Syrian Foreign Policy between Regional Conflict and European Partnership', *Review of International Affairs*, 3 (2), 2003, 191.
10. Fred Halliday, *The Middle East in International Relations: Power, Politics and Ideology* (Cambridge: Cambridge University Press, 2005), p. 6.
11. Arthur Goldschmidt, Jr, *A Concise History of the Middle East* (Boulder, CO: Westview Press, 1996).
12. John M. Hobson, *The Eastern Origins of Western Civilisation* (Cambridge: Cambridge University Press, 2004), p. 32.
13. Arthur Goldschmidt, Jr, *A Concise History of the Middle East*, op. cit., p. 20.
14. Maxine Rodinson, *Islam and Capitalism* (Harmondsworth: Penguin, 1977), p. 56.
15. John M. Hobson, *The Eastern Origins of Western Civilisation*, op. cit., p. 36.
16. Abd-El-Kader Cheref, 'Globalization and the Islamic World', *The Opinion*, 9 October 2002, 3.
17. Franz Fanon, *The Wretched of the Earth* (Harmondsworth: Penguin, 1967), p. 172.
18. Francis Fukuyama, *The End of History and the Last Man* (London: Penguin, 1992), p. 237.

19 Peter Mandaville, *Transnational Muslim Politics: Reimagining the Umma* (New York: Routledge, 2004), p. 81.
20 Karl Marx, 'The British Rule in India', *New York Daily Tribune*, 10 June 1853. Reproduced in Helene Carrere d'Encausse and Stuart R. Schram, *Marxism and Asia* (London: Penguin, 1969), p. 117.
21 Helene Carrere d'Encausse and Stuart R. Schram, *ibid.*, pp. 8–9.
22 Bill Warren, *Imperialism: Pioneer of Capitalism* (London: New Left Books, 1980), pp. 61–62.
23 Bill Warren, *Imperialism: Pioneer of Capitalism*, op. cit., p. 9.
24 Tatu Vanhanen, *Prospects of Democracy: A Survey of 172 Countries* (New York: Routledge, 1997), pp. 117–18. It should be countered, however, that for over a century nationalists and Islamists alike have argued that it was colonialism and imperialism that caused the region's backwardness, not its religion and values. An influential text from this school was published in 1953, making a concerted attack on the West for its drive to deprive the region of its Islamic heritage. See Mustafa al-Khalidi and Umar Farroukh, *The Missionary Movements and Colonialism in the Arab Countries (al-Tabshir w'al-Isti'mar fil-Buldan al-Arabiyya)* (Beirut: al-Maktabah al-Ilmiyyah, 1953).
25 Hisham Sharabi, *Neopatriarchy: A Theory of Distorted Change in Arab Society* (Oxford: Oxford University Press, 1988), p. 17.
26 James A. Bill and Rebecca Bill Chavez, 'The Politics of Incoherence: The United States and the Middle East', *Middle East Journal*, 56 (4), 2002, 562–75.
27 Barry Rubin, 'Globalization and the Middle East: Part One', *YaleGlobal Online*, 16 January 2003, p. 1.
28 Iqbal Sacranie, Secretary General of the Muslim Council of Britain, issued this statement on 13 January 2003. For details see *The Guardian*, 14 January 2003.
29 *The Guardian*, 30 August 2003.
30 See, for example, the debate in the *New Statesman*, 24 September 2001.
31 'Measuring Globalization: Who's Up, Who's Down?', *Foreign Policy*, January/February 2003.
32 See *The National Security Strategy of the United States of America* (Washington, DC: The White House, 2002). See also Sandy Tolan, 'Beyond Regime Change', *Los Angeles Times*, 1 December 2002.
33 Americans, of course, did not need much convincing for, as Pinto notes, as early as 1979–80 'amorphous fears of a threat emanating from Islamic religious "fanatics" ... [was already] widespread among the Americans'. Maria do Céu Pinto, *Political Islam and the United States: A Study of U.S. Policy towards Islamist Movements in the Middle East* (Reading: Ithaca Press, 1999), p. 156.
34 Douglas E. Streusand, 'Abraham's other Childern: Is Islam an Enemy of the West?', *Policy Review*, 50, Fall 1989.
35 Daniel Pipes, 'The Muslims are Coming! The Muslims are Coming!', *National Review*, 19 November 1990, 28–31.
36 Fawaz A. Gerges, *America and Political Islam: Clash of Cultures or Clash of Interests?* (Cambridge: Cambridge University Press, 1999), p. 27.
37 Samuel P. Huntington, 'The Age of Muslim Wars', *Newsweek*, 17 December 2001.
38 The United States Air Force was one of many government institutions to commission in-depth analysis of the Muslim world after 9/11. Their massive report, 500 pages long, was published in 2004 by Angel M. Rabasa *et al.* under the title *The Muslim World after 9/11* (Santa Monica, CA: RAND, 2004).
39 Neil MacFarquhar, 'Qaeda Chief Warns U.S.; Paris Scarf Ban Assailed', *International Herald Tribune*, 25 February 2004.
40 John Thornhill and John Burton, 'Mahathir Despairs at "Racist" War', *Financial Times*, 17 September 2002.

41 Faisal Bodi, 'The West, not Islam, is the Real Enemy of Democracy', *The Guardian*, 13 January 2003.
42 *Arab News*, 22 November 2002.
43 Comments made by Mahfouz Azzam, Vice-President of the Islamist al-Aamal Party in Egypt and uncle of the Al-Qaida leader al-Zawahri, in September 2002. See Hossam El-Hamalawy, 'Whither Political Islam?', *Cairo Times*, 12–18 September 2002.
44 Shibley Telhami, *The Stakes: America and the Middle East* (Boulder, CO: Westview Press, 2002).
45 Gamil Mattar, 'Cold War Defrost', *Al-Ahram Weekly*, 5–11 February 2004.
46 Quoted by Dana Milbank, 'Hawks Chide Bush over Islam', *International Herald Tribune*, 2 December 2002.
47 M. Levy, *Modernization and the Structure of Societies* (Princeton, NJ: Princeton University Press, 1966), p. 36.
48 Leslise Sklair, *Sociology of the Global System* (Hemel Hemstead: Harvest Wheatsheaf, 1991), p. 7.
49 S. Nawabzadeh, 'The Taleban Tumor', *Echo of Islam*, 173, December 1998, 18.
50 Quoted in *The Guardian*, 12 October 2002.
51 *ibid.*
52 Al-Jazeera, 3 November 2001.
53 Al-Qaida has been assisted in this strategy, it has to be said, by President Bush's 'be with us or against us' stance, which has left very little room for manoeuvre for the beleaguered leaders of the less-than-stable Muslim countries.
54 M. A. Muqtedar Khan, 'Globalization as "Glocalization"', www.islamonline.net.

1 Globalization: System or Process?

1 I use the term 'unexpected' because many pundits in the 1970s and 1980s were writing the obituary of the American economy as a twentieth-century has-been. Ironically, both the American economy and its military outlays grew considerably in the last quarter of the twentieth and early twenty-first centuries. See Paul Kennedy, *The Rise and Fall of Great Powers: Economic Change and Military Conflict From 1500 to 2000* (London: Fontana Press, 1989) and Torbjørn L. Knutsen, *The Rise and Fall of World Orders* (Manchester: Manchester University Press, 1999).
2 Francis Fukuyama, *The End of History and the Last Man* (London: Penguin, 1992), p. xiii.
3 Graham E. Fuller and Ian O. Lesser, *A Sense of Siege: The Geopolitics of Islam and the West* (Boulder, CO: Westview Press, 1995), pp. 34–38.
4 Simon W. Murden, *Islam, the Middle East, and the New Global Hegemony* (Boulder, CO: Lynne Rienner, 2002).
5 *The Guardian*, 29 November 2002.
6 Bruce Hoffman, 'What Can we Learn from the Terrorists?', *Global Agenda*, January 2004, 32.
7 V. I. Lenin, *Imperialism, The Highest Stage of Capitalism* (Moscow: Progress Publishers, 1968), p. 9.
8 *ibid.*, p. 119.
9 Jean-Paul Sartre, 'Preface', in Franz Fanon, *The Wretched of the Earth* (Harmondsworth: Penguin, 1967), p. 10.
10 Ian Clark, *Globalization and International Relations Theory* (Oxford: Oxford University Press, 1999), p. 34.
11 See the 34-page survey of globalization, 'Globalisation and its Critics', *The Economist*, 29 September 2001.

12 Susan Strange, *The Retreat of the State: The Diffusion of Power in the World Economy* (Cambridge: Cambridge University Press, 1996).
13 John Micklethwait and Adrian Wooldridge, 'From Sarajevo to September 11', *Policy Review*, 117, 2003, 2–3.
14 El-Sayed a-Aswad, 'Sanctified Cosmology: Maintaining Muslim Identity with Globalism', *Journal of Social Affairs*, 20 (80), 2003, 67.
15 Kenichi Ohmae, *The End of the Nation State: The Rise of Regional Economies* (London: HarperCollins, 1995), p. 79.
16 Malcolm Waters, *Globalization* (London: Routledge, 1996) p. 3.
17 Winfried Ruigrok and Rob van Tulder, *The Logic of International Restructuring* (London: Routledge, 1995), p. 169.
18 Howard H. Lentner, 'Politics, Power and States in Globalization', in Henri Goverde, Philip G. Cerny, Mark Haugaard and Howard H. Lentner (eds) *Power in Contemporary Politics: Theories, Practices, Globalizations* (London: Sage, 2000), p. 203.
19 Kenneth N. Waltz, 'Globalization and Governance', *PS: Political Science and Politics*, 32 (4), 1999, 697.
20 Ali Mazrui, 'Globalisation and the Future of Islamic Civilisation', *Discourse*, October 2000, 11.
21 David Held, *Models of Democracy* (Cambridge: Polity Press, 1996), p. 340.
22 Jan Pronk, 'Globalization: A Developmental Approach', in Jan Nederveen Pieterse (ed.) *Global Futures: Shaping Globalization* (London: Zed Books, 2000), p. 43.
23 Malcolm Waters, *Globalization*, op. cit., p. 136.
24 Albert Paolini, 'Globalization', in Phillip Darby (ed.) *At the Edge of International Relations: Postcolonialism, Gender and Dependency* (New York: Continuum, 2000), pp. 33–60.
25 Leslie Sklair, *Sociology of the Global System* (Hemel Hemstead: Harvest Wheatsheaf, 1991).
26 Leslie Sklair and Peter T. Robbins, 'Global Capitalism and Major Corporations from the Third World', *Third World Quarterly*, 23 (1), 2002, 82.
27 Joseph Stiglitz, *Globalization and Its Discontents* (London: Penguin, 2002), p. 53.
28 Philip G. Cerny, 'Globalization and the Changing Logic of Collective Action', *International Organization*, 49 (4), 1995, 596.
29 R. J. Barry Jones, *Globalisation and Interdependence in the International Political Economy: Rhetoric and Reality* (New York: Pinter, 1995).
30 Glenn D. Hook, Julie Gilson, Christopher W. Hughes and Hugo Dobson, *Japan's International Relations: Politics, Economics and Security* (London: Routlege, 2001), p. 34.
31 Anthony Giddens, *Runaway World: How Globalisation is Shaping our Lives* (London: Profile Books, 2002).
32 Paul Masson, *Globalization: Facts and Figures*, IMF Policy Discussion Paper PDP/01/4 (Washington, DC: International Monetary Fund, October 2001).
33 Philip G. Cerny, 'Globalization and the Changing Logic of Collective Action', op. cit., 595–625.
34 Sir Paul Judge, '250 Years of Globalisation', *RSA Journal*, January 2004, 36.
35 William I. Robinson, 'Globalisation: Nine Theses on Our Epoch', *Race and Class*, 38 (2), 1996, 17.
36 Richard L. Kugler, 'Controlling Chaos: New Axial Strategic Principles', in Richard L. Kugler and Ellen L. Frost (eds) *The Global Century: Globalization and National Security*, Volume I (Washington, DC: National Defense University Press, 2001), p. 78.

37 James H. Mittelman, 'How Does Globalization Work?', in James H. Mittelman (ed.) *Globalization: Critical Reflections* (Boulder, CO: Lynne Rienner, 1996), p. 237.
38 Don D. Marshall, 'Understanding Late-Twentieth-Century Capitalism: Reassessing the Globalization Theme', *Government and Opposition*, 31 (2), 1996, 197.
39 Richard Stubbs, 'States, Sovereignty and the Response of Southeast Asia's "Miracle" Economies to Globalization', David A. Smith, Dorothy J. Solinger and Steven C. Topik (eds) *States and Sovereignty in the Global Economy* (London: Routledge, 1999), p. 229.
40 Immanuel Wallerstein, 'States? Sovereignty? The Dilemmas of Capitalists in an Age of Transition', in *ibid.*, p. 21.
41 Giovanni Arrighi, 'Globalization, State Sovereignty, and the "Endless" Accumulation of Capital', in *ibid.*, p. 53.
42 Michael Cox, 'Whatever Happened to the New World Order?', *Journal of Social Theory*, 25, 1993, 85–95.
43 Malcolm Waters, *Globalization, op. cit.*, p. 3.
44 David Barboza, 'When Golden Arches are too Red, White, and Blue', *New York Times*, 14 October 2001.
45 Marc F. Plattner, 'Globalization and Self-government', *Journal of Democracy*, 13 (3), 2002, 65.
46 Anthony Giddens, *The Consequences of Modernity* (Cambridge: Polity Press, 1990), p. 64.
47 John Micklethwait and Adrian Wooldridge, 'From Sarajevo to September 11', *op. cit.*
48 Mohammed El-Nawawy and Adel Iskandar, *Al-Jazeera: How the Free Arab News Network Scooped the World and Changed the Middle East* (Boulder, CO: Westview Press, 2002).
49 Andrew Hurrell and Ngaire Woods, 'Globalisation and Inequality', *Millennium: Journal of International Studies*, 24 (3), 1995, 447–70.
50 Robert Gilpin, *The Challenge of Global Capitalism: The World Economy in the 21st Century* (Princeton, NJ,: Princeton University Press, 2000), pp. 295–96.
51 David Held and Anthony McGrew, *Globalization/Anti-Globalization* (Cambridge: Polity Press, 2002); Alan Shipman, *The Myth of Globalization* (Cambridge: Icon Books, 2002); Ralph Miliband and Leo Panitch (eds) *New World Order? Socialist Register 1992* (London: Merlin Press, 1992).
52 Sir Paul Judge, '250 Years of Globalisation', *op. cit.*, p. 38.
53 Leslie Sklair and Peter T. Robbins, 'Global Capitalism and Major Corporations from the Third World', *op. cit.*, p. 86.
54 Robert W. Cox, 'A Perspective on Globalization', in James H. Mittelman (ed.) *Globalization: Critical Reflections, op. cit.*, p. 24.
55 David Apter, 'Globalization, Marginality, and the Specter of the Superfluous Man', *Journal of Social Affairs*, 18 (71), 2001, 87.
56 Malcolm Waters provides a handy digest of Kerr *et al.*'s arguments, which can be found in their original form in C. Kerr, J. Dunlop, F. Harbison and C. Myers, *Industrialism and Industrial Man* (Harmondsworth: Penguin, 1973). See Malcolm Waters, *Globalization, op. cit.*
57 Manuel Castells, *End of Millennium* (Oxford: Basil Blackwell, 1998), p. 82.
58 Ankie Hoogvelt, *Globalization and the Postcolonial World: The New Political Economy of Development* (Houndmills: Palgrave Macmillan, 2001), p. xiii.
59 Alfed Kleinknecht and Jan T. Wengel, 'The Myth of Economic Globalisation', *Cambridge Journal of Economics*, 22 (4), 1998, 637–47.

60 Theodore Pelagidis and Harry Papasotiriou, 'Globalisation or Regionalism? States, Markets and the Structure of International Trade', *Review of International Studies*, 28 (3), 2002, 520.
61 Ankie Hoogvelt, *Globalization and the Postcolonial World, op. cit.*, p. 138.
62 Thomas L. Friedman, 'Anti-terror Fight has to be a Marathon Run on Wilsonian Principles, Not Cheap Oil', *YaleGlobal*, 7 February 2003.
63 John Micklethwait and Adrian Wooldridge, 'From Sarajevo to September 11', *op. cit.*, 4.

2 Globalization and Strategic Interdependence

1 For a detailed analysis of regional perspectives on globalization, see Marcus Noland and Howard Pack, 'Islam, Globalization, and Economic Performance in the Middle East', *International Economics Policy Briefs*, No. PB04-4, June 2004.
2 Kathleen Ridolfo, 'The Arab World: Economic Progress and Struggle', in Richard L. Kugler and Ellen L. Frost (eds) *The Global Century: Globalization and National Security*, Volume II (Washington, DC: National Defense University Press, 2001), p. 918.
3 Turki Abdullah al-Sudairi, 'Being Invaded by a Satanic Civilization', *Arab News*, 3 February 2001.
4 Islamic Republic News Agency (IRNA), report of speech by Kamal Kharrazi, Rome, 18 January 2001.
5 M. H. Manzarpour, 'Globalisation Yes, Americanization No', *Tehran Times*, 5 May 2000.
6 Islamic Republic News Agency (IRNA), report of speech by Ayatollah Seyed Ali Khamenei, 28 May 2002.
7 Associated French Press, Interview with Prince Walid bin Talal of Saudi Arabia, 7 December 1999.
8 'Saudi Prince Backs Globalisation', *BBC News*, 29 October 2002.
9 Personal observations, and comments from 'Globalisation Brings New Ideas', *Gulf News*, 30 October 2002.
10 'A Pact for Reforming the Arab Condition', *Arab News*, 17 January 2003.
11 *The Kingdom of Saudi Arabia Newsletter* (London), June 2001.
12 Lubna Olayan, 'A Saudi Vision for Growth', Jeddah Economic Forum, 17 January 2004.
13 Sheikh Mohammed bin Rashid al-Maktoum, speech to Dead Sea World Economic Forum meeting, May 2004, World Economic Forum press release, 16 May 2004.
14 Mehran Kamrava, 'Structural Impediments to Economic Globalization in the Middle East', *Middle East Policy*, XI (4), 2004, 109.
15 Islamic Republic News Agency (IRNA), 31 October 2001.
16 Comments made by Egypt's Foreign Minister Amr Moussa at the ninth G15 summit. See Dina Ezzat, 'Globalisation Fails its Promise', *Al-Ahram Weekly*, 11–17 February 1999.
17 Raymond Hinnebusch, 'Explaining International Politics in the Middle East: The Struggle of Regional Identity and Systemic Structure', in Gerd Nonneman (ed.) *Analyzing Middle East Foreign Policies and the Relationship with Europe* (London: Routledge, 2005), pp. 243–44.
18 Chandra Muzaffar, 'Globalization and Religion: Some Reflections', IslamOnline.net, 19 June 2002, pp.1–2.
19 Mohamed Khodr, 'Muslims Must Surrender to Israel, America, and Globalization', IslamOnline.net, 2 August 2001, p. 4.
20 David Held, *Models of Democracy* (Cambridge: Polity Press, 1996), p. 341.

21 Clement M. Henry and Robert Springborg, *Globalization and the Politics of Development in the Middle East* (Cambridge: Cambridge University Press, 2001), p. 14.
22 Marc F. Plattner, 'Globalization and Self-government', *Journal of Democracy*, 13 (3), 2002, 56.
23 Thomas Michel, 'Islam in Asia', message posted to InterfaithInteraction (interactive e-faith community), http://groups.yahoo.com/group/Interfaith-Interaction/message/908, 14 November 2003.
24 Mohamed El-Shibiny, *The Threat of Globalization to Arab Islamic Culture: The Dynamics of World Peace* (Pittsburgh, PA: Dorrance Publishing, 2005).
25 Fauzi Najjar, 'The Arabs, Islam and Globalization', *Middle East Policy*, XII (3), 2005, 91–106.
26 Glenn D. Hook, Julie Gilson, Christopher W. Hughes and Hugo Dobson, *Japan's International Relations: Politics, Economics and Security* (London: Routledge, 2001), p. 385.
27 William Engdahl, *A Century of War: Anglo–American Oil Politics and the New World Order* (London: Pluto Press, 2004).
28 See John Williams, *The Ethics of Territorial Borders: Drawing Lines in the Shifting Sands* (New York: Palgrave Macmillan, 2006).
29 Robert J. Holton, *Globalization and the Nation-State* (London: Macmillan, 1998). Holton states that 'certain aspects of national sovereignty, but not the institution of the nation-state itself, have undoubtedly been eroded by economic globalization' (p. 101).
30 Stephen D. Krasner, 'Globalization and Sovereignty', in David A. Smith, Dorothy J. Solinger and Steven C. Topik (eds) *States and Sovereignty in the Global Economy* (London: Routledge, 1999), p. 35.
31 Kenneth N. Waltz, 'Globalization and Governance', *PS: Political Science and Politics*, 32 (4), 1999, 698.
32 *ibid.*, pp. 696–97.
33 Thomas L. Friedman, *The Lexus and the Olive Tree* (New York: Farrar, Straus, Giroux, 1999).
34 Robert L. Heilbroner, 'A Look at the Future of Capitalism', in Nicholas X. Rizopoulos (ed.) *Sea-Changes: American Foreign Policy in a World Transformed* (New York: Council on Foreign Relations Press, 1990), p. 115.
35 In May 2004 the USA introduced direct economic sanctions against Syria for Damascus's alleged support for terrorism.
36 The example I had in mind was Iraq's invasion of Kuwait in 1990.
37 Patricia M. Goff, 'Invisible Borders: Economic Liberalization and National Identity', *International Studies Quarterly*, 44 (4), 2000, 533–62.
38 William Pfaff, 'If Globalization Means Westernizing, Then it Means Trouble', *International Herald Tribune*, 2 January 1997.
39 Richard Falk, 'The Monotheistic Religions in the Era of Globalization', *Global Dialogue*, 1 (1), 1999, 140.
40 James A. Bill and Rebecca Bill Chavez, 'The Politics of Incoherence: The United States and the Middle East', *Middle East Journal*, 56 (4), 2002, 568.
41 Olivier Roy, *The Failure of Political Islam* (London: I. B. Tauris, 1995), p. 83.
42 Mehdi Mozaffari, 'Can a Declined Civilization be Reconstructed?', in Stephen Chan, Peter G. Mandaville and Roland Bleiker (eds) *The Zen of International Relations: IR Theory from East to West* (London: Palgrave Macmillan, 2001), pp. 129–56.
43 Rachel Bronson, 'Understanding US–Saudi Relations', in Paul Aarts and Gerd Nonneman (eds) *Saudi Arabia in the Balance: Political Economy, Society, Foreign Affairs* (London: Hurst & Co., 2005), pp. 372–98.
44 Robin Allen, 'Gulf Between Friends', *Financial Times*, 9–10 November 2002.

45 Victor Davis Hanson, 'Our Enemies, the Saudis' *Commentary*, 114 (1), July–August 2002.
46 Robert Jervis, 'An Interim Assessment of September 11: What has Changed and What has Not?', *Political Science Quarterly*, 117 (1), 2002, 45.
47 'Bush Throws Gauntlet at Saudis with Middle East Plan', *The Global Intelligence Report*, 25 June 2002, p. 3.
48 Paul Aarts, 'Events versus Trends: The Role of Energy and Security in Sustaining the US–Saudi Relationship', in Paul Aarts and Gerd Nonneman (eds) *Saudi Arabia in the Balance, op. cit.*, pp. 399–429.
49 Tim Niblock, *Saudi Arabia: Power, Legitimacy and Survival* (New York: Routledge, 2006).
50 Quoted by Robert Dreyfuss, 'Just the Beginning: Is Iraq the Opening Salvo in a War to Remake the World?', *The American Prospect*, 14 (3), 4 March 2003.
51 See the special issue of *Global Dialogue*, 5 (1–2), 2003, dedicated to the question 'American Empire?'
52 Robert Singh, 'The Bush Doctrine', in Mary Buckley and Robert Singh (eds) *The Bush Doctrine and the War on Terrorism* (New York: Routledge, 2006), pp. 12–31.
53 Richard Crockatt, *America Embattled: September 11, Anti-Americanism and the Global Order* (New York: Routledge, 2003).

3 The MENA Regional System in Crisis

1 Richard Higgott, 'The International Political Economy of Regionalism: The Asia–Pacific and Europe Compared', in William D. Coleman and Geoffrey R. D. Underhill (eds) *Regionalism and Global Economic Integration: Europe, Asia and the Americas* (London: Routledge, 1998), p. 56.
2 Barry Buzan and Ole Waever, *Regions and Powers: The Structure of International Security* (Cambridge: Cambridge University Press, 2003).
3 Some of the definitional and conceptual difficulties of identifying a 'region' are ably discussed by Edward D. Mansfield and Helen V. Milner, 'The New Wave of Regionalism', *International Organization*, 53 (3), 1999, 589–627; Jean Grugel and Wil Hout (eds) *Regionalism Across the North–South Divide* (London: Routledge, 1999); Louise Fawcett and Andrew Hurrell (eds) *Regionalism in World Politics* (Oxford: Oxford University Press, 1995).
4 Halim Barakat, *The Arab World: Society, Culture, and State* (Los Angeles, CA: University of California Press, 1993), p. 33.
5 Fred Halliday, *The Middle East in International Relations: Power, Politics and Ideology* (Cambridge: Cambridge University Press, 2005), p. 87.
6 See Malcolm Kerr's classic study, *The Arab Cold War: Jamal Abd al-Nasir and his Rivals, 1958–1967* (Oxford: Oxford University Press, 1971).
7 Bahgat Korany, 'Political Petrolism and Contemporary Arab Politics, 1967–83', in Baha Abu-Laban and Sharon McIrvin Abu-Laban (eds) *The Arab World: Dynamics of Development* (Leiden: E. J. Brill, 1986), p. 72.
8 Raymond Hinnebusch, *The International Politics of the Middle East* (Manchester: Manchester University Press, 2003), p. 183.
9 See Ali Çarkoğlu, Mine Eder and Kemal Kirişci, *The Political Economy of Regional Cooperation in the Middle East* (New York: Routledge, 1998).
10 For a discussion of the three variables mentioned, see Andrew Hurrell, 'Regionalism in Theoretical Perspective', in Louise Fawcett and Andrew Hurrell (eds) *Regionalism in World Politics* (Oxford: Oxford University Press, 1995), p. 41.

11 A good example is the regional Middle East trade talks of the mid-1990s, which led to the doomed Taba declaration of February 1995, in which all the parties (four Arab states and Israel) had agreed to take steps towards deeper economic co-operation and exchanges. Julian Ozanne, ' "Separation" mars Middle East Integration', *Financial Times*, 9 February 1995.
12 Muhammed H. Heikal, *The Sphinx and the Commissar: The Rise and Fall of Soviet Influence in the Middle East* (New York: Harper and Row, 1978).
13 The implications of this in terms of regional co-operation modalities are discussed by Charles Tripp, 'Regional Organizations in the Arab Middle East', in Louise Fawcett and Andrew Hurrell (eds) *Regionalism in World Politics* (Oxford: Oxford University Press, 1995), pp. 283–308.
14 Bahgat Korany, 'The Arab World and the New Balance of Power in the New Middle East', in Michael C. Hudson (ed.) *Middle East Dilemma: The Politics and Economics of Arab Integration* (London: I. B. Tauris, 1999), pp. 35–59.
15 Abdul Khaleq Abdulla, 'The Gulf Cooperation Council: Nature, Origin, and Process', in Michael C. Hudson (ed.) *Middle East Dilemma*, op. cit., p. 155.
16 John Duke Anthony, 'The Gulf Cooperation Council: Constraints', *GulfWire Perspectives*, 4 February 2004.
17 F. Gregory Gause III and Jill Crystal, 'The Arab Gulf: Will Autocracy Define the Social Contract in 2015?', in Judith Yaphe (ed.) *The Middle East in 2015: The Impact of Regional Trends on U.S. Strategic Planning* (Washington, DC: National Defense University Press, 2002), pp. 163–93.
18 The problem also has an extra-regional dimension, for no sooner had the GCC customs union been signed, the USA and Bahrain announced the signing of their own bilateral free trade agreement.
19 Abdul Khaleq Abdulla, 'The Gulf Cooperation Council: Nature, Origin, and Process', op. cit., p. 159.
20 Phebe Marr, 'The Persian Gulf after the Storm', in Phebe Marr and William Lewis (eds) *Riding the Tiger: The Middle East Challenge After the Cold War* (Boulder, CO: Westview Press, 1993), p. 109.
21 The most notorious of such episodes on record was the briefing by Laurent Murawiec to the Pentagon's Defense Policy Board on 10 July 2002. See Thomas E. Ricks, 'Briefing Depicted Saudis as Enemies: Ultimatum Urged to Pentagon Board', *Washington Post*, 6 August 2002; Jack Shafer, 'The PowerPoint that Rocked the Pentagon', *Slate*, 7 August 2002.
22 Issues pertaining to Libya's international policies had proved to be a real problem for the AMU from the early 1990s, so much so that this strategically important member of the organization effectively turned its back on it when, in 1992, its fellow members accepted to impose United Nations sanctions on the country for its involvement in the bombing of flight PAN AM 103 over Scotland in December 1989.
23 I. William Zartman, 'The Ups and Downs of Maghrib Unity', in Michael C. Hudson (ed.) *Middle East Dilemma*, op. cit., pp. 171–86.
24 *ibid.*, p. 182.
25 Paul Noble, 'The Prospects for Arab Cooperation in a Changing Regional and Global System', in Michael C. Hudson (ed.) *Middle East Dilemma*, op. cit., p. 74.
26 Ismail Sirageldin, *Globalization, Regionalization and Recent Trade Agreements: Impact on Arab Economies*, ERC Working Paper 9817 (Cairo: Economic Research Center, undated).
27 Serge Sur, 'An Analysis of American "Hegemony"', *Journal of Social Affairs*, 19 (76), 2002, 55–105.

28 See Laura Guazzone (ed.) *The Middle East in Global Change: The Politics and Economics of Interdependence versus Fragmentation* (London: Macmillan, 1997).
29 David Seddon, 'Unequal Partnership: Europe, the Maghreb and the New Regionalism', in Jean Grugel and Wil Hout (eds) *Regionalism Across the North–South Divide, op. cit.*, pp. 134–51.
30 For a discussion of developments in East Asia see Richard Stubbs, 'Asia–Pacific Regionalism versus Globalization: Competing Forms of Capitalism', in William D. Coleman and Geoffrey R. D. Underhill (eds) *Regionalism and Global Economic Integration, op. cit.*, pp. 68–80.
31 See Allen Scott, *Regions and the World Economy: The Coming Shape of Global Production, Competition, and Political Order* (Oxford: Oxford University Press, 2000).
32 Ali Çarkoğlu, Mine Eder and Kemal Kirişci, *The Political Economy of Regional Cooperation in the Middle East, op. cit.*, p. 31.
33 Roger Owen, *State, Power and Politics in the Making of the Modern Middle East* (New York: Routledge, 2004), p. 233.
34 In his 2006 State of the Union address, President Bush again underlined this trademark of his administration by saying 'the only way to defeat the terrorists is to defeat their dark vision of hatred and fear by offering the hopeful alternative of political freedom and peaceful change. So the United States of America supports democratic reform across the broader Middle East. Elections are vital, but they are only the beginning. Raising up a democracy requires the rule of law, and protection of minorities, and strong, accountable institutions that last longer than a single vote'. Office of the Press Secretary of the White House, 31 January 2006.
35 Anoushiravan Ehteshami and Raymond Hinnebusch, *Syria and Iran: Middle Powers in a Penetrated Regional System* (London: Routledge, 1997).
36 Paul Aarts, *Dilemmas of Regional Cooperation in the Middle East*, Lancaster Papers No. 4 (Lancaster: Lancaster University, 1999), p. 1.

4 Geopolitical Tectonics: the Greater Middle East on the Margins of Eurasia

1 Zbigniew Brzezinski, *The Grand Chessboard: American Primacy and its Geostrategic Imperatives* (New York: Basic Books, 1997), p. 31.
2 Fred Halliday, 'The End of the Cold War and International Relations: Some Analytical and Theoretical Conclusions', in Ken Booth and Steve Smith (eds) *International Relations Theory Today* (Cambridge: Polity Press, 1995), p. 44.
3 For other definitions and detailed analyses of the phenomena of regionalism, see Louise Fawcett and Andrew Hurrell (eds) *Regionalism in World Politics: Regional Organization and International Order* (Oxford: Oxford University Press, 1997).
4 Ronald Steel, 'Europe after the Superpowers', in Nicholas X. Rizopoulos (ed.) *Sea-Changes: American Foreign Policy in a World Transformed* (New York: Council on Foreign Relations, 1990), p. 7.
5 For detailed analyses of the impact of the Kuwait crisis on western European states and their security and strategic thinking, see Nicole Gnesotto and John Roper (eds) *Western Europe and the Gulf* (Paris: Institute for Security Studies of the WEU, 1992).
6 Ernest Wistrich, *The United States of Europe* (London: Routledge, 1994). See also *Europe Without Frontiers – The Completing of the Internal Market* (Luxembourg: Office for Official Publications of the Communities, 1989).

7 Richard McAllister, *From EC to EU: An Historical and Political Survey* (London: Routledge, 1997).
8 Martin J. Dedman, *The Origins and Development of the European Union 1945–95* (London: Routledge, 1996).
9 William Clark, 'The Real Reason Why Iran is the Next Target: The Emerging Euro-denominated International Oil Market', *Energy Bulletin*, 27 October 2004.
10 The EU accounted not only for just over 30 per cent of world output in 1995, but also for 20 per cent of world trade as well. See *The Economist*, 29 March 1997, p. 118.
11 Denis O'Hearn, 'Global Restructuring, Transnational Corporations and the "European Periphery": What has Changed?', in David A. Smith and József Böröcz (eds) *A New World Order? Global Transformations in the Late Twentieth Century* (Westport, CT: Praeger, 1995), p. 71.
12 The rather apt term 'economic balkanisation' has been borrowed from an Economist Intelligence Unit report entitled, 'The Economic Balkanisation of Europe', *European Trends*, 2, 1983, 31–35.
13 This term comes from Michael Zürn, 'The Challenges of Globalization and Individualization: A View from Europe', in Hans-Henrik Holm and Georg Sørensen (eds) *Whose World Order? Uneven Globalization and the End of the Cold War* (Boulder, CO: Westview Press, 1995), pp. 137–63.
14 For a discussion, see Christian-Peter Hanelt, Giacomo Luciani and Felix Neugart (eds) *Regime Change in Iraq* (Florence: Robert Schuman Center for Advanced Studies, 2004).
15 Peter A. Gourevitch, 'The Pacific Rim: Current Debates', *The Pacific Region: Challenges to Policy and Theory, Annals of the American Academy of Political and Social Science*, 505, 1989, 8–23.
16 A reality that may not be apparent from international trade statistics, in which the MENA region accounts for 3.6 per cent of world trade (below the Latin American and Eastern European totals). See Sinclair Road, 'World Trade and the Middle East', *Middle East International*, No. 532, 1996, 18–20.
17 Halford Mackinder (ed.) *Democratic Ideals and Reality* (New York: W. W. Norton, 1962).
18 Frederick S. Starr, 'Making Eurasia Stable', *Foreign Affairs*, 75 (1), 1996, 80–92.
19 Robert S. Chase, Emily B. Hill, and Paul Kennedy, 'Pivotal States and U.S. Strategy', *Foreign Affairs*, 75 (1), 1996, 33–51.
20 Despite the Arab–Israeli peace process, in every year since 1990, the official end of the Cold War era, MENA-related tensions have in one way or another threatened the stability of the international system. It is not too surprising that of the six so-called 'pariah' states in the world in the mid-1990s, four were Middle Eastern ones (Iran, Iraq, Libya, and Sudan).
21 For a useful survey of foreign investment in the MENA region, see Raed Safadi, *Global Challenges and Opportunities facing MENA Countries at the Dawn of the 21st Century*, Working Paper Series 199624 (Cairo: Economic Research Forum, 1996).
22 UNCTAD, *World Investment Report 2005: Transnational Corporations and the Internationalization of R&D* (Geneva: UN Conference on Trade and Development, 2005).
23 See International Institute for Strategic Studies, *Strategic Survey 1991–1992* (London: Brassey's, 1992), p. 5.
24 The statement of Irish Foreign Minister Brian Cowan, the holder of the EU Presidency at the time of the Bush–Sharon agreement. Judy Dempsey, 'EU Warns US–Israel Plan will Hit Peace Hopes', *Financial Times*, 15 April 2004.

25 For a discussion of the region's new restructuring phase, see Yezid Sayigh, '"System Breakdown" in the Middle East?', in Martin Kramer (ed.) *Middle East Lectures – Number Two* (Tel Aviv: Tel Aviv University, 1997), pp. 57–68.
26 Muhammad Faour, *The Arab World after Desert Storm* (Washington, DC: US Institute of Peace, 1993); Anoushiravan Ehteshami, 'The Arab States and the Middle East Balance of Power', in James Gow (ed.) *Iraq, the Gulf Conflict and the World Community* (London: Brassey's, 1993), pp. 55–73.
27 Kenneth Katzman, *The Persian Gulf: Issues for U.S. Policy, 2002* (Washington, DC: CRS, The Library of Congress, 2002). See also David E. Long and Christin Koch (eds) *Gulf Security in the Twenty-First Century* (Abu Dhabi: Emirates Center for Strategic Studies and Research, 1997).
28 See Paul Cornish (ed.) *The Conflict in Iraq, 2003* (New York: Palgrave Macmillan, 2004).
29 See Nader Entessar, 'The Post-Cold War US Military Doctrine: Implications for Iran', *Iranian Journal of International Affairs*, VIII (2), 1996, 393–419.
30 Statement issued on 19 December 2003.
31 For some ideas on this issue, see Gerd Nonneman (ed.) *The Middle East and Europe: The Search for Stability and Integration* (London: Federal Trust, 1993).
32 Lionel Barber and Bernard Gray, 'Nato Turns its Attention to Turbulent Moslem South', *Financial Times*, 9 February 1995.
33 Michel Chatelus, 'Economic Co-operation Among Southern Mediterranean Countries', in Roberto Aliboni, George Joffé and Tim Niblock (eds) *Security Challenges in the Mediterranean Region* (London: Frank Cass, 1996), p. 85; Bichara Khader, 'Les Échanges économiques Euro-Arabes', in Nazih N. Ayubi (ed.) *Distant Neighbours: The Political Economy of Relations Between Europe and the Middle East/North Africa* (Reading: Ithaca Press, 1995), pp. 21–35. According to the Arab League, inter-Arab trade in 1992 stood at 8.6 per cent of the Arab countries' total trade. See 'Euro–Arab Relations', *Arabfile*, 3 (3), 1993, 5–7.
34 Tim Niblock, 'North–South Socio-economic Relations in the Mediterranean', in Roberto Aliboni, George Joffé and Tim Niblock (eds) *Security Challenges in the Mediterranean Region, op. cit.*, pp. 115–36.
35 European Commission, 'Bilateral Trade Relations', European Union database, 2004. See also IMF, *Direction of Trade Statistics* (Washington, DC: International Monetary Fund, 2001).
36 European Commission, 'Bilateral Trade Relations', *op. cit.*, 2004.
37 *ibid.*
38 Giacomo Luciani and Tobias Schumacher, *Relations Between the European Union and the Gulf Cooperation Council States: Past Record and Promises for the Future* (Dubai: Gulf Research Center, 2004).
39 Rodney Wilson, 'The Economic Relations of the Middle East: Toward Europe or Within the Region?', *Middle East Journal*, 48 (2), 1994, 268–87.
40 Roberto Aliboni, *European Security Across the Mediterranean*, Chaillot Papers 2 (Paris: Institute for Security Studies of the WEU, 1991).
41 European Commission, 'Bilateral Trade Relations', *op. cit.*, 2004.
42 Hugh Corbet, 'European Integration and the Integration of the World Economy', *British Journal of International Studies*, 3 (1), 1977, 65.
43 For some early predictions on the impact of the treaty on the MENA region, see Ellen Laipson, 'Europe's Role in the Middle East: Enduring Ties, Emerging Opportunities', *Middle East Journal*, 44 (1), 1990, 7–17.
44 George Joffé 'The European Union and the Maghreb', in Richard Gillespie (ed.), *Mediterranean Politics – Volume I* (London: Pinter, 1994), pp. 22–45.
45 'The Treaty of Maastricht: What it Says and What it Means', *The Independent on Sunday*, 11 October 1992.

46 At the 34th session of the Federation of Arab Chambers of Commerce and Industry meeting in March 1997, for example, it was agreed that the Arab world would need to create a single trade and business environment, a common market of its own, if it was to emulate the successes of the European model. See *Gulf States Newsletter*, 22 (557), 1997, 10.
47 Emma C. Murphy, 'The Arab–Israeli Conflict and the New World Order', in Haifa Jawad (ed.) *The Middle East in the New World Order* (London: Macmillan, 1994), pp. 81–98.
48 See, for instance, *EC Support for the Middle East Peace Process* (Brussels: Commission of the European Communities, 29 September 1993).
49 François D'Alançon, 'The EC Looks to a New Middle East', *Journal of Palestine Studies*, XXIII (2), 1994, 41–51.
50 *The Commission Proposes the Establishment of a Euro–Mediterranean Partnership* (Brussels: European Commission, 19 October 1994).
51 *ibid.*, p. 1.
52 The reassessment process resulted in a major report on the south (with policy recommendations), produced in 1989 and updated in 1990, entitled *Redirecting the Community's Mediterranean Policy* (Brussels: European Commission, 1989). The EC Council adopted the 'New Mediterranean Policy' advocated by the Commission in December 1990.
53 Claire Spencer, *The Maghreb in the 1990s*, Adelphi Paper 274 (London: Brassey's for International Institute for Strategic Studies, February 1993).
54 Rosemary Hollis, 'The Politics of Israeli–European Economic Relations', *Israel Affairs*, 1 (1), 1994, 118–34.
55 Shada Islam, 'Europe Spurned', *Middle East International*, No. 535, 1996, 6–7.
56 Ironically, in early 1996 the Israeli Labour government had welcomed the EU's more interventionist policy in the Middle East, hoping that through its trade negotiations with Syria it could encourage Damascus to return to the negotiating table.
57 The resolution was drafted by France, Portugal, Sweden and the UK. The US veto in the Security Council resulted in the tabling of an alternative resolution to the General Assembly, which was adopted on 13 March by a vote of 130 in favour and two against, with two abstentions. See *News Summary (NS/4/97)* (London: UN Information Centre, 1-14/3/1997).
58 Shada Islam, 'EU and Israel: Battered Relationship', *Middle East International*, No. 546, 1997, 6–7.
59 The Mykonos trial refers to a 4-year-long legal and criminal investigation in Germany, which ended on 10 April 1997. A Berlin court ruling on that day implicated Iran's senior leaders in the murder of four Iranian Kurds in a Berlin restaurant in 1992, causing an immediate rupture in EU–Iranian relations. Ironically, the EU's steps to suspend critical dialogue and to reduce its diplomatic exchanges with Tehran coincided with the Clinton administration's review of its Iran policy, and calls in the USA for application of a more constructive policy towards the Islamic Republic. But the US initiatives proved to be short-lived.
60 Anne Penketh, 'Target Iran', *The Independent*, 10 April 2006.
61 Mahmoud Muawad, *Al-Ahram*, 30 January 2003.
62 See Richard Latter, *Mediterranean Security* (London: HMSO, December 1991); Roberto Aliboni, *European Security Across the Mediterranean*, *op. cit.*
63 Bichara Khader, *L'Europe et la Méditerranée: géopolitique de la proximité* (Paris: L'Harmattan, 1994).
64 Ghassan Salamé, 'Torn Between the Atlantic and the Mediterranean: Europe and the Middle East in the Post-Cold War Era', *Middle East Journal*, 48 (2), 1994, 226–49; George Joffé, 'Low-Level Violence and Terrorism', in Roberto

Aliboni, George Joffé and Tim Niblock (eds) *Security Challenges in the Mediterranean Region, op. cit.*, pp. 139–60.
65. Geoffrey Kemp, 'Europe's Middle East Challenges', *The Washington Quarterly*, 27 (1), 2003–04, 163–77.
66. Rodrigo de Rato, 'Co-operation and Security in the Mediterranean', *North Atlantic Assembly – Political Committee* (Brussels: North Atlantic Assembly, October 1995), pp. 1–16.
67. Werner Weidenfeld (ed.) *Europe and the Middle East* (Gütersloh: Bertelsmann Foundation, 1995).
68. The Barcelona Declaration (Barcelona: Conferencia EuroMediterranea, 1995).
69. In early 1996, the European Parliament had approved the admission of Turkey to the European Customs Union, and by November 1996 the EU had reached new 'partnership pacts' with several Mediterranean countries including Israel, Morocco, and Tunisia.
70. *Middle East Economic Digest*, 24 November 1995.
71. France's pressures on its EU partners to adopt a more active political role in the Middle East had already led to the appointment of an EU special envoy (Miguel Moratinos) for the Middle East in 1996, the Union's first such appointment.
72. The French Foreign Minister Hervé de Charette, quoted in Shada Islam, 'Europe a Go-between?', *Middle East International*, No. 537, 1996, 5.
73. Term used by Martin J. Dedman, *The Origins and Development of the European Union, op. cit.*, p. 128.
74. Ronald S. Asmus, F. Stephen Larrabee and Ian O. Lesser, 'Mediterranean Security: New Challenges, New Tasks', *NATO Review*, 44 (3), 1996, 27.
75. Issues such as monetary union, a single European foreign and security policy, the extension of the EU eastwards, and the future role of NATO in Europe, are some of the obstacles in the way of creating a unified, single, federated, regional body that the EU has the potential to become.
76. See Hugh Corbet, 'European Integration and the Integration of the World Economy', *op. cit.*, pp. 55–69.
77. J. A. R. Marriott wrote in 1921 that the 'root of the ['Eastern Question'] is to be found in the presence, embedded in the living flesh of Europe, of an alien substance – the Ottoman Turk. Akin to the European family neither in creed, in race, in language, in social custom, nor in political aptitudes and traditions, the Ottomans have long presented to the European Powers a problem, now tragic, now comic, now bordering on burlesque, but always baffling and paradoxical. How to deal with this alien substance has been for five hundred years the essence and core of the problem of the Near East'. *Europe and Beyond: A Preliminary Survey of World-Politics in the Last Half-Century 1870–1920* (London: Methuen, 1921), p. 47.
78. Turkey, it should be remembered, has enjoyed advantages (active membership of the NATO alliance, control of vast tracts of continental European territory in the past and a long tradition of interaction with other European civilizations) that today's aspirants from the Mediterranean do not enjoy.
79. Quoted by Meltem Müftüler, 'Turkey and the European Community: An Uneasy Relationship', *Turkish Review Quarterly Digest*, 7 (33), 1993, 39.
80. Stephen Kinzeer, 'Kinkel Tells Turkey it's not Ready for EU', *International Herald Tribune*, 27 March 1997.
81. Lionel Barber, John Barham and Bruce Clark, 'Turkey: Nato Enlargement Threat Over EU', *Financial Times*, 20 January 1997.
82. Sarah Helm, 'EU Smoothes the Path to Membership', *The Independent*, 17 March 1997. In response to the European view, US State Department spokesman Nicholas Burns stated that 'We strongly believe the European

Union should allow for the possibility of Turkish membership ... Turkey's future, we believe, ought to be grounded in Europe'. Reuters, 11 March 1997.
83 The establishment of a European Economic Area, which arose from an agreement between the EC and the European Free Trade Association in May 1992, is another testimony to the EU's strategy. The EEA is the world's largest and most integrated economic zone.
84 Felix Neugart, *The Future of European Policies in the Middle East after the Iraq War* (Munich: Bertelsmann Group for Policy Research and Center for Applied Policy Research, 2003), pp. 22–23.
85 'Trade Liberalization under GATT and by the EC: Implications for Israel', in Ephraim Ahiram and Alfred Tovias (eds) *Whither EU–Israeli Relations? Common and Divergent Interests* (Frankfurt: Peter Lang, 1995), p. 66.
86 Robert Jervis, 'The Remaking of a Unipolar World', *The Washington Quarterly*, 29 (3), 2006, 7.
87 To appreciate the potential economic power of China, look no further than Trish Saywell, 'China: Powering Asia's Growth', *Far Eastern Economic Review*, 2 August, 2001.
88 Michael Scott Doran, 'Somebody Else's Civil War', *Foreign Affairs*, 81 (1), 2002, 22–42.
89 See his State of the Union Address, January 2002.
90 Michael Yahuda, *The International Politics of the Asia–Pacific, 1945–1995* (London: Routledge, 1996), pp. 257–58.
91 David Kerr, 'Greater China and East Asian Integration: Regionalism and Rivalry', *East Asia: An International Quarterly*, 21 (1), 2004, 75–92.
92 'China's Economic Power: Enter the Dragon', *The Economist*, 10 March 2001, p. 26.
93 'China's Confident Bow', *The Economist*, 10 March 2001, p. 79.
94 International Institute for Strategic Studies, *The Military Balance, 2001–2002* (Oxford: Oxford University Press for IISS, 2001, p. 177. The Chinese 2002/03 defence budget increased by a further 17 per cent.
95 Stockholm International Peace Research Institute, *SIPRI Yearbook 2000: Armaments, Disarmament and International Security* (Oxford: Oxford University Press for SIPRI, 2000), p. 372.
96 Martha Brill Olcott, *Central Asia's New States: Independence, Foreign Policy, and Regional Security* (Washington, DC: US Institute of Peace Press, 1996).
97 Richard Weitz, 'Averting a New Great Game in Central Asia', *The Washington Quarterly*, 29 (3), 2006, 155–67.
98 Donald L. Berlin, 'India in the Indian Ocean', *Naval War College Review*, 59 (2), 2006, 58–89.
99 For a discussion of the concept of 'strategic interdependence' and its consequences for the wider Middle East region, see Anoushiravan Ehteshami, *Nuclearisation of the Middle East* (London: Brassey's, 1989).
100 The Iran–Russia nuclear partnership is at the heart of Russia's West Asia presence. A Russian commentator has observed that 'partnership with Iran is becoming one of the key foreign policy tasks of Russia': Gelb Ivashentsov, quoted by Vladimir A. Orlov and Alexander Vinnikov, 'The Great Guessing Game: Russia and the Iranian Nuclear Issue', *The Washington Quarterly*, 28, (2), 2005, 49–66.
101 See Chapter 9 of Robert Gilpin, *The Challenge of Global Capitalism: The World Economy in the 21st Century* (Princeton, NJ: Princeton University Press, 2000).
102 Ray Dafter, 'Pricing Paradox Costs Asia', *Far Eastern Economic Review*, 26 April 2001.
103 According to reliable estimates, 'between 1987 and 1997, energy consumption in the Asia–Pacific region grew 4.5% annually, compared to a world average of

1.5%. It is estimated that energy demand will grow 3.4% annually from 1997 to 2010. At this rate of growth, [the Asia–Pacific] region will become the largest energy-consuming region in the world by 2010'. See Kim Hak-Su, 'Energizing Asia's Growth', *Far Eastern Economic Review*, 23 November 2000. Equally interesting is his assessment that, by 2005, the annual investment requirement of the energy industry in East Asia alone will be 'between $150 billion and $200 billion', an astonishing sum.
104 Quoted by Victor Mallet, 'Power Hungry: Asia's Surging Energy Demand Reverberates Around the World', *Financial Times*, 12 May 2004.
105 Saudi Oil Minister Ali al-Naimi, speaking at an inter-Asian energy conference in New Delhi: Reuters, 6 January 2005.
106 Michael Piskur, 'Iran's Nuclear Plans Complicate China's Energy Security', *Power and Interest News Report (PINR)*, 13 March 2006 (www.pinr.com/report.php?ac = view_report&report_id = 456&language_id = 1)
107 It is said that Indian and Chinese demand is likely to climb sharply to between 20 million and 30 million tonnes a year after 2010, and rise more steeply by 2020. 'It's going to be a quick build-up. Really, this is very big consumption', according to the Director of General Affairs at Indonesia's state-owned Pertamina. ohn McBeth, 'Fuel of the Future', *Far Eastern Economic Review*, 14 September 2000.
108 Hassan M. Fattah, 'Hu's Saudi Visit Signals a Change in Gulf', *New York Times*, 24 April 2006.
109 Alkman Granitsas, 'Barrels of Trouble', *Far Eastern Economic Review*, 30 March 2000.
110 The reasons are a more competitive oil market in Europe and North America; more diverse suppliers; and the fact that all crude prices are based on what are known as 'marker prices', but the actual prices oil sells for are conditioned by oil quality and transport costs. As a consequence, Asia–Pacific countries buying crude at the 'East of Suez' pricing formulae find themselves currently paying, on average, US$1.38 per barrel more than European importers and US$1.21 per barrel more than US customers.
111 Even these estimates are viewed sceptically by many commentators. See Geoffrey Kemp, 'The Persian Gulf Remains the Strategic Prize', *Survival*, 40 (4), 1998–99, 132–49.
112 Jan Kalicki, for example, states that Kazakhstan's Tengiz oil field, 75 per cent owned by US oil interests, is worth more than US$10 billion. Jan H. Kalicki, 'Caspian Energy at the Crossroads', *Foreign Affairs*, 80 (5), 2001, 120–34.
113 Whereas in the Persian Gulf extraction costs fall below US$1 per barrel, in the Caspian the cost is likely to be around or above US$5 per barrel, on a par with North Sea costs.
114 *BP 1997: Statistical Review of World Energy* (London: BP, 1998).
115 President Ilham Aliyev's first formal visit to the USA in April 2006, after his election victory of 2003, was portrayed in geopolitical terms by commentators and US officials alike. One leading news source put it in these terms: 'Sandwiched between Russia and Iran, Azerbaijan's geopolitical status as a western-friendly, Muslim-majority country sitting on oil and gas riches makes it too important to shun despite the risk of charges of double standards in how the US deals with autocrats'. Guy Dinmore and Demetri Sevastopulo, 'Geopolitics Wins Aliyev First White House Visit', *Financial Times*, 24 April 2006.
116 In March 2000, Iran announced its most effective counter-attack yet: the building of a new US$400 million oil pipeline by a Chinese–Swiss consortium, with French financial backing, from its Caspian seaport of Neka to one of its

principal refineries in northern Iran (the Rey complex near Tehran). Under its oil-swap programme with the Caspian trio, Iran is hoping to be able to shift as much as 370,000 bpd of Caspian oil to its refining network, and export an equivalent amount from its Persian Gulf deposits on behalf of its Caspian neighbours. Russia has also been pushing ahead with its own pipeline plans: to complete the 1.3 million bpd capacity Tengiz–Novorossiysk oil pipeline, to complete the new line from Kazakhstan and Novorossiysk, and to build a 312 km pipeline around Chechnya to provide a new link between Baku and Novorossiysk. On the US side, only the Baku–Supsa pipeline has been built. Michael Lelyveld, 'Russia: Kremlin Determined to Stay in Race for Caspian Oil', Radio Free Europe/Radio Liberty, 2 November 1999 (www.rferl.org); 'US Loses Influence Over Caspian Basin Oil', *Global Intelligence Update*, 24 March 2000 (Strategic Forecasting, www.stratfor.com).

117 For a useful discussion of the reserves issue, see OECD, *The Changing Face of Energy Politics* (Paris: Organisation for Economic Co-operation and Development, 2000).

118 The US Secretary Energy, quoted by Amy Myers Jaffe and Robert A. Manning, 'The Myth of the Caspian "Great Game": The Real Geopolitics of Energy', *Survival*, 40 (4), 1998–99, 112.

119 Statement of Counsellor Jan Kalicki, Chief Government CIS Energy Strategist based in the US Department of Commerce. Press release, February 1998.

120 Associated Press, 18 and 20 August 2005; *Xinhua*, 18 August 2005.

121 India and Israel have gone even further, holding joint exercises to test the prowess of India's Su-30MKI fighters against Israel's F-16s, which also happen to be in Pakistan's arsenal. See 'India–Israel Alliance Firming Up', *Jane's Intelligence Digest*, 2 March 2005; Siddharth Srivastava, 'Gunning for Peace in South Asia', *Asia Times*, 13 August 2005.

122 Quoted by Robert Olson, 'The Turkey–Israel Alliance: Is Iran Now the Target?', *Middle East International*, No. 657, 2001, 24.

123 *ibid.*

124 Doug Struck and Glenn Kessler, 'Korea Atom Effort: U.S. Knew Early On', *International Herald Tribune*, 19–20 October 2002.

125 Susumu Ishida, 'Japan's Oil Strategy in the Gulf without Arms Deals', in Charles E. Davies (ed.) *Global Interests in the Arab Gulf* (Exeter: University of Exeter Press, 1992), pp. 179–201; Anoushiravan Ehteshami, 'The Rise and Convergence of the "Middle" in the World Economy: The Case of the NICs and the Gulf States', in Charles E. Davies (ed.), *ibid.*, pp. 132–68.

126 Vivienne Walt, 'Iran: Looks East', *Fortune Magazine*, 21 February 2005.

127 *The Daily Star*, 19 December 2005.

128 Ed Blanche, 'A New World Order?', *Arabies Trends*, May 2006.

129 Farhan Bokhari, 'Dubai in Huge Pakistan Investment', *Financial Times*, 3 June 2006.

130 Keith Bradsher and Christopher Pala, 'Chinese Beat India for Kazakh Oil Fields', *International Herald Tribune*, 23 August 2005.

131 See Hannah Carter and Anoushiravan Ehteshami (eds), *The Middle East's Relations with Asia and Russia* (London: RoutledgeCurzon, 2004).

132 Michael E. Bonine, 'Population Growth, the Labor Market and Gulf Security', in David E. Long and Christian Koch (eds), *Gulf Security in the Twenty-first Century* (Abu Dhabi: Emirates Center for Strategic Studies and Research, 1997), pp. 226–64.

133 Abdullah Al-Madani, 'The Gulf and the Policy of "Looking East"', *Gulf Yearbook 2005–2006* (Dubai: Gulf Research Center, 2006), pp. 297–305; G. Parthasarathy, 'India's Stakes in the Persian Gulf', *Tribune*, 8 September 2005.

134 Buce A. Elleman and Sarah C. M. Paine, 'Security pact with Russia Bolsters China's Power', *International Herald Tribune*, 6 August 2001.
135 James Ridgeway with Camelia E. Fard, 'The New World Order', *Village Voice*, 19–25 September 2001.
136 One example is the emergence of ties between Israel and Pakistan. In 2003, the Pakistani leader called on his people to recognize the fact of the existence of Israel, and since then Pakistani officials have talked in terms of relations with Israel and the US Jewish lobby helping to improve Pakistan's image in the USA and also to deepen its security partnership with the latter. See Graham Usher, 'It's India Again', *Al-Ahram Weekly*, 17–23 November 2005.
137 For a critical analysis of the balance of 'forces' debate in the post-Cold-War era, see James M. Goldgeier and Michael McFaul, 'A Tale of Two Worlds: Core and Periphery in the Post-Cold War Era', *International Organization*, 46 (2), 1992, 467–91.
138 Deutsch and Singer argued in this vein back in the 1960s. See Karl W. Deutsch and J. David Singer, 'Multipolar Power Systems and International Stability', in James N. Rosenau (ed.) *International Politics and Foreign Policy* (New York: Free Press, 1969), pp. 315–24.
139 Richard Rosecrane, 'Bipolarity, Multipolarity, and the Future', in James N. Rosenau (ed.) *International Politics and Foreign Policy* (New York: Free Press, 1969), p. 331.
140 Kenneth Waltz, 'International Structure, National Force, and the Balance of Power', in James N. Rosenau (ed.), *ibid.*, pp. 304–14.
141 Anwar Abdel-Malek, 'While We Were Sleeping', *Al-Ahram Weekly*, 13–19 October 2003.

5 Government and Governance in the Era of Globalization

1 John Micklethwait and Adrian Wooldridge, 'From Sarajevo to September 11', *Policy Review Online*, No. 117, 2003. www.policyreview.org/feb03/micklethwait.html
2 See Peter R. Odell, *Oil and World Power* (New York: Penguin, 1986).
3 James Petras and Henry Veltmeyer, *Globalization Unmasked: Imperialism in the 21st Century* (London: Zed Books, 2002), p. 70.
4 *ibid.*, p. 110. Although, in making their case, the authors have their eye on the political regimes of Latin America, their argument does find resonance in the Arab world as well. Note Algeria's experience in the early 1990s, for example, where the elite rejected the outcome of the country's elections and imposed indirect military rule because the population had not delivered the desired result.
5 For a detailed analysis, see Anoushiravan Ehteshami and Emma C. Murphy, 'Transformation of the Corporatist in the Middle East', *Third World Quarterly*, 17 (4), 1996, 753–72.
6 Victor Lavy and Eliezer Sheffer, *Foreign Aid and Economic Development in the Middle East: Egypt, Syria and Jordan* (New York: Praeger, 1991).
7 Nadim Kawach, 'Arab Budgets Reel Under Heavy Spending on Defence', *Gulf News*, 1 February 2004. The data are based on a report jointly produced by the Arab League and the Arab Fund for Economic and Social Development.
8 Saskia Sassen, *Losing Control? Sovereignty in an Age of Globalization* (New York: Columbia University Press, 1996).
9 Saskia Sassen, 'Losing Control? The State and the New Geography of Power', *Global Dialogue*, 1 (1), 1999, 78–88.
10 Charles Tripp, 'States, Elites and the "Management of Change"', in Hassan Hakimian and Ziba Moshaver (eds) *The State and Global Change: The Political*

Economy of Transition in the Middle East and North Africa (Richmond: Curzon Press, 2001), p. 227.
11 A Western diplomat speaking to the Financial Times. Roula Khalaf, 'Saudis Start to Question Society that Leaves Women Marginalised', *Financial Times*, 30 October 2002.
12 Gowher Rezvi, 'South Asia and the New World Order', in Hans-Henrik Holm and Georg Sørensen (eds) *Whose World Order? Uneven Globalization and the End of the Cold War* (Boulder, CO: Westview Press, 1995), p. 84.
13 Sean L. Yom, 'Civil Society and Democratization in the Arab World', *Middle East Review of International Affairs*, 9 (4), 2005, 14–33.
14 For a detailed analysis, see Anoushiravan Ehteshami, 'Is the Middle East Democratizing?', *British Journal of Middle Eastern Studies*, 26 (2), 1999, 199–217.
15 Thomas Carothers, 'The End of the Transition Paradigm', *Journal of Democracy*, 13 (1), 2002, 8.
16 John Peterson, *The Emergence of Post-Traditional Oman*, Durham Middle East Paper No. 78 (Durham: University of Durham, 2005).
17 Female members of the Kuwaiti elite, such as Sheikha Amthal al-Sabah, announced in early 2004 that the government would ensure women have full political rights in that country by end of 2005. *Kuwait* (London), No. 118, February 2004. This pledge was realized in May 2005.
18 Mai Yamani, 'In Kuwait, Succession and a Parliamentary Revolution', *The Daily Star*, 3 February 2003.
19 Mohammed al-Muhanna, *The Saudi Majlis ash-Shura: Domestic Functions and International Role* (PhD thesis, Institute for Middle Eastern and Islamic Studies, Durham University, 2005).
20 In June 2003, the King granted the Majlis al-Shura the right to propose and debate, but not pass, new bills or proposed amendments to existing laws without the permission of the King. In October, the Saudi authorities announced that they would prepare for elections for half the members of each municipal council within one year.
21 Recently, the then Crown Prince Abdullah received participants of the Makkah dialogue forum at his palace in Riyadh. 'The reform effort has been developing for some time in the mind of the Crown Prince. But the real thrust seems to have come after the May [2003] terrorist attacks in Saudi Arabia. These attacks, and particularly the one against the Muslim compound this past fall, have brought the Royal Family, the businessmen and the average Saudi citizen together in opposition to the threat to the state, to moderation and to the tactic of terrorism. In June, the Crown Prince declared a reform initiative calling for self-reform and the development of political participation through a National Dialogue. The Crown Prince told me that this effort included all elements of the society including Shiites and other sects of the Islamic faith. He called this a process of the intellect to bring people together in consensus behind reform rather than a political process that tends to divide people on ideological lines'. Edward S. Walker, 'The Quiet Revolution – Saudi Arabia', *Middle East Institute Perspective* (Washington, DC: The Middle East Institute, 2004).
22 See *Qatar News*, No. 3, January 2003.
23 *ibid.*
24 The words of Qatar's Foreign Minister, Sheikh Hamad bin Jassim bin Jabr al-Thani. *Qatar News*, 3 January 2003.
25 Gerd Nonneman, *Political Reform in the Gulf Monarchies: From Liberalisation to Democratisation? A Comparative Perspective*, Durham Middle East Paper No. 80 (Durham: University of Durham, 2006), p. 31.

26 Many of the contributors to the following make this point strongly. See Larry Diamond, Marc F. Plattner and Daniel Brumberg (eds) *Islam and Democracy in the Middle East* (Baltimore, MD: Johns Hopkins University Press, 2003).
27 Daniel Brumberg, 'The Trap of Liberalized Autocracy', in *ibid.*, pp. 35–47.
28 President Bush's address at the National Endowment of Democracy, *Washington Post*, 6 November 2003.
29 Daniel Brumberg, *Liberalization Versus Democracy: Understanding Arab Political Reform*, Working Paper No. 37 (Washington, DC: Carnegie Endowment for Peace, 2003), p. 3.
30 President Bush's address at the National Endowment of Democracy, *op. cit.*
31 Leon T. Hadar, 'The "Green Peril": Creating the Islamic Fundamentalist Threat', *Policy Analysis*, No. 177, 1992, 29.
32 President Bush's address at the Whitehall Palace, London, 19 November 2003. White House Press Secretary.
33 *Akidati*, 11 November 2003.
34 *Al-Ahram*, 10 November 2003.
35 *Al-Wafd*, 11 November 2003.
36 *Teshreen*, 12 November 2003.
37 *Teshreen*, 8 November 2003.
38 *International Herald Tribune*, 19–20 October 2002.
39 Frank Griffel, 'Globalization and the Middle East: Part Two', *YaleGlobal Online*, 21 January 2003, http://yaleglobal.yale.edu/display.article?id = 771
40 *ibid.*
41 These observations are based on interviews with Islamists in several Arab countries, their representatives in western Europe, and members of exiled groups.
42 *The Guardian*, 16 October 2002.
43 *The Daily Telegraph*, 17 October 2002.
44 Counter-terrorism expert Jonathan Stephenson, quoted by *The Guardian*. Owen Bowcott, 'Suicide Bombings Highlight Dangers for America's Closest Allies', *The Guardian*, 18 November 2003.
45 Bin Laden's tape was translated by the BBC, 12 February 2003.
46 This was the title of an editorial in the *Al Watan* newspaper (10 November 2003).
47 Bin Laden's tape, *op. cit.*
48 *ibid.* The following view was expressed by an Egyptian university student in November 2003: 'It is very obvious that Israel, America's pampered child, has become more bold since the US occupation of Iraq, committing more bloody crimes against the Palestinians and threatening Syria and Lebanon'. See Gihan Shahine, 'Appreciating Resistance', *Al-Ahram Weekly*, 13–19 November 2003. The similarity may be remarkable, but should not be surprising.

6 Economic Internationalization and the Changing Balance of Economic Power in the Middle East

1 Fauzi Najjar, 'The Arabs, Islam and Globalization', *Middle East Policy*, XII (3), 2005, 91–106.
2 Jan Nederveen Pieterse, *Globalization or Empire?* (London: Routledge, 2004), p. 109.
3 Toby Dodge and Richard Higgott, 'Globalization and its Discontents: The Theory and Practice of Change in the Middle East', in Toby Dodge and Richard Higgott (eds) *Globalization and the Middle East: Islam, Economy,*

Society and Politics (London: Royal Institute of International Affairs. 2002). pp. 13–35.
4 Clement M. Henry and Robert Springborg, *Globalization and the Politics of Development in the Middle East* (Cambridge: Cambridge University Press, 2001), p. 59.
5 See the special issue of *Finance and Development*, 'The Middle East: On the Threshold of Change', 40 (1), 2003.
6 Economist Intelligence Unit, *Business Environment Ranking* (London: EIU, 2000).
7 For a Middle East-based analysis of these data, see Nirmala Janssen, 'Bahrain, Kuwait and the UAE Rank High in Survey', *Gulf News*, 7 January 2005.
8 Daniel Epps, 'World Bank Gives Lebanon Poor Marks in Governance', *The Daily Star*, 8 July 2005.
9 E. Riordan, U. Dadush, J. Jalali, S. Streifel, M. Brahmbhatt and K. Takagaki, 'The World Economy and its Implications for the Middle East and North Africa', in N. Shafik (ed.) *Prospects for Middle Eastern and North African Economies: From Boom to Bust and Back?* (New York: St Martin's Press, 1998).
10 Mehran Kamrava, 'Structural Impediments to Economic Globalization in the Middle East', *Middle East Policy*, XI (4), 2004, 96–112.
11 *BBC News*, 29 October 2002.
12 Sahar Aloul, 'Reform Can't Take Place Until Palestinian, Iraqi Issues Solved', *The Jordan Times*, 17 May 2004.
13 United Nations Development Programme/Arab Fund for Economic and Social Development, *Arab Human Development Report 2002*, (New York: UNDP, 2002), p. 85.
14 Another report, released in 2002, put the Arab unemployment rate at 20 per cent, noting that 6.5 million jobs were needed simply to cut the current unemployment rate. See 'Middle East Faces Jobs Challenge', *BBC News*, 9 October 2002. The figure of 80 million new jobs in 10 years emerged in the course of several debates at the World Economic Forum meeting in Jordan, 15–17 May 2004.
15 Alan Richards, 'Socioeconomic Roots of Middle East Radicalism', *Naval War College Review*, LV (4), 2002, 1.
16 Oded I. Remba, 'Basic Conflict of Economic Development in the Middle East', in J. H. Thompson and R. D. Reischauer (eds) *Modernization of the Arab World* (Princeton, NJ: D. Van Nostrand, 1966), p. 61.
17 The World Bank, *Claiming the Future: Choosing Prosperity in the Middle East and North Africa* (Washington, DC: International Bank for Reconstruction and Development, 1995), p. 33.
18 *ibid.*, p. 34.
19 M. S. El Azhary, 'Introduction', in M. S. El Azhary (ed.) *The Impact of Oil Revenues on Arab Gulf Development* (Beckenham: Croom Helm, 1984), p. 12.
20 Abbas Alnasrawi, 'Dependency Status and Economic Development of Arab States', in Baha Abu-Laban and Sharon McIrvin Abu-Laban (eds) *The Arab World: Dynamics of Development* (Leiden: E. J. Brill, 1986), p. 19.
21 *ibid.*, p. 23.
22 *ibid.*, p. 25.
23 John Duke Anthony notes that 'Saudi Arabia's banks account for approximately forty per cent of the entire Arab world's capital. Tiny Bahrain, however, hosts ... the largest number of international banking units [in the Gulf region]. Moreover, Kuwait, Saudi Arabia and the UAE all have extensive investments overseas as well as impressive funds that play major developmental, economic assistance and humanitarian roles among the world's poorer countries and peoples'. John Duke Anthony, 'The Gulf Cooperation Council: Constraints', *GulfWire Perspectives*, 4 February 2004.

24 *ibid.*, p. 29. Labour remittances to Egypt rose from US$6.4 million in 1971 to US$1.9 billion 8 years later.
25 Rodney Wilson, *Economic Development in the Middle East* (London: Routledge, 1995).
26 Ahmed Boudroua, 'Outlook for Industrialization of the Arab World', in Baha Abu-Laban and Sharon McIrvin Abu-Laban (eds) *The Arab World: Dynamics of Development* (Leiden: E. J. Brill, 1986), p. 33.
27 The World Bank, *World Bank Development Report 1994: Infrastructure for Development* (Oxford: Oxford University Press, 1994). In the cases of Egypt, Syria, Sudan and Yemen, petroleum has come to play a bigger economic share since the mid-1990s.
28 Saifur Rahman, 'Gulf Must Device Strategies to Lure Foreign Direct Investment', *Gulf News*, 30 October 2002.
29 International Monetary Fund, *IMF Staff Country Report, Iran* (Washington, DC: IMF, No. 98/27), p. 19.
30 Sherine Abdel-Razek, 'Glass Half-full', *Al-Ahram Weekly*, 5–11 February 2004.
31 Ismail Sirageldin and Rana Al-Khaled, *The Challenges of Globalization and Human Resource Development in the Arab World: Myth and Reality*, Working Paper 9712 (Cairo: Economic Research Forum, 1996).
32 David Turner, 'World Unemployment Increases to 180m', *Financial Times*, 24 January 2003.
33 Martin Hvidt, 'Limited Success of the IMF and the World Bank in Middle Eastern Reforms', *Journal of Social Affairs*, 21 (81), 2004, 77–103.
34 The problem is highlighted by the plight of one of the region's most dynamic economies, Kuwait, which in the period since the 1960s has seen the share of the private sector decline from 80 per cent to no more than 15 per cent today, according to Ibrahim Dabdoud, Chief Executive Officer of National Bank of Kuwait. World Economic Forum, Jordan, 15–17 May 2004.
35 Karen Pfeifer and Marsha Pripstein Posusney, 'Arab Economies and Globalization: An Overview', in Eleanor Abdella Doumato and Marsha Pripstein Posusney (eds) *Women and Globalization in the Middle East: Gender, Economy, and Society* (Boulder, CO: Lynne Rienner, 2003), pp. 25–54.
36 Fouad Ajami, *The Arab Predicament: Arab Political Thought and Practice Since 1967* (Cambridge: Cambridge University Press, 1993), p. 147.
37 Mohammad Ja'far, 'National Formations in the Arab Region: A Critique of Samir Amin', *Khamsin*, No. 6, 1978, 82.
38 For a discussion of this phenomenon, see Leslie Sklair, *The Transnational Capitalist Class* (Oxford: Blackwell, 2001).
39 Meliha Benli Altunişik and Özlem Tür, *Turkey: Challenges of Continuity and Change* (New York: RoutledgeCurzon, 2005), p. 86.
40 For an excellent analysis of this, see Warwick Knowles, *Jordan Since 1989: A Study in Political Economy* (London: I. B. Tauris, 2005).
41 Arab debt servicing stood at US$16 billion in 2002. *Gulf News*, 1 February 2003.
42 Jahangir Amuzegar, *Oil Exporters' Economic Development in an Interdependent World*, Occasional Paper No. 18 (Washington, DC: International Monetary Fund, 1983).
43 Sana Abdallah, 'Oil Troubles', *Middle East International*, No. 717, 23 January 2004, p. 18.
44 Economic Research Forum for the Arab Countries, Iran and Turkey, *Economic Trends in the MENA Region* (Cairo: Economic Research Forum, 1998), p. 65.
45 Meliha Benli Altunişik and Özlem Tür, *Turkey: Challenges of Continuity and Change*, op. cit.
46 Matthew Karnitschnig, 'European Companies Feel Pressure Over Iran, *The Wall Street Journal*, 28–30 January 2005.

47 *BBC News*, 29 October 2002.
48 Philip G. Cerny, 'Globalization and the Changing Logic of Collective Action', *International Organization*, 49 (4), 1995, 595–625.
49 United Nations Development Programme/Arab Fund for Economic and Social Development, *Arab Human Development Report 2003* (New York: UNDP, 2003), p. 40.
50 World Bank, *World Development Report* (Oxford: Oxford University Press, 1997), p. 136.
51 Figure quoted by Mervat Tallawi, Undersecretary General of the Economic and Social Commission for Western Asia (ESCWA). Osama Habib, 'ESCWA Urges More Trade Between Arab States', *The Daily Star*, 8 July 2005.
52 Weis notes that Bahrain is already the Arab world's most open economy and the UAE is more 'wired' than even Israel. Despite its substantial oil reserves, 75 per cent of Dubai's GDP comes from non-oil sources today. See Stanley A. Weiss, 'Sheiks Give Modernity a Try', *International Herald Tribune*, 15 April 2004.
53 Although with over 45 per cent of their exports destined for the EU, Japan and the USA, and around 60 per cent of their imports originating in the same, this point can be overplayed.
54 Byron and Seiji Naya, 'Why East Asian Economies Have Been Successful: Some Lessons for Other Developing Counties', in Heba Handoussa (ed.) *Economic Transition in the Middle East: Global Challenges and Adjustment Strategies* (Cairo: American University in Cairo Press, 1997), p. 47.
55 World Bank, *The Asian Miracle: Economic Growth and Public Policy* (Oxford: Oxford University Press, 1993), pp. 37–39.
56 See Hassan Hakimian, 'From MENA to East Asia and Back: Lessons of Globalization, Crisis and Economic Reform', in Hassan Hakimian and Ziba Moshaver (eds) *The State and Global Change: The Political Economy of Transition n the Middle East and North Africa* (Richmond: Curzon Press, 2001), pp. 80–108.
57 Mohamed El-Erian and Mahmoud El-Gamal, *Attracting Foreign Investments to Arab Countries: Getting the Basics Right*, Working Paper No. 9718 (Cairo: MEF, July 1997).
58 Fred Halliday, 'The Middle East and the Politics of Differential Integration', in Toby Dodge and Richard Higgott (eds), *Globalization and the Middle East*, op. cit., p. 55.
59 Merrill Lynch has estimated that the GCC's 185,000 millionaires dispose of wealth of around US$718 billion, with some two-thirds of it amassed by Saudi Arabia's 78,000 millionaires. *Gulf States Newsletter* 22 (557), 1997, 10.
60 John Duke Anthony, 'The Gulf Cooperation Council: Constraints', *GulfWire Perspectives*, 4 February 2004.
61 Ghaida Ghantous and Barbara Lewis, 'OPEC Investors Mature, Keep Petrodollars at Home', *Saudi Gazette*, 31 January 2006.
62 Complete data for 2005 suggest that GCC stock markets more than doubled their total capitalization to stand at US$1.46 trillion, recording a massiveincrease of some 118 per cent since 2004. The six GCC markets had stood at just US$119 billion in 2000. The largest GCC bourse, in Saudi Arabia, stood at US$660 billion at end of 2005. 'Gulf Stock Markets Make Historic Gains in 2005', *The Daily Star*, 9 January 2006.
63 Roula Khalaf, William Wallis and Gillian Tett, 'Sky-high: Arab Economies are Booming', *Financial Times*, 5 July 2005.
64 Daniel Hanna, 'A New Fiscal Framework for GCC Countries ahead of Monetary Union', *International Economics Programme Briefing Paper IEP BP 06/02* (London: Royal Institute of International Affairs).

65 A. F. Alhajji, *The GRC Monthly Oil Report – December 2005* (Dubai: Gulf Research Center, 2005).
66 See *SHUAA Capital Economic Bulletin*, December 2005.
67 Osama Habib, 'ESCWA Urges More Trade Between Arab States', *The Daily Star*, 8 July 2005.
68 Pete W. Moore, 'The International Context of Liberalization and Democratization in the Arab World', *Arab Studies Quarterly*, 16 (3), 1994, 43–66.
69 Toby Dodge, 'Bringing the Bourgeoisie Back in: Globalization and the Birth of Liberal Authoritarianism in the Middle East', in Toby Dodge and Richard Higgott (eds) *Globalization and the Middle East: op. cit.*, p. 174.
70 Nazih Ayubi, 'Etatisme versus Privatization: The Changing Economic Role of the State in Nine Arab Countries', in Heba Handoussa (ed.) *Economic Transition in the Middle East, op. cit.*, p. 162.

7 Culture Clash: Globalization and the Geopolitics of Identity in the Middle East

1 It is, in this sense, the cultural underpinning for Muslims. For our purposes, culture is defined as 'the comprehensive worldview through which one perceives and interacts with the outside world'. See Douglas M. Johnston, 'Religion and Culture: Human Dimensions of Globalization' in Richard L. Kugler and Ellen L. Frost (eds) *The Global Century: Globalization and National Security*, Volume II (Washington, DC: National Defense University Press, 2001), p. 666.
2 Bassam Tibi, *The Challenge of Fundamentalism: Political Islam and the New World Disorder* (Berkeley, CA: University of California Press, 2002).
3 Barry Rubin, 'Globalization and the Middle East: Part One', *YaleGlobal Online*, 16 January 2003, p. 3.
4 Farhad Nomani and Ali Rahnema, *Islamic Economic Systems* (London: Zed Books, 1994).
5 It has, however, been suggested that the challenge of globalization 'is perceived primarily as religious and secondarily as cultural'. See Maha Azzam, 'Between the Market and God: Islam, Globalization and Culture in the Middle East', in Toby Dodge and Richard Higgott (eds) *Globalization and the Middle East: Islam, Economy, Society and Politics* (London: Royal Institute of International Affairs, 2002), p. 153.
6 Barry Rubin, 'Globalization and the Middle East: Part One', *op. cit.*
7 Turki Abdullah Al-Sudairi, 'Being Invaded by a Satanic Civilization', *Arab News*, 3 February 2001.
8 Mike Featherstone, *Undoing Culture: Globalization, Postmodernism and Identity* (London: Sage, 1995).
9 Leslie Sklair, *Sociology of the Global System* (London: Harvester Wheatsheaf, 1991).
10 John Tomlinson, *Cultural Imperialism: A Critical Introduction* (London: Pinter, 1991).
11 *Al-Ahram*, 1 November 2003.
12 Yusuf al-Qaradawi, *Al-Muslimun wa al-Awlamah* (Muslims and Globalization) (Cairo: Dar al-Tawzi wa Nashr al-Islamiyya, 2000).
13 Galal Amin, *Globalization, Consumption Patterns and Human Development in Egypt*, Working Paper 9929 (Cairo: Economic Research Forum, undated).
14 Diaa Hadid, 'Recruiters Averse to Hiring Women with Headscarf', *Gulf News*, 7 January 2005.

15 For a fascinating analysis of McDonald's and East Asian cultural norms, see James L. Watson, *Golden Arches East: McDonald's in East Asia* (Stanford, CA: Stanford University Press, 1997).
16 Hassan M. Fattah, 'Ramadan's Beginning to Look A lot Like ... ', *International Herald Tribune*, 12 October 2005.
17 A different emphasis is put on the same issue by Richard Thomas, 'As Hostility Towards America Grows, Will the World Lose its Appetite for Coca-Cola, McDonald's and Nike?', *Financial Times*, 27 March 2003.
18 United Nations Development Programme/Arab Fund for Economic and Social Development, *Arab Human Development Report 2002* (New York: UNDP, 2002), p. 8.
19 *ibid.*, p. 9.
20 See Keith Griffin, 'Culture and Economic Growth: The State and Globalization', in Jan Nederveen Pieterse (ed.) *Global Futures: Shaping Globalization* (London: Zed Books, 2000), pp. 189–202.
21 The Pew Global Attitudes Project, *The Great Divide: How Westerns and Muslims View Each Other* (Washington, DC: Pew Research Center, 2006), p. 17.
22 An excellent starting point would be Simon W. Murden's *Islam, the Middle East, and the New Global Hegemony* (Boulder, CO: Lynne Rienner, 2002), and Bryan S. Turner's *Orientalism, Postmodernism and Globalism* (London: Routlege, 1994).
23 *Associated Free Press*, 7 December 1999.
24 Islamic Republic News Agency (IRNA), 2 January 2003.
25 Islamic Republic News Agency (IRNA), various reports in January and October 2003.
26 Editor of the Saudi-based *Arab News* daily newspaper quoted in Roula Khalaf, 'Saudis Start to Question Society that Leaves Women Marginalised', *Financial Times*, 30 October 2002.
27 *The Daily Star*, 9 January 2006.
28 See Joel Benin and Joe Stork (eds) *Political Islam: Essays From Middle East Report* (Berkeley, CA: University of California Press, 1997), p. 321.
29 Paul Dresch, 'Introduction: Societies, Identities and Global Issues', in Paul Dresch and James Piscatori (eds) *Monarchies and Nations: Globalisation and Identity in the Arab States of the Gulf* (London: I. B. Tauris, 2005), p, 7.
30 For a fascinating discussion of the situation in the UAE, see Christopher M. Davidson, *The United Arab Emirates: A Study in Survival* (Boulder, CO: Lynne Rienner, 2005).
31 The prominent sociologist Moussa Shleiwi, quoted in: 'Jordan's Westernized Youths use English to Broach Taboos', *The Daily Star*, 19 December 2005.
32 *ibid*.
33 Heather Sharp, 'Phone Technology Aids UAE Dating', *BBC News*, 29 July 2005.
34 See *Women, the State, and Political Liberalization: The Moroccan, Jordanian, and Tunisian Cases* (New York: Columbia University Press, 1998); Eleanor Abdella Doumato and Marsha Pripstein Posusney (eds) *Women and Globalization in the Arab Middle East: Gender, Economy and Society* (Boulder, CO: Lynne Rienner, 2003).
35 Mary Ann Tétreault, 'Kuwait: Sex, Violence, and the Politics of Economic Restructuring', in Eleanor Abdella Doumato and Marsha Pripstein Posusney (eds) *Women and Globalization in the Arab Middle East, op. cit.*, p. 227.
36 Emma C. Murphy, 'Women in Tunisia: Between State Feminism and Economic Reform', in Eleanor Abdella Doumato and Marsha Pripstein Posusney (eds) *Women and Globalization in the Arab Middle East, op. cit.*, pp. 169–93.
37 *ibid.*, p. 190.

38 Summary of session, 'Reform Agenda', at the Dead Sea World Economic Forum meeting, 16 May 2004.
39 Mary Ann Tétreault and Haya al-Mughni, 'Gender, Citizenship and Nationalism in Kuwait', *British Journal of Middle Eastern Studies*, 22 (1&2), 1995, 72.
40 Riffat Hassan, 'Feminist Theology: The Challenges for Muslim Women', *Critique: Journal for Critical Studies of the Middle East*, No. 9, 1996, 53–65.
41 Eleanor Abdella Doumato, 'Education in Saudi Arabia: Gender, Jobs, and the Price of Religion', in Eleanor Abdella Doumato and Marsha Pripstein Posusney (eds) *Women and Globalization in the Arab Middle East*, op. cit., p. 255. In Iran there is even a current among its clerics who are 'intent on finding an Islamic solution for the "women's question"'. See Ziba Mir-Hosseini, 'Rethinking Gender: Discussions with Ulama in Iran', *Critique: Journal for Critical Studies of the Middle East*, No. 13, 1998, 45–59.
42 *Arab News*, 20 January 2004.
43 Quotations are from Shahla Haeri, 'Obedience versus Autonomy: Women and Fundamentalism in Iran and Pakistan', in Martin E. Marty and R. Scott Appleby (eds) *Fundamentalisms and Society* (Chicago, IL: University of Chicago Press, 1993), pp. 182–91.
44 Frauke Heard-Bey, 'An Insider's View on Globalization in the Gulf', *Journal of Social Affairs*, 21 (83), 2004, 61.
45 Bassam Tibi, *The Challenge of Fundamentalism: Political Islam and the New World Disorder* (Berkeley, CA, USA: University of California Press, 2002), p. 6.
46 'Fear of Fundies', *The Economist*, 15 February 1992.
47 Jim Hoagland, 'Washington's Algerian Dilemma', *Washington Post*, 6 February 1992.
48 Amos Perlmutter, 'Wishful Thinking about Islamic Fundamentalism', *Washington Post*, 19 January 1992.
49 Leon T. Hadar, *The 'Green Peril': Creating the Islamic Fundamentalist Threat*, Policy Analysis No. 177 (Washington, DC: Cato Institute, 1992), p. 3.
50 Louay Safi, *Tensions and Transitions in the Muslim World* (Lanham, MD: University Press of America, 2003).
51 Maria do Céu Pinto, *Political Islam and the United States: A Study of U.S. Policy towards Islamist Movements in the Middle East* (Reading: Ithaca Press, 1999), p. 10.
52 Bernard Lewis, 'The Roots of Muslim Rage', *The Atlantic Monthly*, 266 (3), 1990, 49.
53 Bernard Lewis, 'License to Kill: Usama bin Ladin's Declaration of Jihad', *Foreign Affairs*, 77 (6), 1998, 19.
54 Margaret Thatcher, 'Islamism is the New Bolshevism', *The Guardian*, 12 February 2002. Her piece had first appeared in the *New York Times*.
55 It is worth noting that it was Libya, in early 1998, that issued the first international warrant for the arrest of bin Laden. A spokesman for the Crown Prince Abdullah of Saudi Arabia, on the other hand, described the anti-Saudi climate in the USA as bordering on hate, an anti-Saudi 'feeding frenzy'. See *International Herald Tribune*, 4 December 2002.
56 Ian Black, 'Turkey Must be Kept Out of the Union, Giscard Says', *The Guardian*, 9 November 2002.
57 Edward S. Walker Jr, 'Gloomy Mood in Egypt and Saudi Arabia', *Middle East Institute Perspective*, January 22 2003.
58 Francis Fukuyama, *The End of History and the Last Man* (London: Penguin, 1992), p. 235.
59 Kathleen Ridolfo, 'The Arab World: Economic Progress and Struggle', in Richard L. Kugler and Ellen L. Frost (eds) *The Global Century*, op. cit..

8 Globalization and International Politics of the Greater Middle East

1. Geoffrey Kemp and Robert E. Harkavy, *Strategic Geography and the Changing Middle East* (Washington, DC: Brookings Institution Press, 1997), p. 349.
2. Saul Cohen, *Geography and Politics in a World Divided* (New York: Random House, 1963), p. 233.
3. L. Carl Brown, *International Politics and the Middle East: Old Rules, Dangerous Game* (Princeton, NJ: Princeton University Press, 1984), p. 16.
4. Fred Halliday, 'The Middle East, the Great Powers, and the Cold War', in Yezid Sayigh and Avi Shlaim (eds) *The Cold War and the Middle East* (Oxford: Oxford University Press, 1997), pp. 6–26.
5. Bahgat Korany, 'The Middle East Since the Cold War: Torn Between Geopolitics and Geoeconomics', in Louise Fawcett (ed.) *International Relations of the Middle East* (Oxford: Oxford University Press, 2005), p. 75.
6. CIA National Intelligence Council Discussion paper, from the December 2003 Commonwealth Conference: 'The Middle East to 2020'. *MERIA News*, 8 (2), 2004.
7. The report notes that 'the Middle East now plays, and is likely to continue to play, at least as large a part in US foreign policy discourse as ever before'.
8. *The National Security Strategy of the United States of America* (Washington, DC: The White House, March 2006).
9. Shafeeq N. Ghabra, 'It's Time to Tear Down the 'Arab Wall', private communication, 23 November 2003.
10. Philippe Legrain, *Open World: The Truth About Globalisation* (London: Abacus, 2003).
11. Michael Scott Doran, 'The Saudi Paradox', *Foreign Affairs*, 83 (1), 2004, 35–51.
12. Nawaf Obaid, 'The Clerics Cannot be Allowed to Block Reform', *International Herald Tribune*, 23 April 2003.
13. 'Iran: Supremely Subversive', *The Guardian*, 19 February 2004.
14. Emma Murphy, 'Old Lessons in a New World Order', *Today*, 10 May 2004.
15. Ankie Hoogvelt, *Globalization and the Postcolonial World: The New Political Economy of Development* (London: Palgrave Macmillan, 2001).
16. See Emma C. Murphy, 'Governance and Development', *Internationale Politik* (transatlantic edition), 3 (4), 2002, 69–76; Peter Thiery, 'Good Governance – No Luxury', *Internationale Politik* (transatlantic edition), 3 (4), 2002, pp. 77–80.
17. Final statement of the 'Arab Reform Issues: Vision and Implementation' conference, Alexandria, Egypt, 12–14 March 2004.
18. United Nations Development Programme/Arab Fund for Economic and Social Development, *Arab Human Development Report 2002* (New York: UNDP, 2002), p. 27.
19. See David Tresilian, 'Wake up Call for Development', *Al-Ahram Weekly*, 25–31 December 2003.
20. United Nations Development Programme/Arab Fund for Economic and Social Development, *Arab Human Development Report 2003* (New York: UNDP, 2003), p. 22.
21. *ibid.*, p. 23.
22. United Nations Development Programme/Arab Fund for Economic and Social Development, *Arab Human Development Report 2003, op. cit.*, p. 28.
23. It is instructive that the first joint trade accord between Israel and Egypt was signed in December 2004, 25 years after the signing of the peace treaty between them, and only after positive and sustained US intervention. As a

result of this accord, a jointly established Israeli–Egyptian free trade zone is entitled to send goods to the USA duty-free. *TurkishPress.com*, 14 December 2004.
24 Rodney Wilson, *Economic Development in the Middle East* (London: Routledge, 1995), p. 16.
25 The cumulative effects of the Palestinian *intifadah* and capital flight have been compared by analyst Shlomo Swirski with that of the 'structural changes introduced into eastern Europe countries in the aftermath of the collapse of the Soviet Union, or to the structural changes imposed by international financial institutions on countries that had undergone severe financial crises'. Chris McGreal, 'Hidden Costs of Israel's Occupation Policies', *The Guardian*, 25 February 2005.
26 Rosemary Hollis, 'Getting Out of the Iraq Trap', *International Affairs*, 79 (1), 2003, 23–35.
27 Insights gained from conversations with several senior Iraqi officials participating in the World Economic Forum, Davos, 20–23 January 2004.
28 Jon B. Alterman, 'Not in My Backyard: Iraq's Neighbors' Interests', *The Washington Quarterly*, 26 (3), 2003, 149–60.
29 Mohammed Ayoob, 'The War Against Iraq: Normative and Strategic Implications', *Middle East Policy*, X (2), 2003, 27–39.
30 See Marina Ottaway and Thomas Carothers, 'The Greater Middle East Initiative: Off to a False Start', *Policy Brief*, No. 29, March 2004, (Washington, DC: Carnegie Endowment for International Peace).
31 George P. Shultz, 'A Changed World', E-note, Foreign Policy Research Institute, 22 March 2004. www.fpri.org/enotes/20040322.americawar.shultz.changedworld.html
32 United Nations Development Programme/Arab Fund for Economic and Social Development, *Arab Human Development Report 2003*, op. cit., pp. 51–56.
33 *ibid.*, p. 144.
34 Hamid Zangeneh, 'Economic Consequences of Student Unrest in Iran', *Journal of Iranian Research and Analysis*, 15 (2), 1999, 135.
35 *Ettela'at International*, 15 September 2005.
36 United Nations Development Programme/Arab Fund for Economic and Social Development, *Arab Human Development Report 2003*, op. cit., p. 62.
37 This is how Grand Ayatollah Hussein Ali Montazeri explains the media scene in Iran: 'Today in Iran, there is no freedom of the press. They have closed more than a hundred publications; honest and knowledgeable people have been deprived of their jobs. They have reduced newspapers to self-censorship. For instance, they are forbidden to write about me. If they do, they [the editors] are immediately summoned. There is repression, as before the Revolution'. *Il Corriere della Sera*, January 30 2004.
38 See Mohammed El-Nawawy and Adel Iskandar, *Al-Jazeera: How the Free Arab News Network Scooped the World and Changed the Middle East* (Boulder, CO: Westview Press, 2002).
39 Vali Nasr, 'Regional Implications of Shi'a Revival in Iraq', *The Washington Quarterly*, 27 (3), 2004, 7–24.
40 'Please know ye, may God have mercy on you, that fasting on the 10th day in the month of Muharram [the first month of the new Hegira year, which began on 21 February 2004] atones for the sins of the two previous years. Fast on that day and also on the day before or after it. This is the tradition of your Prophet Muhammad, May the peace and blessings of God be upon him. He fasted on this day to thank God for saving Moses and his people and drowning the Pharaoh and his people. *It is a strange paradox that this happy occasion has been transformed by a Muslim faction [i.e., the Shia] into*

continuous mourning and ceaseless wailing, in a picture that clearly shows ignorance of religion and following misleading persons without a good reason. O Ye, correct the path to God and follow the guidance of the prophet'. (emphasis added). This undisguised attack on the Shia was delivered by Shaykh Salih Bin-Mohammad Al Talib in the holy mosque in Mecca and carried live on TV1 of Saudi Arabia on 27 February 2004. Foreign Broadcast Information Service, 27 February 2004.
41 This strategy was the main focus of discussions at two Hudson conferences: 'Saudi Vulnerability: The Source of Middle Eastern Oil and the Eastern Province', in April 2002; 'Oil, Terrorism, and the Problem of Saudi Arabia', in June 2002.
42 Ashraf Fahim, "Liberating' Saudi Shi'ites (and Their Oil)', *Middle East International*, No. 722, 2 April 2004.
43 *ibid.*
44 Stephen Glain, *Dreaming of Damascus: Merchants, Mullahs, and Militant in the New Middle East* (London: John Murray, 2003), p. 20.
45 Asher Susser, 'The Decline of the Arabs', *Middle East Quarterly*, Autumn 2003, p. 6.
46 Israel's assassination of Sheikh Ahmed Yassin on 22nd of March 2004 and its repercussions for peace talks was given as one reason for the abrupt cancellation of the Tunis Arab League summit by the host country. See *BBC News*, 28 March 2004.
47 'Libya', declared its leader at the May 2004 Arab League Summit in Tunis, 'is currently absorbed in its African space and it is planning to be the bridge between Africa and Europe'. It had no intention of turning towards the Arab world. See Dina Ezzat, 'Surprise, Surprise', *Al-Ahram Weekly*, 27 May–2 June 2004.
48 Muhammad Ahsan, 'Globalization and the Underdeveloped Muslim World', in Ali Mohammadi (ed.) *Islam Encountering Globalization* (London: Routledge-Curzon, 2002), p. 189.
49 Stephen Philip Cohen, 'The Jihadist Threat to Pakistan', *The Washington Quarterly*, 26 (3), 2003, 7–25.
50 Clement M. Henry, 'The Clash of Globalisations in the Middle East', in Louise Fawcett (ed.) *International Relations of the Middle East, op. cit.*, p. 127.

9 Globalization and the Middle East in Perspective

1 L. Carl Brown, *International Politics of the Middle East: Old Rules, Dangerous Game* (Princeton, NJ: Princeton University Press, 1984), p. 4.
2 Clement M. Henry, 'The Clash of Globalisations in the Middle East', in Louise Fawcett (ed.) *International Relations of the Middle East* (Oxford: Oxford University Press, 2005), pp. 105–29.
3 Hisham Sharabi, *Neopatriarchy: A Theory of Distorted Change in Arab Society* (Oxford: Oxford University Press, 1988), p. 60.
4 Halim Barakat, The *Arab World: Society, Culture, and the State* (Berkeley, CA: University of California Press, 1993), p. 157.
5 'President Discusses War on Terror'. Speech delivered at the National Defense University, Washington, DC, 8 March 2005.
6 *ibid.*, p. 271.
7 Nazih N. Ayubi, *Over-stating the Arab State: Politics and Society in the Middle East* (London: I. B. Tauris, 1995), p. 402.
8 Ayubi does, however, foresee a situation in which 'defensive' democratization – say in response to US and EU pressures since 9/11 – coinciding with 'the need

for positive and pro-active democratic transition' at home, come together to forge a proper democratic framework: *ibid.*, p. 414.
9   Simon W. Murden, *Islam, the Middle East, and the New Global Economy* (Boulder, CO: Lynne Rienner, 2002), p. 205.
10 Anthony H. Cordesman, 'Ten Reasons for Reforging the US and Saudi Relationship', *Saudi–American Forum*, 1 February 2004.
11 Monica Malik and Tim Niblock, 'Saudi Arabia's Economy: The Challenge of Reform', in Paul Aarts and Gerd Nonneman (eds) *Saudi Arabia in the Balance: Political Economy, Society, Foreign Affairs* (London: Hurst, 2005), p. 110.
12 'Iran's Stagnant Economy', IranMania.com, 12 January 2004.
13 According to Cordesman, 'The US Census Bureau estimates that Saudi Arabia's population has climbed from 6 million in 1970 to 22 million in 2004. Even if birth rates decline significantly in future years, it is expected to rise to 31 million in 2010, 42 million in 2020, and 55 million in 2030. The number of young Saudis between 15 and 24 years of age will nearly double from 3.6 million in 2000 to 6.3 million in 2025. This is in a society where the government estimates that unemployment for native Saudi males is already 12%, and many experts privately estimate that real and disguised unemployment is in excess of 20%'. See note 10.
14 Figures are drawn from Nicholas Nesson, 'The Next Generation', *Arabies Trends*, May 2006, 60–68.
15 Robin Wright, 'U.S. Readies Push for Mideast Democracy Plan', *Washington Post*, 28 February 2004.
16 *Arab News*, 17 January 2003.
17 *ibid.*
18 Author's conversations with officials from Egypt, Iran, Iraq, Jordan, Saudi Arabia, and the UAE.
19 To address such fears, US Secretary of State Colin Powell told the US-funded Al-Hurra Arabic satellite television that 'I agree with the Egyptians and the Saudis that reform can not be imposed from outside, and that it has to be accepted from within. The initiative must be acceptable to all the countries in the region'. Quoted by Gamal Essam El-Din, 'Asserting Home-grown Reform', *Al-Ahram Weekly*, 4–10 March 2004.
20 Robin Wright, 'U.S. Readies Push for Mideast Democracy Plan', *op. cit.*
21 Gamal Essam El-Din, 'Asserting Home-grown Reform', *op. cit.*
22 Khaled Ezzelarab, 'Everyone Else Wants Reform', *Cairo Times*, 26 February–3 March 2004.
23 'The Wrong Way to Sell Democracy to the Arab World', *New York Times*, 8 March 2004. He further added that 'There are other reasons to be wary of the administration's plan. Democracy, impatiently imposed, can lead to unintended consequences. If the Palestinians were able to choose a leader in truly free elections, might they not opt for the head of Hamas? If free elections were soon held in Saudi Arabia, would Crown Prince Abdullah, a reformer, prevail over Osama bin Laden or another militant Islamic leader? If not genuinely accepted and reinforced by traditions of constitutionalism, democracy can degenerate into plebiscites that only add legitimacy to extremism and authoritarianism'.
24 Gamal Essam El-Din, 'Reform and Reformulating', *Al-Ahram Weekly*, 19–24 February 2004.
25 In terms of a sequence of events, in January American and European officials met in Washington to work out the project's details. For EU diplomats the meeting had clarified an ambitious post-Iraq war idea being debated by the US administration. It was German Foreign Minister Joshka Fischer who

announced on 7 February 2004, however, that the US–EU GMEI was based largely on linking the existing NATO Mediterranean dialogue with the European Union's Barcelona process (the former includes Israel, Egypt, Jordan, and four North African states, while the latter also adds Syria and Lebanon). Fischer announced in several briefings that NATO would offer a security partnership, while the Barcelona process would lay the foundation for an economic partnership and a free-trade area beginning in 2010.

26 Gamal Essam El-Din, 'Reform and Reformulating', *op. cit.*
27 Nader Fegani, quoted by Glenn Kessler and Robin Wright, 'Arabs and Europeans Question 'Greater Middle East' Plan', *Washington Post*, 22 February 2004.
28 The importance of the difference is highlighted by Völker Perthes 'America's "Greater Middle East" and Europe: Key Issues for Dialogue', *Middle East Policy*, XI (3), 2004, 85–97.
29 'President Bush Delivers State of the Union Address', Office of the Press Secretary, the White House, 31 January 2006, p. 3.
30 Stephen E. Ambrose, *Rise to Globalism: American Foreign Policy Since 1938* (New York: Penguin, 1985), p. xviii.
31 *ibid.*: 'We don't deny that the Arab world is still a long way from being a complete democracy, but we think it is the conflict with Israel that basically breeds terrorism and undemocratic politics', added the Chairman of Egyptian parliament's Arab Affairs Committee.
32 German Foreign Minister Joschka Fischer, speaking at a conference in Munich in February 2004, underlined the same point: 'The key regional conflict, namely the Middle East conflict, should neither be set aside nor allowed to block this initiative from the outset'. Glenn Kessler and Robin Wright, 'Arabs and Europeans Question "Greater Middle East" Plan', *Washington Post*, 22 February 2004.
33 If more proof were still needed of the corroding impact on the region of the Arab–Israeli conflict, let us not look any further than the military violence that again visited the region in June–July 2006. The violence that encompassed Palestine, Lebanon, and Israel had left over 500 people dead, and had displaced around 500,000 million in Lebanon (one-quarter of its entire population), around 100,000 in Israel, and countless others in Gaza within a week of its commencement. By the end of its second week, the number of displaced persons in Lebanon had risen to over 800,000 and the damage to its economy over US$4 billion. Apart from the appalling humanitarian disaster caused by Israel's military actions in Lebanon, the bombings also devastated the economic infrastructure of one of the most liberal states in the Arab world (causing over US$2 billion worth of damages in the first 7 days of bombardment), accelerated capital flight on a massive scale from Lebanon and Syria, and set the clock of economic progress back some years. Within days of the fighting, the Cairo stock exchange had to halt trading as its benchmark index dipped by as much as 9.5 per cent in a day; the Dubai bourse slipped to a 19-month low, and Qatar's main index fell 6.1 per cent on the fifth day of fighting. The Jordanian and Lebanese bourses were equally badly hit, sending shock waves across the region, and halting in its tracks the oil price-induced growth that had been spreading beyond the GCC to fuel economic activity elsewhere. Internationally, the crisis increased the pressure on oil prices, boosting it to an all-time high of US$78 per barrel on 17 July and also threatening earnings in the USA and other industrialized countries. The fallout raised the geopolitical stakes, spreading the crisis to Iran (Hezbollah's main non-Arab ally) and the oil-rich Persian Gulf subregion, and also brought condemnation from the Muslim states of South and Southeast Asia, adding to extremism. The fires lit in the

Arab–Israeli arena spread rapidly, regionally and internationally, directly affecting world security, economics and politics. 'Conflict transfer' is the flipside of exchange in a globalized world and, so long as this conflict is not settled to the satisfaction of all the parties, instability will continue to be the region's main export.

Select Bibliography

Paul Aarts and Gerd Nonneman (eds) *Saudi Arabia in the Balance: Political Economy, Society, Foreign Affairs* (London: Hurst and Co., 2005).
Abdul Khaleq Abdulla, 'The Gulf Cooperation Council: Nature, Origin, and Process', in Michael C. Hudson (ed.) *Middle East Dilemma: The Politics and Economics of Arab Integration* (London: I. B. Tauris, 1999).
Baha Abu-Laban and Sharon McIrvin Abu-Laban (eds) *The Arab World: Dynamics of Development* (Leiden: E. J. Brill, 1986).
Ephraim Ahiram and Alfred Tovias (eds) *Whither EU–Israeli Relations? Common and Divergent Interests* (Frankfurt: Peter Lang, 1995).
Muhammad Ahsan, 'Globalization and the Underdeveloped Muslim World', in Ali Mohammadi (ed.) *Islam Encountering Globalization* (London: RoutledgeCurzon, 2002).
Fouad Ajami, *The Arab Predicament: Arab Political Thought and Practice Since 1967* (Cambridge: Cambridge University Press, 1993).
Fouad Ajami, 'The Sentry's Solitude', *Foreign Affairs*, 80 (6), 2001.
Roberto Aliboni, *European Security Across the Mediterranean*, Chaillot Papers 2 (Paris: Institute for Security Studies of WEU, March 1991).
Roberto Aliboni, George Joffé and Tim Niblock (eds) *Security Challenges in the Mediterranean Region* (London: Frank Cass, 1996).
Abbas Alnasrawi, 'Dependency Status and Economic Development of Arab States', in Baha Abu-Laban and Sharon McIrvin Abu-Laban (eds) *The Arab World: Dynamics of Development* (Leiden: E. J. Brill, 1986).
Jon B. Alterman, 'Not in My Backyard: Iraq's Neighbors' Interests', *The Washington Quarterly*, 26 (3), 2003, 149–60.
Stephen E. Ambrose, *Rise to Globalism: American Foreign Policy Since 1938* (New York: Penguin, 1985).
Galal Amin, *Globalization, Consumption Patterns and Human Development in Egypt*, Working Paper 9929 (Cairo: Economic Research Forum, undated).
Jahangir Amuzegar, *Oil Exporters' Economic Development in an Interdependent World*, Occasional Paper No. 18 (Washington, DC: International Monetary Fund, 1983).
John Duke Anthony, 'The Gulf Cooperation Council: Constraints', *GulfWire Perspectives*, 4 February 2004.
David Apter, 'Globalization, Marginality, and the Specter of the Superfluous Man', *Journal of Social Affairs*, 18 (71), 2001.

Select Bibliography

Giovanni Arrighi, 'Globalization, State Sovereignty, and the "Endless" Accumulation of Capital', in David A. Smith, Dorothy J. Solinger and Steven C. Topik (eds) *States and Sovereignty in the Global Economy* (London: Routledge, 1999).

Ronald S. Asmus, F Stephen Larrabee, Ian O. Lesser, 'Mediterranean Security: New Challenges, New Tasks', *NATO Review*, 44 (3), 1996, 25–31.

Mohammed Ayoob, 'The War Against Iraq: Normative and Strategic Implications', *Middle East Policy*, X (2), 2003, 27–39.

Nazih N. Ayubi (ed.) *Over-stating the Arab State: Politics and Society in the Middle East* (London: I. B. Tauris, 1995).

Nazih N. Ayubi (ed.) *Distant Neighbours: The Political Economy of Relations Between Europe and the Middle East/North Africa* (Reading: Ithaca Press, 1995).

Maha Azzam, 'Between the Market and God: Islam, Globalization and Culture in the Middle East', in Toby Dodge and Richard Higgott (eds) *Globalization and the Middle East: Islam, Economy, Society and Politics* (London: Royal Institute of International Affairs, 2002).

Benjamin R. Barber, *Jihad vs. McWorld: Terrorism's Challenge to Democracy* (London: Corgi, 2003).

Igor Belikov, 'Soviet Scholars' Debate on Socialist Orientation in the Third World', *Millennium: Journal of International Studies*, 20 (1), 1991, 23–39.

Joel Benin and Joe Stork (eds) *Political Islam: Essays From Middle East Report* (Berkeley, CA: University of California Press, 1997).

Donald L. Berlin, 'India in the Indian Ocean', *Naval War College Review*, 59 (2), 2006.

Jagdish Bhagwati, *In Defense of Globalization* (Oxford: Oxford University Press, 2004).

James A. Bill and Rebecca Bill Chavez, 'The Politics of Incoherence: The United States and the Middle East', *Middle East Journal*, 56 (4), 2002, 562–75.

Ken Booth and Steve Smith (eds) *International Relations Theory Today* (Cambridge: Polity Press, 1995).

Ahmed Boudroua, 'Outlook for Industrialization of the Arab World', in Baha Abu-Laban and Sharon McIrvin Abu-Laban (eds) *The Arab World: Dynamics of Development* (Leiden: E. J. Brill, 1986).

L. Carl Brown, *International Politics and the Middle East: Old Rules, Dangerous Game* (Princeton, NJ: Princeton University Press, 1984).

Daniel Brumberg, *Liberalization Versus Democracy: Understanding Arab Political Reform*, Working Paper No. 37 (Washington, DC: Carnegie Endowment for Peace, 2003).

Zbigniew Brzezinski, *The Grand Chessboard: American Primacy and its Geostrategic Imperatives* (New York: Basic Books, 1997).

Mary Buckley and Robert Singh (eds) *The Bush Doctrine and the War on Terrorism* (New York: Routledge, 2006).

Barry Buzan and Ole Waever, *Regions and Powers: The Structure of International Security* (Cambridge: Cambridge University Press, 2003).

Thomas Carothers, 'The End of the Transition Paradigm', *Journal of Democracy*, 13 (1), 2002, 5–21.

Hannah Carter and Anoushiravan Ehteshami (eds) *The Middle East's Relations with Asia and Russia* (London: RoutledgeCurzon, 2004).

Manuel Castells, *End of Millennium* (Oxford: Basil Blackwell, 1998).

Philip G. Cerny, 'Globalization and the Changing Logic of Collective Action', *International Organization*, 49 (4), 1995, 595–625.

Ian Clark, *Globalization and International Relations Theory* (Oxford: Oxford University Press, 1999).
Stephen Philip Cohen, 'The Jihadist Threat to Pakistan', *The Washington Quarterly*, 26 (3), 2003, 7–25.
William D. Coleman and Geoffrey R. D. Underhill (eds) *Regionalism and Global Economic Integration: Europe, Asia and the Americas* (London: Routledge, 1998).
Michael Cox, 'Whatever Happened to the New World Order?', *Critique: Journal of Social Theory*, No. 25, 1993.
Robert W. Cox, 'A Perspective on Globalization', in James H. Mittelman (ed.) *Globalization: Critical Reflections* (Boulder, CO: Lynne Rienner, 1996).
Robert S. Chase, Emily B. Hill and Paul Kennedy, 'Pivotal States and U.S. Strategy', *Foreign Affairs*, 75 (1), 1996, 33–51.
Michel Chatelus, 'Economic Co-operation among Southern Mediterranean Countries', in Roberto Aliboni, George Joffe and Tim Niblock (eds) *Security Challenges in the Mediterranean Region* (London: Frank Cass, 1996).
Richard Crockatt, *America Embattled: September 11, Anti-Americanism and the Global Order* (New York: Routledge, 2003).
Ali Çarkoğlu, Mine Eder and Kemal Kirişci, *The Political Economy of Regional Cooperation in the Middle East* (New York: Routledge, 1998).
François D'Alançon, 'The EC Looks to a New Middle East', *Journal of Palestine Studies*, XXIII (2), 1994, 41–51.
Phillip Darby (ed.) *At the Edge of International Relations: Postcolonialism, Gender and Dependency* (New York: Continuum, 2000).
Martin J. Dedman, *The Origins and Development of the European Union 1945–95* (London: Routledge, 1996).
Karl W. Deutsch and J. David Singer, 'Multipolar Power Systems and International Stability', in James N. Rosenau (ed.) *International Politics and Foreign Policy* (New York: Free Press, 1969).
Toby Dodge, 'Bringing the Bourgeoisie Back in: Globalization and the Birth of Liberal Authoritarianism in the Middle East', in Toby Dodge and Richard Higgott (eds) *Globalization and the Middle East: Islam, Economy, Society and Politics* (London: Royal Institute of International Affairs, 2002).
Toby Dodge and Richard Higgott (eds) *Globalization and the Middle East: Islam, Economy, Society and Politics* (London: Royal Institute of International Affairs, 2002).
Michael Scott Doran, 'Somebody Else's Civil War', *Foreign Affairs*, 81 (1), 2002, 22–42.
Michael Scott Doran, 'The Saudi Paradox', *Foreign Affairs*, 83 (1), 2004, 35–51.
Eleanor Abdella Doumato, 'Education in Saudi Arabia: Gender, Jobs, and the Price of Religion', in Eleanor Abdella Doumato and Marsha Pripstein Posusney (eds) *Women and Globalization in the Arab Middle East: Gender, Economy and Society* (Boulder, CO: Lynne Rienner, 2003).
Eleanor Abdella Doumato and Marsha Pripstein Posusney (eds) *Women and Globalization in the Middle East: Gender, Economy, and Society* (Boulder, CO: Lynne Rienner, 2003).
Robert Dreyfuss, 'Just the Beginning: Is Iraq the Opening Salvo in a War to Remake the World?', *The American Prospect*, 14 (3), 2003, www.prospect.org/print/V14/3/dreyfuss-r.html.
Economic Research Forum for the Arab Countries, Iran and Turkey, *Economic Trends in the MENA Region* (Cairo: Economic Research Forum, 1998).

Select Bibliography

Anoushiravan Ehteshami, 'The Rise and Convergence of the "Middle" in the World Economy: The Case of the NICs and the Gulf States', in Charles E. Davies (ed.) *Global Interests in the Arab Gulf* (Exeter: University of Exeter Press, 1992).

Anoushiravan Ehteshami, 'The Arab States and the Middle East Balance of Power', in James Gow (ed.) *Iraq, the Gulf Conflict and the World Community* (London: Brassey's, 1993).

Anoushiravan Ehteshami, 'Is the Middle East Democratizing?', *British Journal of Middle Eastern Studies*, 26 (2), (1999), 199–217.

Anoushiravan Ehteshami and Raymond Hinnebusch, *Syria and Iran: Middle Powers in aPenetrated Regional System* (London: Routledge, 1997).

Anoushiravan Ehteshami and Emma C. Murphy, 'Transformation of the Corporatist State in the Middle East', *Third World Quarterly*, 17 (4), 1996, 753–72.

M. S. El Azhary (ed.) *The Impact of Oil Revenues on Arab Gulf Development* (Beckenham: Croom Helm, 1984).

Mohamed El-Erian and Mahmoud El-Gamal, *Attracting Foreign Investments to Arab Countries: Getting the Basics Right* (Cairo: Market, Economics and Finance Unit, Working Paper 9718, 1997).

Mohammed El-Nawawy and Adel Iskandar, *Al-Jazeera: How the Free Arab News Network Scooped the World and Changed the Middle East* (Boulder, CO: Westview Press, 2002).

Nader Entessar, 'The Post-Cold War US Military Doctrine: Implications for Iran', *Iranian Journal of International Affairs*, VIII (2), 1996.

Richard Falk, 'The Monotheistic Religions in the Era of Globalization', *Global Dialogue*, 1 (1), 1999, 148.

Muhammad Faour, *The Arab World after Desert Storm* (Washington, DC: United States Institute of Peace, 1993).

Louise Fawcett (ed.) *International Relations of the Middle East* (Oxford: Oxford University Press, 2005).

Louise Fawcett and Andrew Hurrell (eds) *Regionalism in World Politics* (Oxford: Oxford University Press, 1995).

Mike Featherstone, *Undoing Culture: Globalization, Postmodernism and Identity* (London: Sage, 1995).

John W. Fox, Nada Nourtada-Sabba and Mohammed al-Mutawa (eds) *Globalization and the Gulf* (London: Routledge, 2006).

Thomas L. Friedman, 'Anti-terror Fight has to be a Marathon Run on Wilsonian Principles, Not Cheap Oil', YaleGlobal Online, 8 February 2003, http://yaleglobal.-yale.edu/display.article?id = 913.

Thomas L. Friedman, *The World is Flat: The Globalized World in the Twenty-First Century* (London: Penguin Books, 2006).

Francis Fukuyama, *The End of History and the Last Man* (London: Penguin, 1992).

Katja Füllberg-Stolberg, Petra Heidrich and Ellinor Schöne (eds) *Dislocation and Appropriation: Responses to Globalization in Asia and Africa* (Berlin: Das Arabische Buch, 1999).

Graham E. Fuller and Ian O. Lesser, *A Sense of Siege: The Geopolitics of Islam and the West* (Boulder, CO: Westview Press, 1995).

F. Gregory Gause III and Jill Crystal, 'The Arab Gulf: Will Autocracy Define the Social Contract in 2015?', in Judith Yaphe (ed.) *The Middle East in 2015: The Impact of Regional Trends on U.S. Strategic Planning* (Washington, DC: National Defense University Press, 2002).

Anthony Giddens. *The Consequences of Modernity* (Cambridge: Polity Press. 1990).
Anthony Giddens, *Runaway World: How Globalisation is Shaping our Lives* (London: Profile Books, 2002).
Richard Gillespie (ed.), *Mediterranean Politics – Volume I* (London: Pinter, 1994).
Robert Gilpin, *The Challenge of Global Capitalism: The World Economy in the 21st Century* (Princeton, NJ: Princeton University Press, 2000).
Stephen Glain, *Dreaming of Damascus: Merchants, Mullahs, and Militant in the New Middle East* (London: John Murray, 2003).
Nicole Gnesotto and John Roper (eds) *Western Europe and the Gulf* (Paris: Institute for Security Studies of WEU, 1992).
James M. Goldgeier and Michael McFaul, 'A Tale of Two Worlds: Core and Periphery in the Post-Cold War Era', *International Organization*, 46 (2), 1992, 467–91.
Arthur Goldschmidt, Jr, *A Concise History of the Middle East* (Boulder, CO: Westview Press, 1996).
Patricia M. Goff, 'Invisible Borders: Economic Liberalization and National Identity', *International Studies Quarterly*, 44 (4), 2000, 533–62.
Peter A. Gourevitch, 'The Pacific Rim: Current Debates', *The Pacific Region: Challenges to Policy and Theory – Annals of the American Academy of Political and Social Science*, 505, 1989, 8–23.
Henri Goverde, Philip G. Cerny, Mark Haugaard and Howard H. Lentner (eds) *Power in Contemporary Politics: Theories, Practices, Globalizations* (London: Sage, 2000).
James Gow (ed.) *Iraq, the Gulf Conflict and the World Community* (London: Brassey's, 1993).
Frank Griffel, 'Globalization and the Middle East: Part Two', YaleGlobal Online, 21 January 2003, http://yaleglobal.yale.edu/display.article?id = 771
Keith Griffin, 'Culture and Economic Growth: The State and Globalization', in Jan Nederveen Pieterse (ed.) *Global Futures: Shaping Globalization* (London: Zed Press, 2000).
Jean Grugel, 'Democratization Studies and Globalisation: The Coming of Age of a Paradigm', *British Journal of Politics and International Relations*, 5 (2), 2003, 258–83.
Jean Grugel and Wil Hout (eds) *Regionalism Across the North-South Divide* (London: Routledge, 1999).
Laura Guazzone (ed.) *The Middle East in Global Change: The Politics and Economics of Interdependence versus Fragmentation* (London: Macmillan, 1997).
Leon T. Hadar, 'The "Green Peril": Creating the Islamic Fundamentalist Threat', Cato Policy Analysis No. 177, 27 August 1992, www.cato.org/pubs/pas/pa-177.html
Shahla Haeri, 'Obedience versus Autonomy: Women and Fundamentalism in Iran and Pakisan', in Martin E. Marty and R. Scott Appleby (eds) *Fundamentalisms and Society* (Chicago, IL: University of Chicago Press, 1993).
Hassan Hakimian, 'From MENA to East Asia and Back: Lessons of Globalization, Crisis and Economic Reform', in Hassan Hakimian and Ziba Moshaver (eds) *The State and Global Change: The Political Economy of Transition in the Middle East and North Africa* (Richmond: Curzon Press, 2001).
Hassan Hakimian and Ziba Moshaver (eds) *The State and Global Change: The Political Economy of Transition in the Middle East and North Africa* (Richmond: Curzon Press, 2001).

Fred Halliday, 'The End of the Cold War and International Relations: Some Analytical and Theoretical Conclusions', in Ken Booth and Steve Smith (eds) *International Relations Theory Today* (Cambridge: Polity Press, 1995).

Fred Halliday, 'The Middle East and the Politics of Differential Integration', in Toby Dodge and Richard Higgott (eds) *Globalization and the Middle East: Islam, Economy, Society and Politics* (London: Royal Institute of International Affairs, 2002).

Fred Halliday, *The Middle East in International Relations: Power, Politics and Ideology* (Cambridge, UK: Cambridge University Press, 2005).

Khair el-Din Haseeb et al., *The Future of the Arab Nation: Challenges and Options* (New York: Routledge, 1991).

Riffat Hassan, 'Feminist Theology: The Challenges for Muslim Women', *Critique: Journal for Critical Studies of the Middle East*, No. 9, 1996, 53–65.

Muhammed H. Heikal, *The Sphinx and the Commissar: The Rise and Fall of Soviet Influence in the Middle East* (New York: Harper and Row, 1978).

David Held, *Models of Democracy* (Cambridge: Polity Press, 1996).

David Held and Anthony McGrew, *Globalization/Anti-Globalization* (Cambridge: Polity Press, 2002).

Richard Higgott, 'The International Political Economy of Regionalism: The Asia–Pacific and Europe Compared', in William D. Coleman and Geoffrey R. D. Underhill (eds) *Regionalism and Global Economic Integration: Europe, Asia and the Americas* (London: Routledge, 1998).

Clement M. Henry and Robert Springborg, *Globalization and the Politics of Development in the Middle East* (Cambridge: Cambridge University Press, 2001).

Raymond Hinnebusch, *The International Politics of the Middle East* (Manchester: Manchester University Press, 2003).

Raymond Hinnebusch and Anoushiravan Ehteshami (eds) *The Foreign Policies of Middle East States* (Boulder, CO: Lynne Rienner, 2002).

John M. Hobson, *The Eastern Origins of Western Civilisation* (Cambridge: Cambridge University Press, 2004).

Rosemary Hollis, 'The Politics of Israeli–European Economic Relations', *Israel Affairs*, 1 (1), 1994, 118–25.

Rosemary Hollis, 'Getting Out of the Iraq Trap', *International Affairs*, 79 (1), 2003, 23–35.

Hans-Henrik Holm and Georg Sørensen (eds) *Whose World Order? Uneven Globalization and the End of the Cold War* (Boulder, CO: Westview Press, 1995).

Robert J. Holton, *Globalization and the Nation-State* (London: Macmillan, 1998).

Ankie Hoogvelt, *Globalization and the Postcolonial World: The New Political Economy of Development* (London: Palgrave Macmillan, 2001).

Glenn D. Hook, Julie Gilson, Christopher W. Hughes and Hugo Dobson, *Japan's International Relations: Politics, Economics and Security* (London: Routlege, 2001).

Michael C. Hudson (ed.) *Middle East Dilemma: The Politics and Economics of Arab Integration* (London: I.B. Tauris, 1999).

Andrew Hurrell, 'Regionalism in Theoretical Perspective', in Louise Fawcett and Andrew Hurrell (eds) *Regionalism in World Politics* (Oxford: Oxford University Press, 1995).

Andrew Hurrell and Ngaire Woods, 'Globalisation and Inequality', *Millennium: Journal of International Studies*, 24 (3), 1995, 447–70.

Susumu Ishida, 'Japan's Oil Strategy in the Gulf Without Arms Deals', in Charles E. Davies (ed.) *Global Interests in the Arab Gulf* (Exeter: University of Exeter Press, 1992).

Mohammad Ja'far, 'National Formations in the Arab Region: A Critique of Samir Amin', *Khamsin*, No. 6, 1978.
Amy Myers Jaffe and Robert A. Manning, 'The Myth of the Caspian "Great Game": The Real Geopolitics of Energy', *Survival*, 40 (4), 1998–99.
Robert Jervis, 'An Interim Assessment of September 11: What has Changed and What has Not?', *Political Science Quarterly*, 117 (1), 2002, 37–54.
George Joffé, 'Low-Level Violence and Terrorism', in Roberto Aliboni, George Joffe and Tim Niblock (eds) *Security Challenges in the Mediterranean Region* (London: Frank Cass, 1996).
R. J. Barry Jones, *Globalisation and Interdependence in the International Political Economy: Rhetoric and Reality* (New York: Pinter, 1995).
Sir Paul Judge, '250 Years of Globalisation', *RSA Journal*, January 2004.
Jan H. Kalicki, 'Caspian Energy at the Crossroads', *Foreign Affairs*, 80 (5), 2001, 120–34.
Geoffrey Kemp, 'The Persian Gulf Remains the Strategic Prize', *Survival*, 40 (4), 1998–99, 132–49.
Geoffrey Kemp, 'Europe's Middle East Challenges', *The Washington Quarterly*, 27 (1), 2003–04, 163–77.
Paul Kennedy, *The Rise and Fall of Great Powers: Economic Change and Military Conflict From 1500 to 2000* (London: Fontana Press, 1989).
Gilles Kepel, *Jihad: The Trail of Political Islam* (Cambridge, MA: Harvard University Press, 2002).
C. Kerr, J. Dunlop, F. Harbison and C. Myers, *Industrialism and Industrial Man* (Harmondsworth: Penguin, 1973).
David Kerr, 'Greater China and East Asian Integration: Regionalism and Rivalry', *East Asia: An International Quarterly*, 21 (1), 2004, 75–92.
Malcolm Kerr, *The Arab Cold War: Jamal Abd al-Nasir and his Rivals, 1958–1967* (Oxford: Oxford University Press, 1971).
Bichara Khader, *L'Europe et la Méditerranée: Géopolitique de la Proximité* (Paris: l'Harmattan, 1994).
Bichara Khader, 'Les Échanges économiques Euro-Arabes', in Nazih N. Ayubi (ed.) *Distant Neighbours: The Political Economy of Relations Between Europe and the Middle East/North Africa* (Reading, UK: Ithaca Press, 1995).
M. A. Muqtedar Khan, 'Globalization as "Glocalization"', IslamOnline.net, www.islamonline.net/iol-english/dowalia/american-24-10/american2.asp
Mohamed Khodr, 'Muslims Must Surrender to Israel, America, and Globalization', IslamOnline.net, 2 August 2001, www.islamonline.net/english/Views/2001/08/article2.shtml
Michael Klare, *Blood and Oil: How America's Thirst for Petrol is Killing Us* (London: Hamish Hamilton, 2004).
Alfed Kleinknecht and Jan ter Wengel, 'The Myth of Economic Globalisation', *Cambridge Journal of Economics*, 22 (4), 1998, 637–47.
Torbjørn L. Knutsen, *The Rise and Fall of World Orders* (Manchester: Manchester University Press, 1999).
Bahgat Korany, 'Political Petrolism and Contemporary Arab Politics, 1967–83', in Baha Abu-Laban and Sharon McIrvin Abu-Laban (eds) *The Arab World: Dynamics of Development* (Leiden: E. J. Brill, 1986).
Bahgat Korany, 'The Arab World and the New Balance of Power in the New Middle East', in Michael C. Hudson (ed.) *Middle East Dilemma: The Politics and Economics of Arab Integration* (London: I.B. Tauris, 1999).

Stephen D. Krasner. 'Globalization and Sovereignty', in David A. Smith, Dorothy J. Solinger and Steven C. Topik (eds) *States and Sovereignty in the Global Economy* (London: Routledge, 1999).

Sai Felicia Krishna-Hensel (ed.) *The New Millennium: Challenges and Strategies for aGlobalizing World* (Burlington, VT: Ashgate, 2000).

Richard L. Kugler and Ellen L. Frost (eds) *The Global Century: Globalization and National Security* (Volumes I and II) (Washington, DC: National Defense University Press, 2001).

Ellen Laipson, 'Europe's Role in the Middle East: Enduring Ties, Emerging Opportunities', *Middle East Journal*, 44 (1), 1990, 7–17.

Richard Latter, *Mediterranean Security* (London: HMSO, December 1991).

Victor Lavy and Eliezer Sheffer, *Foreign Aid and Economic Development in the Middle East: Egypt, Syria and Jordan* (New York: Praeger, 1991).

Philippe Legrain, *Open World: The Truth About Globalisation* (London: Abacus, 2003).

M. Levy, *Modernization and the Structure of Societies* (Princeton, NJ: Princeton University Press, 1966).

Bernard Lewis, 'The Roots of Muslim Rage', *Atlantic Monthly*, 266 (3), 1990, 47–60.

Bernard Lewis, 'License to Kill: Usama bin Ladin's Declaration of Jihad', *Foreign Affairs*, 77 (6), 1998, 14–19.

David E. Long and Christian Koch (eds) *Gulf Security in the Twenty-first Century* (Abu Dhabi: Emirates Center for Strategic Studies and Research, 1997).

Halford Mackinder (ed.) *Democratic Ideals and Reality* (New York: W. W. Norton, 1962).

Peter Mandaville, *Transnational Muslim Politics: Reimagining the Umma* (New York: Routledge, 2004).

Edward D. Mansfield and Helen V. Milner, 'The New Wave of Regionalism', *International Organization*, 53 (3), 1999, 589–627.

Phebe Marr, 'The Persian Gulf After the Storm', in Phebe Marr and William Lewis (eds) *Riding the Tiger: The Middle East Challenge After the Cold War* (Boulder, CO: Westview Press, 1993).

Phebe Marr and William Lewis (eds) *Riding the Tiger: The Middle East Challenge After the Cold War* (Boulder, CO: Westview Press, 1993).

J. A. R. Marriott, *Europe and Beyond: A Preliminary Survey of World-Politics in the Last Half-Century 1870–1920* (London: Methuen, 1921).

Don D. Marshall, 'Understanding Late-Twentieth-Century Capitalism: Reassessing the Globalization Theme', *Government and Opposition*, 31 (2), 1996, 193–215.

Martin E. Marty and R. Scott Appleby (eds) *Fundamentalisms and Society* (Chicago, IL: University of Chicago Press, 1993).

Paul Masson, *Globalization: Facts and Figures*, IMF Policy Discussion Paper PDP/01/4, October 2001.

Ali Mazrui, 'Globalisation and the Future of Islamic Civilisation', *Discourse*, October 2000.

Richard McAllister, *From EC to EU: An Historical and Political Survey* (London: Routledge, 1997).

John Micklethwait and Adrian Wooldridge, 'From Sarajevo to September 11', *Policy Review*, No. 117, 2003.

Ralph Miliband and Leo Panitch (eds) *New World Order? Socialist Register 1992* (London: Merlin Press, 1992).

Ziba Mir-Hosseini, 'Rethinking Gender: Discussions with Ulama in Iran', *Critique: Journal for Critical Studies of the Middle East*, No. 13, 1998, 45–60.

James H. Mittelman, 'How Does Globalization Work?', in James H. Mittelman (ed.) *Globalization: Critical Reflections* (Boulder, CO: Lynne Rienner, 1996).
James H. Mittelman (ed.) *Globalization: Critical Reflections* (Boulder, CO: Lynne Rienner, 1996).
Pete W. Moore, 'The International Context of Liberalization and Democratization in the Arab World', *Arab Studies Quarterly*, 16 (3), 1994, 43–67.
Ali Mohammadi (ed.) *Islam Encountering Globalization* (London: RoutledgeCurzon, 2002).
Mehdi Mozaffari, 'Can a Declined Civilization be Reconstructed? Islamic Civilization or Civilized Islam?', *International Relations*, XIV (3), 1998, 31–50.
Mehdi Mozaffari, 'Mega Civilization: Global Capital and the New Standard of Civilization', in Sai Felicia Krishna-Hensel (ed.) *The New Millennium: Challenges and Strategies for aGlobalizing World* (Burlington, VT: Ashgate, 2000).
Simon W. Murden, *Islam, the Middle East, and the New Global Economy* (Boulder, CO: Lynne Rienner, 2002).
Emma C. Murphy, 'The Arab–Israeli Conflict and the New World Order', in Haifa Jawad (ed.) *The Middle East in the New World Order* (London: Macmillan, 1994).
Emma C. Murphy, 'Governance and Development', *Internationale Politik* (Transatlantic edition), 3 (4), 2002, 69–76.
Emma C. Murphy, 'Women in Tunisia: Between State Feminism and Economic Reform', in Eleanor Abdella Doumato and Marsha Pripstein Posusney (eds) *Women and Globalization in the Arab Middle East: Gender, Economy and Society* (Boulder, CO: Lynne Rienner, 2003).
Meltem Müftüler, 'Turkey and the European Community: An Uneasy Relationship', *Turkish Review Quarterly Digest*, 7 (33), 1993, 31–41.
Chandra Muzaffar, 'Globalization and Religion: Some Reflections', IslamOnline.net, 19 June 2002, www.islamonline.net/english/Contemporary/2002/06/Article3.shtml
Fauzi Najjar, 'The Arabs, Islam and Globalization', *Middle East Policy*, XII (3), 2005, 91–106.
Vali Nasr, 'Regional Implications of Shi'a Revival in Iraq', *The Washington Quarterly*, 27 (3), 2004, 7–24.
Felix Neugart, *The Future of European Policies in the Middle East after the Iraq War* (Munich: Bertelsmann Group for Policy Research and Center for Applied Policy Research, 2003).
Tim Niblock, 'North–South Socio-economic Relations in the Mediterranean', in Roberto Aliboni, George Joffé and Tim Niblock (eds) *Security Challenges in the Mediterranean Region* (London: Frank Cass, 1996).
Tim Niblock, *Saudi Arabia: Power, Legitimacy and Survival* (New York: Routledge, 2006).
Paul Noble, 'The Prospects for Arab Cooperation in a Changing Regional and Global System', in Michael C. Hudson (ed.) *Middle East Dilemma: The Politics and Economics of Arab Integration* (London: I.B. Tauris, 1999).
Gerd Nonneman (ed.) *The Middle East and Europe: The Search for Stability and Integration* (London: Federal Trust, 1993).
Gerd Nonneman (ed.) *Analyzing Middle East Foreign Policies and the Relationship with Europe* (New York: Routledge, 2005).
Kenichi Ohmae, *The End of the Nation State: The Rise of Regional Economies* (London: HarperCollins, 1995).

Denis O'Hearn, 'Global Restructuring, Transnational Corporations and the "European Periphery"': What has Changed?', in David A. Smith and József Böröcz (eds) *A New World Order? Global Transformations in the Late Twentieth Century* (Westport, CT: Praeger, 1995).

Martha Brill Olcott, *Central Asia's New States: Independence, Foreign Policy, and Regional Security* (Washington, DC: US Institute of Peace Press, 1996).

Marina Ottaway and Thomas Carothers, *The Greater Middle East Initiative: Off to a False Start*, Policy Brief No. 29, March 2004 (Washington, DC: Carnegie Endowmment for International Peace).

Albert Paolini, 'Globalization', in Phillip Darby (ed.) *At the Edge of International Relations: Postcolonialism, Gender and Dependency* (New York: Continuum, 2000).

Theodore Pelagidis and Harry Papasotiriou, 'Globalisation or Regionalism? States, Markets and the Structure of International Trade', *Review of International Studies*, 28 (3), 2002, 519–35.

James Petras and Henry Veltmeyer, *Globalization Unmasked: Imperialism in the 21st Century* (London: Zed Books, 2002).

Karen Pfeifer and Marsha Pripstein Posusney, 'Arab Economies and Globalization: An Overview', in Eleanor Abdella Doumato and Marsha Pripstein Posusney (eds) *Women and Globalization in the Middle East: Gender, Economy, and Society* (Boulder, CO: Lynne Rienner, 2003).

Jan Nederveen Pieterse (ed.) *Global Futures: Shaping Globalization* (London: Zed Press, 2000).

Jan Nederveen Pieterse, *Globalization or Empire?* (London: Routledge, 2004).

Maria do Céu Pinto, *Political Islam and the United States: A Study of U.S. Policy towards Islamist Movements in the Middle East* (Reading: Ithaca Press, 1999).

Daniel Pipes, 'The Muslims are Coming! The Muslims are Coming!', *National Review*, 19 November 1990.

Marc F. Plattner, 'Globalization and Self-government', *Journal of Democracy*, 13 (3), 2002, 54–67.

Jan Pronk, 'Globalization: A Developmental Approach', in Jan Nederveen Pieterse (ed.) *Global Futures: Shaping Globalization* (London: Zed Books, 2000).

Yusuf al-Qaradawi, *Al-Muslimun wa al-Awlamah* (Muslims and Globalization) (Cairo: Dar al-Tawzi wa Nashr al-Islamiyya, 2000).

Rodrigo de Rato, 'Co-operation and Security in the Mediterranean', *North Atlantic Assembly – Political Committee* (Brussels: North Atlantic Assembly, October 1995).

Gowher Rezvi, 'South Asia and the New World Order', in Hans-Henrik Holm and Georg Sørensen (eds) *Whose World Order? Uneven Globalization and the End of the Cold War* (Boulder, CO: Westview Press, 1995).

Alan Richards, 'Socioeconomic Roots of Middle East Radicalism', *Naval War College Review*, LV (4), 2002, 23–38.

E. Riordan, U. Dadush, J. Jalali, S. Streifel, M. Brahmbhatt and K. Takagaki, 'The World Economy and its Implications for the Middle East and North Africa', in N. Shafik (ed.) *Prospects for Middle Eastern and North African Economies: From Boom to Bust and Back?* (New York: St Martin's Press, 1998).

William I. Robinson, 'Globalisation: Nine Theses on Our Epoch', *Race and Class*, 38 (2), 1996, 13–31.

Maxine Rodinson, *Islam and Capitalism* (Harmondsworth, UK: Penguin, 1977).

Richard Rosecrane, 'Bipolarity, Multipolarity, and the Future', in James N. Rosenau (ed.) *International Politics and Foreign Policy* (New York: Free Press, 1969).

James N. Rosenau (ed.) *International Politics and Foreign Policy* (New York: Free Press, 1969).
James N. Rosenau, *The Study of World Politics: Globalization and Governance* (New York: Routledge, 2006).
Olivier Roy, *The Failure of Political Islam* (London: I. B. Tauris, 1995).
Barry Rubin, 'Globalization and the Middle East: Part One', YaleGlobal Online, 16 January 2003, http://yaleglobal.yale.edu/display.article?id = 744.
Winfried Ruigrok and Rob van Tulder, *The Logic of International Restructuring* (London: Routledge, 1995).
Ghassan Salamé, 'Torn Between the Atlantic and the Mediterranean: Europe and the Middle East in the Post-Cold War Era', *Middle East Journal*, 48 (2), 1994, 226–49.
Louay Safi, *Tensions and Transitions in the Muslim World* (Lanham, MD: University Press of America, 2003).
Raed Safadi, *Global Challenges and Opportunities facing MENA Countries at the Dawn of the 21st Century*, Working Paper Series No. 199624 (Cairo: Economic Research Forum, 1996).
Saskia Sassen, *Losing Control? Sovereignty in an Age of Globalization* (New York: Columbia University Press, 1996).
Saskia Sassen, 'Losing Control? The State and the New Geography of Power', *Global Dialogue*, 1 (1), 1999, 197–214.
Yezid Sayigh, '"System Breakdown" in the Middle East?', in Martin Kramer (ed.) *Middle East Lectures – Number Two* (Tel Aviv: Tel Aviv University, 1997).
an Aart Scholte, *Globalization: A Critical Introduction* (New York: Palgrave Macmillan, 2005). Allen Scott, *Regions and the World Economy: The Coming Shape of Global Production, Competition, and Political Order* (Oxford: Oxford University Press, 2000).
David Seddon, 'Unequal Partnership: Europe, the Maghreb and the New Regionalism', in Jean Grugel and Wil Hout (eds) *Regionalism Across the North–South Divide* (London: Routledge, 1999).
N. Shafik (ed.) *Prospects for Middle Eastern and North African Economies: From Boom to Bust and Back?* (New York: St Martin's Press, 1998).
Ian Shapiro, *Democratic Justice* (New Haven, CT: Yale University Pres, 1999).
Hisham Sharabi, *Neopatriarchy: A Theory of Distorted Change in Arab Society* (Oxford: Oxford University Press, 1988).
Alan Shipman, *The Myth of Globalization* (Cambridge: Icon Books, 2002).
George P. Shultz, 'A Changed World', *Foreign Policy Research Institute*, E-note, 22 March 2004.
Ismail Sirageldin, *Globalization, Regionalization and Recent Trade Agreements: Impact on Arab Economies*, Working Paper 9817 (Cairo: Economic Research Forum, 1998).
Ismail Sirageldin and Rana Al-Khaled, *The Challenges of Globalization and Human Resource Development in the Arab World: Myth and Reality*, Working Paper 9712 (Cairo: Economic Research Forum, 1996).
Leslie Sklair, *Sociology of the Global System* (London: Harvester Wheatsheaf, 1991).
Leslie Sklair, *The Transnational Capitalist Class* (Oxford: Blackwell, 2001).
Leslie Sklair and Peter T. Robbins, 'Global Capitalism and Major Corporations from the Third World', *Third World Quarterly*, 23 (1), 2002, 81–100.
David A. Smith and József Böröcz (eds) *A New World Order? Global Transformations in the Late Twentieth Century* (Westport, CT: Praeger, 1995).

David A. Smith, Dorothy J. Solinger and Steven C. Topik (eds) *States and Sovereignty in the Global Economy* (London: Routledge, 1999).
Claire Spencer, *The Maghreb in the 1990s*, Adelphi Paper 274 (London: Brassey's for IISS, February 1993).
Frederick S. Starr, 'Making Eurasia Stable', *Foreign Affairs*, 75 (1), 1996, 80–92.
Ronald Steel, 'Europe after the Superpowers', in Nicholas X. Rizopoulos (ed.) *Sea-Changes: American Foreign Policy in a World Transformed* (New York: Council on Foreign Relations, 1990).
Joseph Stiglitz, *Globalization and its Discontents* (London: Penguin, 2002).
Susan Strange, *The Retreat of the State: The Diffusion of Power in the World Economy* (Cambridge: Cambridge University Press, 1996).
Douglas E. Streusand, 'Abraham's Other Childern: Is Islam an Enemy of the West?', *Policy Review*, No. 50 (1989).
Richard Stubbs, 'Asia–Pacific Regionalism versus Globalization: Competing Forms of Capitalism', in William D. Coleman and Geoffrey R. D. Underhill (eds) *Regionalism and Global Economic Integration: Europe, Asia and the Americas* (London: Routledge, 1998).
Shibley Telhami, *The Stakes: America and the Middle East* (Boulder, CO: Westview Press, 2002).
Mary Ann Tétreault, 'Kuwait: Sex, Violence, and the Politics of Economic Restructuring', in Eleanor Abdella Doumato and Marsha Pripstein Posusney (eds) *Women and Globalization in the Arab Middle East: Gender, Economy and Society* (Boulder, CO: Lynne Rienner, 2003).
Mary Ann Tétreault and Haya al-Mughni, 'Gender, Citizenship and Nationalism in Kuwait', *British Journal of Middle Eastern Studies*, 22 (1&2), 1995, 64–80.
Peter Thiery, 'Good Governance – No Luxury', *Internationale Politik* (Transatlantic edition), 3 (4), 2002.
J. H. Thompson and R. D. Reischauer (eds) *Modernization of the Arab World* (Princeton, NJ: Van Nostrand, 1966).
John Tomlinson, *Cultural Imperialism: A Critical Introduction* (London: Pinter, 1991).
Charles Tripp, 'States, Elites and the "Management of Change"', in Hassan Hakimian and Ziba Moshaver (eds) *The State and Global Change: The Political Economy of Transition in the Middle East and North Africa* (Richmond: Curzon Press, 2001).
Bryan S. Turner, *Orientalism, Postmodernism and Globalism* (London: Routlege, 1994).
United Nations Development Programme/Arab Fund for Economic and Social Development, *Arab Human Development Report 2002* (New York: UNDP, 2002).
United Nations Development Programme/Arab Fund for Economic and Social Development, *Arab Human Development Report 2003* (New York: UNDP, 2003).
Edward S. Walker Jr, 'Gloomy Mood in Egypt and Saudi Arabia', *Middle East Institute Perspective*, January 22, 2003.
Immanuel Wallerstein, 'States? Sovereignty? The Dilemmas of Capitalists in an Age of Transition', in David A. Smith, Dorothy J. Solinger and Steven C. Topik (eds) *States and Sovereignty in the Global Economy* (London: Routledge, 1999).
Kenneth Waltz, 'International Structure, National Force, and the Balance of Power', in James N. Rosenau (ed.) *International Politics and Foreign Policy* (New York: Free Press, 1969).
Kenneth N. Waltz, 'Globalization and Governance', *PS: Political Science and Politics*, 32 (4), 1999, 693–700.

Malcolm Waters, *Globalization* (London: Routledge, 1996).
James L. Watson, *Golden Arches East: McDonald's in East Asia* (Stanford, CA: Stanford University Press, 1997).
Werner Weidenfeld (ed.) *Europe and the Middle East* (Gütersloh: Bertelsmann Foundation, 1995).
Richard Weitz, 'Averting a New Great Game in Central Asia', *The Washington Quarterly*, 29 (3), 2006, 155–67
Paul White and William S. Logan (eds) *Remaking the Middle East* (New York: Berg, 1997).
John Williams, *The Ethics of Territorial Borders: Drawing Lines in the Shifting Sands* (New York: Palgrave Macmillan, 2006).
Rodney Wilson, 'The Economic Relations of the Middle East: Toward Europe or Within the Region?', *Middle East Journal*, 48 (2), 1994, 268–87.
Rodney Wilson, *Economic Development in the Middle East* (London: Routledge, 1995).
Ernest Wistrich, *The United States of Europe* (London: Routledge, 1994).
World Bank, *The Asian Miracle: Economic Growth and Public Policy* (Oxford: Oxford University Press, 1993).
World Bank, *Claiming the Future: Choosing Prosperity in the Middle East and North Africa* (Washington, DC: IBRD, 1995).
Michael Yahuda, *The International Politics of the Asia–Pacific, 1945–1995* (London: Routledge, 1996).
Judith Yaphe (ed.) *The Middle East in 2015: The Impact of Regional Trends on U.S. Strategic Planning* (Washington, DC: National Defense University Press, 2002).
Hamid Zangeneh, 'Economic Consequences of Student Unrest in Iran', *Journal of Iranian Research and Analysis*, 15 (2), 1999, 132–41.
I. William Zartman, 'The Ups and Downs of Maghrib Unity', in Michael C. Hudson (ed.) *Middle East Dilemma: The Politics and Economics of Arab Integration* (London: I.B. Tauris, 1999).
Michael Zürn, 'The Challenges of Globalization and Individualization: A View from Europe', in Hans-Henrik Holm and Georg Sørensen (eds) *Whose World Order? Uneven Globalization and the End of the Cold War* (Boulder, CO: Westview Press, 1995).

Index

Aarts, Paul 59, 204n48, 206n36
Abdallah, Sana 218n43
Abdel-Malek, Anwar 60, 214n141
Abdel-Razek, Sherine 218n30
Abdellah, Mohamed 194
Abdulla, Abdul Khaleq 205n15
Abdullah, Crown Prince of Saudi Arabia 170, 192, 215n21, 222n55, 226n23
Abdullah, King of Jordan 180
Achaemenids 5
Adelman, Kenneth 16
Afghanistan 10, 14, 16–17, 43, 48, 72, 89–90, 106; civilian targeting by terrorists in 125; elections in 116; Sunni domination in 179; as terrorist base 124; US attack on 18
Africa 7, 16, 38, 89, 95, 131, 162; North African internal divisions 51; Sub-Saharan 33, 68, 136; *see also* MENA
AHDR (2002) *see* Arab Human Development Report
Ahiram, Ephraim and Tovias, Alfred 211n85
Ahmed, Qazi Hussain 16
Al-Ahram Weekly 60, 121, 193, 216n34, 220n11
Ahsan, Muhammad 182–83, 225n48
Ajami, Fouad 137, 218n36
Akidati 216n33
al-Arabiya TV 28, 156
al-Jazeera TV 28, 156, 199n52
al-Manar TV 156
al-Qaeda 12, 13, 17–18, 40, 53–54, 70, 162, 181, 199n53; civilian targeting by 125; globalization as midwife 21–22; Iraq War and 127; MENA and operations of 128–29

Al-Wafd 216n35
Al Watan 216n46
Albania 81
Alexander the Great 5
Alexandria 5
'Alexandria Declaration' (March, 2004) 173, 223n17
Algeria 12, 49, 50, 51, 73, 82, 115; elections in 116; global economic ranking 131; Islamist defeat in 123; key actor in MENA 183; petrodollar plenty in 147
Alhajji, A.F. 220n65
Ali, Mohammed 189
Aliboni, Roberto 208n40, 209n63
Aliyev, President Ilham 212n115
Allen, Robin 204n44
Allen, Woody 34
Alnasrawi, Abbas 134, 217n20
Aloul, Sahar 217n12
Alterman, Jon B. 224n28
Altunišik, M.B. and Tūr, Ō. 218n39
Ambrose, Stephen E. 194, 227n30
Amin, Galal 220n13
Amuzegar, Jahangir 218n42
Andalusia 6
Anthony, John Duke 146, 205n16, 217n23, 218n24, 219n60
anti-imperialism 22–23
APEC (Asia-Pacific Economic Cooperation) 37–38, 80
Apter, David 201n55
Arab Charter for Anti-Terrorism 174
Arab Co-operation Council (ACC) 50–51, 54–55
Arab Human Development Report (2002) 132, 143, 152, 173–74, 178, 193, 217n13, 219n49, 221n18, 223n20

Index 243

Arab-Israeli conflict 76–81, 181–82; corroding impact on region 227n33; and future for Middle East 195–96
Arab-Israeli peace process 68–69
Arab League 48
Arab Maghreb Union (AMU) 54, 69
Arab News 199n42, 202n10
Arab World and MENA 48–49
'Arabizi' 154–55
Arafat, Yasser 195
Arafat-Netanyahu summit (Washington, October 1996) 78–79
Armenia 100
Arrighi, Giovanni 201n41
ASEAN (Association of South-East Asian Nations) 51, 61–62, 94
Al-Asheikh, Grand Mufti Sheikh Abdul Aziz 158
Asia: Asia-Pacific Economic Cooperation (APEC) 37–38, 80; Asia-Pacific train 66; Central Asian Republics 10, 45, 48, 67, 71, 72, 84, 90, 94, 175; geopolitical vacuum in 92–93; core-periphery 89; energy sector 95–99; Euro-Asian struggle 66–67; geopolitics in action 89–94, 106; investment and trade 101–2; labour and migration 102–4; military partnerships and arms trade 99–101; petrodollar investments in 101–2; post-Cold War strategic landscape 91, 93–94; pre-eminence, race for 107–8; relations across Asian region 94–106; religion 104–6; South and Southeast 17; Southeast 45, 66, 67–68, 88, 96; tiger economies of 66–67; US Central Asian strategy 106; WMD in regional security 101
Aslam, Mian 16
Asmus, Ronald S. 210n74
al-Assad, President Bashar 111
al-Assad, President Hafez 111
assimilation, regional barriers to 175–84
Associated Free Press 221n23
Associated Press 213n120
Assyria 6
a-Aswad, El-Sayed 200n14
Atlantic Monthly 165
Attaturk, Kamal 189
Australia 18, 96
Austria 83
authoritarianism (and 'neo-authoritarianism') 111, 115, 132, 174, 226n23

al-Awwa, Salim 150
Ayoob, Mohammed 224n29
Ayubi, Nazih N. 148, 188, 220n70, 225n7, 226n8
Azerbaijan 72, 98
El Azhary, M.S. 133, 217n19
Azzam, Maha 220n5
Azzam, Mahfouz 199n43

Baaysir, Abu Bakar 123
Baghdad 5, 11, 17, 33, 44, 53, 55, 127–28, 180, 182
Bahrain 44, 48, 50, 57, 70, 117; accommodation with globalization 130, 131; elections in 116; geopolitical realignment of 127; preservation of US external prop 119
Baku-Ceyhan pipeline 98
Bali, bombing in 18, 123
Balkan states 81
Barakat, Halim 48, 188, 204n4, 225n4
Barber, Lionel, *et al.* 210n81
Barber, Lionel and Gray, Bernard 208n32
Barboza, David 201n44
Barcelona Conference (1995) 82, 83, 210n68
El-Baz, Osama 193
BBC News 156, 202n8
Bekaa Valley 45
Benin, Joel and Stork, Joe 221n28
Bergen, Peter 22
Berlin, Donald L. 211n98
Berlin Wall, fall of 21, 38, 78
Bill, J.A. and Chavez, R.B. 11, 33, 42, 198n26, 203n40
bin Laden, Osama 17, 22, 43–44, 104, 125, 127, 128–29, 153, 216n47, 222n55, 226n23
Black, Ian 222n56
Black Sea Grouping 72
Blair, Tony 71
Blanche, Ed 213n128
Bodi, Faisal 199n41
Bokhari, Farhan 213n129
Bonine, Michael E. 213n132
Bosnia 14
Boudroua, Ahmed 135, 218n26
Bourgiba, Habib 189
Bower, Ernest 107–8
Bradsher, Keith and Pala, Christopher 213n130
Brazil 67
Britain 48, 64, 75; mandate in Iraq 171

244 Index

Bronson, Rachel 203n43
Brown, Carl E. 2, 166, 196, 223n3
Brown, L. Carl 197n3, 225n1
Brownback, Sam 180
Brumberg, Daniel 120, 216n27
Brzezinski, Zbigniew 60–61, 87–88, 193, 206n1
Bullock, A. and Stallybrass, O. 197n2
Burns, Nicholas 210n82
Bush, President George W. 15, 39, 70, 71, 79, 91, 105, 142, 163, 166, 171, 187, 194; democratization and the 'war on terror' 120–22; State of Union Address (2006) 206n34
Bush administration 14, 45–46, 128, 188, 194
Bush Sr, President George 69–70, 121
Business Environment Ranking 217n6
Buzan, B. and Waever, O. 204n2
Byzantium (and Byzantine Empire) 5, 6

Cairo 5
Cairo Times 193
Canada 42
capitalism 30–31; despotism and 9; domination of market capitalism 172–75; globalization and 20–22; liberating force of 9; unstoppable march of 21; world system of oppression 22–23
Çarkoğlu, A. *et al.* 204n9, 206n32
Carothers, Thomas 215n15
Carrere d'Encausse, H. and Schram, S.R. 9, 198n21
Carter, Hannah and Ehteshami, Anoushiravan 213n131
Carter, President J.E. 39
Caspian hydrocarbon reserves 96, 97–98
Caspian Sea States Organization 72
Castells, Manuel 30, 201n57
CATO Institute 44
CBS TV 16
Central Asia 106
Cerny, Philip G. 26, 200n28, 219n48
Céu Pinto, Maria do 222n51
Chase, R.S., *et al* 207n19
chastity *(namous)* 156
Chatelus, Michel 208n33
Chechnya 14
Cheney, Dick 142, 163, 191
Cheref, Abd-El-Kader 7, 197n16
Chicago School 26
China, People's Republic of 7, 9, 45, 57, 66–67, 72, 88, 90, 94–96, 99, 106, 168, 175; Asian powerhouse 91–92; military ties with Middle East 99–100; as model for MENA 172; Moscow-Beijing axis 94; *National Defence in 2000* 91; regional focus of 107–8; Sino-Russian relations 92
China National Petroleum Corporation 102
Chirac, President Jacques 79
Clark, Ian 24, 199n10
Clark, William 207n9
Clinton, President William J. 34
CNN 28, 156
Cobler, Martin 193
Cohen, Saul B. 166, 197n1, 223n2
Cohen, Stephen Philip 225n49
Cold War 13; impact on strategic map of Middle East 107; superpowers and MENA 48–49
colonialism and MENA 48–49
Commentary 44
communications networks, role of 178–79
competitiveness deficit 136
Conference on Security and Co-operation in the Middle East 68
Corbet, Hugh 74, 208n42, 210n76
Cordesman, Anthony H. 190, 226n10
Cordoba 5
core-periphry 31, 56
Cornish, Paul 208n28
cosmetic political reform 111–12
cosmopolitanism 5, 6, 7, 138, 151; youth cosmopolitanism 154–55
Cowan, Brian 207n24
Cox, Michael 201n42
Cox, Robert W. 201n54
Crockatt, Richard 204n53
cross-border linkages 43
cross-cultural contacts 167
crossroads of struggle, Middle East as 66–67
Crusades 5, 13–14
Cuba 80
cultural assimilation 155
cultural geography and American power 17–19
cultural obstacles to integration 178–79
cultural space of states, impingement on 37
culture clash in identity 149–56
Cyprus 81, 82, 84

Dabdoud, Ibrahim 218n34
Dafter, Ray 211n102

The Daily Star 213n127, 221n27
The Daily Telegraph 216n43
D'Alançon, François 209n49
Damascus 5, 57, 153, 203n25, 209n56
Dar el-Islam 8–10
Davidson, Christopher M. 221n30
de Charette, Hervé 210n72
de Rato, Rodrigo 210n66
de-territorialization 25, 109–10
de Villepin, Dominique 195
Dead Sea World Economic Forum (2004) 36
Dedman, Martin J. 207n8, 210n73
defence costs 113–14
Demko, G.J. and Wood, W.B. 197n1
demography 167
despotism 8, 9, 10, 187
Deutsch, K.W. and Singer, J.D. 214n138
Diamond, Larry, *et al.* 216n26
El-Din, Gamal Essam 226n19, 227n26
Dinmore, Guy and Sevastopulo, Demitri 212n115
Dodge, Toby and Higgott, Richard 216n3
Dodge, Tony 220n69
Doha 4
Doran, Michael Scott 169–70, 211n88, 223n11
Doumato, E.A. and Posusney, M.P. 221n34
Dresch, Paul 221n29
Dreyfuss, Robert 204n50
Dubai 4, 102, 151, 153; Dubai Strategy Forum (2002) 35, 131–32; economic miracle in 36
Duomato, Eleanor Abdella 222n41

East Timor 18
Easternization and MENA 67
Economic and Social Commission for Western Asia (ESCWA) 144
Economic Co-operation Organization (ECO) 55, 72
Economic Research Forum 141
economics: Asia-Pacific train 66; Asian tigers 66–67; Chicago School 26; competitive lag in MENA region 136; competitiveness deficit 136; conditions in MENA region 130–32; Dubai Strategy Forum (2002) 131–32; economic autocracy 4–5; 'economic balkanisation' 207n12; economic internationalization and balance of power 130–48; economic obstacles to integration 175–76; economic regionalism 51–52; Economic Trends in the MENA Region 218n44; future prospects 143–48; geopolitics and globalization, visible change 141–43; global currencies, shifts in 64–65; global rankings of MENA economies 131; globalization as negative economic force 130–31; imperialism revisited 130–31; import substitution industrialization (ISI) 137; internationalization and balance of power 130–48; knowledge production 143; liberalization of trade 2, 37, 70, 75, 112–13, 143–44, 148; marginalization 130–31; natural resources, dependence on 135–36; neo-colonialism revisited 130–31; North-South debates 37; oil and balance of power 132–35; oil geo-economics 137–41; open trade and economic growth 145; political economy and shaping of Middle East 2; political instability 132; powerlessness 130–31; price of prosperity through globalization 148; rentier-dependent economics 111, 138; stagnation in MENA region 131–32; state-led economic activities 136–37; subjugation 130–31; trade barriers 136–37; underemployment 136–37; World Economic Summit (2004) 131–32; world economy 1
The Economist 160, 199n11, 207n10, 211n92
Egypt 5, 6, 40, 50, 71, 73, 81, 82, 110; Egypt-Israel accommodation 50; elections in 116; Gema'a al-Islamiya in 154; geopolitical realignment, marginalization and 127; global economic ranking 131; Gulf capital investment in 147; Islamist defeat in 123; key actor in MENA 183
Ehteshami, A. and Hinnebusch, R. 206n35
Ehteshami, A. and Murphy, E.C. 214n5
Ehteshami, Anoushiravan 211n99, 213n125, 215n14
elections 116–17
elite legitimacy, challenge to 115–16
Elleman, B.A. and Paine, S.C.M. 214n134

246 *Index*

emasculation of regional actors 41
Engdahl, William 203n27
English language, cultural tradition and 153
Entessar, Nader 208n29
entrepreneurs within GME 35
Epps, Daniel 217n8
El-Erian, Mohamed and El-Gamal, Mahmoud 219n57
Eritrea 82
ethnic and religious division of, potential for 127–28
Eurasia 7, 60–62, 106, 108, 168; Asian geo-strategic dynamics 87–89; economic space and GME 39
Euro-Mediterranean Partnership (1994) 78
European Commission 65, 69, 79, 208n35, 209n48
European Economic Area (EEA) 211n83
European Parliament 210n69
European Union (EU) 42, 52, 57, 61, 175, 194, 210n75; Arab-Israeli peace process, position on 78; divisions within 84; Europe and MENA 53, 56, 61–62, 64–65; evolution of 64–66; expansion, implications for Middle East 69, 83–87; global actor 62–66; integration in 63–64; international transformations and EU-MENA relations 66–69; Iran, relations with 80; Israel, relations with 79; Maastricht and MENA 74–76; Mediterranean initiatives 83–84; Mediterranean security concerns 81–83; Mediterranean trade 74, 76; Middle East, EU relations with 72–73; 'Neighbourhood Policy' 65; regional problems 84–85; strategic dilemmas for EU-MENA relations 81–83, 107; strategic weakness of 70–71; systemic change shaping destiny of 63–64; tariff regime in 144; tensions with US on Arab-Israel peace process 78–80
Exxon Mobil 101
Ezzat, Dina 202n16, 225n47
Ezzelarab, Khaled 226n22

Fahd (ibn Abd al-Aziz), King of Saudi Arabia 118, 192
Fahim, Ashraf 225n42
al-Faisal, Prince Turki 157
Falk, Richard 3, 42, 197n7, 203n39
Falwell, Jerry 15, 16
Fanon, Franz 8, 10, 23, 197n17

Faour, Muhammad 208n26
Far Eastern Economic Review 97
Fattah, Hassan M. 212n108, 221n16
Fawcett, L. and Hurrell, A. 204n3, 205n13, 206n3
FDI (foreign direct investment) 136, 146
fear of globalization 2–3
Featherstone, Mike 220n8
Fegani, Nader 227n27
Finance and Development 217n5
Finland 83
Fischer, Joshka 226–27n25
Foreign Affairs 149, 161
Foreign Policy 198n31
fragmentation 25, 28, 39, 40, 42, 50, 51, 57, 62, 69, 78
France 13–14, 48, 64, 75, 81, 210n71; Arab-Israeli peace process, position on 79
Frank, Andre Gundur 1
Freedom House 173
Friedman, Thomas L. 31, 202n62, 203n33
Frum, David 180
Fukuyama, Francis 8, 164, 197n18, 199n2, 222n58
Füllberg-Stolberg, Katja *et al.* 197n8
Fuller, G.E. and Lesser, I.O. 199n3

GATT (General Agreement on Tariffs and Trade) 37–38, 144
Gauze III, F.G. and Crystal, J. 205n17
Gauzzone, Laura 206n28
GCC (Gulf Cooperation Council) 35, 69, 70, 74, 84, 103; citizen money and investment in 146–47; international system, engagement with 145; MENA and 52–53, 55; stock markets 147, 219n62; tariffs and free-trade initiatives 144–45; wealth disposition 219n59
gender-segregated societies 156–57
geo-culture and globalization 42–43
geo-economics of globalization 39–40
geopolitics 1–2; Arab-Israel conflict 76–81; Asia: energy sector 95–99; geopolitics in action 89–94, 106; investment and trade 101–2; labour and migration 102–4; military partnerships and arms trade 99–101; pre-eminence, race for 107–8; relations across Asian region 94–106; religion 104–6; US Central Asian strategy 106; Eurasia 60–62; Asian

geo-strategic dynamics 87–89;
European Union: EU-MENA
relations: implications of EU
expansions 83–87; international
transformations and 66–69; strategic
dilemmas 81–83, 107; global actor
62–66; Maastricht and MENA 74–76;
geopolitical context of GME 179–84;
geopolitical future of Middle East
183–84; geopolitical pressures within
MENA 41; globalization and, visible
change 141–43; Iraq: Persian Gulf
security and 69–71; militant Islam
and impact of 9/11 18–19; pan-
Islamism 126; Soviet Union,
implosion of 71–74; *see also* identity,
geopolitics of
Gerges, Fawaz A. 13, 198n36
Germany 64, 75, 81
Ghabra, Shafeeq N. 223n9
Ghantous, Ghaida and Lewis, Barbara
219n61
Giddens, Anthony 28, 200n31, 201n46
Gilpin, Robert 28, 201n50, 211n101
Giscard d'Estaing, Valéry 162
Glain, Stephen 225n44
global currencies, shifts in 64–65
Global Dialogue 204n51
Global Intelligence Report 204n47
Global Intelligence Update 212–13n116
*Global Paradox: The Bigger the World
Economy, the More Powerful its
Smallest Players* (Naisbitt, J.) 47
global rankings of MENA economies 131
global society 24
Global Trends 2015 167
global village 24–25
globalist *jihad*, challenge of 123–29
globalization 1–2; as al-Qaeda midwife
21–22; Arab cultural exports through
155–56; assessment of 31; capitalism
and 20–22; communications
networks, role of 178–79; in context
of MENA 130–31; core-periphry and
31; corrosive impacts on Muslim
social regulation 38; costs of
unfettered embrace 145–46; as
cultural construct 150; cultural
space of states, impingement on 37;
de-territorialization and 25; Dead
Sea World Economic Forum (2004)
36; domination through, fear of 2–3,
7; Dubai Strategy Forum 35;
endgame or conceptual framework?
23–31; essence of 26; fear of 2–3;
fragmentation and 28, 41–42, 51;
fruits of, uneven distribution of 28–31;
geo-culture and 42–43; geo-
economics of 39–40; Gulf Cooperation
Council (GCC) 35; hard and soft
globalization 24–25; in history 5–7;
ideologically-rooted concept 29;
imperialism, capitalism and 22–23;
individualism and 38–39;
industrialization and 30;
interdependence and 5, 33–46;
international financial institutions
(IFIs) and 38; international politics
and 165–84; internationalization of
capital 26; as invasion by 'Satanic
civilization' 34–35; Jeddah
Economic Forum (2004) 36; *jihad*
and 123–26; levelling and 26; liberal
value system, acceptance of 38–39;
limits of 12, 20; local separation
and 12; localization and 27; male-
driven cultural values, challenge to
156–60; media role 178–79; MENA
states and 36–39; Middle East fallout
of politics of 40–42; and Middle East
in perspective 185–96; multi-
disciplinary paternity of 24;
multinational business and 37–38, 39;
myth of 24–25; as negative economic
force 130–31; neo-liberal economics
26; origins of 26–28; politics of 40–
42; price of economic prosperity
through 148; processes of 25–26;
public good and 142–43; re-
Islamization and 42–43; regional
organization of states and 33–34;
regional politics and strategic
interdependence 43–46;
regionalization and 63; safety nets,
provision and 143; secularization
and 37; 'socialization of production'
and 23; Soviet collapse and 20, 26–
27, 62–63, 68, 71–74, 86, 89–92,
108, 161, 178, 182, 192; strategic
interdependence 43–46, 166–67;
structures of 25–26, 29–30; system
and process? 31–32; time, space and
26, 28; transformation patterns 38;
transnational corporations and 37–38,
39; transnationalism and 25;
universalism of 3–4; US hegemonic
ambition and 27–28; US National
Security Strategy analysis 168–69;

Western values and 20–21; *see also* economics; geopolitics; GME; governance; identity, geopolitics of; MENA; Middle East
Globalization and the Nation-State (Holten, R.) 40
GME (greater Middle East) 1, 2, 25, 45–46, 58–59, 60, 108; alternative futures for 169–72, 172–73; assimilation, regional barriers to 175–84; capitalism, domination of market capitalism 172–75; conflict, intensive and harmful 167–68; cross-cultural contacts 167; cultural geography and American power 17–19; cultural obstacles 178–79; demography 167; economic obstacles 175–76; entrepreneurs within 35; Eurasian economic space and 39; geopolitical context 179–84; geopolitics of identity in 160–64; global context 165–66; globalization and international politics 165–84; GMEI (Greater Middle East Initiative) 70, 121, 185, 190, 191, 193–94, 224n30; insecurity, transmission of 166; and MENA 48; natural resources, allocation of 167; political elites, objectives of 169–70; political obstacles 176–77; post 9/11 context 174; reform and dynamism of globalization 169; regional environment and US power 170–71; regional organization of states and 33–34; regional politics in global context 165–72; religious elites, objectives of 169–70; shaping the region, influential factors 167–68; social relations, tight knit in 4; socio-political contradictions 169–71; strategic context, 9/11 and globalization 10–19; strategic interdependence 166–67; strategic unit 10–11; terrorism and geopolitics, 9/11 effect 15–17; US policies towards 163–64; *see also* MENA; Middle East
Gnesotto, N. and Roper, J. 206n5
Goff, Patricia M. 203n37
Goldgeier, J.M. and McFaul, M. 214n137
Goldschmidt Jr, Arthur 197n11
good governance indicators 131
Gourevitch, Peter A. 207n15

governance: Bush administration, effects of policies 120–22; cosmetic political reform 111–12; de-territorialization 109–10; defence costs 113–14; elections 116–17; elite legitimacy, challenge to 115–16; globalist *jihad,* challenge of 123–29; 'good governance' indicators, MENA region 131; government in era of globalization 109–29; hereditary republicanism 111; judicial review 119–20; 'marketization' of states 112–15; oil income 110–11; political dynamism 117–18; political reform, liberalization and 116–20; power and economic controls 114; pressures of globalization for 112–13, 114–15; protectionist pressures 125–26; rentier-dependence 111, 138; states 109–12; tax revenues 113; tensions of globalization for 113, 114–15; terrorism, globalization and the state 123–29; transnational *jihadist* challenges 123–26; *see also* economics; geopolitics; globalization; GME; identity, geopolitics of; MENA; Middle East
Graham, Franklin 15–16
Granada 5
Granitsas, Alkman 212n109
Greater Arab Free Trade Area (GAFTA) 58, 144, 147
Greater Middle East Initiative (GMEI) 70, 121, 185, 190, 191, 193–94, 194, 224n30, 226–27n25
Greece 85
'green peril' of Islamic terror 160–64
Griffel, Frank 123, 216n39
Griffin, Keith 152, 221n20
Grugel, J. and Hout, W. 204n3
G7 79
The Guardian 171, 198n29, 199n5, 199n50, 216n42
Gulf News 202n9, 218n41
Gulf States Newsletter 209n46
Gulf War (1991) 76–77

Habib, Osama 219n51, 220n67
Hadar, Leon T. 161, 216n31, 222n49
Haddah, Sheikh Ahmed Abdelaziz 151
Hadid, Diaa 220n14
Hadjor, Kofi Buenor 1
Haeri, Shahla 222n43

Haikal, Muhammad Hassanain 143
Hajj festival 7
Hakimian, Hassan 219n56
Halliday, Fred 4, 62, 146, 197n10, 204n5, 206n2, 219n58, 223n4
El-Hamalawy, Hossam 199n43
Hamas 40
Hanelt, Christian-Peter, et al. 207n14
Hanna, Daniel 219n64
Hanson, Victor Davis 44, 204n45
Hassan, Riffat 222n40
Heard-Bey, Frauke 160, 222n44
Heikal, Muhammed H. 205n12
Heilbroner, Robert L. 203n34
Held, D. and McGrew, A. 201n51
Held, David 38, 200n21, 202n20
Hellenic civilization 5, 6
Helm, Sarah 210n82
Henry, Clement M. 183, 225n50
Henry, C.M. and Springborg, R. 38, 203n21, 217n4
hereditary republicanism 111
Heritage Foundation 44; Index of Economic Freedom 131
Heseltine, Lord Michael 11
Higgott, Richard 47, 204n1
Hinnebusch, Raymond 50, 197n9, 202n17, 204n8
Hizbul Tahrir 40
Hoagland, Jim 222n47
Hobson, John M. 6, 7, 197n12
Hoffman, Bruce 199n6
Hollis, Rosemary 209n54, 224n26
Holten, Robert 40
Holton, Robert J. 3, 197n5, 203n29
Hong Kong 145, 175
honour *(namous)* 156
Hoogvelt, Ankie 31, 201n58, 202n61, 223n15
Hook, G.D., et al. 39, 40, 200n30, 203n26, 203n36
Hudson Institute 180
Hunaidi, Rima Khalaf 131–32
Huntington, Samuel P. 13, 18–19, 149, 161, 198n37
Hurrell, A. and Woods, N. 201n49
Hurrell, Andrew 204n10
Hussein, Ouday 111
Hussein, Qusay 111
Hussein, Saddam 51, 55, 70, 80, 82, 111, 121, 126
Hussein ibn Talal, King of Jordan 55
Hvidt, Martin 218n33
hydrocarbons 89, 95–99, 110

IAEA (International Atomic Energy Agency) 71, 75
identity, geopolitics of 149–64; 'Arabizi' 154–55; chastity *(namous)* 156; cultural assimilation 155; culture clash 149–56; English language, cultural tradition and 153; gender-segregated societies 156–57; globalization as cultural construct 150; GME, geopolitics of identity in 160–64; 'green peril' of Islamic terror 160–64; honour *(namous)* 156; Islam, religion and way of life 149; male-dominated division of labour 156–57; manhood *(rujula)* 156; 'Muslim identity' 159–60; Muslim patterns of social organization 158–59; Muslim perceptions of globalizing world 153; patrimony and globalization 156–60; sex as marketing tool 151; tourist activities, threats to traditions 154; traditional values and globalizing world 152–53; Western consumerism 150, 151–52; Western ways, penetration of 150–51; youth cosmopolitanism 154–55; *see also* geopolitics; globalization
IMF (International Monetary Fund) 38, 112, 218n29
imperialism 8–9; capitalism and 22–23; imperialism revisited 130–31
Imperialism: Highest Stage of Capitalism (Lenin, V.I.) 22
Imperialism: Pioneer of Capitalism (Warren, W.) 9
import substitution industrialization (ISI) 137
India 45, 88, 90, 94, 95, 99, 106; subcontinental superpower 93
Indian Oil and Natural Gas Corporation 102
individualism and globalization 38–39
Indonesia 18, 96, 97, 107, 123; women in 158
industrialization and globalization 30
insecurity, transmission of 166
inter-Arab trade relations 72–74
interdependence and globalization 5
international financial institutions (IFIs) 38
International Herald Tribune 216n38
International Labour Organization (ILO) 136

internationalization: and balance of power 130–48; of capital 26; *see also* globalization
intra-Arab problems 49–50
investment activity 67–68
Iran 10, 14, 19, 43, 45, 61, 71, 75, 88, 90, 96, 99, 106, 107, 168, 207n20; brain drain from 178; containment of 41; elections in 116; EU as 'strategic partner' 74; EU relations with 80; geopolitical realignment, marginalization and 127; global economic ranking 131; Iranian Revolution 49–50; oil-exporting agreements 101–2; parliamentary elections (2004) 170–71; petrodollar plenty in 147; Revolutionary Guards in 153; sanctions, deleterious effects of 141–42; Shia domination in 181; Sino-Russian cooperation with 99; women in 158
Iran-Iraq War 50, 51
Iraq 12, 14, 19, 40, 43, 44–45, 49, 56, 61, 96, 115, 207n20; adventurism of 51; Ba'athist Iraq 47; British mandate in 171; civilian targeting by terrorists in 125; containment of 41; division of, potential for 127–28; future for 176; geo-cultural slant of terror in 179; global economic ranking 131; key actor in MENA 183; Persian Gulf security and 69–71; as terrorist base 124; US-UK invasion of 126–27
Ishida, Susumu 213n125
Islam 10, 90, 123, 160–64; corrosive impacts on Muslim social regulation 38; Dar el-Islam 8–10; impacts of globalization on Muslim social regulation 38; Islamic banking 102; Islamic Empires 6–7; 'Islamic nationalism' 3; Islamic support for Taleban 90; Islamist radicalism 14–15, 43, 120, 123, 132, 161, 187; militant Islam and impact of 9/11 18–19; pan-Islamism 126; re-Islamization and globalization 42–43; religion and way of life 149; revivalists and Muslim *umma* 8; rise of 7; Salafi Islam 17, 90, 128, 181, 183; Shia Islam 17, 49, 127–28, 158, 176, 179–81, 224–25n40; socio-cultural domination by West, fears of 21; Sunni Islam 17, 90, 127–28, 153, 176,

179–81; *ummah* (entire Islamic world) 8, 126; US suspicions of 12–13, 14; Wahhabii Islam 17, 169, 170, 179, 180
Islam, Shada 209n55
Islam in a Globalizing World (Simons Jr, T.W.) 20
Islamic Republic News Agency (IRNA) 202n4, 221n24
Israel 10, 50, 71, 73, 82, 107, 171, 209n56; accommodation with globalization 130, 131; Arab-Israeli peace process 68–69, 76; economy of 175–76; EU trading partner 74; Israel-Egypt trade accord 224n23; Israeli-Turkish security axis 57; military partnership with India and China 100; Palestine-Israel, dispute between 68–69; Palestine-Israel, peace in 57; regional political economy and 41; Sharon-Bush agreement (2004) 68–69; Six Day War 52; skilled labour, influx of 178; Turkish-Israeli alliance 106
Italy 48
Ivashentsov, Gelb 211n100

Ja'far, Mohammad 137, 218n37
Jaffe, A.M. and Manning, R.A. 213n118
Jane's Intelligence Digest 213n121
Janssen, Nirmala 217n7
Japan 45, 57, 65, 66, 88, 95, 145, 175
Jassim bin Jabral-Thani, Sheikh Hamad bin 215n24
Jeddah Economic Forum (2004) 36, 158
Jemaah Islamiyah 123
Jervis, Robert 87, 204n46, 211n86
jihad and globalization 123–26
Joffé, George 76, 208n44
Johnston, Douglas M. 220n1
Jones, Paula 34
Jones, R.J. Barry 200n29
Jordan 12, 50, 57, 82, 110; accommodation with globalization 130; al-Qaeda target 128–29; civilian targeting by terrorists in 125; election in (2003) 117; geopolitical realignment of 127; Gulf capital investment in 147; Islamist defeat in 123; 'oil deficit' in 140–41; preservation of US external prop 119; women in 158; youth cosmopolitanism 154–55
Jordanian-Israeli Peace Treaty (1994) 77

Judge, Sir Paul 26, 29, 200n33, 201n52
judicial review 119–20

Kalicki, Jan 212n112, 213n119
Kamrava, Mehran 37, 131, 202n14, 217n10
Karnitschnig, Matthew 218n46
Kashmir 14, 90, 93
Katzman, Kenneth 208n27
Kawach, Nadim 214n7
Kazakhstan 72, 96, 98, 102, 107
Kemp, G. and Harkavy, R.E. 223n1
Kemp, Geoffrey 81, 210n65, 212n111
Kennedy, Paul 199n1
Kenya 22
Kerr, C., et al. 30, 201n56
Kerr, David 211n91
Kerr, Malcolm 204n6
Kessler, Glenn and Wright, Robin 227n32
Khader, Bichara 74, 208n33, 209n63
Khalaf, Roula 215n11, 221n26
Khalaf, Roula, et al. 219n63
al-Khalidi, M. and Farroukh, U. 198n24
Khamenei, Ayatollah Seyed Ali 34, 37, 202n6
Khan, M.A. Muqtedar 199n54
Khan, Reza 189
Kharrazi, Kamal 34, 202n4
Khatami, President Seyed Mohammad 34, 178
Khodr, Mohamed 202n19
Khomeini, Ayatollah Ruhollah 123, 158–59
Kim Hak-Su 212n103
Kinzeer, Stephen 210n80
Kirdar, Nemir 35
Kleinknecht, A. and Wengel, J.T. 201n59
knowledge deficit 178
knowledge production 143
Knowles, Warwick 218n40
Knutsen, Torbjørn L. 199n1
Kol, Jacob 87
Korany, Bahgat 49, 166, 204n7, 205n14, 223n5
Krasner, Stephen D. 40, 203n30
Kugler, Richard L. 26, 200n35
Kuwait 44, 50; elections in 116; Iraqi invasion 68, 126, 203n36; negative impact of Gulf War (1991) 142; preservation of US external prop 119; women's rights in 157

Laipson, Ellen 208n43
Latin America 67–68
Latter, Richard 209n62
Lavy, Victor and Sheffer, Eliezer 214n6
Lebanese Broadcasting Corporation 156
Lebanon 45, 50, 82; elections in 116; Gulf capital investment in 147; Hizbollah in 153; women in 158; youth cosmopolitanism in 155
Legrain, Philippe 223n10
Lelyveld, Michael 212–13n116
Lenin, V.I. 9, 22–23, 32, 199n7
Lentner, Howard H. 24, 200n18
levelling and globalization 26
Levy, M. 16, 199n47
Lewinsky, Monica 34
Lewis, Bernard 161, 222n52
liberal value system, acceptance of 38–39
liberalization of trade 2, 37, 70, 75, 112–13, 143–44, 148
Libya 14, 19, 41, 45, 49, 71, 80, 82, 115, 205n22, 207n20; non-confrontational stance 182; petrodollar plenty in 147; regional mood swings 51
limits of globalization 12
localization and globalization 27
Long, David E. and Koch, Christine 208n27
Los Angeles Times 198n32
Luciani, G. and Schumacher, T. 208n38

Maastricht Treaty 208n45
McAllister, Richard 207n7
McDonalds 27
MacFarquhar, Neil 198n39
Mackinder, Halford 207n17
Al-Madani, Abdullah 213n133
Madonna 34
Madrid Conference (1991) 57, 71, 77
Maghreb states 51, 52, 54, 69, 73, 96, 170, 182
Mahathir bin Mohamad 14
al-Maktoum, Sheikh Mohammed bin Rashid 36, 202n13
Malaysia 96, 97; women in 158
male-dominated division of labour 156–57
male-driven cultural values 156–60
Malik, Monica and Niblock, Tim 226n11
Mallet, Victor 212n104
Malta 82
Manama 4
Mandaville, Peter 198n19
manhood *(rujula)* 156
Mansfield, E.D. and Milner, H.V. 204n3
Manzarpour, M.H. 202n5

Mao Tse Tung 9
Marcos, President Ferdinand 39
marginalization 127, 130–31
Marin, Manuel 79
'marketization' of states 112–15
Marr, Phebe 53, 205n20
Marriott, J.A.R. 210n77
Marshall, Don D. 26, 201n38
Marx, Karl 8, 9, 10, 198n20
Mashreq 52, 58, 61, 151, 170
Masson, Paul 200n32
Mattar, Gamil 199n45
Maududi, Maulana 159
Mauretania 73
Mazrui, Ali 24–25, 200n20
Mecca 7, 163
media role in globalization 178–79
Medina 7
MENA (Middle East and North Africa) 1–3, 25, 28, 45–46, 60; accommodation to globalization 56–57; al-Qaeda operations and 128–29; as analysis unit 47; Arab Co-operation Council (ACC) 50–51, 54–55; Arab Maghreb Union (AMU) 54, 69; Arab World and 48–49; challenge and opportunity for West, post 9/11 19; China as model for 172; civilizations of 6; Cold War superpowers and 48–49; colonialism and 48–49; cross-border linkages 43; Easternization, Westernization and 67; economic autocracy 4–5; Economic Co-operation Organization (ECO) 55; economic regionalism 51–52; Egypt-Israel accommodation 50; emasculation of regional actors 41; Europe and 61–62, 64–65; European Union and 53, 56; FDI (foreign direct investment) flows 136; fragmentation 51; fusion and fission within 62; GCC 52–53, 55; geopolitical pressures within 41; globalization in context of 36–39, 130–31; GME and 48; good governance indicators 131; Greater Arab Free Trade Area 58; inter-Arab trade relations 72–74; intra-Arab problems 49–50; investment activity 67–68; Iran-Iraq War 50, 51; Iranian Revolution 49–50; knowledge deficit 178; 'metropolization' of economic activity 56–57; neo-patriarchy in Arab world 10; 9/11 and Muslim sense of purpose 16–17; non-Arab disruptions 50; North African internal divisions 51; 'oil deficit' in 140–41; oil economies of 39; Pakistan, role in MENA region 182–83; petrodollar politics 49–50, 52; politico-cultural responses to globalization 4, 7, 10; post 9/11 fragility 56; region without regionalism 47–52; regional politics and strategic interdependence 43–46; regionalism and selective co-operation 57–59; sanctions, deleterious effects of 141–42; security and volatility 58–59; socio-economic crisis in region 132; state of MENA states 36–39; strategic shift, Saudi Arabia and US 44–46; subregionalism 52–57; subregions 48; tariff reductions, benefits from 144; territorial divisions within 47–48; *thawra* (revolution) and *tharwa* (riches) in 52–56; underemployment 136; United Arab Republic 49; US motivations, Arab and Muslim fears of 15–16; Western demands of 70; *see also* GME; Middle East
MENACA (Middle East, North Africa and Central Asia) 67
MERCO-SUR 51
'metropolization' of economic activity 56–57
Michel, Thomas 203n23
Micklethwait, John and Wooldridge, Adrian 28, 200n13, 201n47, 202n63, 214n1
Middle East: Arab-Israeli conflict and future for 195–96; authoritarianism 115; challenge of globalization for 7; Conference on Security and Co-operation in the Middle East 68; consolidation of globalization 128; crossroads of struggle between Europe, Asia and US 66–67; dysfunctional, dismembered states, potential for 128; Economic Co-operation Organization (ECO) 72; economic internationalization and balance of power 130–48; ethnic and religious division of, potential for 127–28; EU expansion, implications for 69; EU-Middle East relations 72–73; fallout of politics of globalization 40–42; FDI (foreign

direct investment) in 146; geopolotical future 183–84; globalization and Middle East in perspective 185–96; historical exposure to outside influences 7; military ties with China 99–100; opportunities of globalization 185–90; political peace as prefix of globalization 194–95; shock and horror at 9/11 14; 'swing powers' 107; transition, reform and new rules 190–94; *see also* GME; MENA
Middle East Broadcasting Centre 156
Middle East Economic Digest 210n70
Middle East Journal 33
Milbank, Dana 199n46
Miliband, R. and Panitch, L. 201n51
military ties with China 99–100
Mir-Hosseini, Ziba 222n41
Mittelman, James H. 26, 201n37
MMA (Muttahida Majlis-e-Amal) 17–18
Montazeri, Grand Ayatollah Hussein Ali 224n37
Moore, Pete W. 220n68
Moratinos, Miguel 79
Morocco 11, 12, 50, 57, 73, 82; accommodation with globalization 130; al-Qaeda target 129; civilian targeting by terrorists in 125; geopolitical realignment of 127; Gulf capital investment in 147; Islamist defeat in 123; parliamentary elections (2002) 117; preservation of US external prop 119; women in 158
Moussa, Amr 202n16
Mozaffari, Mehdi 203n42
MTV 28
Muawad, Mahmoud 209n61
Mubarak, President Husni 180, 192
Müftüler, Meltem 210n79
al-Muhanna, Mohammed 215n19
multi-disciplinarity 24
multinational business 37–38, 39
Murawiec, Laurent 205n21
Murden, Simon W. 199n4, 221n22, 226n9
Murphy, Emma C. 171, 209n47, 221n36, 223n14
Muslim Arab Empires 6–7
Muslim Brotherhood 40
'Muslim identity' 159–60
Muslim patterns of social organization 158–59
Muslim perceptions of globalizing world 153

Muzaffar, Chandra 202n18
Mykonos trial 80, 209n59
myth of globalization 24–25

NAFTA (North American Free Trade Area) 51, 57, 80
al-Naimi, Ali 212n105
Naisbitt, John 47, 51–52, 56
Najjar, Fauzi 203n25, 216n1
Nasr, Vali 224n39
Nasrallah, Hassan 153
Nasser, Gamal Abdel 52
National Intelligence Council 167–68
The National Security Strategy of the United States (White House publication) 198n32
NATO (North Atlantic Treaty Organization) 61, 72–73, 79, 80, 81, 82, 86, 192, 194
natural resources: allocation of 167; dependence on 135–36
Nawabzadeh, S. 199n49
El-Nawawy, Mohammed and Iskandar, Adel 201n48, 224n38
Naya, Byron and Seiji 219n54
Naya, Seiji 145, 219n
Nayef, Prince of Saudi Arabia 170
neo-colonialism 130–31
neo-liberal economics 26
neo-patriarchy in Arab world 10
Nesson, Nicholas 226n14
Neugart, Felix 211n84
New Perspectives in North-South Dialogues: Essays in Honour of Olof Palme (Hadjor, K.B., Ed.) 1
New Statesman 198n30
New York Daily Tribune 8
Niblock, Tim 204n49, 208n34
Nigeria 129
9/11: GME, post 9/11 context 174; MENA, post 9/11 fragility 56; Middle East shock and horror at 9/11 14; militant Islam and impact of 18–19; and Muslim sense of purpose 16–17; strategic context, 9/11 and globalization 10–19; terrorism and geopolitics, 9/11 effect 15–17; US motivations, post 9/11 15
Noble, Paul 55, 205n25
Noland, M. and Pack, H. 202n1
Nomani, Farhad and Rahnema, Ali 220n4
Nonneman, Gerd 208n31, 215n25
North-South debates 37

Obaid, Nawaf 223n12
Odell, Peter R. 214n2
OECD (Organization for Economic Cooperation and Development) 96, 97, 146, 175, 185, 213n117
O'Hearn, Denis 65, 207n11
Ohmae, Kenichi 24, 200n15
oil: and balance of power 132–35; economies of MENA 39; geo-economics of 137–41; income from 110–11; 'oil deficit' in MENA 140–41; *see also* hydrocarbons; petrodollars
Olayan, Lubna 130, 135, 158, 202n12
Olcott, Martha Brill 211n96
Olson, Robert 100, 213n122
Oman 119
OPEC (Organization of Petroleum Exporting Councties) 134, 139, 140, 147
open trade and economic growth 145
origins of globalization 26–28
Orlov, V.A. and Vinnikov, A. 211n100
OSCE (Organization for Security and Co-operation in Europe) 72–73, 86
Ottaway, Marina and Carothers, Thomas 224n30
Ottoman Empire 210n77
Owen, Roger 58, 206n33
Ozanne, Julian 205n11

Pahlavi, Shah Mohammad Reza 39
Pakistan 10, 12, 17, 45, 48, 50, 90, 93, 94, 99, 106, 107; al-Qaeda target 129; brain drain from 178; civilian targeting by terrorists in 125; Jamaat-i Islami in 159; role in MENA region 182–83; Sunni domination in 179; as terrorist base 124
Palestine 14, 40, 50, 57, 78, 82, 110; elections in 116, 117; *intifadah* in 224n25; Palestine-Israel Accords (1993) 77; Palestine-Israel dispute 68–69; violence in Occupied Territories 79–80
Paolini, Albert 25, 200n24
patrimony and globalization 156–60
Pelagidis, Theodore and Papasotiriou, Harry 31, 202n60
Penketh, Anne 209n60
Perle, Richard 180
Perlmutter, Amos 161, 222n48
Persia 6
Persian Gulf oil reserves 96, 97, 98

Persian-Roman rivalries 5
Perthes, Völker 227n28
Peterson, John 117, 215n16
Petras, James and Veltmeyer, Henry 29, 111, 214n3
petrodollars: petrodollar plenty 147; petrodollar politics 49–50, 52
Pew Global Attitudes Project (2006) 152, 221n21
Pfaff, William 42, 203n38
Pfeifer, K. and Posusney, M.P. 218n35
Philippines 107
Phoenicia 6
Pieterse, Jan Nederveen 216n2
Pinto, Maria do Céu 198n33
Pipes, Daniel 13, 198n35
Piskur, Michael 212n106
Plattner, Marc F. 27–28, 38, 201n45, 203n22
Poland 84
politics: dynamism and governance 117–18; elites, objectives of 169–70; of globalization 40–42; instability and economics 132; liberalization 111, 115, 172; obstacles to integration 176–77; peace as prefix of globalization 194–95; political economy and shaping of Middle East 2; politico-cultural responses to globalization 4, 7, 10; reform, liberalization and 116–20; regional politics in global context 165–72; strategic interdependence 43–46, 166–67
The Politics of Incoherence: United States and Middle East (Bill, J.A. and Chavez, R.B.) 33
Polk, William R. 165
Polynesia 7
Portugal 85
Powell, Colin 120, 226n19
power and economic controls 114
powerlessness in economics 130–31
pressures of globalization 112–13, 114–15
price of economic prosperity 148
processes of globalization 25–26
Pronk, Jan 200n22
Prophet Muhammad 7, 16, 224n40
protectionist pressures 125–26
public good and globalization 142–43

Qaddafi, Colonel Muammer 139
al-Qaradawi, Yusuf 150, 220n12
Qatar 44, 57, 96; elections in 116; geopolitical realignment of 127;

petrodollar plenty in 147; pluralism in 118–19
Qatar News 215n22
al-Qosaibi, Ambassador Dr Ghazi 36

Rabasa, Angel M. *et al.* 198n38
Rabin, Itzhak 78
Rahim-Safavi, Yahya 153
Rahman, Saifur 218n28
RAND Corporation 44
al-Razzuqi, Hisham 136
re-Islamization and globalization 42–43
Reagan, President Ronald 194
regional environment: elites, objectives of 169–70; organization of states and globalization 33–34; region without regionalism 47–52; regional politics and strategic interdependence 43–46, 166–67; regional politics in global context 165–72; selective co-operation 57–59; shaping the region, influential factors 167–68; and US power 170–71
Remba, Oded I. 132, 134, 217n16
rentier-dependence 111, 138
Rezvi, Gowher 115, 215n12
Richards, Alan 132, 136, 217n15
Ricks, Thomas E. 205n21
Ridgeway, J. and Fard, C.E. 214n135
Ridolfo, Kathleen 202n2, 222n59
Riordan, E., *et al.* 217n9
The Rise and Fall of the Great Powers: Economic Change and Military Conflict (Kennedy, P.) 199n1
The Rise and Fall of World Orders (Knutsen, T.L.) 199n1
Road, Sinclair 207n16
Robertson, Pat 15, 16
Robinson, William I. 26, 200n34
Rodinson, Maxine 6, 197n14
Rosecrane, Richard 107, 214n139
Roy, Olivier 42–43, 203n41
Rubin, Barry 149, 198n27, 220n3
Ruigrok, W. and van Tulder, R. 200n17
Russia 88, 96, 99, 106, 168; Asian growth of military links 93–94; Moscow-Beijing axis 94; Sino-Russian relations 92

Saba 5
al-Sabah, Sheikh Jaber 117–18
al-Sabah, Sheikha Amthal 215n17
Sacranie, Iqbal 198n28
Sadat, President Mohammed Anwar 137

Safadi, Raed 207n21
safety nets 143
Safi, Louay 222n50
Salamé, Ghassan 209n64
Samarquand 5
sanctions, deleterious effects of 141–42
Sarhan, Haitham 155
Sartre, Jean-Paul 8, 23, 199n9
Sasanids 6
Sassen, Saskia 114, 214n8
'Satanic civilization' 34–35
al-Saud, Prince Walid bin Talal 131, 142, 153
Saudi Arabia 12, 17, 19, 45, 49–50, 53–54, 70, 71, 81, 95, 96, 106, 162, 215n20; 'Arab Charter' of 35–36; civilian targeting by terrorists in 125; dichotomy of power elites in 169–70; elections in 116; global economic ranking 131; Islamist defeat in 123; key actor in MENA 183; *Kingdom of Saudi Arabia Newsletter* 202n11; petrodollar plenty in 147; reform, debate on introduction of 118; strategic shift, US and 44–46; US-Saudi relations 43–44, 45; women in 157, 158
Saudi Aramco 101
Sayigh, Yezid 208n25
Saywell, Trish 211n87
Scott, Allen 206n31
secularization and globalization 37
security and volatility 58–59
Seddon, David 206n29
sex as marketing tool 151
Sha'aban, Buthaina 122
Shafer, Jack 205n21
Shahina, Gihan 216n48
Shamali, Nasser 122
Shanghai Co-operation Organization 72, 99
Sharabi, Hisham 10, 188, 198n25, 225n3
Sharon, Ariel 79
Sharon-Bush agreement (April 2004) 68–69
Sharp, Heather 221n33
El-Shibiny, Mohamed 197n4, 203n24
Shipman, Alan 201n51
Shleiwi, Moussa 221n31
Shultz, George P. 177, 224n31
Silk Road 5
Simons Jr, Thomas W. 20
Singapore 145, 175
Singer, Max 180
Singh, Robert 204n52

Sinopec, China 101
Sirageldin, Ismail 205n26
Sirageldin, Ismail and Al-Khaled, Rana 218n31
Sklair, L. and Robbins, P.T. 200n26, 201n53
Sklair, Leslie 16, 25, 150, 199n48, 200n25, 218n38, 220n9
social relations 4, 28, 31, 90, 156, 158
'socialization of production' 23
socio-economics 21, 121, 137, 169, 188; American culture 27; change 26; crises 116, 132, 186; fabric of states 2, 19, 93; failings of 47; globalization as phenomenon 32; 'pan-Arab' structures 58; problems 191; reform 173, 177, 185; rentier relationships 2; security 190; stability 104; structures 110, 186; US as force in Iraq 179
socio-political contradictions 169–71
Solana, Javier 75
Somalia 14; as terrorist base 124
South Korea 57, 88, 95, 107, 145, 175
Soviet Union 17, 28, 42, 43, 48, 55, 69–70, 88, 224n25; Afghanistan occupation by 43, 124, 163; collapse of 20, 26–27, 62, 63, 68, 86, 89–92, 108, 161, 178, 182, 192; expansionist zeal of 194; external prop for left-leaning states 115; implosion of 71–74; Marxist-Leninists in 9
Spartacus 12
Spencer, Claire 209n53
Srivastava, Siddharth 213n121
stagnation in MENA region 131–32
Starr, Frederick S. 67, 207n18
state governance 109–12
state-led economic activities 136–37
Steel, Ronald 206n4
Stephenson, Jonathan 216n44
Stiglitz, Joseph 25, 200n27
Stockholm International Peace Research Institute (SIPRI) 211n95
Strange, Susan 24, 200n12
strategic context, 9/11 and globalization 10–19
strategic interdependence 43–46, 166–67
strategic shift, Saudi Arabia and US 44–46
Strategic Studies, International Institute for 211n94
Strategic Survey 1991–92 (IISS) 207n23
strategic unit, GME as 10–11
Streusand, Douglas E. 13, 198n34

Struck, Doug and Kessler, Glenn 213n124
Stubbs, Richard 26–27, 201n39, 206n30
subjugation 130–31
subregionalism 48, 52–57
Al-Sudairi, Turki Abdullah 202n3, 220n7
Sudan 14, 19, 41, 50, 51, 82, 110, 207n20; as terrorist base 124
Sur, Serge 205n27
Susser, Asher 225n45
Sweden 83
'swing powers' 107
Swirski, Shlomo 224n25
Syria 19, 41, 45, 50, 61, 71, 81, 82, 110, 115, 209n56; Ba'athist Syria 47; EU trading partner 74; geopolitical realignment, marginalization and 127; Gulf capital investment in 147; key actor in MENA 183; US economic sanctions against 203n35

Taiwan 88, 100, 145, 175
Taleban 16–17, 21, 89, 106; Islamic support for 90
Al Talib, Shaykh Salih Bin-Mohammad 224n40
Tallawi, Mervat 219n51
tariff reductions, benefits from 144
tax revenues 113
technological change 24, 30, 36, 39–40, 65, 143, 169, 179
Telhami, Shibley 199n44
tensions of globalization 113, 114–15
territorial divisions 47–48
terrorism 22; and geopolitics, 9/11 effect 15–17; globalization and the state 123–29
Teshreen 122, 216n36
Tétreault, M.A. and al-Mughni, H. 222n39
Tétreault, Mary Ann 157, 221n35
al-Thani, Sheikh Hamad bin Khalifa, Emir of Qatar 118
Thatcher, Margaret 161–62, 222n54
thawra (revolution) and *tharwa* (riches) in 52–56
Thomas, Richard 221n17
Thornhill, J. and Burton, J. 198n40
Tibi, Bassam 149, 220n2, 222n45
time, space and globalization 26, 28
The Times 109
Tolan, Sandy 198n32
Tomlinson, John 220n10
tourist activities 154

trade barriers 136–37
traditional values and globalizing world 152–53
transformation patterns 38
transition, reform and new rules 190–94
transnational corporations 37–38, 39
transnational *jihadist* challenges 123–26
transnationalism and globalization 25
Tresilian, David 223n19
Tripp, Charles 114, 205n13, 214n10
Tunisia 12, 73, 82; accommodation with globalization 130; al-Nahda movement in 157; civilian targeting by terrorists in 125; Gulf capital investment in 147; Islamist defeat in 123; women in 158
Turkey 10, 50, 57, 61, 71, 74, 82, 84, 107, 175, 210n69, 210n78; accommodation with globalization 130; Arab relationships 100; civilian targeting by terrorists in 125; elections in 116; EU relationship with 85, 162, 163; geopolitical realignment, marginalization and 127; global economic ranking 131; ISI system dismantlement 141; Sunni domination in 179; Turkish-Israeli alliance 106; women in 158
Turkmenistan 72, 96, 98
Turner, Bryan S. 221n22
Turner, David 218n32

ummah (entire Islamic world) 8, 126
underemployment 136–37
unemployment and new jobs 217n14
United Arab Emirates 17, 106; accommodation with globalization 130, 131; mobile phones and cultural assimilation 155; petrodollar plenty in 147
United Arab Republic 49
United Nations 18; UN Security Council 77, 79, 209n57; UNCTAD 207n22
United States 42, 56, 57, 60, 65, 95, 99, 124, 162; anti-globalization radicals, target of 16; attack on Afghanistan 18–19; CENTCOM (Central Command) 88; Central Asian strategy 106; cultural exports 34; D'Amato Bill (1996) 75; dominant military power in GME 168; free-trade initiatives 144–45; global hyper-power 45; GME regional environment and US power 170–71; Greater Middle East Initiative (2004) 70; hegemonic ambition and globalization 27–28; imperial over-reach 45–46; liberalist strategy 39–40; motivations, Arab and Muslim fears of 15–16; National Security Strategy 168; non-resident dominance of 107; Pax Americana 45; perceptions of 11–12; Persian Gulf, military strength in 70–71; policies towards GME 163–64; strategic shift, Saudi Arabia and 44–46; support for Afghan Mujahedeen 90; suspicions of Islam 12–13, 14; tariff regime in 144; tensions with EU on Arab-Israel peace process 78–80; terrorism and 123; US-ASEAN Business Council 107; US Central Command in Bahrain 48; US National Security Strategy analysis 168–69; victim and aggressor 43; war on terror 14
universalism of globalization 3–4
Usher, Graham 214n136
Uzbekistan 12, 72

Vanhanen, Tatu 198n24
Venice Declaration (1980) 77
Voice of America 156

Al-Wafd 122
Walid bin Talal, Prince of Saudi Arabia 35, 202n7
Walker, Edward S. 44–45, 215n21, 222n57
Wall Street Journal 142
Wallerstein, Immanuel 27, 201n40
Walt, Vivienne 213n126
Waltz, Kenneth N. 25, 40–41, 107, 200n19, 203n31, 214n140
Warren, Bill 9, 32, 198n22
Warsaw Pact 71–72, 84, 124
Washington Institute for Near East Policy 44
Waters, Malcolm 27, 200n16, 201n43
Watson, James L. 221n15
Weidenfeld, Werner 210n67
Weiss, Stanley A. 219n52
Weitz, Richard 211n97
Western consumerism 150, 151–52
Western demands of MENA 70
Western European Union 86
Western values and globalization 20–21
Western ways, penetration by 150–51
Westernization and MENA 67

Weyrich, Paul 15
Williams, John 203n28
Wilson, Rodney 175, 208n39, 218n25, 224n24
Wistrich, Ernest 206n6
World Bank 217n17, 218n27, 219n50, 219n55
World Economic Summit (2004) 131–32
World Investment Report 68
World Travel and Tourism Council 153
The Wretched of the Earth (Fanon, F.) 23
Wright, Robin 226n15
WTO (World Trade Organization) 37–38, 75, 112, 144, 176

Xie, Andy 97

Yahuda, Michael 91, 211n90
Yamani, Mai 117–18, 180, 215n18
Yassin, Sheikh Ahmed 225n46
Yemen 50, 51, 82, 110, 115; al-Qaeda target 129; as terrorist base 124
Yom, Sean L. 215n13
youth cosmopolitanism 154–55
Yunesi, Hojjatoleslam Ali 153

Zangeneh, Hamid 224n34
Zartman, I. William 54, 205n23
Zeta-Jones, Catherine 34
Zürn, Michael 207n13

eBooks – at www.eBookstore.tandf.co.uk

A library at your fingertips!

eBooks are electronic versions of printed books. You can store them on your PC/laptop or browse them online.

They have advantages for anyone needing rapid access to a wide variety of published, copyright information.

eBooks can help your research by enabling you to bookmark chapters, annotate text and use instant searches to find specific words or phrases. Several eBook files would fit on even a small laptop or PDA.

NEW: Save money by eSubscribing: cheap, online access to any eBook for as long as you need it.

Annual subscription packages

We now offer special low-cost bulk subscriptions to packages of eBooks in certain subject areas. These are available to libraries or to individuals.

For more information please contact webmaster.ebooks@tandf.co.uk

We're continually developing the eBook concept, so keep up to date by visiting the website.

www.eBookstore.tandf.co.uk